POVERTY AND WEALTH IN EAST AFRICA

Poverty and Wealth in East Africa

A Conceptual History

Rhiannon Stephens

DUKE UNIVERSITY PRESS
Durham and London 2022

© 2022 Duke University Press
Typeset in Garamond Premier Pro by PageMajik

Library of Congress Cataloging-in-Publication Data

Names: Stephens, Rhiannon, [date] author.
Title: Poverty and wealth in East Africa : a conceptual history / Rhiannon Stephens.
Description: Durham : Duke University Press, 2022. | Includes bibliographical references and index.
Identifiers: LCCN 2022001174 (print)
LCCN 2022001175 (ebook)
ISBN 9781478016199 (hardcover)
ISBN 9781478018827 (paperback)
ISBN 9781478024514 (ebook)
Subjects: LCSH: Development economics. | Uganda—Economic conditions. | Uganda—Social conditions. | Uganda—Economic policy. | BISAC: HISTORY / Africa / East
Classification: LCC HC870 .S747 2022 (print) | LCC HC870 (ebook) | DDC 338.96761
—dc23/eng/20220625
LC record available at https://lccn.loc.gov/2022001174
LC ebook record available at https://lccn.loc.gov/2022001175

Cover art: Banana fiber weaving. Photograph by the author.

For Jarod and Menna

CONTENTS

Acknowledgments ix

Introduction 1

CHAPTER ONE
Methodologies and Sources for a Conceptual History of
Economic Difference over the *Longue Durée* 22

CHAPTER TWO
Excavating Early Ideas about Poverty and Wealth 45

INTERCHAPTER
Overview of Climate Developments 64

CHAPTER THREE
The Bereft and the Powerful: Greater Luhyia Concepts of
Poverty and Wealth through the Nineteenth Century 72

CHAPTER FOUR
Gender and Honor: North Nyanza Concepts of Poverty and Wealth through
the Nineteenth Century 99

CHAPTER FIVE
Orphans and Livestock: Nilotic Concepts of Poverty and Wealth
through the Nineteenth Century 120

CHAPTER SIX
Wealth, Poverty, and the Colonial Economy:
Nineteenth and Early Twentieth Centuries 144

Conclusion 167

Appendix: Reconstructed Vocabulary 171

Notes 207

Bibliography 253

Index 277

ACKNOWLEDGMENTS

This book has its earliest origins in a talk at a series on "Rethinking Poverty in Africa" at the Centre for African Studies, Cambridge University, back in 2009, and so I have accumulated multiple people and institutions to thank over the years, including Derek Peterson and Megan Vaughan, who invited me and prompted me to stop and rethink poverty in early Ugandan history. The next impetus came from an invitation from Axel Fanego Palat and Bo Stråth to join the ConceptAfrica project. The meetings we had were instrumental in pushing my thinking and my decision to pull both wealth and poverty into the same frame. I thank all the participants in those meetings for their comments and conversations, and in particular Axel Fanego Palat, Pamela Khanakwa, Ana Lúcia Sá, and Anne Mager. I also benefited from feedback on various parts and versions of what became this book at a number of different venues. These include the Makerere Institute for Social Research, the Fung Global Fellows Program at Princeton University, the University Seminar Studies in Contemporary Africa at Columbia University, the Uganda Society, Medieval Africa? Middle Ages in the Wider World Conference at the University of California at Berkeley, the New Directions in Economic History panel at the African Studies Association Annual Meeting in Philadelphia, the 6th International Conference on Bantu Languages at the University of Helsinki, the Rethinking Economic Concepts in Southern and Eastern African History panel at the African Studies Association Annual Meeting in Washington, DC, the Beyond Words and Things: Archaeology and Historical Linguistics panel at the Society of Africanist Archaeologists 24th Biennial Meeting at the University of Toronto, the African History Workshop at Columbia University, and "Extracting the Past from the Present": International and Interdisciplinary Conference on African Precolonial History at the University of Ghent. The conversations we had through the Undocumented Stories workshop series, with Zoë Crossland, Severin Fowles, and Caterina Pizzigoni, and all our invited speakers, especially Jan Bender Shetler and Adria LaViolette, helped shape my thinking. And I thank Emily Callaci, Cymone Fourshey, Raevin Jimenez, Neil Kodesh, Kate de Luna, Andreana

Prichard, David Schoenbrun, Yaari Felber Seligman, and Constanze Weise for our ongoing conversations about research.

Funding for the research for this project came from Columbia University, including from the Lenfest Faculty Development Grant. The Makerere Institute for Social Research and the Department of History, Archaeology and Heritage Studies gave me research affiliations, for which I am very grateful. Research in Uganda was approved by the Uganda National Council for Science and Technology and an Institutional Review Board exemption was awarded by the Human Research Protection Office at Columbia University. While writing, I benefited from a fellowship at the Heyman Center for the Humanities, Columbia University, and I thank my cofellows for their thoughtful feedback on my work. Over the past year, I have benefited from an Andrew W. Mellon Foundation New Directions Grant, which allowed me to complete an MA in Climate and Society at Columbia University that has been pivotal in enhancing my understanding of past climate change.

Shobana Shankar helped improve the book proposal I submitted to Duke University Press. Adria LaViolette, Kate de Luna, and Jarod Roll read the entire manuscript and gave me invaluable feedback. I am deeply indebted to the three of them, but most especially to Jarod Roll. Will Fitzsimons read parts of the manuscript and I am very appreciative for his feedback and our ongoing conversations on Ateker questions in particular. Marcia Wright's feedback on what became my article in the *American Historical Review* continued to inform my thinking as I wrote this book. Jason Smerdon read the interchapter, offered important feedback, and has generally been critical in enhancing my knowledge and understanding of paleoclimatology. I also thank the three anonymous reviewers for Duke University Press, who pushed me to improve the manuscript and offered thoughtful and helpful comments. I'm grateful to Elizabeth Ault at Duke for her interest in the project from our first conversation and to Ihsan Taylor for shepherding it through production. I also thank Paula Durbin-Westby for the index. Any errors are, of course, mine.

Along the way, a number of people have been exceptionally generous with their time and resources. I thank Christopher Ehret, David William Cohen, Ron Atkinson, Susan Reynolds Whyte, Michael Marlo, Kevin Alulu, Hannah Chazin, and Jeff Hantman for their help. In Uganda, I have been privileged to meet and listen to many exceptional people who gave their time to contribute to my research and from whom I learned a tremendous amount: Hihubbi Adam, Stephen Akabway, Gesa Aristarchus, Kasango Banuli, Kurwa Charles,

Jimmy Eribu, Gudoi Esau, Adyango Freda, Okalany David Hannington, Tazenya Henry, Carol Ilako, Helen Kagino, Peter Kamuron, Veronica Kanyana, Joyce Kawuledde, John Kunena, Joseph Lomongin, Samsom Luvunya, Henry Aloysius Mafwabi, Henry Maganda, Tom Masaba, Madete Mohammed, Henry Mongo, Masai Moses, Joram Mpande, Samuel Mubbala, Peter Michael Muloit, Yokulamu Mutemere, Sam Mwigo, Rehema Nakaima, Harriet Nakibanda, Florence Naasambu, Peter Namaondo, Laury Ocen, George Okambo, Charles Okumu, Musumba Ouma, Robert Osega, John Owor, Mutemo Robert, Samuel Siminyu, Ephraim Talyambiri, James Kangala Tuumuwa, Wanende, Timothy Wangusa, Abel Wanzige, Sarah Maswere Wasake, Cornelius Wekunya, Gertrude Yanga, and Gershom Ngolobe Zablon. Charles Okumu has been especially generous in continuing our conversations over email. Most of all I thank Pamela Khanakwa, who has been a friend and colleague since my first visit to Uganda over twenty years ago, and all her family, especially Kasango Banuli, for their hospitality and kindness.

I want to thank all the graduate students I've worked with at Columbia; my conversations with them and their feedback on parts of my work have challenged me and reshaped much of my thinking for the better: Sarah Runcie, Sam Daly, Devon Golaszewski, Halimat Somotan, Yayra Sumah, Thomas Zuber, Rebecca Glade, Conor Wilkinson, Luz Colpa, Jealool Amari, and Jessie Cohen. I especially thank Conor Wilkinson for his comments on various parts of the manuscript. My colleagues, Gregory Mann, Abosede George, and Mamadou Diouf, in particular, read parts of this and have listened to me talk about this project for many years and have been influential in my thinking. I am grateful for their support. Caterina Pizzigoni, Kavita Sivaramakrishnan, Zoë Crossland, Frank Guridy, Laura Fair, Hannah Farber, and Sailakshmi Ramgopal have been wonderful friends as well as colleagues. Zoom writing sessions with my colleague and friend Adria LaViolette kept me on track. I also thank Rebecca Barrett-Fox and her Any Good Thing monthly writing challenge, which helped ensure that words kept appearing on pages and revisions kept happening, even in the midst of teaching and everything else life brings.

This book is dedicated to Menna and Jarod, who remind me every day that a life full of love is a life full of wealth.

Parts of the introduction first appeared in "Poverty's Pasts: A Case for *Longue Durée* Studies," *Journal of African History* 59, no. 3 (2018): 399–409. Those parts are reprinted with permission from Cambridge University Press.

Parts of chapter 2 and chapter 3 first appeared in "Bereft, Selfish, and Hungry: Greater Luhyia Concepts of the Poor in Precolonial East Africa," *American Historical Review* 123, no. 3 (2018): 789–816. Those parts are reprinted with permission from Oxford University Press.

INTRODUCTION

Poverty and Wealth in East Africa is a conceptual history of poverty and wealth and of the poor and the wealthy over the past two millennia. It demonstrates the dynamism and diversity of people's thinking about inequality in the region long before colonial conquest or incorporation into global trade networks. Sub-Saharan Africa's economic woes and the poverty of its inhabitants have become familiar narratives.[1] But how did African people understand wealth and poverty and how have those understandings changed across time? In this book, I ask that question for people living in eastern Uganda and examine how they sustained and changed their ways of thinking about wealth and its absence. Drawing on the methods of historical linguistics alongside others, I have been able to reconstruct some of the ways in which people conceived of economic difference over the past two thousand years and more, and I have been able to do so for a region for which the written record is only a little more than a century old. The answers I lay out here challenge much of the received wisdom about the nature and existence of economic and social inequality in East Africa's deeper past. In eastern Uganda, a region that is roughly the size of Switzerland, and only a little larger than Guinea-Bissau, people had—and still have—a startlingly wide array of concepts about poverty and wealth and about the poor and the rich. For example, speakers of one language, Lunyole, use fifteen different word roots to talk about poverty. We can compare that to the one root that speakers of Welsh, a language of similar antiquity, use for the same purpose.[2] More importantly, the different roots found in Lunyole reflected different conceptualizations of poverty, from connecting poverty and bereavement to conceiving of the poor as deceitful. In reconstructing the conceptual history of poverty and wealth in eastern Uganda, I show the complexity of people's intellectual engagements with these concepts. I also demonstrate that this kind of history can be written for periods long before those for which we have documentary archives.

Extremes of poverty and wealth appear to have preoccupied the thoughts of many people in eastern Uganda for a very long time. That preoccupation has not been static. In fact, people's understandings and framings of these economic concepts have changed significantly over time, even while some understandings have endured across centuries. In the following chapters, I explore the diverse and dynamic ways that people conceived of poverty and wealth across the *longue durée* and across communities that differed in the languages they spoke, in the kinds of economic activities they prioritized, and in the ways that they organized their political lives. This study focuses on thirteen modern languages that belong to two of Africa's major language families: Bantu and Nilotic. Lugwere, Lusoga, Rushana, Lunyole, Lugwe, Lusaamia, Lumasaaba, Lubukusu, and Ludadiri make up the Bantu languages, and Ateso, Ngakarimojong, Kupsabiny, and Dhopadhola make up the Nilotic languages (see map 1.1). Historically the economic foci of communities in the area ranged widely, from transhumant pastoralism to mixed agriculture to fishing, hunting, and gathering. They also traded in products such as iron tools or ceramic pots, in foodstuffs such as grain and fish, and in wild resources such as honey. Politically, these communities and those speaking their ancestral languages ranged from small monarchies to lineage-based or age-grade- and age-set-based politics. This was by no means a homogenous region in the past, just as it is not homogenous in the present. Instead, it was characterized by high levels of diversity across all aspects of human society. That diversity shaped the ways in which people living in the region since around the start of the Common Era have understood what it meant to be poor or rich, both within their own societies and between their society and those of their neighbors. By taking a regional approach to this study, rather than one defined by a particular language group, it becomes possible to see that diversity and the ways in which some concepts were shared or borrowed across communities.

Until the COVID-19 pandemic, sub-Saharan Africa's poverty rate was said by the World Bank to be steadily declining with GDP (gross domestic product) on an upward trajectory.[3] At the same time, the Gini coefficient that measures wealth disparities has been increasing in some countries, even as it decreases in others. Any visitor to Uganda's capital city in the twenty-first century would be struck by the profound and jarring difference between the shopping malls with their Belgian patisseries and multiplex cinemas and the experience of so many of Kampala's residents who live in informal settlements without sanitation or electricity. Yet recent developments are not the first major economic transformation in Ugandan societies. The modern era saw the introduction of cash crops and the construction of railway and road infrastructure to facilitate transportation to global markets in the twentieth century, colonial conquest and the pillaging and taxing that accompanied it in the nineteenth and twentieth centuries, and the nineteenth-century extension of direct East African and Indian Ocean trade networks to Buganda and eastern Uganda. A little earlier, in the eighteenth

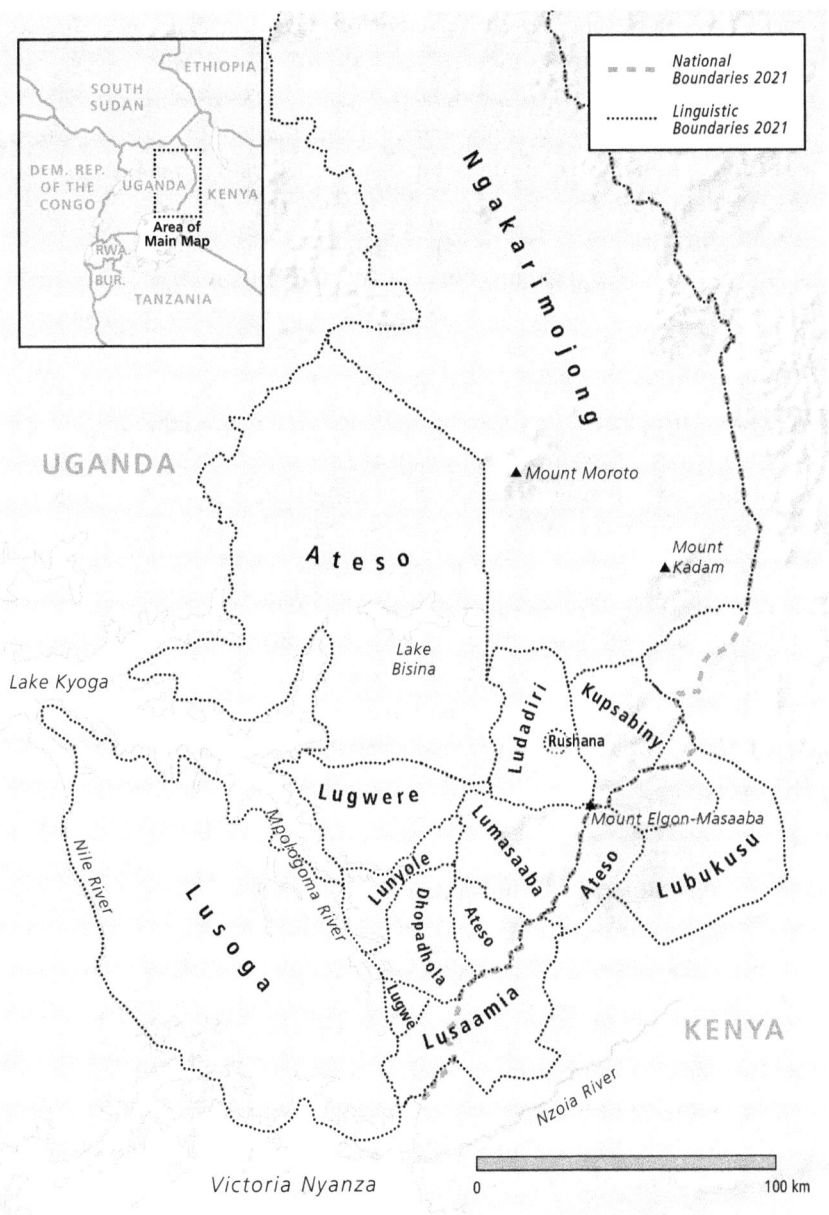

MAP I.I. Relief map of eastern Uganda with modern languages. Map created by Nat Case.

century, we might consider the wars of expansion in Buganda and Bunyoro, which led to what historian Nakanyike Musisi has termed "elite polygyny" as chiefly and royal households overflowed with captive women—women who constituted wealth for those who laid claim to them.[4] Each of these developments led to an intensification of inequality and a reconceptualization of wealth, and each was in turn challenged by those who were not the beneficiaries of the new socioeconomic reality. In the deeper past, periods of state formation, new kinds of control over land and resources by clans and lineages, or migrations to settle in unfamiliar areas would have had similar effects, as would have economic and social responses to climate change. *Poverty and Wealth in East Africa* explores how communities made sense of these dramatic changes, as well as more modest yet no less consequential ones, through the words and concepts that people drew on to talk about the wealthy and the poor and about wealth and its absence.

Both poverty and wealth have histories in eastern Uganda and those histories are of significant antiquity. Yet, despite scholarship showing the dynamism of Africa's economic history, the continent continues to be depicted as having always been impoverished.[5] Such ahistorical projections about poverty and about local understandings of poverty in Africa remain problematic. This depiction, in part, grows out of colonialism. Colonial officials, at the start of the twentieth century, argued that the only way to overcome poverty was to more effectively exploit Uganda's natural wealth by coercing its people into various forms of labor. The explicit racism of colonial officials shaped their belief that poverty was a product of indolence. Scholars, by contrast, have shown how colonialism contributed to the impoverishment of entire communities, causing them to enter into structural poverty, the kind of poverty from which it was almost impossible to escape because the prior mechanisms available to remedy that poverty no longer existed or no longer functioned.[6] This is also true in eastern Uganda. Communities in the region have certainly not always been poor. We know this, not least because they have an ancient vocabulary for wealth, but also because they have long had distinct ways of classifying the poor, something that would not have been necessary if everyone was equally impoverished. That is, it is neither the case that everyone was destitute, nor that no one was. And just as the material conditions of poverty and wealth have long histories in eastern Uganda, there are also long intellectual histories of those conditions, ones that can be recovered through a conceptual history approach.

Despite this, in parallel with the continued depiction of Africa as eternally poor exists the perception that life in precolonial Africa was largely egalitarian and that mechanisms of poverty alleviation were generally effective.[7] It is easy to counter this with examples of fundamental socioeconomic inequality in the stone-towns of the Swahili coast, the royal capitals of Buganda and Rwanda, and, further afield, in Great Zimbabwe and Asante. Inequality could also be found in Mali, whose fourteenth-century ruler Mansa Musa is frequently given as an example of such extreme wealth that his spending on the hajj led to inflation and an economic crisis across the Mediterranean world. But economic and social difference were not historically limited to these cases that saw the large-scale centralization of wealth and power. Indeed, linguists who have carefully reconstructed vocabulary to Proto-Bantu (a language spoken some five thousand years ago in what is today the borderlands of Cameroon and Nigeria) identified words both for poverty and for being rich.[8] That this vocabulary was created and used by speakers of Proto-Bantu, people who farmed without iron tools and who lived in small communities, tells us that they must have understood there to be differences in economic status of some significance. What precisely those differences meant, however, is a different and, to my mind, more compelling question. It is that question, one grounded in the intellectual work done by people in eastern Uganda as they conceived and reconceived of what it meant to be poor and to be rich, that I address here.

Poverty and Wealth in Eastern Uganda

Modern evidence provides a glimpse into the diverse ways in which people in eastern Uganda have understood what poverty and wealth meant and also reflects the historical complexity of these concepts in the region. In Bunyole in the 1970s, the anthropologist Susan Reynolds Whyte observed prayers offered by men to their ancestors at a funeral ceremony:

> We are begging here for wealth, we are begging that the children here may study and learn, here we also would like a motorcar to drive. Wherever we plant millet, wherever we plant sesame, wherever we plant sorghum, may it come quickly and soon. Here let us elope with women, we are begging here for facility in getting wives, here we beg for reproduction, may we strike two by two so that we may have a twin ceremony everyday. Let us be well, you give us life and let us be free from cold.[9]

The prayer began with a plea for wealth, specifically for kinds of wealth that could not have been conceived of in the region before the twentieth century: formal education and cars. Because these were not ubiquitous in Bunyole in the 1970s, they served as clear markers of high socioeconomic status. But the men's prayer quickly moved onto pleas for other forms of wealth, ones that would have been familiar to their ancestors who lived in the nineteenth century and, indeed, much earlier still. These were pleas for plentiful harvests; in this case the pleas were for the staple crops millet and sorghum and for the cash crop sesame. These requests represented a melding of old forms and concepts of wealth with new ones. The prayer for a successful growing season of millet and sorghum reflected the need to sustain a household through unreliable harvests and, ideally, a season that generated a surplus which could be converted into other forms of wealth, such as livestock or a fishing boat. Sesame, however, although long cultivated in East Africa, was grown in the twentieth century as a cash crop and thus represented a more recent form of wealth, one that could be transformed into education, cars, and other newer markers of status.

The men's prayer then shifted to marriage and childbirth, with a request for wives married through elopement and, therefore, without, seemingly, the transfer of bridewealth (the wealth transferred to the woman's family from the man's family) that formalized marriage. Bridewealth could be a point of tension between younger and older men, especially if fathers chose to use livestock to marry additional wives themselves, keeping sons in the limbo of junior status. Elopement was a means for younger—and poorer—men to circumvent the restrictions bridewealth placed on their ability to marry and thus begin to build their own wealth in a form that will be familiar to many—namely wealth in people.[10] In asking their ancestors for fertility, these men specifically requested twin births, suggesting that normal rates of reproduction would not allow them to become wealthy at the pace or in the ways that they desired.

Further north, but still in eastern Uganda, historians collecting oral histories in Teso communities, in the late 1960s, interviewed three men, Nasanairi Arugai, Omodoi, and Toroma, who offered their thoughts on trade and wealth. They talked about a man named Ibwala: "The hoe trade was before the war with Ocopo [1890s]; the war didn't interfere with the trade. Ibwala became wealthy on this trade and his family is still wealthy, has many cattle."[11] In the nineteenth century, Ibwala had managed to translate the wealth he had acquired through trading iron hoes into wealth in cattle. His descendants remained wealthy long after Ibwala's original trading success: as much as a century later, they still had many cattle. Wealth was understood as the possession of cows, bulls, and calves. But why would people who understood wealth to take the form of livestock seek to acquire hoes through trade? Iteso women and men did not understand there to be a single form of wealth nor did they view forms of wealth as immutable. By the seventeenth century, early Ateso speakers had developed a concept of wealth in crops or wealth in food (using the Ugandan English meaning of food as a staple starch, like millet bread) which they called *amio*. Hoes enabled them to grow millet and sorghum, both crops that were understood to form *amio* wealth.

The trio also talked about the hoe trade itself: "The red hoes were brought by Basoga passing through Opiu from Mbale side. Basoga came in groups of twenty and carried the hoes and carried away the tusks. They went to all homes which had ivory."[12] Here we find different ideas about what constituted wealth, at least in terms of the material forms it took. The Basoga traders had an abundance of hoes and so valued them primarily for their trade value, notably for the ivory for which they could be exchanged. For Iteso women and men who did not produce their own metal tools, however, the iron hoes brought by Basoga traders were of greater value than the ivory tusks they traded for them. This was the case, in part at least, because Iteso used the hoes to generate *amio* (wealth in crops) that they could then translate into *abar* (wealth in cattle)—as was the case for Ibwala who managed to pass his substantial *abar* wealth on to his descendants. From an outside perspective, trading ivory tusks for iron hoes may seem to have been a short-sighted decision on the part of Iteso women and men—after all, demand in Europe, the Americas, and South Asia for elephant ivory in the nineteenth century was very high.[13] But this outside perspective does not account for the different ways in which people in eastern Uganda historically conceived of wealth, value, and what it meant to be rich—and conversely, how they conceived of poverty and what it meant to be poor.[14] A conceptual history approach allows us to not only understand what poverty and wealth meant to people in eastern Uganda in the nineteenth century, but also how people's concepts of them changed over time to accommodate shifting social, political, and material realities.

Conceptual History of Poverty and Wealth

Conceptual history foregrounds the intellectual work of ordinary people.[15] But it goes further by understanding that concepts are not mere indicators. As Melvin Richter wrote, concepts "affect political and social change because it is through concepts that a horizon is constituted against which structural changes are perceived, evaluated, and acted upon."[16] In this, it offers "an opportunity to take seriously peoples' intellectual activity as part of historical processes."[17] Language not only serves as a possible historical source; it is a critical source for history, because it helps us understand how people made sense of and reshaped their worlds. Conceptual history thus places eastern Ugandans at the center of their own history, instead of centering those outsiders who wrote about them and their homes. As was the case in my and Axel Fanego Palat's previous work, *Doing Conceptual History in Africa*, I am working from the assumption that language is inherently social and produced by people. The concepts that people hold in the language or languages they speak, and even the grammatical structures that they use, may contribute to shaping what is possible for them to conceptualize. At the same time, language offers people the possibility to reshape those concepts and structures and thus move the horizon Richter described.

The categories of poverty and wealth, of the poor and the rich, are not only about economic status, just as economics cannot be isolated from society, culture, and politics. These categories are in a dynamic relationship with the social and political, with social status creating or reinforcing economic status and vice versa. The work of defining who is poor and who wealthy—and struggles over that work—is as much about the ideological basis for these categories as it is a question of quantification based on clear metrics. Poverty, poor, wealth, and wealthy are thus concepts that can be—and have been—contested within and across communities. Terence Ranger wrote several decades ago, "An answer to the problem of poverty [in Africa] is not to be found by means of an exclusive concentration upon production history. The study of changing concepts is also very relevant. African history needs to make a connection not only with the material way of life of the people but also with their modes of thought."[18] Whether or not a conceptual approach to poverty will help answer the problem of poverty is a question I set aside. A conceptual history approach can, however, bring to light the complexity of people's understandings and ideological views of poverty and wealth. Indeed, it is in the complexity of a concept that history can be found. As Friedrich Nietzsche wrote with reference to punishment, "all ideas, in which a whole process is promiscuously comprehended, elude definition; it is only that which has no history, which can be defined."[19] As will become clear in the following chapters, both poverty and wealth are complex concepts that "elude definition." Starting from their multiple meanings across communities—rather than any external definitions—allows me to bring to the fore the complexity of the concepts, as they were understood and remade by people in eastern Uganda.

This is a book about a remarkably diverse region, even by African standards. Eastern Uganda, defined here as stretching from the Nile to the Nzoia River and from Lake Victoria Nyanza to north of Mount Moroto, is an area of some 41,000 square kilometers (16,000 square miles). The languages spoken there belong to two major language families: Bantu and Nilotic—although English is today also predominant given its status as the official language of Uganda.

The Bantu languages are further divided between Greater Luhyia Bantu and North Nyanza Bantu, both of which are branches of Great Lakes Bantu. The Nilotic languages are divided between Eastern Nilotic (represented by the Ateker branch), Western Nilotic (represented by the Southern Luo branch), and Southern Nilotic (represented by the Kalenjin branch). As a result of this diversity, the reconstruction of relevant terms to protolanguages, and hence to different moments in the past, is complicated. That complexity is productive, because it allows us to trace concepts that have been borrowed across linguistic, social, and economic frontiers and to see commonalities and differences across and between speaker communities. In eastern Uganda, most people are and historically have long been multilingual; they have traded across ecotones and economic specializations, they have married outside of their immediate communities, and they have gone to war over control of resources or people. Words and concepts have migrated across languages through these processes. Understanding how and why that happened is an important part of this story.

How eastern Ugandans understood poverty and wealth, and how they made sense of what it meant to be poor or rich, has varied widely across time and space. That variation speaks to the dynamism of the concepts and, in particular, to the intellectual engagement of the speakers of the languages covered in this book with questions of economic and social difference. In parallel with the dynamism and diversity, it is also evident from the linguistic record that some ways of understanding poverty and wealth have proved highly durable, remaining in place, although not entirely unchanged, across millennia of human experience. And for all the variety, it is possible to discern three broad themes among the many conceptualizations of poverty and wealth that cut across time and across linguistic divisions, albeit in tangled and overlapping ways: people understood poverty and wealth in social terms, in material terms, and in emotional terms.

Social understandings of poverty included concepts that referenced kinlessness or ones that emphasized that the poor lacked the ability to marry, and hence engage in socially recognized reproduction. But they also included perceptions of the poor as posing a threat to the collective, whether through their demands on resources, their disruptive behavior, or their inability to contribute to the social reproduction of the community. Social anxieties about the presence of poor people in communities resulted in some framing the poor as not fully human and others framing them as cheats. Gendered concepts of poverty and of the poor also fit into the broad framework of the social. Women who contravened social norms of appropriate gender behavior as a result of poverty, for example, could be named with words not used for poor men and that were often condemnatory. The particular implications for a woman who married into a poor household were also marked through specific terms for poor women.

Gender and the gendered division of labor were similarly fundamental to many social concepts of wealth. Tracing the etymologies of words for bridewealth shows how some wealth was explicitly conceived of as taking the form of girls and women. The same root that was used to form the word meaning bridewealth, for example, was used to form the word for a widow, a woman who would be inherited by her husband's heir on his death. The root was also used to describe women and girls abducted in warfare and distributed as spoils by the victorious side. But this is not to say that the concept of wealth in eastern Uganda was such that only men could be wealthy. Indeed, one speaker community coined a new word to describe wealthy women specifically. Along with naming wealthy women, that speaker community also added a new definition of wealth that was grounded (quite literally) in the fields worked by women and the crops they harvested. Social concepts of wealth also included the framing of wealth as a result of composition, of threading together distinct pieces into a new whole. While that composition involved material wealth and livestock, creating compositions of people was an integral element as well. Connected to that were concepts of wealth as power and as leadership. However, while some concepts of wealth fit, directly or indirectly, into the theoretical framework of wealth in people, for the most part this was not how the historical speaker communities of eastern Uganda talked about what it meant to be rich.

Concepts of poverty grounded in material understandings focused in large part on the absence of necessities; that is, they focused on lack. This concept is an ancient one in eastern Uganda, and it emerged during a period of prolonged drought when people who came to speak Proto-Greater Luhyia established new communities in the region some two thousand years ago. The form that lack took in people's concepts of poverty was not uniform. But one example is that those who placed great economic and social value in livestock began to understand poverty as the absence of cattle, goats, and sheep. For some, poverty was hunger and the physical manifestation of hunger on the human body. But, perhaps surprisingly, this was by no means a universal conceptualization of the condition. It may have been one that fluctuated with changes in climate, as there is some evidence to suggest that concepts of poverty as emaciation emerged during periods of pronounced climate stress. Elsewhere and at other times, people began to envision poverty as a natural phenomenon and not the consequence of political choices, again emphasizing its material rather than social aspects.

Wealth was understood as taking material form when speakers of different languages articulated concepts of it as material possessions, as land, as crops, and as livestock. At times and in some speaker communities, these concepts coexisted with the concept of wealth in people, but the latter was by no means dominant. At the same time, wealth in one form could be transformed into wealth in a different form, whether that involved wealth in crops being transformed into wealth in livestock, or wealth in land being transformed into wealth as power. The reality of wealth as power could be displayed through insignia, such as copper or brass armlets, that were named with the same root used to name both a wealthy person and a powerful person. The boundaries between social and material concepts of poverty and wealth were porous, as were their boundaries with emotional concepts.

Both poverty and wealth were conceived of in emotional terms across the linguistic communities of eastern Uganda and across the centuries although in a wide range of ways. Among the oldest concepts of poverty was one that framed it as suffering, placing it alongside other experiences such as bereavement and sickness. Other conceptualizations foregrounded bereavement in particular, emphasizing the economic as well as emotional consequences for those whose parents died when they were still young or women whose husbands died, leaving them vulnerable. This was a concept that cut across the division of languages into Nilotic and Bantu, and across economic classifications into pastoralist and agriculturalist. In general, emotional understandings of wealth were positive, framing the wealthy as honorable or worthy of respect. But more negative emotions toward the wealthy also made their way into the language people used to talk about them.

Sources and Methods

In the East African interior—and in eastern Uganda in particular—written sources go back a little over a hundred years. To write this history for societies without written records before the late nineteenth century, therefore, requires an interdisciplinary approach. I drew on a diverse range of sources and methods to reconstruct the conceptual history of wealth and poverty, as well as the contexts for that history. I started with the words themselves and the methods of comparative historical linguistics.[20] These methods have allowed me to reconstruct the words and meanings used by people in the past to talk about poverty and wealth and about the poor and the rich. The first step in this process involved the genetic classifications of modern languages—that is, which languages emerged from a common ancestral or protolanguage and the particular sequences by which related languages diverged. The next step was to look at cognate words (those inherited from a common ancestral language) across modern languages and use established sound changes to posit the form (in terms of sounds or phonemes) that words had in the protolanguage. Alongside determining the form of words, it was necessary to look at the range of meanings the cognates hold and use insights from diachronic and cognitive semantics to posit the meaning attached to the form in the protolanguage. This approach is often referred to as words-and-things. It is worth emphasizing the plurals in this phrase because in any language there are often many words for the same thing (or meaning) and many things (meanings) for the same word. For conceptual history, this reality is highly productive. By tracing, to the fullest extent possible, all the meanings associated with a word that also meant wealth, poverty, rich person, or poor person, we can see the intellectual work that went into the naming of these concepts. Similarly, by tracing all the synonyms for each of these concepts we can see reflected in them competing ideas within a single speaker community about socioeconomic difference and its causes and consequences.

With the evidence from comparative historical linguistics in place, I turned to other sources and approaches. These are archaeology, climate data, oral traditions and literature, local histories, and ethnography. Each of these offers a particular form of evidence that speaks to different aspects of socioeconomic inequality in the past. Archaeology, for example, is very useful for understanding changes in the material cultures and economies of societies, although an archaeology of poverty remains to be developed for eastern Uganda and, indeed, Africa.[21] Climate data can help suggest ways in which long-term ecological pressures and opportunities might have reshaped socioeconomic dynamics or strained mechanisms for aid within a community. Oral traditions can offer insight into social and political dynamics as well as into economic changes. Ethnography, when used comparatively and very carefully, can help us explain the contexts in which particular words were used. Each of these, thus, forms its own layer of evidence that I overlay on the linguistic data to see whether, for example, I can correlate a new settlement or a change in political organization with the adoption of a new word for poverty. Or whether emergent tensions around wealth might have happened at the same time as a multidecadal drought, excessive rainfall, or the adoption of a new crop.

Histories of Poverty, Histories of Wealth

This book is the first conceptual history of poverty and wealth over the *longue durée* in Africa. Indeed, it is a rare African history of these concepts in any time frame.[22] Earlier generations of historians of Africa have demonstrated the longevity of economic inequality on the African continent. K. O. Diké wrote in the 1950s of "land hunger" in Igbo-speaking regions spurring migration to the city states of the Niger Delta in the nineteenth century.²³ In the 1970s, A. G. Hopkins, while focused on economic history questions of production and distribution, nonetheless noted that wealth was not equally shared in precolonial West Africa.²⁴ Robin Palmer, Neil Parsons, and the contributors to their edited volume on central and southern Africa were explicitly focused on the question of poverty and its transformation over the *longue durée*, as the region was ever more entangled in global trade networks.²⁵ And in the 1980s, John Iliffe surveyed the history of poverty across the continent, often through the lens of charity and almsgiving. While limited in the most part to areas with written sources prior to colonial conquest, Iliffe clearly demonstrated the breadth of poverty across the continent and of the existence of people who lived in persistent and deep poverty.²⁶ The transatlantic slave trade and colonial conquest marked important turning points in the economic history of Africa writ large, as was documented decades ago by scholars such as Samir Amin and Walter Rodney, and as has been the focus of much subsequent study.²⁷ These turning points did not, however, mark the origin of poverty or economic inequality. Jan Vansina traced the emergence of concepts of wealth and poverty in West Central Africa back some two thousand years.²⁸ Palmer and Parsons, meanwhile, argued that it was possible to "begin to distinguish between rich and poor, in a class sense, within the same society" as long ago as the Early Iron Age.²⁹

Some who have argued that poverty did not exist in Africa prior to colonial conquest recognized the possibility of scarcity, but asserted that those who were without the basic necessities to survive were always given aid by others in their community. Julius Nyerere, for example, believed that whatever poverty may have existed in Tanzania before colonialism was egalitarian, in that "all the basic goods were held in common, and shared among all members of the unit ... no one could go hungry while others hoarded food."³⁰ This perception is enduring. Elizabeth Amoah has argued that "the African traditional way of land use has its own internal mechanism for ensuring that no one lives in abject poverty" and that "the community's resources (material and nonmaterial) are mobilized to ensure the welfare of all the members of the community."³¹ But there are powerful counterexamples to this narrative, including from East Africa. John Lonsdale, for example, drew on proverbs to argue that "the rules of social obligation" in nineteenth-century Gikuyu society "scorned charity" and disparaged the poor as having "no heart, no friends and would have no posterity." Indeed, their "hunger kept nobody else awake."³² Even in contexts where the poor were given aid, the reciprocity expected in labor or other payments in kind and the long-term obligations aid entailed suggest that, as elsewhere, charity was self-interested and created new hierarchies.[33]

The wealthy leave much more behind them in the way of historical evidence than the poor, whether documentary, material, or oral, and the scholarship reflects this. Historians, anthropologists, and archaeologists have written about currencies, whether copper-cross ingots, cloth, or iron bars, that circulated in precolonial Africa.[34] Others have focused on the exportation of wealth from Africa through the Indian Ocean, Atlantic Ocean, and trans-Saharan trades, whether gold, ivory, tortoiseshells, grains, or—infamously and tragically—people.[35] Christopher Ehret, noting that exports from Africa were primarily raw materials while imports tended to be manufactured commodities, argued that the imbalance in trade between raw and manufactured goods, so visible in modern economic history, already existed in the last millennium BCE.[36] Still, Jane Guyer's question from "Wealth in People, Wealth in Things—Introduction" remains relevant: "What were people's own concepts for wealth?"[37] *Poverty and Wealth in East Africa* offers many answers to this question and shows that whatever frameworks we may use to help ourselves make sense of wealth in the past, the reality is that there were myriad ways in which people conceived of wealth. This is, then, one response to the late historian Ogbu Kalu's call for scholars "to define poverty and wealth from an indigenous African perspective."[38] Even so, as dynamic concepts, they elude any attempt at definitive definition.

It is anthropologists who have been at the forefront of developing theoretical frameworks for wealth in Africa. Wealth in people is the most important of these and the most ubiquitous in the literature. Initially developed in the context of slavery and then applied to the context of marriage and household composition, wealth in people has been used widely in varying contexts and for varying periods across the continent.[39] As Guyer and S. M. Eno Belinga neatly summarize, the phrase "offers a useful descriptive term for the well-appreciated fact that interpersonal dependents of all kinds—wives, children, clients and slaves—were valued, sought and paid for at considerable expense in material terms in pre-colonial Africa."[40] Historians have adopted wealth in people to explain perceptions of wealth in precolonial Africa, sometimes in categorical terms. For example, Joseph Miller argued that "Africans' unwavering view of wealth as people, if increasingly also as trade goods, complemented an equally set Portuguese view of wealth as money, specie and currencies, in the eighteenth century."[41] Guyer and Belinga, in applying the model to Equatorial Africa, argued that it needed nuancing, in particular to pay attention to the different qualities that made or make people valuable. Furthermore, attention should be paid to how those who were able to do so chose to compose the various people who made up their wealth.[42] Drawing on this approach, Kathryn de Luna has used "wealth in people as wealth in knowledge" to "imagine why local leaders and peers recognized and celebrated distinctive hunters for the meat, skins, excitement, and renown they brought to the community" between the eighth and thirteenth centuries in South Central Africa.[43]

Poverty and Wealth in East Africa builds on this scholarship, but I take as my starting point the particular and varied meanings with which historical communities have imbued wealth and demonstrate that wealth in people was only one of many meanings. Crucially, this approach allows for the interaction of locally developed concepts with regional and global notions. In this, I take inspiration from work by Parker Shipton, who has unpacked meanings of credit, debt, and land in western Kenya to show how these global economic ideas have particular and locally embedded meanings.[44] Thus, at the book's core, *Poverty and Wealth in East Africa* explains the effects of large-scale changes, such as long-distance trade or zoological epidemics, and of local dynamics, such as gender and generational conflicts, on people's concepts of wealth and poverty. But also inspired by Shipton's work, alongside that of Guyer, I do not take a narrow economic approach to the concepts of wealth and poverty. Shipton's work on debt in Luo communities of western Kenya demonstrates that a primarily economic approach, even to concepts like land and money, is inadequate because social relations and ideology structure these concepts just as much as does economics. Development plans in those communities that were based on a market in land failed because they did not account for "ideologies of attachment."[45]

Historians of Europe and the Middle East have engaged the concepts of poverty and wealth more extensively, especially with reference to the deeper past. Histories of the conceptualization of poverty in ancient Rome and in medieval Europe have shown how major historical events, such as the adoption of Christianity or the large-scale migration of the rural poor to urban areas, changed social perceptions of the economically marginal.[46] Whether in oral or literate contexts, in ancient or modern times, the poor have tended to leave little trace in the historical record. Historians thus have "to identify the empty spaces, the gaps and cracks in society" that were inhabited by the poor.[47] A number of historians of Europe and the Middle East facing this difficulty have turned to linguistic evidence as one method of identifying those gaps and cracks and overcoming the limitations of the archives. Michel Mollat, for example, in his landmark studies of poverty in the European Middle Ages, showed how changes in the usage of terms, including antonyms, synonyms, and related words, reflected "deep-seated alterations in the notions they designate."[48] These scholars have turned to linguistic evidence in literate contexts, even while literacy was limited to elites.[49] Here, I offer an approach to writing about changes in people's understandings of economic inequality in the absence of a long documentary record. In so doing, I build on scholarship that takes an interdisciplinary approach to the history of precolonial Africa.[50] The focus on the history of concepts, however, is a move in a new direction and the methodological discussion in chapter 1 addresses this.

Historians of East Africa have written about communal attitudes toward the poor and the wealthy, whether among speakers of Gigikuyu, Luganda, or Kiswahili. Because of the sources they drew on—notably proverbs transcribed in the late nineteenth and early twentieth centuries and dictionaries—they offer synchronic snapshots of indigenous attitudes in the mid- to late nineteenth century.[51] Those snapshots are useful in developing a baseline for understanding changes from the late nineteenth century onward as the region was subjected to colonial conquest and rule by European powers. Laura Fair, drawing on songs performed by Siti binti Saad and her band in the 1920s, explored the enduring nature of hierarchical attitudes toward the poor in post-abolition Zanzibar. Abolition changed some things, but disdain for the poor remained a powerful force, as captured in the song "The Poem of What Poverty Does": "Poverty is powerlessness . . . You are always treated as dumb and useless." The wealthy, by contrast, were granted respect: "A rich person is always among those who are counted without even having to speak."[52] The continuities with 1880s Mombasa, as written about by Jeremy Prestholdt, are striking. Drawing on the poetry of Muyaka bin Haji and Johann Krapf's dictionary of Kiswahili, Prestholdt noted that residents of Mombasa conceived of poverty as "the condition of a lack of respectability and its signifying objects."[53] The archaeological record brings to light a different perspective on wealth from that offered by Siti binti Saad, highlighting the multiplicity of concepts in play. Stephanie Wynne-Jones has argued that the material evidence indicates that "the accumulation of material wealth seems to have been subordinated to the social prestige and power available through its appropriate usage."[54] The wealthy may have been counted but they were nonetheless subject to social expectations that inhibited their ability to accumulate without limits. As these examples show, drawing on diverse sources of evidence makes possible a dynamic history of concepts of poverty and wealth, an approach that is foundational to *Poverty and Wealth in East Africa* and its exploration of continuities and transformations in eastern Ugandan people's concepts of poverty and wealth.

Chapter Outlines

This study differs somewhat from many other histories of precolonial Africa that draw on evidence from comparative historical linguistics in that it focuses closely on concepts of poverty and wealth across a broad and diverse set of languages. Chapter 1, "Methodologies and Sources for a Conceptual History of Economic Difference over the *Longue Durée*," addresses my approach. In it, I set out the methodological and evidentiary basis for writing a conceptual history of oral societies over the *longue durée*. It presents the genetic classification of the languages in the study, including my own classifications of the North Nyanza and Greater Luhyia languages. As part of the genetic classification of each language family (North Nyanza, Greater Luhyia, Eastern Nilotic, Southern Nilotic, Western Nilotic), the chapter provides contextual information on the communities that spoke the protolanguages, locating them in space and time as the evidence allows. Chapter 1 also explores the different forms of evidence used in *Poverty and Wealth in East Africa*—historical linguistic reconstructions, climate data, archaeological evidence, oral traditions, ethnographic material—and addresses what each of them does and does not allow us to say about the past. Because this is a conceptual history, the chapter sets out how the methods of diachronic semantics can help us better understand how the meanings attached to particular words—or clusters of sounds—can change over time.

After this methodological overview, the book moves in chapter 2, "Excavating Early Ideas about Poverty and Wealth," to some of the oldest concepts of poverty and wealth held by people who spoke the languages ancestral to the ones spoken in eastern Uganda today. The chapter serves as a baseline, setting out the concepts of wealth and poverty in Proto-Greater Luhyia, Proto-West Nyanza, Proto-Eastern Nilotic, Proto-Western Nilotic, and Proto-Southern Nilotic. It shows how, for example, people speaking Proto-Western Nilotic did not distinguish between poverty and other kinds of suffering. And, while we can assume that they had terms for forms of wealth, none of those can be reconstructed today. The chapter also sets out how people speaking Proto-Greater Luhyia invented an entirely new vocabulary for poverty, even though they drew on words that they had inherited to do so. By contrast those who spoke Proto-West Nyanza continued to use older vocabularies of poverty and wealth alongside their innovations of new words for, and concepts of, these economic binaries. Drawing on archaeological evidence and evidence from climate science, the linguistic reconstructions are contextualized in the changing physical and social landscapes inhabited by speakers of the various protolanguages.

I then pause to explore in more detail the evidence for historical climate change until the late nineteenth century in the interchapter, "Overview of Climate Developments." We know only too well the devastating consequences of an unpredictable climate for communities in East Africa and elsewhere in the present.[55] The communities of eastern Uganda in the centuries covered by this book lived by growing food, raising livestock, hunting and fishing, and gathering wild foods. All of these activities required intimate knowledge of their local environments and the seasons if they were to be successful. Changes in rainfall patterns, a shift from reliable rains in the short and long rainy seasons to multidecadal failures of rains interspersed with intense, destructive precipitation, for example, fundamentally challenged established ways of life. But the inverse was also true, as more reliable rains enabled people to expand into areas that were previously uncultivable or unable to sustain livestock. This is categorically not to argue that climate determined the history of the people of eastern Uganda any more than their environment did. What fluctuations in climate did do, however, was change the range of the possible. How people responded depended on multiple factors, including whether they prioritized—economically and culturally—certain crops over others, or pastoralism over agriculture, or fishing over hunting. Their responses also depended on how they organized the work of producing food in their households and communities. Drawing on a wide range of scholarship that has examined changes in East Africa's climate over the past two thousand years and more, the interchapter offers a synthesis of this research, setting out the major patterns it has discerned.

The next three chapters, respectively, trace the concepts of poverty and wealth for the languages that emerged from Proto-Greater Luhyia, Proto-West Nyanza, and the three Nilotic protolanguages: Southern, Eastern, and Western. In all three of these chapters, I focus on the languages that are spoken in eastern Uganda today and their protolanguages. While evidence from related languages spoken elsewhere in Uganda, as well as in Kenya and beyond, is included—as it must be for the purposes of reconstructions—I have stuck with this regional focus. Doing so makes it feasible to look across a wider range of languages, both Bantu and Nilotic, and understand how these economic concepts moved across linguistic, cultural, and economic divides—and how they did not.

Chapter 3, "The Bereft and the Powerful: Greater Luhyia Concepts of Poverty and Wealth through the Nineteenth Century," covers developments in these concepts in the languages that emerged from Proto-Greater Luhyia after the sixth century. The chapter opens with Lunyole, one of four languages to emerge from Proto-Greater Luhyia, the others being Proto-North Luhyia, Proto-Gwe-Saamia and Proto-Luyia. Over the many centuries that Lunyole has existed as a language, its speakers developed an extensive vocabulary for poverty and wealth. Some of that vocabulary represented a continuation from earlier concepts, and some reflected new—and more negative—attitudes toward the poor in particular. Wealth continued to be understood in gendered terms as intimately associated with marriage and reproduction through bridewealth. At the same time, it was increasingly conceived of in material terms and in terms of the ability to eat without restraint. The chapter then moves on to Proto-North Luhyia and two of the modern languages to emerge from it: Lumasaaba and Lubukusu. Here, too, a more negative concept of poverty and of the poor emerged, this time of the poor as selfish and disruptive, even while poverty was understood as a condition of a lack of essentials. In marked contrast, speakers of Proto-North Luhyia conceived of the wealthy as honorable and worthy of respect; indeed, they drew a connection between wealth and leadership. Suggesting tensions regarding economic disparities within their communities, however, Lubukusu speakers later added a concept of the rich as those who had displaced others. Finally, the chapter turns to Proto-Gwe-Saamia, whose speakers focused on a material conceptualization of poverty, but who understood wealth as accruing to elders and understood the wealthy as powerful.

In chapter 4, "Gender and Honor: North Nyanza Concepts of Poverty and Wealth through the Nineteenth Century," we turn to Proto-North Nyanza and the languages that emerged from it after around 1200 CE: Proto-South Kyoga, Proto-East Kyoga, Lusoga, and Lugwere. Speakers of Proto-North Nyanza appear to have been especially sensitive to gradations of poverty, perhaps a consequence of more people experiencing profound economic uncertainty during a time of pronounced aridity across much of the region. At the same time, they coined a new word in such a way that it marked poverty as both having physical consequences for the poor and described it as a natural phenomenon, rather than a product of political decisions or human actions. The Proto-North Nyanza speaker community conceived of wealth as gendered and as acquired through violence, but they also conceived of it in more generic terms as something obtained. Reflecting new connections with neighboring communities, people who spoke Proto-South Kyoga—one of the languages that emerged from Proto-North Nyanza along with Luganda—borrowed words from their neighbors to expand their vocabulary for poverty. And in a sign of an altered political context, they no longer conceived of wealth as the product of plunder. Lusoga speakers, after the dissolution of Proto-South Kyoga, emphasized the naturalness of poverty, but also recognized it as part of a broad spectrum of suffering. Wealth was highly gendered for the Lusoga speaker community and it is also only there that we find the concept of wealth in people expressed through specific vocabulary. In Proto-East Kyoga, the other language to emerge from Proto-South Kyoga, we see its speakers narrowing their concept of poverty to focus on the distinction between the poor and the very poor. Finally, speakers of Lugwere made several changes to their vocabulary for poverty, reflecting their shifting conceptualizations of the condition. They expanded their vocabulary for the very poor or destitute and borrowed other words to express new concepts of poverty.

The last of these three chapters is chapter 5, "Orphans and Livestock: Nilotic Concepts of Poverty and Wealth through the Nineteenth Century." It looks at how people speaking languages that emerged from Proto-Southern, Proto-Eastern, and Proto-Western Nilotic conceived of the poor and the rich. The speaker community of Proto-Kalenjin, a language that emerged from Proto-Southern Nilotic, understood poverty as connected with both being an orphan and being a beggar. But they also chose to name, in particular, the kind of poverty involved in not owning cattle and they connected this with death. Later, people speaking Proto-Elgon-Mau Kalenjin borrowed a word from their Bantu-speaking neighbors that allowed them to connect wealth with elderhood. Those who spoke Eastern Nilotic languages emphasized suffering and punishment in their concepts of poverty and the possession of livestock in their concepts of wealth, as we see for the Proto-Ateker speaker community. Later, Ateso speakers coined a new word to specify a poor woman and held a highly negative concept of the poor in general. They also understood poverty to be a condition of misery. The Ateso speaker community specified forms of wealth by distinguishing between wealth in food crops and wealth in livestock. And they connected wealth with skillfulness. People speaking Ngakarimojong, another Ateker language, placed greater emphasis on the possession of livestock, or lack thereof, in their concepts of wealth and poverty, reflecting the cultural and economic role of transhumant pastoralism in Karimojong communities. For those speaking the Western Nilotic language Dhopadhola, poverty was a condition of suffering, but one that also disturbed those who lived alongside the poor. They conceived of wealth, by contrast, in positive terms, connected as it was for them with visiting and gift exchange.

In the last chapter of the book, I focus on the developments of the nineteenth and early twentieth centuries when eastern Uganda was integrated into wider-reaching trade networks and came into the purview of European imperial ambitions. Chapter 6, "Wealth, Poverty, and the Colonial Economy: Nineteenth and Early Twentieth Centuries," thus moves away from a focus on particular groups of languages and their speakers to look at the region more broadly, drawing on examples from specific speaker communities to illustrate larger developments. It traces how some concepts of poverty and wealth continued despite some of the profound disruptions of this period, including prolonged, severe drought at the start of the nineteenth century and shorter, but pronounced drought at its end. The period of more regular and plentiful rainfall in between these events brought abundant wealth to some, but also saw the arrival of coastal traders seeking primarily ivory and slaves. The devastation wrought by the rinderpest epidemic at the end of the nineteenth century, following as it did on the heels of other livestock diseases and drought, posed a clear threat to concepts of wealth in both pastoralist and agricultural communities, with gendered overtones. Colonial conquest and rule further disrupted and undermined communities, but introduced new ways to acquire wealth—and hence speaker communities adapted their concepts of it. At the same time, older concepts endured and colonial officials found themselves working within those concepts, even if they did so unintentionally.

CHAPTER ONE

Methodologies and Sources for a Conceptual History of Economic Difference over the *Longue Durée*

> Languages don't change; people change language through their actions.
>
> —William Croft, *Explaining Language Change: An Evolutionary Approach* (2000)

> Whether records are written or embodied in folk lore and tradition, behind them lie real human history.
>
> —K. O. Diké, "African History and Self-Government" (1953)

How can we know what a farmer meant fifteen hundred years ago when she used the word **omutambi* to describe someone? How can we know the different meanings her listeners held in their minds for that noun and, thus, the range of assumptions they may have made about her choice to use **omutambi* rather than **omutaki*? Both words, after all, referred to a poor person. Or how can we know what a fisher meant a thousand years ago when he referred to wealth as **obugaiga* and how that differed from wealth he referred to as **omwaandu*? We do not have recordings or transcriptions of any conversations that occurred at those times, or even during far more recent ones. What we do have are the words of people speaking languages descended from the one our farmer spoke and ones descended from the one spoken by our fisher. Those words offer us a window onto the intellectual work performed by people whose names we cannot know. They are people who spoke languages descended from Proto-Great Lakes Bantu and from Proto-Nilotic. The meanings that they ascribed to particular words have been inherited by those who speak the modern languages of eastern Uganda. In the intervening centuries, speakers changed some meanings of words, adding new meanings and dropping others, so that they are lost to us. Over those centuries, too, people changed the way they spoke some of those words. Changes in meaning and pronunciation were passed on to subsequent generations of speakers, who in turn made their own changes as well as keeping some sounds and meanings the same.

So long as people kept using words inherited from previous generations of speakers of their language and kept teaching them to their children, those words reached all the way to the present and into the modern languages of eastern Uganda. Because of this continuity, we can trace them back in time, both in terms of the specific clusters of sounds that formed words and the meanings that those words held. When we add to these reconstructions evidence gleaned from archaeology and comparative ethnography, we can learn about some of the contexts in which people used *omutambi*, *omutaki*, *obugaiga*, and *omwaandu*, and all the other words—and there are many of them—that people in eastern Uganda have used to talk about the poor and the rich. We can learn from those words and contexts about what it meant to live in poverty and what it meant to have wealth. As we get closer to the present, oral traditions offer us additional insights. The farmers and fishers and herders and potters and smelters of eastern Uganda told stories to each other about their histories, about how they came to live where and the way they did. They passed those on through their children and grandchildren. In narrating and remembering those stories, they also tell us about social differences and economic differences in their communities and what those differences meant.

As with all histories of places without long documentary traditions, writing the history of eastern Uganda before the twentieth century poses methodological challenges.[1] Overcoming those challenges, however, highlights the possibilities that do exist for writing history and that allow us to write different kinds of histories.[2] Writing a conceptual history of economic difference in eastern Uganda might be seen as raising particular challenges because it requires the reconstruction of commonly held ideas rather than of material worlds. The roots of conceptual history as a field are deeply planted in highly literate contexts in Europe.[3] Nonetheless, exploring different approaches to conceptual history beyond the contemporary documentary archive demonstrates how the existence of other kinds of sources should challenge historians of Europe and elsewhere to reconsider their heavy reliance on documentary archives.[4] Conceptual history in colonial and postcolonial Africa is sometimes only possible with, and is certainly enriched by, a move beyond the archive, as work by Pamela Khanakwa on Uganda and Ana Lúcia Sá on Equatorial Guinea has demonstrated so effectively.[5] For all that archives offer, they represent only a partial record of the past, and other sources, such as those generated through historical linguistic reconstruction, bring new evidence to the table.

There is a perception that one of the methods historians of precolonial Africa have turned to, often referred to as "words and things," "works best when the words designate, for example, plants and tools; less well when they refer to social and cultural values."[6] The evidentiary basis for this perception is weak and not borne out by linguistic principles. But using historical linguistic evidence to write conceptual history does require a considered and careful methodological approach that goes well beyond the one-to-one matching of lexical and material items. When used appropriately, linguistic evidence holds great potential for writing historically about cultural and social values in the absence of contemporaneous documentation.

Despite challenges, the sources that are available allow for the reconstruction of a nuanced history of the concepts of poverty and wealth in eastern Uganda over the past two millennia. The most prominent of these sources, for this study, is an archive of reconstructed words for the ancestral languages—usually referred to as protolanguages—of the modern languages spoken in the region today. In particular, this archive is composed of the words people used to name, debate, and discuss the concepts of poverty and wealth and related ideas and material realities. Below I set out in some detail how I constructed this archive and how, with regard to conceptual history in particular, I focused on the changes in meanings attached to words to gain insight into the different ideas people held about socioeconomic difference in the past and how those ideas altered over time.

What makes this reconstructed vocabulary such a productive source is that rather than having to read the silences in, or read against the grain of, documents written by outsiders and elites, we can turn to the very words people used. We can, that is, take the words out of the minds and mouths of people whose names we will never know, but whose life experiences and opinions shaped and reshaped the meanings that they attached to words for a poor person or a wealthy one, for example. The historian Kathryn de Luna has noted that the histories we can write from these words are limited to the "social unit of the speech community" in ways that can frustrate explorations of individual agency.[7] Her work has demonstrated, however, how individual attributes, like talent, can be recovered even if the names and biographies of those who possessed those attributes are lost to us.[8] We can also find in the reconstructed vocabulary contestations and struggles over the meanings attached to a particular word. Those contestations and struggles were ones between individuals and groups of individuals, and they bring to light divisions and conflicts over economic and social inequality between speakers of a language, alongside examples of consensus.

That said, an honest accounting of the challenges involved in researching and writing this book is an important starting point for moving beyond them. The most obvious challenge emerges from the fact that the people in eastern Uganda lived in oral societies until the twentieth century when Christianity and colonialism contrived to bring writing to bear on them and their languages. Unlike many parts of Africa and other places in the world, these oral societies remained largely unwritten about by outsiders until the very end of the nineteenth century. It is not, therefore, possible to draw on the kinds of early detailed accounts of economic practices such as those the historian Edda Fields-Black used in her groundbreaking history of the West African rice coast.[9] However compromised the journals of slave-ship captains are by their authors and the contexts of their production, they nonetheless offered Fields-Black a late eighteenth-century baseline from which she could work backward with her linguistic data. The documentary baseline for this book is a hundred years or so later, in the late nineteenth century.

Another challenge emerges from a historical aversion in eastern Uganda toward large-scale political centralization. While various forms of governance existed across the different societies in the region and across time, these forms are not ones that have given rise to the kinds of oral traditions associated with the famous states of Buganda, Bunyoro, Rwanda, and, further afield, Mali, Luba, and Asante.[10] The epic of Sundiata is not, of course, a straightforward source to use in writing the history of the founding of the Mali empire in the thirteenth century, any more than Alexis Kagame's twentieth-century transcriptions of the oral traditions of Rwanda's dynastic families are straightforward sources for understanding their history and that of the wider area they dominated.[11] Oral traditions are by their very nature ripe for multiple and contradictory interpretations, as evidenced by the very different histories of Buganda that draw on the same body of texts.[12] And yet, they are an invaluable source for writing about Africa's deeper past. The extant oral traditions of eastern Uganda are, however, fewer and more disparate than for the states to the west.

Archaeology has also proven valuable for writing the history of places as far apart as Nigeria, the Swahili coast, and South Central Africa, even when research has been sparse.[13] Eastern Uganda has not been the site of extensive archaeological excavation, although there has been considerably more research done in western Kenya. Where archaeological work has been done in the region, much of it has tended to focus on the transition to pastoralism and agriculture from subsistence practices of fishing, gathering, and hunting, as discussed below. Archaeologists have not generally been able to identify and excavate individual houses, for example.[14] This means that we do not have the kind of detail about household structures and domestic architecture or about differences between the material goods found in households that could illuminate the material realities of people's lives in the more distant past, including realities of material difference.

This accounting of the evidentiary challenges should not discourage the historian of precolonial eastern Uganda—or any other comparable region in terms of availability of sources—because the reality that I uncovered was that (for all that I may have wished for more of this or that kind of evidence) I was in fact working with a lot of evidence.

History from Words, Words from History

Language structures how we understand and interact with the world we inhabit. This is particularly the case for what is called social reality. As the philosopher Jan Ifversen notes, "this is the difference between, on one hand, mountains, rivers, and gravitational attraction," which exist outside of human interaction, "and marriage and property, on the other. Without a social decision of some kind, a convention—or an institution, as sociologists would say—money would only be paper, and complex social institutions like marriage and property would not make any sense."[15] Because of this, language offers us a window not only into past material worlds, but also into past conceptual and intellectual worlds.

While words are the medium for most of the evidence historians draw on to write about the past, whether as documents, inscriptions, or oral histories, those of us who use words themselves as sources are far fewer in number. To do so, we step into the world of linguistics and, more specifically, into the world of comparative historical linguistics. This disciplinary and methodological bridging can mean that how we acquire our evidence and, in particular, how we analyze it becomes opaque to historians accustomed to documentary archives and tighter chronologies. The historian David Schoenbrun has written about how reading work that draws on technically complex genetic evidence has given him insight into how "some must feel when they read the parts of my work that rest on historical linguistics."[16] Once we have become conversant with them, it can be easy to forget how impenetrable other disciplines are to those less familiar with the methodological assumptions made and the technically specific language used. It is worth, therefore, devoting some space to a discussion of method such that the evidence and analysis in the following chapters is as transparent as possible to readers without training in historical linguistics. The purpose is not, however, to offer a how-to guide to using linguistic data in writing history. This is necessarily only a brief introduction.[17]

The vast majority of the words we use today are ones that we have inherited from people who spoke our languages—and languages ancestral to them—in the past. Each generation of speakers changes the language in some ways, forgetting some words, borrowing words from other languages, and inventing new words. Each generation also makes changes in pronunciation, leading dialects of languages to emerge and, over time, become separate languages. Languages that emerged out of a common protolanguage retain shared features from that language, whether words (lexical items), sounds (phonology and phonetics), or grammar (morphology and syntax), even as speakers made and make changes to their languages. Because of this historical fact, it is possible to reconstruct substantial elements of that protolanguage. For scholars working on Indo-European and other language families with long histories of writing, the task is facilitated by the ability to cross-check reconstructions with words and sentences written down in the past. This has allowed the subfield of comparative historical linguistics to develop robust and tested methodologies for reconstructing the lexicon, phonology, morphology, and syntax of protolanguages that were not documented in writing. In order to do so, we need to first know the relationship of the relevant modern languages to each other.

Linguists classify languages in two ways: typological and genetic. Typological classifications arrange languages according to common features—for example, all those that order simple declarative sentences by starting with the subject, followed by the object, and ending with the verb. This enables linguists to make comparisons across languages and identify universal features of language. For historians, however, it is genetic classifications that offer us the possibility of writing about the deeper past of oral societies. Genetic classifications of languages trace which languages developed out of a common ancestral language, the protolanguage, and what were the intervening stages of development and branching. This draws on the biological terminology of genetic relatedness and so it is essential to emphasize that while a set of languages may be genetically related to each other, their speakers need not be.[18]

What the genetic classification of languages gives us is the historical relationship between modern languages and protolanguages at various periods in the past. Taking the Indo-European family of languages as an example, Celtic and Italic are both protolanguages descended from Proto-Indo-European. The Celtic languages further divided into Brythonic (the ancestor to Welsh, Breton, and Cornish), Goidelic (the ancestor to Irish, Scots, and Manx Gaelic), and

Gaulish. The Italic languages diverged a number of times until the Latinic family emerged, from which derived the Romance languages that in turn yielded Romanian, French, Spanish, and Italian, among others.[19] Understanding those relationships makes it possible to reconstruct, at least in part, Proto-Romance or Proto-Celtic.[20] Similarly, Kiswahili is descended from Proto-Northeast Coast Bantu and isiZulu is descended from Proto-Nguni, while both those protolanguages are in turn descended from Proto-East Bantu.[21] And understanding those relationships makes it possible to reconstruct—again, at least in part—Proto-East Bantu as well as Proto-Nguni and Proto-Northeast Coast Bantu.[22]

The genetic classification of languages depends on the recognition of inherited features. One method for establishing a genetic classification takes a statistical approach that assumes, based essentially on the principle of Occam's razor, that the higher the percentage of shared core vocabulary across related languages, the closer their relation. This method is generally referred to as lexicostatistics. It involves the comparison of lexical items for a fixed set of meanings between pairs of languages to determine whether two words are cognate (that is, they are inherited from a common protolanguage) or not. In order to minimize the effect of borrowing from contact languages, linguists use a list of one or two hundred items that are understood to be most universal and least subject to change through borrowing. This includes words such as rain, sun, moon, woman, stone. Often called the Swadesh list, after the linguist Morris Swadesh who first developed it in the mid-twentieth century, this list of core vocabulary has been amended several times with the aim of removing geographically and culturally specific items, such as snow.[23]

Once we have collected the words for the items on the core vocabulary list for the languages being studied as well as those neighboring them, the process of determining which are cognate can begin. For example, we can take the lexical item *white* and compare it across Lubukusu, Ludadiri, Lumasaaba, Lugwe, Lusaamia, and Lunyole, as shown in table 1.1. We then compare the item for each pair of languages. If the word is cognate, we assign it a value of 1. If it is not cognate, we assign it a value of 0. If there is more than one word with the meaning in either language, we identify how many are cognate and assign a value of 0, 1, or a decimal, depending on the result. Here we can see that the item *white* is cognate between Lubukusu and Ludadiri and so is assigned a value of 1, but between Lubukusu and Lumasaaba the value is 0.5 because only one of the words in Lumasaaba exists in Lubukusu. The item is not cognate between Lubukusu and Lugwe and so we assign it a value of 0. If we compare Lumasaaba and Lunyole,

TABLE 1.1. The adjective *white* in select Greater Luhyia languages

English	Lubukusu	Ludadiri	Lumasaba	Lugwe	Lusaamia	Lunyole
white	-waanga	-waanga	-wanga -khose	-lafu	-lafu -rachari	-bbece -xoosa

we again assign a value of 0.5 because *-khose* and *-xoosa* are cognate, but *-wanga* and *-bbece* are not.

This process is repeated for all pairs of languages and for the full list of one or two hundred items. When an item is not found in a language—or the data is incomplete—we do not assign a value and instead remove the item from the calculation (basing it on 99, say, rather than 100). The results are then put into a matrix of the percentages of cognates between each pair of languages. The matrix for the Greater Luhyia languages is in figure 1.1. Based on this, it is possible to identify groupings of languages descended from a common protolanguage because they have higher rates of cognation. Importantly, it is also possible to identify subgroupings within a larger language group. We can, furthermore, identify the boundaries between one group of languages and another if they are related at a deeper time depth (as are Greater Luhyia and West Nyanza) by seeing where cognate percentages fall significantly. Similarly, it is possible to identify if the languages are entirely unrelated by seeing where cognation falls away completely, as would be the case, for example, between Greater Luhyia and Western Nilotic languages.[24]

A second method for establishing genetic relatedness between languages and classifying them is the comparative method. The comparative method is also the foundation for reconstructing portions of a protolanguage (it is never possible to fully reconstruct an undocumented protolanguage due to the reality that parts of it simply disappear when they stop being used by speakers). The first step is determining—typically from shared morphology—that a group of languages is likely related. Then we compare possible cognate words and morphological paradigms. If a word or morphological element is shared by a subgroup of languages and no others, then an initial assumption can be made that those languages have a common protolanguage whose speakers innovated a new word or morphological element. One example of shared innovation is weak evidence of a genetic relationship between languages. Multiple examples of shared innovation, however, form strong evidence that a group of languages has a common protolanguage. Morphology is a good indicator of genetic linguistic relationship because there is a very low likelihood of a feature being common across several languages by chance.[25] The

M	65									Key
										N: Lunyole
M	65									M: Lumasaaba
D	63	85								D: Ludadiri
B	62	81	78							B: Lubukusu
G	68	67	69	69						G: Lugwe
S	66	65	66	69	90					S: Lusaamia
K	60	63	64	66	75	78				K: Lukisa
W	58	61	63	64	71	73	97			W: Luwanga
Ts	58	62	63	66	72	76	98	95		Ts: Lutsotso
I	53	56	56	57	62	65	81	79	79	I: Lwidakho
L	54	56	57	57	64	68	76	75	75	77	L: Lulogooli
Ti	53	57	56	59	60	63	73	71	72	79	80	Ti: Lutirichi
	N	M	D	B	G	S	K	W	Ts	I	L

FIGURE 1.1. Matrix of cognation between Greater Luhyia languages

comparative method, thus, as with lexicostatistics, allows us to determine the limits of relatedness and the specific relationships among languages. The most reliable genetic classifications are those done through the comparative method, but lexicostatistical classifications are highly useful for establishing initial groupings that can then be tested by the comparative method. If a subgroup proposed through lexicostatistics does not have any shared innovations that are unique to it, then it cannot be held up as a valid subgroup. On the other hand, the more unique shared innovations within a subgroup, the stronger the classification.

The last twenty years have seen significant further developments in the genetic classification of languages, with linguists drawing on analogies with biological evolution and dramatically enhanced computing capacity to apply phylogenetic methods in this area.[26] This is especially useful at higher levels in classifications, such as the Bantu family which is made up of some five hundred individual languages. The computing capacity also allows for the application of Bayesian statistics, which results in a classification "based on *maximum likelihood*, i.e., which parameters are the most likely to produce the observed data."[27] Research by the linguist Rebecca Grollemund in this field has resulted in an important, new classification of Bantu languages that has implications for the ancestry of Great Lakes Bantu languages, although it does not speak to the subclassifications of West Nyanza and Greater Luhyia.[28]

The people living in eastern Uganda today speak languages belonging to two distinct language families: Atlantic-Congo and Nilotic.[29] Proto-Nilotic diverged into three branches, generally termed Eastern, Southern, and Western.[30] Proto-Eastern Nilotic further diverged, yielding Bari and Tung'a, with Proto-Tung'a dividing into Lotuko-Maa and Ateker.[31] Among the modern languages that descended from Proto-Lotuko-Maa are Lotuko, Maa, and Ongamo, spoken in South Sudan and Kenya. We now have a well-developed classification of the Ateker branch of Tung'a thanks to historian William Fitzsimons's extensive fieldwork and analysis. Proto-Ateker first saw a two-way split into Proto-Ateso and Proto-Northern Ateker. Proto-Northern Ateker further divided into Proto-Highland Northern Ateker and Proto-Lowland Northern Ateker. It is the former that is of relevance for this study, yielding as it did the modern language Ngakarimojong, with the closely related dialect Jie. Proto-Ateso ultimately gave rise to Atesyo (Tororo) and the three Ateso dialects of Pallisa, Usuku, and Ngora—here these are collectively referred to as Ateso.[32]

Proto-Southern Nilotic diverged into Proto-Tato or Proto-Omotik-Datooga (yielding Omotik, now extinct, and the Datooga dialect cluster spoken in north central Tanzania) and Proto-Kalenjin. Proto-Kalenjin then diverged into Proto-Northern Kalenjin, which gave rise to Päkot and the Marakwet languages, and Proto-Elgon-Mau Kalenjin. Proto-Elgon-Mau Kalenjin in turn yielded three protolanguages: Proto-Elgon Kalenjin, Proto-Central Kalenjin (with languages such as Nandi and Kipsigis), and Proto-Southern Kalenjin (with languages such as Akie and Kinare). It is the former that is of interest here. Proto-Elgon Kalenjin diverged into Proto-Kony-Sapiny, yielding Kony and Sapiny, and Proto-Pok-Ong'om, yielding Pok and Ong'om.[33]

Finally, Proto-Western Nilotic has three main branches, Northern, Luo, and Dinka-Nuer, although scholars disagree on the precise relationship between them. The problem is primarily grounded in a lack of documentation for some languages, but a recent classification sees a two-way divide into Nuer-Dinka and Luo-Burun, with the former giving rise to Jieng (Dinka) and Naadh (Nuer) and the latter dividing again into Luo and Burun. Luo then divided into North and South branches, with the former, including Ocolo (Shilluk) and Anywa, spoken in South Sudan and the latter, including Acholi, Dholuo, Dhopadhola, Lango, and Kumam, spoken across northern and eastern Uganda and western Kenya.[34] Please see figure 1.2 for full listing and a visualization of these genetic relationships that highlights the relevant modern Nilotic languages for this study.

Proto-Nilotic

I. Eastern Nilotic
  A. Bari
  B. Tung'a
    1. Lotuko-Maa
      Lotuko, Maa, Ongamo
    2. Ateker
      a. Teso
        i. Kyoga-Bisina Teso
          α. ***Ateso*** *(Pallisa)*
          β. Nuclear Teso
            Ateso *(Usuku),* ***Ateso*** *(Ngora)*
        ii. ***Atesyo*** *(Tororo)*
      b. Northern Ateker
        i. Highland Northern Ateker
          Najie, ***Ngakarimojong****, Dodos?*
        ii. Lowland Northern Ateker
          Toposa, Nyangatom, Turkana

II. Southern Nilotic
  A. Tato
  B. Kalenjin
    1. Northern Kalenjin
      a. *Päkot*
      b. Marakwet
    2. Elgon-Mau Kalenjin
      a. Elgon Kalenjin
        i. Kony-Sapiny
          Kony, ***Kupsabiny*** *(also Kupsapiny)*
        ii. Pok-Ong'om
          Pok, Ong'om
      b. Central Kalenjin
        i. *Kipsigis*
        ii. *Barao*
        iii. Plateau Central Kalenjin
      c. Southern Kalenjin (provisional)
        i. Plains Southern Kalenjin
        ii. Highland Southern Kalenjin

III. Western Nilotic
  A. Nuer-Dinka
  B. Luo-Burun
    1. Luo
      a. North
      b. South
        Acholi, Dholuo, ***Dhopadhola****,*
        Lango, Kumam
    2. Burun

KEY: Italics denote modern languages or dialect clusters. Bold denotes languages spoken in eastern Uganda and that are the primary focus of this study. Note that not all languages are listed for each subgroup. The question mark after Dodos indicates that there is still uncertainty about its classification.

FIGURE 1.2. Genetic classification of Nilotic languages

The Atlantic-Congo languages spoken in eastern Uganda are all Bantu languages that belong to two different branches of the Great Lakes Bantu family: Greater Luhyia and West Nyanza.[35] Unlike the putative Nilo-Saharan phylum, the Atlantic-Congo one is well-established and the place of the Bantu languages within it even more so. Proto-Bantu emerged from the Bantoid subbranch of the Benue-Congo. While debates about the divergence of Proto-Bantu have been waged for a number of decades, the evidence increasingly points toward a relatively late emergence of Proto-East Bantu from the Western Bantu branch.[36] Proto-East Bantu then diverged into a number of languages, one of which was Proto-Northeast Savanna Bantu or Proto-Kaskazi Bantu, the ancestral language to many of the modern Bantu languages spoken in Kenya and Tanzania, as well as Uganda. Proto-Great Lakes Bantu emerged from Proto-Kaskazi and

Proto-Great Lakes Bantu

I. Western Lakes

II. West Nyanza
   A. Rutara
   B. North Nyanza
     1. *Luganda*
     2. South Kyoga
       a. *Lusoga*
       b. East Kyoga
         Lugwere, Rushana

KEY: Italics denote modern languages or dialect clusters. Bold denotes languages spoken in eastern Uganda that are the focus of this study.

III. Pre-Gungu

IV. East Nyanza

V. Greater Luhyia
   A. North Luhyia
     Lubukusu, Lumasaaba, Ludadiri
   B. **Lunyole**
   C. Gwe-Saamia
     Lugwe, Lusaamia
   D. Luyia
     1. Kisa-Wanga-Tsotso
       Lukisa, Luwanga, Lutsotso
     2. *Lutirichi*
     3. *Lwidakho*
     4. *Lulogooli*

FIGURE 1.3. Genetic classification of West Nyanza and Greater Luhyia languages

itself diverged into five languages: Proto-Western Lakes, Proto-West Nyanza, pre-Gungu, Proto-East Nyanza, and Proto-Greater Luhyia. The West Nyanza languages formed two different branches: Rutara, including Runyoro, Kihaya, and Kizinza, spoken in Uganda and Tanzania, and North Nyanza. Proto-North Nyanza initially diverged into two languages, early Luganda and Proto-South Kyoga, with the latter yielding Lusoga and Proto-East Kyoga. East Kyoga finally split into the modern languages of Lugwere and Rushana. All the modern North Nyanza languages are spoken in Uganda.[37]

The Greater Luhyia languages saw an initial four-way split into Proto-North Luhyia, pre-Lunyole, Proto-Gwe-Saamia, and Proto-Luyia. Soon thereafter, Proto-Luyia diverged to yield Lutirichi, Lwidakho, Lulogooli, and the dialect cluster of Lukisa, Luwanga, and Lutsotso, with the latter remaining mutually intelligible to the present. Proto-North Luhyia diverged to yield the modern languages of Lubukusu, Lumasaaba, and Ludadiri, while Proto-Gwe-Saamia yielded the dialects Lugwe and Lusaamia, which also retain high mutual intelligibility.[38] Lumasaaba, Ludadiri, Lunyole, and Lugwere are spoken in Uganda. Lubukusu and Lusaamia are spoken in both Uganda and Kenya, while the Luyia languages are spoken in Kenya. Please see figure 1.3 for the classifications of West Nyanza and Greater Luhyia and their relationship to Great Lakes Bantu languages.

Establishing when people spoke protolanguages in the absence of datable written records is difficult. The most reliable way of doing so takes the assumption about where a language was spoken and correlates reconstructed vocabulary for material objects, including tools, grains, and animal remains, with excavated and dated examples from the archaeological record of that location. The more correlations, the stronger the likelihood that the people who spoke those words were the ones using those tools, growing and consuming the grains, and keeping or hunting the animals. But it is hard to be certain that communities identifiable from the archaeological record are the speaker communities identified from the linguistic record. The way to mitigate that uncertainty is through the most possible data points. Unfortunately for eastern Uganda, that is difficult because of the highly limited archaeological research to date.

The approximate dates for when the various protolanguages that are the focus of this study were spoken thus come from glottochronology. Glottochronology is based on the observation that while each change in the core vocabulary (the basic vocabulary that is posited to be least susceptible to change) is random, the changes accumulate to a normal distribution of 14 percent per five hundred years.[39] Linguists diverge significantly in their acceptance of this method, and there are a number of valid counterexamples in Indo-European, where continued contact, for example, has slowed divergence between languages, skewing the numbers.[40] Like other human sciences, it is imperfect, but in the Great Lakes region the dates derived by this method for Great Lakes Bantu languages correlate well with the archaeological and palynological (pollen) records.[41] Similarly, Fitzsimons's research shows that the glottochronological dates for Ateker languages correlate well with evidence for climate events and chronologies based on generations.[42] In the absence of another method for generating calendar dates, glottochronology offers us broad estimates that can be tested and improved using correlations from archaeological and other data as it is produced. Some of the dates here are ones I calculated from my own lexicostatistical data; some are ones I draw from other scholars.

Reconstructing Sounds

As part of the comparative method, we identify sound correspondences between related languages. Comparing the words *amaaji* and *kameezi* (water) in Lunyole and Lumasaaba respectively allows us to see, for example, that the phoneme /ʒ/ (the sound we commonly represent in English as "j" and that is a voiced post-alveolar fricative) in Lunyole corresponds to /z/ (a voiced alveolar fricative) in Lumasaaba. Similarly, /g/ (a voiced velar plosive) in Lunyole corresponds to /k/ (an unvoiced velar plosive) in Lumasaaba, as in *olwiga* and *lulwika* (horn). With all the sound correspondences in place, we can use the established rules that govern the kinds and directions of sound changes to determine what each phoneme was in the protolanguage and build up the full phonology. This is because if speakers of a language change a sound in one word, they will also change that sound in all other words where it occurs in the same phonetic context.

The reconstruction of the phonology of a protolanguage is not always a straightforward matter, as multiple sound changes can affect the same phonemes of a language. In such cases, it is necessary to identify the order in which the changes occurred if we are to establish the original phoneme. The linguist Martin Mould has noted that the Greater Luhyia languages underwent the sound change known as Dahl's Law. This is a change that involves dissimilation of phonemes in particular contexts.[43] A common example given to illustrate this sound change is the word for the number three, which has been reconstructed to Proto-Bantu as *tátò (where the asterisk indicates that this is a reconstructed and, thus, hypothetical form, rather than a word that has been attested), with the voiceless stop /t/ in the first syllable followed by the same voiceless stop in the second syllable. In Greater Luhyia languages, speakers distinguished between the two by changing the first /t/ to /d/, a voiced stop, yielding *dátò. But when we look at the phonology of modern Greater Luhyia languages, we can see that some of them have a /t/ where Dahl's Law would lead us to expect a /d/. For example, in Lumasaaba the word for three is *taru*. This is because of another sound change known as Luyia Law that saw the second /t/ in the sequence become /r/. This then undid the Dahl's Law change because it was no longer necessary for the purposes of dissimilation and rather than have #daru (where # indicates a nonexistent form), speakers of Lumasaaba, Lubukusu, and other Luyia languages changed the /d/ back to /t/. This example illustrates that it is possible, even with complicated phonological detours, to reconstruct the phonology of protolanguages.

With the phonology in place, we can then turn to words to identify which are cognate and reconstruct the forms they had in the relevant protolanguage. In the absence of any contemporaneous record from when those languages were spoken, these reconstructions remain hypothetical. Nonetheless, grounded as they are in well-established knowledge about phonology and phonetics and about how sounds change, we can have a high degree of confidence in them. While the reconstruction of sounds to protolanguages is based on phonetics and phonology, the reconstruction of meaning depends on semantics. The reconstruction of meaning is always important for historians, but is especially so for conceptual history because the primary interest is in how and why concepts and their meanings have changed.

Concepts, Meaning, and Cognitive Semantics

Diachronic semanticists—linguists who work on how and why meanings change within a language across time—have developed a much better understanding of semantic change in recent decades. Their insights offer important lessons for historians who use linguistic evidence because just as there are constraints on phonological changes, so are there constraints on semantic change. Those constraints take a number of forms—for example, directionality in grammaticalization (when concepts "are expressed as affixes or non-lexical categories," e.g., the concept past is expressed in English by the affix -ed[44])—and mean that semantic change, like phonological and morpho-syntactic change, is regular in that there are predictable patterns of change across languages. Linguists Elizabeth Closs Traugott and Richard Dasher argued that this is because language use at all levels "is constrained by the structural properties of the form in question, and the cognitive and communicative purposes for which language is used."[45] In order to understand how meaning changes, therefore, linguists draw on cognitive linguistics, pragmatics, and discourse analysis.

The kinds of semantic changes that interest Traugott and Dasher and others, notably grammaticalization, are not those that offer much insight for historians. We typically look more at nouns, verbs, and adjectives, because those enable us to reconstruct parts of the physical, social, and metaphysical realities of speakers in the past. When speakers changed the meaning of an existing word to refer to a specific kind of grain or a different hunting technique, this suggests to us there was a change in their material world: a move into savanna environment, for example. When speakers changed the meaning of an existing word to refer to inherited leadership, this suggests a change in their political organization: a move toward monarchy, for example. When speakers changed the meaning of an existing word to refer to territorial spirits this suggests a change in their beliefs: a move away from the ancestral spirits of firstcomers and toward more generalized spirits, for example.[46]

In order to understand how the meaning attached to a particular form has changed over time, we need to understand the different reasons for why meanings change, some of which are internal to language (such as grammaticalization) and others external to language (such as the creation of monarchical leadership). The linguist Andreas Blank has proposed a typology of the motivations for semantic change from a cognitive perspective.[47] These include the need to name a new concept; abstraction expressed through metaphor; and sociocultural change. Other motivations emerge from a close conceptual or factual relation.

Sometimes a "strong and habitual relation between two concepts within a frame makes speakers express them by using only one word."[48] Prototypical changes are when the meaning within the category is either restricted or expanded. Blurred categories occur when "speakers make transfers without being aware of it, because their knowledge about the limits of these concepts and the respective categories is momentarily or permanently blurred—for example, shifts in meaning between rat and mouse in Romance languages.[49] Complexity and irregularity in the lexicon can also lead to changes in meaning. Lexical gaps, "caused by an asymmetric lexical structure," result in semantic change as speakers extend meanings or add new words to balance the perceived asymmetry.[50] Similarly, when speakers encounter "words whose meaning is somewhat untypical for the word class they belong to" they may change the meaning of the word.[51] Finally, euphemism can lead to semantic change, especially around taboos or emotionally freighted words, such as death and dying.[52]

In contrast to Blank's expansive model, the linguist Dirk Geeraerts has focused on prototype theory to explain semantic change.[53] Prototype theory is premised on the fact that, as linguist William O'Grady explained, "Underlying the use of words and sentences to express meaning in human language is a conceptual system capable of organizing and classifying every imaginable aspect of our experience, from inner feelings and perceptions, to cultural and social phenomena, to the physical world that surrounds us."[54] We organize words into concepts or semantic categories, such as animals, dwellings, and intelligence. Furthermore, it is possible to grade the members of any semantic category according to their typicality.[55] The category bird in English, as an example, encompasses a wide range of meanings, some of which are more typical than others. Thus, sparrow, blackbird, and eagle are very typical while penguins and ostriches are less typical. Prototypicality offers us a model for why and how meaning changes over time. According to Geeraerts, speakers can develop "peripheral nuances within given categories" in response to material and intellectual changes and in response to "changing cognitive requirements." The addition of "marginally deviant concepts," such as penguin, "can be peripherally incorporated" and thus do not destabilize the whole category, in this case bird, even while the category changes.[56] In other words, a category can be expanded or peripherally changed yet retain its core meaning. If a peripheral meaning becomes increasingly central, then the entire category can be changed. Thus, if penguin came to be the core meaning of bird, the centrality of flight to the concept bird would no longer hold.

In order to trace changes in the concepts poverty and wealth in eastern Uganda, in the absence of a long history of documentation and, in particular, the rich contextualized data available to conceptual historians of Europe, I compiled detailed semantic maps. I did this for each of the roots associated with the prototype categories poverty, poor person, wealth, and rich person found in all of the thirteen modern languages that are covered by this study, as well as in many more related languages. In developing these semantic maps, I traced polysemous meanings and homonyms, as well as synonyms for each root and meaning. Drawing on insights from diachronic semantics and prototype theory, I used these semantic maps to reconstruct the range of meanings of words used in the past as a way of getting at the broader conceptualization encapsulated in each.

The data I used to make these semantic maps came from more than one hundred interviews I conducted with speakers of relevant languages and from published and unpublished dictionaries and wordlists, as well as from ethnographies and other published materials. Each dictionary compiler, just as each speaker I interviewed, was working with their particular definition of poverty and of wealth. To mitigate the effects of this work of definition, I used as wide a range of sources as possible for each word, and I repeatedly moved back and forth between synonyms and the different meanings ascribed to particular words by asking how people would translate a word back into English and then tracing those different translations back into the original language. By starting with the words people in eastern Uganda today use to talk about poverty and wealth, rather than imposing external models or theories such as wealth in people, pawnship, and debt, the aim was to trace indigenous ways of conceiving of socioeconomic difference, rather than look for evidence to support a particular hypothesis. This approach, as should become clear in the following chapters, led me to some conceptualizations of poverty and wealth that I had not at all anticipated.

Before moving on to the other kinds of evidence used in this book, a brief overview of noun classes in Bantu languages is necessary, because they play an integral role in determining the meaning of words. All nouns in Bantu languages belong to specific classes that are denoted by the use of prefixes and by modifications to other words in the same noun phrase, a feature referred to as a system of agreement markers.[57] Noun classes function in a similar way to grammatical gender in some other languages. With gender, all nouns belong to a category (feminine, masculine, neuter) and the category affects other aspects of morphology (for example, pluralization). In contrast to the two or three categories usually represented by gender, linguists posit up to twenty-three different noun classes across the Bantu languages.[58] Many, although not all, of them are paired in singular and plural forms. Thus, nouns in class one, with the prefix *mu-* (in the Bantu languages of this study) are singular and plurals are formed by changing the prefix to that of noun class two, *ba-*. For example, in Lunyole *omubumbi* means potter and *ababumbi* means potters. The prefixes of adjectives agree with the noun class prefix of the subject as we can see in these examples from Lusoga:

> *omwáná omúleeyí*
> child (noun, s.) prefix–tall (adjective)
> the tall child
> *abáaná abáreeyí*
> children (noun, pl.) prefix–tall (adjective)
> the tall children
> *ekímúlí ekíreeyí*
> flower (noun, s.) prefix–tall (adjective)
> the tall flower
> *ebímúlí ebíreeyí*
> flowers (noun, pl.) prefix–tall (adjective)
> the tall flowers

Verbs agree with the subject, object, or both. Thus, in Lugwere, we find:

> *omuyembe gukula*
> mango tree (noun, s.) subject–marker–grow (verb)–present–tense
> the mango tree is growing
> *omwala agukoma omuyembe*
> girl (noun, s.) subject–marker–object–marker–plant (verb)–present–tense mango tree (noun, s.)
> the girl is planting the mango tree

As we have seen, the meaning of nouns can be changed from singular to plural by changing the noun class. Other changes in meaning can be made by moving a noun from one noun class to another. This is easily illustrated with the root *-soga*, where *omusoga* is a Soga person, *abasoga* are Soga people, *busoga* is Soga country, *lusoga* is the Soga language. This is because noun classes are associated, albeit not in a rigid manner, with categories of meaning. Nouns in classes one (*mu-*) and two (*ba-*) are human beings, nouns in class fourteen (*bu-*) are abstracts or collectives, and some nouns in class eleven (*lu-*) are languages. Another example, from Lugwere this time, is the root *-ntu*, where *omuntu* means person, *abantu* means people, *ekintu* means thing, *ebintu* means things, *akantu* means small thing, and *obuntu* means small things. In addition, changing the noun class of a noun used to refer to a person away from classes one and two can indicate a value judgment, whether positive or negative. Part of tracing the changing meanings of words used to talk about the concepts of poverty, wealth, poor person, and rich person thus involves paying close attention to the noun classes used, especially when words referring to people are not in classes one and two.

Archaeology: Ceramics, Economy, Identity

Archaeology is an invaluable means of learning about the African past, both in contexts where there are written records and in those where there are not. This is in part because archaeological research produces very different evidence about different things from that typically found in archives and other writings. As many others have noted, historians and archaeologists using evidence from comparative historical linguistics for the African context have long turned to the research produced by the other. While this relationship has, at times, been framed rather negatively, such as a sibling rivalry, it has in fact been extremely productive for both disciplines. Nonetheless, it is true that due to the different starting points of research in each discipline—and the sometimes incomplete understanding of the evidence from the other discipline—that some tensions have arisen over how archaeologists have used historical linguistic data produced by historians and how historians have used archaeological data.[59]

Archaeology offers the possibility of dating communities in time and locating them in space. Through methods of carbon dating in particular, archaeologists are able to provide spans of time during which places were inhabited, particular kinds of ceramics were made and used, and particular kinds of food were hunted, gathered, fished, grown, or raised. And, rather obviously, because archaeologists excavate spaces used by people in the past, they produce evidence about specific places. This contrasts with linguistic evidence, such as reconstructed words, that could have been spoken and heard across large spans of space. Matching up a community that emerges from the archaeological record with one that emerges from the linguistic record is fraught with complexity and ideally rests on multiple correlations in the data. Because of the nature of research, the mapping of linguistic and archaeological communities in much of East Africa and beyond remains somewhat conjectural.[60]

While some archaeological research has been conducted in eastern Uganda, the political instability of the 1970s and 1980s in Uganda in general, and of the 1990s and 2000s in parts of the East in particular, has contributed to a general paucity of archaeology in the region. There has, however, been a good deal of research (relatively speaking) in some neighboring areas, especially in western

Kenya and around the littoral and islands of the Victoria Nyanza to the east and west of the region. A major topic for archaeologists in East Africa in particular, and sub-Saharan Africa more generally, is the transition from foraging to food production.[61] A series of excavations in the eastern basin of the Victoria Nyanza in the early 2000s—and drawing on earlier work—provided evidence for ceramic production by hunter-fisher-gatherer communities that depended on fish and shellfish as a regular and predictable source of food that allowed them to become sedentary.[62] These ceramics are called Kansyore ware "and have been intimately associated with a Later Stone Age (LSA) hunter-gatherer lifestyle" in East Africa.[63] Another type, called Urewe ware, consists of "well-made and highly crafted ceramic" with beveled rims, "incised or impressed" decoration "with a wide palette of horizontal banding, cross-hatching, hanging or pendant motifs, and 'covering pattern.'"[64] They have long been associated with Bantu-speaking farmers and, in particular, with iron production during the period referred to as the Early Iron Age in the Great Lakes region.

At one site in particular in Usenge in western Kenya, Kansyore ware that dated to circa 1690–1390 BCE was overlain by what archaeologist Ceri Ashley has termed Contact Urewe ware, dated to circa 410–600 CE. "Although superficially resembling Urewe ceramics in aspects of typology, it is nonetheless clear that the producers of this ceramic, here termed 'Contact Urewe,' did not place the same emphasis on quality of manufacture and finish, thus creating a completely localized and unique variant of Urewe."[65] Furthermore, the archaeological record at Usenge shows that by around fifteen hundred years ago there had been "a clear shift away from reliance on aquatic resources, with the near complete disappearance of shellfish and an increased presence of terrestrial animals, including cattle as well as sheep/goats."[66] Rather than simply suggest the displacement of the older communities by newer ones, Darla Dale and Ceri Ashley noted that the overall record at Usenge instead points to the adoption of new ceramic styles by the existing community. This, they argued, would most likely have been a result of contact with farming communities using Urewe ware in a "frontier situation" in which "certain goods and commodities" as well as "ideas and adaptations (such as cattle-keeping)" were "moving between communities."[67] While remaining somewhat conjectural, we can posit that the farming communities they found themselves sharing the frontier situation with were people speaking Greater Luhyia languages, who built communities in the region from roughly two thousand years ago. Further archaeological and historical research, especially in the southern half of eastern Uganda, would do much to deepen our knowledge of this period.

Oral Traditions: The Past through the Present

A quick glance at *History in Africa: A Journal of Debates, Methods, and Source Analysis* suffices to understand that the use of oral traditions for writing about the past is simultaneously common and contested. In some ways we can think of oral traditions as akin to manuscripts transcribed time and again, with variations made by each scribe and with each transcription. Because earlier versions are so frequently lost to us, we have to rely on later versions that include those variations. "The Periplus of the Erythraean Sea," for example, is attributed to an author in the mid-first century CE, but the earliest extant manuscript dates to the tenth century.[68] Historians wishing to use the "Periplus" to understand first-century trading patterns must do so knowing there is a nine-hundred-year gap in the documentation. Nonetheless, documents do help provide a stability to the text and firm dates from which to start.

Oral traditions, passed down from generation to generation, and only transcribed in the last hundred years or so, and frequently in the last fifty years, sit a little more uncomfortably with the discipline of history. Historians of Africa have taken widely varying approaches to them as sources over the past many decades. Some sought to develop rigorous methodologies that aimed to weed out what they perceived as myths and retain only what they perceived as facts.[69] Others turned to the members of the societies whose traditions they were collecting to develop a single, agreed-upon version, an approach that might today be described as the coproduction of knowledge.[70] Some scholars paid more attention to the contexts in which oral traditions were performed, using ethnographic knowledge to understand how audiences would have made sense of the traditions.[71] There is also wide variety in how communities remembered and performed oral traditions, from highly specialized experts, such as the jeli of the Mande world, to informal transmission across generations in ordinary households. Practices and timing of their transcription vary just as widely. There can, therefore, be no single approach to them as historical sources. While assuming that they cannot be read as straightforward narratives of historical events, we can nonetheless glean much that is useful. And by reading them carefully, by paying attention to the moment of transcription and its political context, we can gain invaluable insight into the past beyond the nineteenth century.

In eastern Uganda, the kinds of oral traditions associated with the monarchy in Buganda are absent, not least because the kind of centralized power the monarchy there represented is also absent. But there are many oral traditions. For the Greater Luhyia societies (and some Kalenjin and Teso societies), those collected by Gideon Were are important, but histories written by other scholars drawing on their own collections of oral traditions are also valuable.[72] The Uganda History Project run from the Makerere University Department of History in the 1960s and 1970s sent undergraduate students to their home areas to collect oral traditions, many of which resulted in BA theses. Some of these remain in the Makerere University Library and some are reproduced in collections, such as the "History of Bugisu."[73] Several historians in the 1960s and 1970s collected what they collectively referred to as Historical Texts across eastern Uganda and western Kenya, covering Busoga, Bugwere, Teso, and Jie, in particular, often with publications on precolonial history resulting.[74] Published and unpublished histories written by local intellectuals in the colonial era also drew on oral traditions.[75] All told, this body of work offers us windows into economic, social, and political history, including into concepts of wealth and poverty.

Ethnography and History

Ethnographic descriptions of societies, especially those undertaken a hundred or so years ago (before the dramatic changes of the twentieth century), can be useful in providing some of the context in which words about the poor and the rich were spoken, heard, and understood. But this must always be undertaken with great care and historicity. While we can identify cultural and social practices that continued into the era of colonial rule—for example, we have early twentieth-century descriptions of dress practices that suggest minimal external influence—it is essential to be attentive to everything that had changed. As early as 1901, a British colonial report noted that the main aim of men, after having large families, in some Greater Luhyia–speaking communities was to join the colonial police force as a means of enhancing their status.[76] While this was likely exaggerated, it does reflect the rapidity with which some changes came about, especially with reference to socioeconomic status—precisely what this book is about.

Aside from the transformations wrought by colonial rule and colonial economies, it is worth repeating the obvious, but often forgotten, fact that the societies of eastern Uganda in the late nineteenth and early twentieth centuries were the products of centuries and millennia of change. Indeed, five hundred years earlier, many of their ancestors lived far outside the region. Thus, any ethnographic data must be used comparatively and anchored with other forms of evidence as far as possible. That said, we have well-documented examples of very long-term continuities of practices in contexts outside of eastern Uganda. One example is that of the dances performed in the worship of the goddess Hathor in Nubia that are documented on the walls of the temple at Philae during the Ptolemaic and Roman periods. The Egyptologist and Nubiologist Solange Ashby has shown continuities in clothing and performance from two thousand years ago to present-day dances.[77] Thus, while we must be very careful and especially attentive to anachronism in our use of comparative ethnographic evidence, to claim that there are no continuities in practice and thought is as wrong-headed as it is to claim that descriptions from the late nineteenth and early twentieth centuries can be readily projected back to early periods.

Ethnographic descriptions for eastern Uganda vary significantly in quantity and quality across the region. Some were written by the missionary-turned-ethnographer John Roscoe, others by other missionaries, travelers, and colonial officials. Later in the twentieth century, professional anthropologists arrived from Europe and eastern Ugandans themselves researched their societies. While ethnographic evidence does not provide the backbone for this book, I have turned to it to provide possible context for some of the concepts of poverty and wealth. When I do so, I make this clear in the text, so readers can decide for themselves what to make of my conclusions.

CHAPTER TWO

Excavating Early Ideas about Poverty and Wealth

WHAT ARE THE OLDEST concepts for wealth and poverty that we can identify for the lands that stretch north of Lake Victoria Nyanza and east of the River Nile in eastern Uganda? What frames of reference did the people using those concepts mobilize as they developed them across centuries and millennia? This chapter answers these questions in order to lay a foundation for the evidence and arguments presented in the subsequent chapters that tell the history of these concepts across time and across the radical transformation of this region's social, political, and economic landscape. To do this, I examine what words people used when they spoke about impoverished people and their condition of poverty and when they talked about wealth and those who possessed it. In so doing, I set out the different ideas that those words encapsulated.

To be able to understand how people's concepts of economic difference changed across the centuries and the ways they endured despite dramatic shifts in the human landscape, in climate, and in economy, we need a baseline from which to build. In this case, focused as it is on the words people used to talk about poverty and wealth in the past, we need to know what those words were in the ancestral or protolanguages of the modern languages of eastern Uganda. From that baseline, it is possible to trace how those words and the concepts they named developed in intermediary protolanguages. The starting point here consists of five protolanguages: Proto-Greater Luhyia, Proto-West Nyanza, Proto-Southern Nilotic, Proto-Eastern Nilotic, and Proto-Western Nilotic. The people who spoke each of these languages developed their own ideas about what poverty meant and what wealth meant, grounded in their particular economic, ecological, social, and cultural realities. Those who spoke languages descended from these protolanguages drew on these ancient concepts as they articulated their own understandings of poverty and wealth.

There are some commonalities that emerge when we look at the vocabulary for wealth and poverty used by people speaking these various ancestral languages, yet it is the diversity among and between them that is most striking. Some people drew on older, inherited vocabularies, sometimes holding on to the exact same meanings as their linguistic ancestors, while others created new vocabularies and ranges of meanings. Most often, the people who spoke any one protolanguage used new words and existing ones alongside each other, melding old and new concepts for economic and social difference. The variances in how people understood poverty and wealth do not fall neatly along the lines of economic specialization, any more than they do along clear linguistic lines. That is, there was no pastoralist concept of poverty and no agriculturalist concept of wealth. Instead, it is possible to discern three broad conceptual themes that cut across lines of linguistic and economic difference. People had emotional, material, and social notions of what it meant to be poor or to be wealthy. These broad themes coexisted in different arrangements. Two thousand years ago and more, the people speaking these protolanguages in East Africa—stretching at the time across what is now South Sudan, Kenya, and Uganda—not only had words for poverty and wealth, they had complex and differing conceptualizations of these categories. That we are able to reconstruct at least some of those concepts offers us new and compelling insights into what it meant to live in these ancient societies.

The Proto-Greater Luhyia Speaker Community

Proto-Greater Luhyia speakers settled in eastern Uganda around two thousand years ago (see map 2.1). They were not the first to live there; the archaeological record tells us that it has been home to people for at least the past eight millennia.[1] The people who spoke Proto-Great Lakes Bantu, the ancestral language of Proto-Greater Luhyia, lived between the Kivu Rift Valley on the western edge of the Great Lakes region and the mouth of the Kagera River on the Victoria Nyanza from around 500 BCE, and gradually settled across the Great Lakes region. Their dialects diverged as they did so, until they could no longer easily understand each other.[2] Given the challenges of circumnavigating the lake on foot, it is reasonable to assume that the people who came to speak Proto-Greater Luhyia traveled the 220 or so kilometers (some 140 miles) to its northeastern shore by water in dugout canoes, perhaps using the many islands in the lake as staging posts.[3] It is impossible to know precisely what that migration looked like. It may have involved an initial migration by a small group—along the lines theorized in anthropologist Igor Kopytoff's model of the "Internal African Frontier."[4] It may have involved a larger initial movement. It certainly was not a single event; rather, new groups arrived in the area and were incorporated into existing communities at various moments across the centuries. Regardless of how they traveled, they took

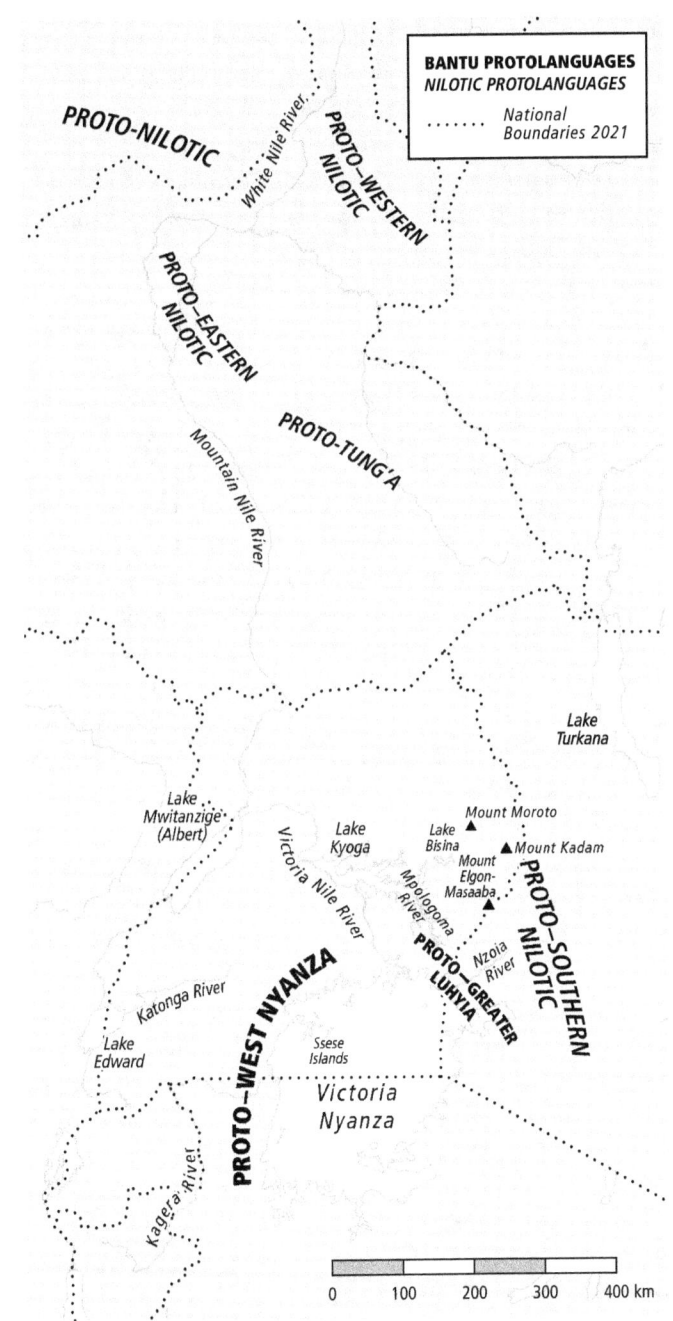

MAP 2.1. Map showing approximate areas of Proto-Greater Luhyia, Proto-West Nyanza, Proto-Nilotic, Proto-Southern Nilotic, Proto-Western Nilotic, Proto-Eastern Nilotic, and Proto-Tung'a. Map created by Nat Case.

with them a deep-rooted and diversified technological skill set that included farming and livestock raising, production of high-quality ceramics known as Urewe ware, and, in all likelihood, iron smelting and forging. They also took with them their knowledge of hunting, foraging, and fishing inherited from their ancestors who had spoken Proto–Great Lakes Bantu. And, crucially, they carried with them a long-established practice of trade and exchange with other communities, including those who spoke unrelated languages.[5]

As Proto–Greater Luhyia speakers settled in this area and gradually formed new speaker communities, they did so in a place where people speaking other, unrelated languages had long engaged in hunting, fishing, and gathering economies. Proto–Greater Luhyia speakers entered into patterns of exchange that helped change how the existing populations—firstcomers—lived, with the changes recorded in the linguistic record as well as in the region's archaeology.[6] It was in this context of exchange, wide-ranging economic activities, and sociocultural diversity that speakers of Proto–Greater Luhyia developed their particular concepts of poverty and of wealth. For all the upheaval they must have experienced in moving across or around the lake, their ability to replicate the economic model they had left behind, rather than assimilate to the one where they settled, and their influence on the way of life of existing populations, suggests that they were starting from a position of some strength and not as destitute refugees. Their capacity to successfully establish themselves, however, depended on their relations with the existing hunter-gatherer-fishing communities who had expertise in the local landscape. This process would not have been entirely straightforward. Indeed, it seems that people speaking Proto–Greater Luhyia did face real challenges as they built their communities in these new lands. Those challenges come across to us in the words they used to talk about economic and social difference.

Living on the northeastern shore and in the hinterland of the Victoria Nyanza from around two thousand years ago, communities who spoke Proto–Greater Luhyia had a diverse vocabulary for talking about poor people and the poverty they experienced. That vocabulary was composed, in part, of words that they had inherited from their Great Lakes Bantu linguistic ancestors and in part by words coined and adapted by Proto–Greater Luhyia speakers themselves. But while they drew on an older vocabulary to talk about poverty, it was not the same set of words used by their linguistic ancestors for that purpose. Instead, they took other words from their lexicon and gave them new meanings. It is worth emphasizing this: not one of the words that Proto–Greater Luhyia speakers used for poverty or for the poor was the same as those used by people speaking Proto-Great Lakes Bantu.⁷ People who spoke Proto-Greater Luhyia felt the need for a new set of words to talk and think about the social experience and material reality of privation and poverty after they settled on the far side of the vast expanse of water that is the Victoria Nyanza, as they established themselves on new lands and as they interacted with existing communities in those lands.

Some of that new vocabulary emphasized the material aspect of privation. Greater Luhyia people used words that they derived from the root *-tak- to talk about poor people (*omutaka, poor person) and about poverty (*obutaka, poverty or lack).⁸ This was a root that they inherited from people who spoke Proto-Bantu up to three thousand years earlier. Proto-Greater Luhyia speakers used it to talk about being in situations of need or lack, of being in want, in addition to using it to talk about poverty and being poor. These are different meanings to those scholars have reconstructed both for the Proto-Great Lakes Bantu reflex of the root, *-sàka ("find food, trade or work for food"), and the original Proto-Bantu root, *-càk- ("desire, wish; search for"), with their emphasis on desiring (another meaning of the English verb want⁹) and searching.¹⁰ When Proto-Greater Luhyia speakers used the root *-tak-, therefore, they invoked a conceptualization of poverty as a condition grounded in an unspecified, yet at least partially material, lack.

The emphasis on poverty as lack—as the absence of something necessary— was likely connected to their settlement to the northeast of the Victoria Nyanza. The centuries around the turn of the era were ones "of pronounced climate variability, with considerable regional differences," but the time around two thousand years ago does seem to have been "a period of extreme aridity." By around eighteen hundred years ago, the situation had improved, with "a transition to slightly wetter conditions" that lasted until about fifteen hundred years ago.¹¹ Whether or not the prolonged drought was a causal factor in the movement of Proto-Greater Luhyia speakers to eastern Uganda, such conditions would have complicated their initial settlement in the region. As people rebuilt communities in an unfamiliar landscape and adjusted their food production and collection to account for local variations in soil quality, rainfall, and temperature, they would have faced an initial period of hardship. Indeed, as they were the ones who left established communities to the west of the lake, they may have already been experiencing some economic and social marginalization, even if they were unlikely to have been entirely destitute. The hardship that they experienced in their new homeland would not have been only material in nature. People left behind social networks that had been established across generations and moved into an area where they could not, initially at least, understand the languages spoken by their new neighbors. Such a lack of networks of support would have had an emotional toll in addition to making survival harder in times of drought, disease, and crop failure. In creating a new vocabulary for poverty from the root *-tak-, Proto-Greater Luhyia speakers thus referenced the search for food found in the Proto-Great Lakes Bantu meaning of *-sàka and they emphasized the more general sense of being in serious need.

Proto-Greater Luhyia speakers developed a second set of words to talk about poverty and the poor from the root *-tamb-, which they inherited from Proto-Great Lakes Bantu, and which can again be traced back to Proto-Bantu.[12] During the time that Proto-Greater Luhyia existed, its speakers radically changed the meaning of this root from the meaning given to it by the members of their ancestral speaker communities. In Proto-Bantu, *-támb- had five separate meanings: "call; take; receive; walk; and play, dance, jump."[13] For speakers of Proto-Great Lakes Bantu, *-támb- had retained two sets of meanings: "walk" with an extension to "travel," and "offer, sacrifice to heal the sick."[14] For those speaking Proto-Greater Luhyia, by contrast, *obutambi meant poverty, *omutambi meant poor person, and the intransitive verb *-tamba meant to be poor. They stopped using it with reference to many of its older meanings, marking a clear break in the semantic history of the root.

When they used words derived from the root *-tamb-, Proto-Greater Luhyia speakers seem to have been drawing a conceptual link between poverty and bereavement. Thus, *omutambi also meant bereaved person and *-tamba also meant to be bereaved. We see this very clearly in the North Luhyia languages and in Lunyole. It is not a conceptualization I could identify in the modern languages in the Gwe-Saamia and Luyia branches and so it is not possible to be certain that this was an innovation of people who spoke Proto-Greater Luhyia. It may instead have been innovated by those who spoke Proto-North Luhyia and borrowed by speakers of Proto-Lunyole (or vice versa) after the sixth century. The regularity of the sound correspondences, however, suggests that it is an inherited form from Proto-Greater Luhyia, in which case it may have been an innovation that occurred not long before the divergence of Proto-Greater Luhyia into its descendant languages.

This conjunction of bereavement and poverty is not unique to Greater Luhyia–speaking or even to Bantu-speaking communities in this region. Nonetheless, that the Proto-Greater Luhyia speaker community used the same root for poverty and bereavement suggests an awareness of particular kinds of vulnerability and a recognition both of suffering and contingency in connection with being bereft. Losing a family member could undermine the economic security of a family, whether it was the death of a parent rendering a child vulnerable to poverty, or of a spouse—especially a husband, in this patrilineal context—making an entire household vulnerable to impoverishment. While such an observation might be seen as commonplace in studies of poverty and household contingency today, speakers of Greater Luhyia languages made this connection as much as fifteen hundred years ago.[15]

In conceiving of poverty as interlinked with bereavement, speakers of Proto-Greater Luhyia also underscored the emotional and material aspects of impoverishment by including grief and pity alongside lack and destitution. While there were undoubtedly profound economic consequences to the loss of a family member who helped sustain the household, this particular concept of poverty, as expressed through the root *-tamb-, emphasized the equal loss of important social and emotional relationships as a result of death.[16] Proto-Greater Luhyia speakers did this by highlighting the bereaved person in this overlapping conceptualization of poverty and loss.

In addition to using these two roots when they discussed poverty, the Proto-Greater Luhyia speaker community innovated a third set of words by drawing on the root *-paat-.[17] They used it in the forms of the verb *-paata meaning be poor and the noun *omupaati meaning poor person. Once again, they used a much older word, all while changing its meaning significantly. This root has been reconstructed to Proto-Bantu in the form of the verb *-pát- and with the meaning "hold."[18] But while in other Great Lakes Bantu languages the root has a wide range of meanings, including ones connected to holding, in Proto-Greater Luhyia it was used only to refer to being poor. The etymological link with the Proto-Bantu meaning "hold" and its derived meaning "be jammed, be wedged" suggests an idea of poverty as resulting from being stuck, although this remains a speculative conclusion because the meaning hold was not one Proto-Greater Luhyia speakers associated with *-paat-.[19] An alternative reading is that the poor person herself or himself was the one doing the jamming, by being unable to participate in the socially necessary circulation of wealth, such as occurred at marriage.[20] This latter interpretation is reflected in the words derived from this root that appear in neighboring languages today, having been borrowed from Greater Luhyia–speaking communities. Those words suggest a negative perception of the poor as lacking in social niceties and also as lacking the right to make demands on the basis of kinship, something discussed in detail in chapter 3.

The existence of *-paat-, with its meanings of poverty, poor person, and to be poor in Proto-Greater Luhyia, alongside the semantically more complex roots

-tak- and *-tamb-*, tells us that poverty merited considerable discussion in this ancient speaker community. Speakers of Proto-Greater Luhyia, some two thousand to fifteen hundred years ago, innovated three separate roots to talk about the condition and those who experienced it, all while abandoning the vocabulary their linguistic ancestors had used. This collective, though not necessarily conscious, decision may have been the result of a general struggle to establish a new community after they settled to the northeast of the Victoria Nyanza. It may also have been the result of the need to build networks of support in unfamiliar lands or a function of more people living in poverty in the community and tensions that arose as a consequence of this. Whatever the impetus, poverty and the existence of poor people were sufficiently important problems for the community that they developed several new words for them. As they coined new nouns, adjectives, and verbs to talk about these issues, Proto-Greater Luhyia speakers were also developing new concepts of poverty and the poor, concepts that were distinct from those held by their linguistic predecessors speaking Proto-Great Lakes Bantu. Central to these new ideas was a recognition of the interrelationship between poverty and death.

Proto-Greater Luhyia speakers, as we have seen, held an idea of society that included material inequality. Directly connected to their holding of this idea, they also developed a new vocabulary for wealth, although it was less expansive than their lexicon for poverty. The vocabulary for wealth that they built contained greater continuities with older terminology than that for poverty, suggesting greater continuity with their linguistic ancestors in how they thought about wealth. The noun *-jàandu*, in noun classes three and four, is an example of that continuity. It was coined by people speaking Proto-Great Lakes Bantu, in the last centuries BCE, to describe wealth or property.[21] Its meanings at that time had a strongly gendered component to them, as the noun referred in particular to wealth in women or wealth associated with the transfer of women, either at marriage or at the death of a husband. The word could be used, for example, to refer to a widow, because she would be inherited by her deceased husband's heir. Furthermore, in Proto-Great Lakes Bantu, it referred to wealth that was durable and heritable, whether it took ritual, material, or spiritual form.[22]

These meanings were retained by Proto-Greater Luhyia speakers, and they also retained the notion that this was a form of wealth that could be transferred to an heir at death. Taking the form *-yaandu* in Proto-Greater Luhyia, the root denoted wealth, as well as holding the more specific meaning of bridewealth. It was also used to talk about bequeathing wealth and inheriting a widow. But speakers of Proto-Greater Luhyia gave the noun other, more narrowly material, meanings of property and possessions. In this way, *-yaandu encapsulated many of the complexities of wealth in Greater Luhyia societies, complexities that have strong echoes across sub-Saharan Africa and beyond. Wealth took the form of material possessions, including the built environment of the homestead, but also other objects that conveyed status and could produce further wealth, such as leopard skins, hunting spears, or jewelry. Wealth took the forms of livestock that were both productive for a household, in terms of food and as a medium of exchange, and reproductive of it, when used as bridewealth. Wealth took the form of people, especially women whose presence in a household signified the past material wealth exchanged for them and future wealth in the form of children. And wealth was that which could be bequeathed to the next generation, both in human form as widows and in the form of material possessions and livestock.[23]

In addition to retaining *-yaandu with its gendered meanings of wealth, the Proto-Greater Luhyia speaker community began developing their own notions of wealth and of being wealthy that were distinct from those of their Proto-Great Lakes Bantu linguistic ancestors. To do so they drew on another ancient root, *-hind-, and once more demonstrated their linguistic and intellectual creativity as they transformed its meanings to address their new social and economic context.[24] This is a root that has been reconstructed to Proto-Bantu in the form of the verb *-pind-, with the primary meanings of "fold, hem, plait" and the secondary meanings of "turn, invert, change."[25] (The meaning plait was retained in Proto-Greater Luhyia in the form of the noun for basket, creating a clear etymological connection.) The root *-pind- has proved simultaneously enduring and productive across a wide range of Bantu languages, with meanings ranging from basketry to revolution.[26]

David Schoenbrun has reconstructed the noun *-hindia, derived from the Proto-Bantu root *-pind- and meaning "authority, power, able person," to Proto-Great Lakes Bantu.[27] But the distributions of form and meaning across modern languages indicate that the root had a wider range of meanings for speakers of Proto-Great Lakes Bantu. These included ones related to threatening behavior and transformation, which connected directly with the Proto-Bantu meanings of turning and changing.[28] Proto-Greater Luhyia speakers changed the meaning of the root and instead used *-hind- to talk about wealth in the form of the nouns *muhinda, meaning rich person, and *buhinda, meaning wealth, riches, and in the form of the adjective *-hinda, meaning rich or wealthy. In so doing they created a clear break with their linguistic ancestors and with their contemporaries speaking related languages. The latter used it to talk about power and authority, but did not use it to refer to wealth. Nonetheless, the etymological connection with the Proto-Great Lakes Bantu noun and its meanings of "authority, power, able person" is apparent: a wealthy person in Greater Luhyia society, as elsewhere, would have wielded at least a degree of power in the community and would have had the ability to act in ways that were not open to a poor neighbor.

With these two roots, *-yaandu and *-hind-, the community of people speaking Proto-Greater Luhyia simultaneously expressed a new, more material, concept of wealth as property and possessions and held onto older notions of it as gendered, not least because some forms of wealth were heritable and so decisions had to be made about who could inherit and what could be inherited. Proto-Greater Luhyia speaker communities appear to have continued the Proto-Great Lakes Bantu practice of patrilineal descent, as all the Greater Luhyia modern societies do so. Lineality is, of course, intimately connected to wealth because it determines who holds it and who controls the transmission of wealth across generations. Speakers of Proto-Greater Luhyia also continued to understand wealth as the cause and result of power. These material aspects echo developments in their concepts of poverty as being about material lack, but in other ways these two socioeconomic concepts continued along distinct tracks. That is, while they existed in relation to each other, they were not understood to be entirely interdependent. In particular, the Proto-Greater Luhyia speaker community appears to have perceived the causes and consequences of poverty and the causes and consequences of wealth to be quite different from each other.

The Proto-West Nyanza Speaker Community

Proto-West Nyanza was spoken around the same time as Proto-Greater Luhyia, but its speakers inhabited the area to the west of the Victoria Nyanza (see map 2.1).[29] The people who spoke Proto-West Nyanza experimented with different forms of food production, with new technologies and new forms of social and political organization, and continued established practices of ironworking, pottery, and trade. Schoenbrun has identified the intercropping of legumes with staples such as cereals and yams and other roots as the most important new forms of food production in this community, but Proto-West Nyanza speakers also expanded their expertise in livestock, especially in the maintenance of large herds of cattle.[30] As to social and political organization, they consolidated the offices under the control of royal leaders, building on the development of hereditary leadership by their ancestors who had spoken Proto-Great Lakes Bantu.[31]

The language of poverty used by Proto-West Nyanza speakers and their descendants was in part an ancient one that they inherited from their linguistic forebears. In contrast to the Proto-Greater Luhyia speaker community, they retained some of the same concepts of poverty as those held by Proto-Bantu speakers up to five thousand years ago. This suggests that during this period of consolidation in familiar lands, Proto-West Nyanza speakers did not face the same challenges and opportunities that their counterparts speaking Proto-Greater Luhyia encountered. We see this continuity in particular in the root *-jolo that was derived from the Proto-Bantu noun *-jódò, which could be used to describe a "weak person," a "smooth person," or a "poor person."³² Linguist Yvonne Bastin and her colleagues also noted a possible related form, *-bódó, with the gloss "poor person." In the derived verbal forms of the root, however, they reconstructed only the meanings "become soft" and "be soft," suggesting that that was its original sense.³³ The distribution of this root in the Greater Luhyia, East Nyanza, and West Highlands branches is such that we can be confident that it held both the meanings smooth and poor when people spoke Proto-Great Lakes Bantu. That community, thus, along with their linguistic descendants who spoke Proto-West Nyanza, perceived a link between being poor and being weak or soft. An especially suggestive connection is that between smoothness and youth. The overlapping meanings of *-jolo may point to a conceptualization of poverty as a status of youth, of those with smooth skin and no facial or body hair, and thus of the poor as not of fully adult status.³⁴

The consequences of poverty and the strategies available to the poor and the destitute in this community emerge from the other roots that Proto-West Nyanza speakers used to talk about it. Schoenbrun has written about how poor people could join the households or families of those who were better off in Great Lakes Bantu society.³⁵ But the unequal relationships that this possibility engendered were made clear to all involved through two Proto-West Nyanza roots, *-bánjà and *-jidù.³⁶ The first tied together access to land, a home, and indebtedness through its meanings "courtyard," "plot of land," and "debt." "That the word for one's home and fields should have been asked to do the work of naming a debt relation as well," noted Schoenbrun, "reveals the connection between inequality and access to land with stark efficiency."³⁷ The second root, *-jidù, meant "(male) follower" or "client" and so marked an unequal relationship where one offered labor or tribute in exchange for access to land, livestock, or simple subsistence. In later centuries, this root took on the even more freighted meanings of slavery and ethnosocial status.³⁸ It also came to be used to refer to the senior wife in a household.³⁹ For the Proto-West Nyanza speaker community, then, a poor person was weak and soft—not fully recognized as an adult, someone who could be acted upon and turned into a client, but also one who needed to be cared for. This last meaning emerged clearly in Proto-North Rutara, a descendant language from Proto-West Nyanza. Its speakers used a causative form—*-jódozi, with the literal meaning of one who causes another to be soft or weak—to name the role of guardian.

Using another root, Proto-West Nyanza speakers connected poverty to particular emotions and to time. To achieve this, they innovated a set of words using the root *-naku, the etymology of which is unclear beyond Proto-West Nyanza, although it does not appear to be Bantu in origin.[40] The nouns *obunaku and *ennaku both referred to poverty and distress, and to time and season, while the noun *omunaku was used to talk about a poor person or a miserable and wretched person. The connection between misery, sorrow, and poverty is a familiar one, but it is nonetheless notable that the Proto-West Nyanza speaker community conceived of them as so interconnected that they coined a new word to be able to talk about them simultaneously. What makes this root especially unusual is that in addition to poverty and misery, Proto-West Nyanza speakers used it to mean time or season. This might suggest a conceptualization of poverty and suffering as temporary or transient through its relation to a cyclical conception of time, most obviously manifest in the periods of hunger that accompanied the seasonal pattern of labor and harvest.[41]

Proto-West Nyanza speakers certainly would have faced food scarcity in the wet months of the long rainy season, before the new crops had ripened and could be harvested. Nonetheless, the linguistic evidence points us in a different direction with regard to *-naku, one of poverty as a long-term experience. In the modern North Rutara languages Runyankore and Rukiga, the noun *obunáku* means chronic misery, time, and period, with the first meaning highlighting an enduring condition. And a Luganda proverb reflects a similar view: "*Ekuba omunaku tekya: esigala ku mutwe*," which translates as, "Rain falling on a poor person does not clear up: it remains on her/his head."[42] Rather than being connected to a regular period of shortage that affected many in the community, this conceptualization of poverty and suffering as interlinked with time instead points to Proto-West Nyanza speakers' understanding of it as affecting particular individuals for prolonged periods. In this, *-naku gets us close in meaning to the structural poor who were the focus of John Iliffe's study, *The African Poor*, rather than the conjunctural poor who also suffered hardship, but did so sporadically.[43]

When it came to talking about wealth and the wealthy, the Proto-West Nyanza speaker community once more combined words they had inherited with ones they innovated themselves to express the range of concepts they held. They shared with their Proto-Greater Luhyia linguistic siblings the noun *-jàandu, inherited from Proto-Great Lakes Bantu.⁴⁴ Proto-West Nyanza speakers retained the gendered meaning the root had in Proto-Great Lakes Bantu and used it to refer specifically to wealth in women. In what may reflect a change in the form, frequency, or scale of armed conflict, however, they began using this noun to talk about wealth obtained as a result of war, what we would gloss in English as plunder or loot. Women formed a significant part of any wealth taken in warfare as they were targeted for capture and enslaved and then, if they survived, passed on to heirs.⁴⁵

Alongside the more specific term *-jàandu, Proto-West Nyanza speakers inherited general terms for wealth and for being wealthy from Proto-Great Lakes Bantu. These were derived from the root *-tung- that Bastin and her colleagues have reconstructed as a Proto-Bantu verbal root with the form *-túng- and the meanings "put through; thread on string; plait; sew; tie up; build; close (in)."⁴⁶ While holding on to those meanings, Proto-Great Lakes Bantu speakers drew on the figurative associations they offered to coin the verb *-tunga meaning be wealthy, as well as the nouns *obutungi and *omutungi meaning wealth and wealthy person, respectively.⁴⁷ Here we can trace an early conceptualization of wealth as the result of composition, whether the composition of different people or of different things or, most likely, both, and, hence, a recognition of it as the result of a creative process.⁴⁸ This marks a strong contrast with the change in meaning of *-jàandu by the Proto-West Nyanza speaker community to name a form of wealth obtained through the violence and destruction of warfare. We can, thus, see in these two roots alone two very different concepts of wealth and how it might be accumulated in a single community of speakers.

Wealth must have been a preoccupation of Proto-West Nyanza speakers, because in addition to these inherited forms, they innovated a new root for it and for the wealthy: *-gàiga.⁴⁹ This root is widely distributed in all branches of the West Nyanza languages and the differences in form are regular; all this evidence indicates that people speaking modern West Nyanza languages inherited it from their linguistic ancestors who spoke Proto-West Nyanza. Despite this, the root is widely perceived as a Luganda loan in the modern West Nyanza languages even when the phonology and the distribution do not support this as an etymology. This perception appears to reflect the disproportionate wealth and power of Buganda over the past two centuries and, in particular, during the time that dictionaries have been compiled. The root is also present in Lugungu, but there it is a loan from Runyoro.⁵⁰ Where the root appears in the Greater Luhyia languages, such as Lunyole, Lumasaaba, Lugwe, and Lusaamia, its form is identical to that in Luganda and it has not undergone the regular sound changes we would expect if they had inherited it from their common linguistic ancestor, Proto-Great Lakes Bantu.[51] The root thus reflects the much more recent economic and political power of Buganda in its folk etymologies in West Nyanza languages and in its borrowing into other languages, such as Greater Luhyia ones. It offers less insight into how people speaking Proto-West Nyanza, some two thousand years ago, conceived of wealth or how they perceived the wealthy in their society. Members of this speaker community used it in the form of the nouns *omugáiga* meaning rich person and *obugáiga* meaning wealth or riches. They may also have used it in a verbal form to mean to be rich or to become rich. But there was no polysemy and no specificity about kinds of wealth, in contrast to *-jàandu* and *-tung-* and we must, therefore, assume that *-gáiga* was used to refer to wealth and riches in general. This innovation may, therefore, mark a change in the prevalence of wealth or in its social salience. That this general meaning underwent significant change in the North Nyanza languages after the eighth century, as we will see in chapter 4, suggests that this altered again at that time.

The elaboration of their vocabulary for wealth and for poverty highlights the growing significance of these socioeconomic categories for Proto-West Nyanza speakers and their linguistic descendants. Terms referencing debt and clientship reflect their awareness of the entangled relationships between rich and poor, something further emphasized by their conceptualization of the poor as soft, smooth, and weak. The gendered nature of wealth, both in its heritability and in the fact that it could take the form of women, whether through marriage or kidnapping in warfare, was surely connected to men seeking to control wealth and its inheritance. But despite these connections between wealth and poverty, it seems it was only the latter that Proto-West Nyanza speakers understood to have an emotional component.

The Nilotic Languages

The ancestral languages Proto-Eastern Nilotic, Proto-Southern Nilotic, and Proto-Western Nilotic all diverged from Proto-Nilotic. The community that spoke Proto-Nilotic existed until more than three thousand years ago and likely lived in what is now Sudan and South Sudan (see map 2.1).[52] Our picture of economic, social, and political life at that time remains sparse, but what we do know is that people speaking Proto-Nilotic herded cattle, sheep, and goats. They also grew and processed grains.[53] Although we know only a limited amount about their economic and social life, we do know that members of the Proto-Nilotic speaker community began using a new root when they talked about poverty: *-can-*.[54] They used it in the form of a verb meaning be poor, in the form of the adjective poor, and as the nouns meaning poverty and poor person. The root held within it the particular notion that poverty was a difficult condition in which people suffered.

In this sense, Proto-Nilotic speakers had a straightforwardly negative view of being poor. More unusually, when they used the root *-can- to talk about poverty, they did not distinguish it from other kinds of suffering, whether as a result of disease, bereavement, or mistreatment. Whatever the cause, it was the fact of suffering that was paramount. The root *-can- is the only root relating to the meanings poverty and wealth that I have been able to reconstruct to Proto-Nilotic.[55] As the three languages, Proto-Eastern Nilotic, Proto-Southern Nilotic, and Proto-Western Nilotic, emerged and further diverged over subsequent centuries, their speakers adapted and changed how they talked about differences in economic status to reflect their changing ideas about the poor and the rich.

Proto-Southern Nilotic was spoken from approximately two thousand years ago until around fifteen hundred years ago.[56] Based on evidence for contact with Eastern Cushitic languages, Christopher Ehret has posited that there must have been an intermediary language, which he has termed pre-Southern Nilotic, that would have been spoken in "the far north of East Africa" or "the Ethiopian highland fringes" between the dissolution of Proto-Nilotic until the turn of the Common Era.[57] Proto-Southern Nilotic speakers lived further south in the Kenyan Rift Valley and western highlands, where they interacted with speakers of Southern Cushitic languages.[58] There has been considerable loss of Southern Nilotic languages over the centuries and this has had the unfortunate effect of skewing our knowledge toward the Kalenjin branch of Southern Nilotic. As a result, it can be hard to know whether a root was innovated when people spoke Proto-Southern Nilotic or when people spoke Proto-Kalenjin.[59] Proto-Southern Nilotic speakers herded cattle, goats, and donkeys, and their pastoral skills included bleeding cattle. They also grew grains, notably sorghum and finger millet (*Eleusine coracana*), and collected honey. They did not have centralized political authority, using age sets as their primary means of social organization.[60]

Poverty, for people speaking Proto-Southern Nilotic, had a clear association with being kinless and lacking social standing. There are two roots that relate to poverty in the Southern Nilotic languages and they point to distinct, albeit complementary, conceptualizations of the condition and of those living in it. The first is *-panan-, which speakers used to derive one noun meaning pauper and another meaning poverty.[61] Ehret has reconstructed *-panan-, glossing as pauper, to Proto-Southern Nilotic and noted that it was a loanword from the Southern Cushitic language Proto-Iraqw where it had the form *pan-.[62] The linguist Franz Rottland has contended that the root can only be reconstructed to the more recent Proto-Kalenjin in the form *-panan- and the dual meaning pauper and orphan.[63] The precise etymology—that is, when the root was first used in Southern Nilotic languages—would benefit from further research.

When people speaking Southern Nilotic languages spoke the words derived from *-panan-, they associated poverty with bereavement and kinlessness, and hence with vulnerability, through the joint meaning orphan. This is a much more specific notion of poverty than their Proto-Nilotic-speaking ancestors articulated through the root *-can-, with its general meaning of poverty. The root *-panan- differs from *-can-, too, in the lack of explicit association with suffering. While we might surmise that an orphan would be poor and would suffer as a result of both conditions, this was neither articulated nor invoked when Proto-Kalenjin speakers, at least, used *-panan- to talk about such an individual. Instead, as we will see in chapter 5, the Proto-Kalenjin speaker community invoked a different association: that of begging, as they used a noun derived from *-panan- to name a beggar and a verb derived from the root to talk about the acts of begging and pleading. The concept of a poor person encapsulated by this root in Proto-Southern Nilotic was thus one of someone who lacked materially and socially, someone who had no immediate support network.

Proto-Eastern Nilotic also diverged from Proto-Nilotic. One of its descendant languages, Proto-Tung'a (the other being Proto-Bari), was likely spoken until around 900 BCE.[64] Speakers of Proto-Tung'a made a number of changes to their concepts of poverty and wealth. After Proto-Tung'a gave way to its descendant languages, including the immediate ancestor to the Eastern Nilotic languages spoken in eastern Uganda, Proto-Ateker, spoken between 900 BCE and 1000 CE, we see further innovation in these domains. These successive waves of innovation highlight the ways in which people adapted and changed their concepts of socioeconomic difference according to their particular experiences.

During the time that they spoke Proto-Eastern Nilotic, people kept livestock and developed an increasingly elaborate vocabulary associated with herding, including for milking. It was people speaking Proto-Tung'a, however, who developed the more specialized pastoralist vocabulary that reflected a new prominence for cattle in their economy and culture. Proto-Eastern Nilotic speakers grew grains, notably *Eleusine* and millet, and ground them into flour for consumption. They also engaged in trade, a fact we know from their vocabulary, including a word meaning buy, and from the pattern of their loanwords from Eastern Cushitic and other languages.[65]

When they talked about poverty, the community that spoke Proto-Eastern Nilotic used the root *-can-, which their Proto-Nilotic-speaking ancestors had coined to talk about various kinds of suffering, including living in poverty. Proto-Eastern Nilotic speakers also used *-can- to talk about other kinds of suffering, such as grief (in the form of the noun *ŋican). However, in a departure from what we know about the way Proto-Nilotic speakers used the root, those speaking Proto-Eastern Nilotic articulated a markedly negative concept of a poor person in the words they coined from *-can-.[66] They used the root to talk about those who caused trouble in their community through adjectives that described someone as disturbing or troubling and through verbs that referred to the act of troubling, disturbing, and annoying another person. This is a development that was also adopted by people speaking Western Nilotic languages and so is complicated to date because the available evidence does not allow us to be sure whether it was a later areal development or an innovation that occurred just before the dissolution of Proto-Nilotic.

The community speaking Proto-Eastern Nilotic took the negative associations with poverty one step further still by using *-can- when they spoke of punishment and even of torture.[67] These meanings suggest that Proto-Eastern Nilotic speakers viewed poor people as inflicting negative consequences on others, as well as suffering themselves. Poverty for this community, then, needs to be recognized as having been understood not only in terms of the physical, social, and emotional consequences of poverty on the poor themselves, but also the social and economic consequences of poverty for the community in general. The Proto-Eastern Nilotic speaker community appears to have been especially concerned about the presence of poor people among them and the uncomfortable implications for others of their presence. As I discuss in chapter 5, people speaking Proto-Ateker developed even more negative views of the impact of poor people on their communities; a development that is reflected in part in their innovation of several roots for the concepts of poverty and poor person. We can, thus, surmise that the existence of poor people in these speaker communities came to be perceived as an increasing problem during the time that the language was spoken, which may have coincided with extended arid events in the region.[68] But it is worth remembering that it was a political decision to choose to label those without the basic means of subsistence as problematic. Colonial officials in the early twentieth century also made political judgments about poor people and about the causes of poverty. Those decisions were, however, rooted in a racist ideology and were imposed from outside and so marked a clear break from earlier periods.

As they held on to this older concept of poverty, speakers of Proto-Tung'a developed a new word to talk about wealth. This was the root *-bar-.[69] They derived it from an older Proto-Nilotic root, which referred to an increase in size. Fitzsimons has pointed out that the semantic shift to the meaning of wealth may have occurred during the time that Proto-Eastern Nilotic was spoken, but that the linguistic evidence is as yet insufficient to demonstrate that.[70] Whether it was new in Proto-Tung'a or inherited, speakers of Proto-Tung'a and of its descendant languages held on to the new meaning of wealth and developed it further as they rethought their concepts of what constituted wealth.

Proto-Western Nilotic was the third language to emerge from Proto-Nilotic, and it gave way in turn to Proto-Northern West Nilotic (the ancestral language of Burun and Mabaan, spoken today in northeastern South Sudan), Proto-Dinka-Nuer (the linguistic ancestor of languages such as Jieng, Naadh, and Atuot, spoken across South Sudan), and Proto-Luo. The last of these, Proto-Luo, divided to form Proto-Northern Luo (the descendant languages of which are today also spoken in South Sudan—for example, Shilluk and Päri) and Proto-Southern Luo. It is languages descended from the last of these that are today spoken in eastern Uganda. The Proto-Western Nilotic speaker community herded livestock, including cattle, and grew grains, like its Eastern and Southern counterparts.[71] It is striking that people who spoke Proto-Western Nilotic and the languages descended from it, in particular the Southern Luo branch, do not appear to have made many changes to the vocabulary that they used when talking about poverty or about paupers. They did, however, coin a new word for wealth, drawing on the root *lim-.[72] When they used words derived from *lim-, Proto-Southern Luo speakers expressed a concept of wealth as intertwined with visiting. Thus, the noun *lim- meant both wealth and visit, while the verb *limo meant visit and receive. The latter meaning suggests a concept of wealth and visiting that sees them as connected to exchange. Given the importance of redistributing wealth through the provision of food and beer to guests as a means of marking status, this dual meaning of *lim- is one that seems an almost common-sense way of expressing this concept. But it was not one that was widely made. Indeed, I have only found this particular articulation in Proto-Southern Luo and its descendant languages. Perhaps speakers of Proto-Southern Luo felt the need to remind the wealthy that they were expected to live up to these redistributive norms because they did not do so in a consistent fashion.

The lack of much of a vocabulary at all—let alone an elaborate one—that can be reconstructed for wealth in the Proto-Nilotic languages is in marked contrast to Proto-Greater Luhyia and Proto-West Nyanza. It is especially striking that it has not been possible to identify any word for wealth for these protolanguages that connects it conceptually with owning cattle. This, as we will see in chapter 5, changed profoundly in more recent centuries. By the time people were speaking Proto-Kalenjin, a shift toward identifying socioeconomic status with cattle ownership had begun, but it took the negative form of marking someone without cattle as poor. Instead, when people speaking Nilotic languages during this earlier period talked about wealth, they referenced growth and exchange. When they talked about the poor, however, they emphasized emotional and social aspects, such as suffering and being without kin.

Conclusion

After this sweeping overview of the protolanguages of Greater Luhyia, West Nyanza, Eastern, Southern, and Western Nilotic, it is useful to pause and return to the three themes of the emotional, the material, and the social in their concepts of poverty, wealth, the poor, and the rich. We see emotional dimensions in the Proto-Greater Luhyia understanding of poverty and bereavement as entwined, in the Proto-West Nyanza view of poverty as sorrow, and in the Proto-Nilotic notion of poverty as a form of suffering. We also see it in the Proto-Eastern Nilotic perception of the poor as creating a disturbance and discomforting others. The material conceptualizations come across in the Proto-Greater Luhyia emphasis on poverty as lack, and in the Proto-West Nyanza concept that the poor owed their labor to those who assisted them. The social is there in the understanding that poverty and bereavement and kinlessness went together in Proto-Southern Nilotic and in Proto-Greater Luhyia. When people speaking Proto-West Nyanza or Proto-Greater Luhyia described some forms of wealth as gendered and as heritable they referenced social norms of lineality and marriage. We see the overlapping nature of these themes, for example, in the fact that the Proto-Eastern Nilotic view of the poor as disruptive was as much a social and political statement as it was an emotional one. This structuring of the different conceptualizations into the themes of the emotional, material, and social thus allows us to see some of the commonalities across these different societies and, in subsequent chapters in particular, across time. But it is just as apparent that often more than one theme was at play in any given notion of poverty or wealth, reflecting the complex ways in which economic difference was marked and in what its multilayered consequences were for all in society.

INTERCHAPTER

Overview of Climate Developments

In the following chapters, I examine how the concepts of poverty and wealth held by people speaking Proto-Greater Luhyia, Proto-West Nyanza, Proto-Eastern Nilotic, Proto-Southern Nilotic, and Proto-Western Nilotic were transformed or retained by their linguistic descendants. Across multiple centuries, people who spoke tongues descended from these protolanguages profoundly transformed how they conceived of economic and social difference. Those shifting conceptualizations were shaped by the experiences and realities lived by people speaking these many languages. They were shaped by changes in climate, changes in landscapes as people settled in new areas, and changes in human geography as people encountered others speaking unfamiliar languages and with different ways of making a living and accumulating wealth. Because these various people lived, for the most part, in what is today eastern Uganda and thus experienced jointly some of these developments, this interchapter sets out some of the major changes in climate as context for chapters 3, 4, 5, and 6, which explore in turn both the shifting and constant ways in which people speaking Great Lakes Bantu and Nilotic languages in the region understood and talked about the poor and the wealthy and about what poverty and wealth meant.

Over the past thirty years, climate scientists have learned a lot about historical changes in East Africa's climate, including for the past two thousand years. The amount of data available has expanded significantly—such that we are no longer solely dependent only on distant proxies like records of the level of the Nile in Egypt—and the understanding of how different aspects of the climate system interact and what specifically particular kinds of evidence can tell us has also come a long way. That said, there remain important gaps in both the evidence and the knowledge of how the climate system worked in the past, and indeed works currently, in East Africa. The former is due to a relative lack of research in comparison to many other world regions. In terms of high-resolution paleoclimatology for the last two millennia, this stems in part from the long emphasis on dendrochronology (the study of tree rings as an indicator of hydroclimate patterns). Tropical trees tend not to have clearly defined rings, creating a lacuna in evidence for paleoclimatologists to study—and those in the eastern African region that have been dated, including some from Ethiopia, tend to be relatively young.[1] Compounding this is the focus on written documentary sources for climate history that has further marginalized regions of the world without long histories of writing. Observational climate records are limited in East Africa, which did not adopt writing until the mid- to late nineteenth century. It may also stem in part from a certain amount of Eurocentrism in research and theorizing of climate change and of the Anthropocene in particular, as anthropologist Kathleen Morrison has argued.[2]

The climate system in East Africa is shaped by multiple factors and, while climate scientists have a good understanding of each of those factors individually, how they interact and thus affect the climate, and how they affect rainfall in particular, is less well understood.[3] East Africa is at the confluence of two major atmospheric convergence zones. The Intertropical Convergence Zone (ITCZ) is where the northern and southern hemisphere trade winds converge. It is an area "of low pressure, convection, rainfall, and consequent transfer of substantial latent heat to the high troposphere. The transfer of heat and moisture from the surface to the upper troposphere occurs chiefly through cumulonimbus clouds, the towering clouds of thunderstorm systems."[4] At the convergence point, warm, moist air rises and cools, which in turn causes the water in the air to condense and precipitate as rainfall. The areas over which the warm, moist air converges and then rises, therefore, experience higher amounts of precipitation than others—hence the rainfall belt around the equator. Once the rising air masses have risen to the top of the troposphere, the air is displaced to higher latitudes (around thirty degrees north and south), where it subsequently descends. This descending air is warm and dry, which helps create deserts in the subtropical latitudes, such as the Sahara. These dynamics of the ITCZ affect the distribution of rain across East Africa because of its annual migration north and south. In austral winter, it rises as far as ten degrees north, which is roughly the border between South Sudan and Sudan. In boreal winter, the ITCZ displaces as far as five degrees south, which is just to the south of Burundi. "In detail, however, the ITCZ undulates through the tropics with longitude and with the seasons," taking precipitation with it.[5]

A second major convergence zone affecting the climate in East Africa is the Congo Air Boundary, where warm, moist Indian Ocean air and Congo Basin air converge. This boundary is again not static and in East Africa its movement particularly affects rainfall along the western edge of Uganda. Interconnected with these convergence zones are the African and Indian Ocean monsoons, which are two important phenomena for East African rainfall. Highlighting their interconnection, the meteorologist Sharon Nicholson, among others, has noted that although there is not consistent usage in the nomenclature, it is more appropriate to use ITCZ to describe the pattern of pressure and wind over the oceans and monsoons to describe it over land.[6]

Two additional patterns of significance for East Africa's climate, and for precipitation in particular, are the El Niño–Southern Oscillation (ENSO) and the Indian Ocean Dipole (IOD). In its El Niño phase, the ENSO system is characterized by a "dramatic and rapid warming [that] occurs in the tropical Pacific Ocean off the coast of Peru and Ecuador," which can amount to a sea surface temperature rise of two to four degrees centigrade in one month.[7] In contrast, during the La Niña phase, the tropical Pacific cools in the east and warms in the west. Although the heating and cooling are locally specific, "the impacts of ENSO are felt globally," causing severe droughts across large swathes in several regions and increasing rainfall in others.[8] In East Africa, El Niño events are linked with increased precipitation, while La Niña events are connected to drought. The IOD is a similar phenomenon, albeit more recently identified, which sees, in its positive phase, anomalously cool sea surface temperatures in the eastern Indian Ocean and anomalously warm sea surface temperatures in the western Indian Ocean. The opposite occurs in its negative phase.[9] Positive phases of the IOD have been connected to flooding in East Africa, while negative phases have been linked to droughts in the region.[10]

The East African climate is further complicated by the region's topography, especially the East African Rift that runs roughly north to south through the region, with two Rift Valleys—an eastern one running through Kenya and Tanzania and a western one running along the west of Uganda to Lake Tanganyika. The latter is especially deep, with Lake Tanganyika reaching a depth of 1,500 meters (about a mile). The eastern Rift Valley is up to 65 kilometers wide (40 miles), but the width varies across its length, and the elevation of the valley floor ranges from 365 meters above sea level (1,200 feet) at Lake Turkana to 1,800 meters (6,000 feet) at Lake Nakuru. The Rift Valleys cause pronounced rain shadows and their formation, millions of years ago, is understood to have been critical to the emergence of savanna environments in the region.[11] There are also several mountain ranges and individual volcanic craters that help shape the region's climate. Related to the topography but having its own effect is the vast amount of water held in the region's lakes, especially the Victoria Nyanza. Together, the topography and water volume create significant variation in the expression of the climate factors and "greatly influence the spatial distribution of seasonal rainfall in the region, especially the March–May long rainy season," and thus affect the viability of rain-fed agriculture and nontranshumant pastoralism.[12] In addition to regionally specific factors, East Africa's climate is, of course, part of the global climate and thus has been affected by past events tied to global radiative forcing conditions that have been better documented in other parts of the world, such as the Medieval Climate Anomaly (circa 950–1250 CE).

From the Start of the Common Era to the Eleventh Century

According to evidence from lake cores and other proxies taken from across East Africa, the region entered "a period of extreme aridity" around 2,000 years ago.[13] Thus, for example, Lake Naivasha's Crescent Island Basin in central Kenya was dry at that time, while Lake Mwitanzige (Edward) in western Uganda "reached its lowest water level of the mid- to late Holocene, about 15 [meters] below present lake level, at about 2000 [calendar years before present]."[14] The evidence is not altogether straightforward, with Rob Marchant and his colleagues noting that "this was a period of pronounced climate variability, with considerable regional differences."[15] Evidence from the Victoria Nyanza, for example, suggests an earlier "extended dry period" between 2,700 and 2,400 years ago, that coincided with "a solar activity minimum that affected climates over much of the planet."[16] But the evidence from diatoms (a form of algae with silica cell walls that are valuable proxies for climate) does not point to a dramatic impact on the levels of the Victoria Nyanza from the very dry period starting 2,000 years ago. The size of the lake and its watershed makes it a complicated measure of climate. The available evidence from the lake does, however, as J. Curt Stager and his colleagues have noted, point to a very "long-term shallowing trend indicated by rising littoral diatom percentages" between 2,700 and 150 years ago.[17] Drawing on fluctuations in the relative abundance of hydrogen and deuterium isotopes in leaf wax conserved in the sediment of Sacred Lake on Mount Kenya, Bronwen Konecky and her colleagues have also identified the first 200 years of the Common Era as ones of drought.[18]

The approximately two century–long period of intense aridity in East Africa that started 2,000 years ago was followed by wetter conditions that lasted from around 1,800 to around 1,500 years ago. Evidence for this comes from "the refilling of the previously dry basin" of Lake Naivasha from circa 200 CE. The lake filled to reach a highstand that lasted until circa 600 CE.[19] This was followed by a sharply drier period. In Kenya, the level of Lake Bogoria declined from circa 700 CE and the lake experienced "multiple prolonged lowstand stages" leaving the central and southern basins as shallow brine pools.[20] Around 1,200 years ago, the level of the Victoria Nyanza abruptly declined and remained low for a period of 600 years.[21] Pollen records from Lake Emakat in northern Tanzania also indicate a long dry period from circa 800 to 1200 CE.[22] It seems clear that the closing centuries of the first millennium were a time of climate stress across East Africa, leading to lower lake levels, even desiccation, and that this would have created long-term challenges for communities that depended on agriculture and pastoralism.

From the Eleventh to the Sixteenth Century

The long period of reduced rainfall that ended the first millennium continued well into the second and was part of a global climate event that paleoclimatologists have identified as the Medieval Climate Anomaly. During this time, from circa 950 to circa 1250 CE, the northern hemisphere experienced a long period of higher temperatures, possibly due in part to increased solar activity.[23] The way this anomaly manifested itself in regional climates varied significantly. In East Africa, it manifested as a period marked by "century-scale droughts."[24] The evidence for reduced rainfall comes from lakes across the region: Naivasha, Emakat, Victoria Nyanza, Mwitanzige (Edward), Kitagata, and Masoko.[25] The sediment record from Lake Naivasha, for example, shows that the almost three centuries from circa 1000 to 1270 were particularly dry in the wider region. After a brief respite in the early fourteenth century, there was a further multidecadal drought from circa 1380 to 1420.[26] Sedimentary evidence from Lake Bogoria indicates that the years circa 950 to 1100 were less dry than the previous three centuries, but "that overall conditions were still highly arid." From circa 1100, however, there was "a relatively abrupt shift to wetter conditions" until circa 1350.[27] Palynological data (from pollen samples) from western Uganda and evidence of vegetation burning (from charcoal samples) from Lake Simbi, near the Victoria Nyanza, as well as from Naivasha, further indicate that there were "generally dry conditions" during this period in the centuries spanning the end of the first and start of the second millennium.[28] Looking at the Victoria Nyanza, we see consecutive periods of markedly reduced rainfall: from circa 1180 to 1240, from circa 1320 to 1340, and again from circa 1360 to 1380.[29] This pattern suggests generational switches from higher to lower rainfall and back again, something that would have affected the effective transmission of specialized knowledge of particular rainfall regimes from one generation to the next.

There is, thus, a clear pattern of prolonged droughts during the Medieval Climate Anomaly, into the first half of the second millennium. While additional research will undoubtedly further illuminate the precise contours of this dry period, the existing body of evidence points reliably in the same direction. This prolonged period of reduced rainfall was followed by a two- to three-century–long period of more regular and reliable rainfall.[30] Without resorting to environmental determinism, we can nonetheless understand that the greater frequency and longer duration of droughts during those early centuries would have helped to create new dynamics within and among communities and would have led to differences across groups and locations. Some would have benefited from the opportunities that shortages offered, centralizing wealth and power, but many others would have suffered significantly from the repeated reduced or failed harvests and the reduced well-being or even death of livestock, as well as from having scarcer wild resources to gather. Long periods of more and more regular rainfall would have expanded agricultural opportunities into new lands and allowed for the grazing and watering of larger herds of livestock. Increased rainfall was not necessarily an uncomplicated blessing for all. It could bring new challenges, such as the risk of deadly fungal contamination of grain crops as was experienced by people in Ukimbu in western Tanzania in the first half of the nineteenth century.[31] Communities that had adapted to drier conditions lasting decades and more would have had to adapt anew when wetter conditions prevailed. How people responded to changes in their climate depended on what they and their ancestors had experienced and the decisions they had made. Those whose ancestors had chosen to prioritize grain cultivation, for example, made different choices to those whose ancestors had prioritized herding. But even within a community, the possibilities open to a family with resources to expend would not have been available to another without them.

From the Sixteenth to the Nineteenth Century

The evidence for climate conditions in the last 500 years suggests that they were highly variable in terms of precipitation. Part of the variability in comparison to earlier periods may be due to the greater availability of paleoenvironmental records, with the higher resolution at the data level allowing for more nuanced interpretations.[32] Looking at the level of the Victoria Nyanza, where more than 90 percent of the total water leaving the lake each year does so through evaporation and is replenished largely through rainfall, in large part due to its massive surface area (68,800 square kilometers or 26,600 square miles), we can see that its levels were low between circa 1630 and 1660, and then at their lowest between circa 1780 and 1850. Conversely, lake levels were highest circa 1400 to 1600 and circa 1700 to 1750.[33] In central Kenya, the Crescent Island crater in Lake Naivasha also fluctuated significantly with a relatively high intake of water until circa 1550 followed by a "pronounced lowstand" between circa 1560 and 1590. A subsequent highstand lasted from circa 1670 to 1770 again followed by a lowstand from circa 1810 to 1850. It reached a historic peak in the late 1880s and 1890s.[34] Lake Bogoria offers evidence that the long drought that started in circa 1350 ended in circa 1500 with the lake's waters being more dilute and at higher levels. This reprieve came to an end in circa 1550 with a return to lower lake levels reflecting drier conditions until circa 1790.[35] Evidence from hydrogen and deuterium isotopes in leaf wax in the sediment of Sacred Lake on Mount Kenya indicates rapid drying around 1450, at the start of the early Little Ice Age, "with pronounced aridity ~1520–1560 C.E." The dry period continued "until the late LIA [Little Ice Age], ~1700 C.E., with decadal-scale droughts at Sacred Lake centered at 1610 and 1680 C.E."[36] Around 1700, the evidence from Sacred Lake indicates an abrupt transition "into pluvial conditions."[37] However, since 1870, leaf wax records changed sharply, "suggesting aridification on Mt. Kenya," which continued to 1895.[38] Overall, there is "a general pattern of substantially increasing lake levels in the nineteenth century CE (150–50 [years before present])."[39]

The centuries from circa 1500 to 1900 were, from a climate perspective, a time of considerable volatility with what appear to have been abrupt switches from multidecadal long periods of increased rainfall to multidecadal long periods of reduced rainfall or even drought. Climate scientists continue to work to understand the causes of these shifts, whether the El Niño–Southern Oscillation, the Indian Ocean Dipole, changes in the migration of the Intertropical Convergence Zone, volcanic eruptions, or some combination of these. Given the complex interactions between different climate and weather phenomena, the most likely answer will lie in some combination of these for any particular shift.

For people living in eastern Uganda between the sixteenth and nineteenth centuries, however, their primary concerns would have centered on the realities of dealing with this variation. For those for whom livestock were the core of their economy and culture, reduced grazing and watering would have necessitated moves to new areas, with the consequent threat of conflict with others, or a move away from pastoralism. While expanded grasslands could have offered new opportunities, expansion across space would likely have required new political formations.[40] Farmers would have had to cope with smaller—or even failed—harvests year after year or conversely with unpredictable heavy rains washing away newly planted crops or destroying crops that were ready to be harvested. But they would also have benefited from adapting to new rainfall regimes and the crop varieties that they developed or new irrigation strategies. All of these realities helped shape how they conceived of poverty and wealth and how they changed those conceptualizations over time.

CHAPTER THREE

The Bereft and the Powerful

Greater Luhyia Concepts of Poverty and Wealth through the Nineteenth Century

Around fifteen hundred years ago, the different dialects forming among speakers of Proto-Greater Luhyia became sufficiently distinct from each other that they were no longer easily mutually intelligible. Four languages emerged as a result of this gradual process of differentiation: pre-Lunyole, Proto-North Luhyia, Proto-Gwe-Saamia, and Proto-Luyia. My focus in this chapter is on the first three of these as they were spoken within the area that, in the twentieth century, came to be eastern Uganda (see map 3.1). Nonetheless, Proto-Luyia and its descendant languages continued to be significant, not least in their ongoing influences on the others. Of similar importance were influences from other speaker communities in the region.

The conceptualizations of poverty and wealth across these different speaker communities and those speaking the modern Greater Luhyia languages varied widely and changed in disparate ways. As we saw for the speakers of Proto-Greater Luhyia and the other protolanguages discussed in chapter 2, however, the broad themes of the material, social, and emotional are useful in making sense of the continuities and changes that unfolded as people adapted to and reshaped their material and social environments. What emerged across the centuries covered here are material concepts of poverty as lack and as hunger, and of wealth as land and property, with distinctions of quantity or intensity. From a social perspective, gender remained part of the conceptualization of wealth, but became less salient. Instead, a concept of wealth as power became more important. By contrast, we see increasingly negative conceptualizations of the poor and their position in society, from the poor as cheats or as greedy people to the poor as those disrupting and disturbing others. The emotional dimensions of concepts of poverty are apparent in the continued association of poverty with bereavement and suffering, but also in the negative perceptions of the poor as

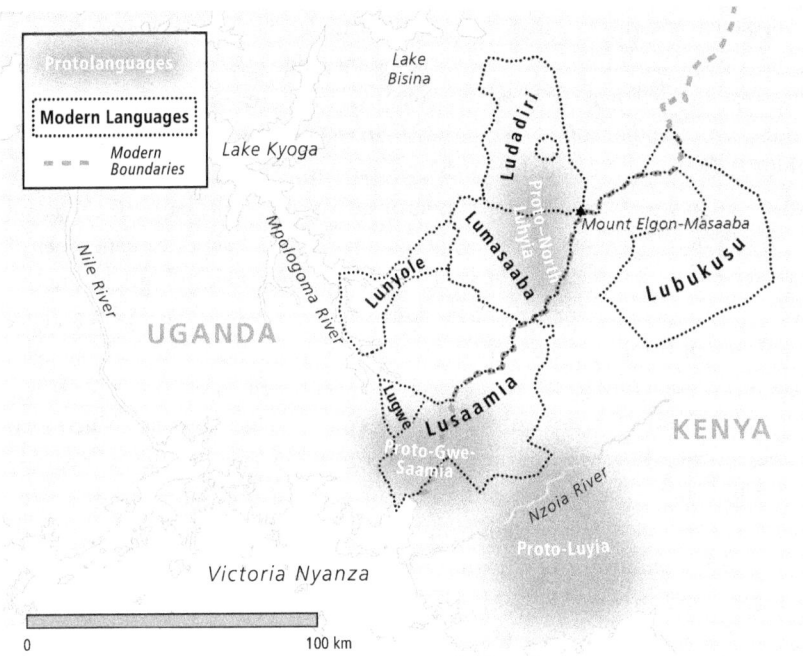

MAP 3.1. Map of Lunyole, Proto-North Luhyia, Proto-Gwe-Saamia, Proto-Luyia, Lumasaaba, Ludadiri, Lubukusu, Lugwe, and Lusaamia. Map created by Nat Case.

selfish. For the wealthy, the emotional dimensions expressed through language were much more positive, with a concept of them as deserving of honor, but there were also tensions and more negative perceptions of the rich.

Most of the changes in people's concepts of poverty and wealth were specific to the protolanguages that emerged from Proto-Greater Luhyia. This occurred as speaker communities responded to new social, environmental, and economic dynamics. But these speaker communities were not sealed off from each other or from those speaking unrelated languages—quite the opposite. Some new concepts spread across all the speaker communities, especially when they faced a common development. The root *-manan- and its meaning is an example of this. Its presence in Greater Luhyia languages was a product of contacts with communities that did not speak Greater Luhyia, contacts that were the result of combined climatic and social pressures. The root yielded modern nouns such as *omumanani* meaning poor person and *owumanani* meaning poverty in Lugwe and verbs such as *khúumanana* meaning to become poor in Lubukusu.[1]

Speakers of Greater Luhyia languages borrowed this root from people who spoke Proto-Kalenjin or one of its descendant languages, for whom it had the form *-panan-.[2] When the word was borrowed into Greater Luhyia languages it underwent a regular sound change in which the /n/ that begins the second syllable ("na") caused the initial /p/ to become an /m/.[3] Speakers of these languages have been living in neighboring communities for at least the past one thousand to fifteen hundred years and Kalenjin languages have a significant number of Greater Luhyia loanwords, not least in the semantic field of agriculture, reflecting their long history of interactions and exchanges.[4] This history, along with the uniformity in the form of the root in the Greater Luhyia languages, makes it challenging to tell when exactly the borrowing occurred. The change in meaning in the Greater Luhyia languages offers a clue, however. Whereas in Proto-Kalenjin, *-panan- meant both pauper and orphan, the latter meaning is not present in the Greater Luhyia languages. This indicates that the word was borrowed once, rather than being borrowed independently by each modern speaker community, because it is unlikely that they would each have made the exact same change. The simplest explanation is that after the divergence of Greater Luhyia into its descendant languages, speakers of Proto-North Luhyia, Proto-Gwe-Saamia, or Proto-Luyia borrowed the word from Proto-Kalenjin speakers and it was then adopted by speakers of the other languages.

In Proto-Kalenjin and its descendant languages, the root *-panan- associates poverty with bereavement and kinlessness, and hence vulnerability, through the meaning orphan.[5] The Kalenjin languages also have an association with begging in this root, both in the form of nouns meaning beggar and in the form of verbs meaning to beg.[6] The concept of a poor person encapsulated by this root in the Kalenjin languages is of someone who lacks materially and socially, who has no immediate support network, and so is reduced to asking others to supply basic needs. None of these meanings were carried into the Greater Luhyia languages in association with the root. This is surprising given that Proto-Lunyole and Proto-North Luhyia speakers also conceived of poverty as intimately linked with bereavement, although not with begging. Why would they borrow a new noun meaning poor person from Kalenjin speakers when they were not borrowing with it a new concept of the poor? The answer may lie in the incorporation of Kalenjin speakers into Greater Luhyia–speaking communities at times of crisis.[7] As refugees from violence or drought, the Kalenjin who were taken in would have been vulnerable and economically impoverished. The noun *omumanani, with its plural form *abamanani, may initially have referred to them in particular and only later acquired a generalized meaning.

Lunyole and Its Speakers

People speaking Proto-Lunyole, or early Lunyole, lived some fifty miles north of the Victoria Nyanza in an area of moderate soil fertility, relatively high annual rainfall, and a landscape of low hills separated by swamps.[8] Their agriculture centered on the cultivation of millet alongside legumes and other crops, and they made use of the swamps and waterways for fish. In more recent centuries, Lunyole speakers experienced relatively high population density with attendant competition for land. Conflicts with neighboring communities over land were recorded in local histories.[9] The available historical traditions suggest that early speakers of Lunyole lived to the west of their current area of settlement, in what is now Busoga. They may have moved into the area that is now Bunyole some three centuries or so ago.[10] It was in this somewhat turbulent context that people speaking Lunyole over the past several centuries elaborated an extensive vocabulary to talk about economic difference. Embedded in that vocabulary were concepts of the poor as bereft but also concepts of the poor as cheaters. Embedded in it, too, were concepts of wealth in material terms—in particular, wealth as manifested by fertile agricultural land.

The words that speakers of Proto-Greater Luhyia derived from the root *-tak- showed that poverty, for them, was a condition of being in want, but they also reflected other forms of lack. People speaking Lunyole, for example, made a conceptual connection between poverty and bereavement in their use of *-tak-.[11] This was not a new conceptual link. People speaking Proto-Greater Luhyia articulated a conceptual overlap between poverty and bereavement through the root *-tamb- (although not via *-tak-), as we saw in chapter 2, an overlap that is also present in Lunyole.[12] When it came to *-tak-, however, Lunyole speakers completely replaced the meaning poverty with that of bereavement. Despite this shift, the broader conceptual connection between death and impoverishment of the bereft remained through the etymology of the root. Lunyole speakers would have initially expanded their use of *-tak- to include bereavement as a peripheral meaning. In so doing, they underscored their recognition of the real connection between the two life experiences by using both of their major root words for poverty to also refer to the experience of suffering the death of a relative or loved one. They then came, perhaps over several centuries, to understand bereavement as the core meaning of *-tak-, with poverty moving to the periphery until it fell out of use entirely as a meaning for this root.[13] Because Lunyole is a very old language that dates back to the initial divergence of Proto-Greater Luhyia into its descendant languages and dialects, this process of expansion and contraction may well have occurred gradually across several centuries.

This intensification of an already strong association between poverty and bereavement through their use of the older roots *-tak- and *-tamb- contrasted, in emotional terms, with the condemnatory concept of the poor that Lunyole speakers articulated through the root *-gad-.[14] Speakers of Proto-Greater Luhyia were the ones who coined *-gad-; they used it as a verb to mean deceive or cheat and as a noun to mean deceit. In addition to those older senses, Lunyole speakers began to also mean poverty, destitution, and poor person when they spoke the nouns derived from this root (*obugadi* for poverty and *omugadi* for poor person). In this way, they articulated a new concept of the poor as those who cheated or deceived. They then changed that concept again. Over time, they stopped using -gad- when they talked about deceit and cheating and used it only to mean poverty and the poor. We cannot know when these changes happened, other than that they occurred after Lunyole diverged from Proto-Greater Luhyia to become its own language. What caused Lunyole speakers to develop a condemnatory notion of poverty and what caused them to then move away from it somewhat? Given that we do not know when exactly those changes happened, we can only speculate, but it is likely that the initial change was related to heightened tensions around inequality. Those tensions may have been exacerbated by drought, such as the multidecadal one at the end of the twelfth century, and by competition for land.[15]

The other words for poverty in Lunyole reflect a negative view of the condition, but do not hold the judgmental attitude that -gad- expressed. One of these words referenced poverty as a condition people fell into; Banyole expanded the meaning of -gwa, a verb that has been reconstructed to Proto-Bantu with the meaning fall, to include the meanings lose wealth and become poor.[16] The original meaning can be found widely across the Greater Luhyia languages as well as across Great Lakes Bantu languages more generally, but it is only in Lunyole that we see this semantic shift to poverty. This association is a familiar one in English, where people frequently talk of someone falling into poverty or descending into squalor.[17] The use of -gwa in this way marked a negative connotation with poverty. Just as significantly, it marked a concept of poverty as a condition a person could move into. The intransitive nature of the verb suggests that this movement into poverty by an individual or a family was not caused by an external agent. That is, a person—in this conceptualization—was not pushed into poverty by someone else, but fell into it, perhaps due to their inattentiveness or simply due to misfortune. Poverty then, in this sense, was not conceived of as a status one was necessarily born into, but was rather a contingent condition. This aspect of contingency is also to be found in another word for poverty that Banyole innovated, one that focused on the physical consequences of deprivation and directly referenced hunger and malnutrition. To make this connection, Lunyole speakers took the Proto-Greater Luhyia root *-ɲat-, which meant become emaciated, and began using it in the form *ohuɲata* to refer to "living a life of poverty."[18] In the absence of significant dialectal variation, it is all but impossible to identify at what point in the existence of Lunyole as a language its speakers made these innovations. Nonetheless, these words offer important insights into the ways in which Banyole understood what it meant to be poor and show the dynamism in that understanding over time.

The question of wealth and the place of the wealthy in society preoccupied Banyole women and men as much as did poverty and the place of the poor. Changes in Lunyole words meaning wealth and rich people captured this preoccupation and its shifting contours. Lunyole speakers retained the root *-yaandu that Proto-Greater Luhyia speakers had inherited from Proto-Great Lakes Bantu, but they stopped using it to mean property or possessions.[19] For Banyole, *omwandu* meant only bridewealth. In more recent times, at least, bridewealth was very much a marker of status, such that the dictionary offers us the phrase: "*Efe Abanyole huhwa omwandu mungi.* 'We Banyole give (marry with) plenty of bridewealth.'"[20] The ethnicization inherent to this phrase points to developments during the twentieth and twenty-first centuries and the mobilization of ethnic identity for political ends.[21] Nonetheless, the reconstruction of the meaning of *omwandu* to limit it to this form of gendered and gender-dependent wealth suggests that in earlier centuries, Banyole parents, and perhaps fathers in particular, sought greater control over the wealth they acquired in exchange for their daughters' productive and reproductive labors.

A Lunyole proverb encapsulates the value of bridewealth brought into a household by one of its daughters: "*Omwana muhaana, ngabo yehyoma; omwana museere luɲerere,*" which translates as, "A daughter in the home is an iron shield; a son is a fence." The explication provided by Sylvester Musimami, the compiler of the proverbs, is: "A daughter brings bride wealth in the home while a son is a guard."[22] In a manuscript on "Family Life and Customs in Bunyole," Y. Nyango echoed this, writing, "A man loved to have as many daughters as possible since the bride price paid for each one added to his wealth." Furthermore, he wrote, "In days of old when the country was full of wars, when people were very hostile, the safest man was that who had many sons and some other male dependents living in his home. They provided the 'security force' and such a home was usually feared to be attacked."²³ Thus, not only was the wealth embodied in daughters, and in the bridewealth they would bring to their natal homes, deeply gendered, but there was also a perceived need to physically defend the gendered wealth of the household. Combined with the elaboration of vocabulary to talk about poverty and the negative conceptualizations several of those words held, we can conclude that Banyole women and men were very concerned about economic precarity, even if they did not all experience it, or at least did not experience it equally.

Lunyole speakers retained and transformed another root used by their ancestors who had spoken Proto-Greater Luhyia to talk about wealth—namely, the root *-hind-.²⁴ Whereas Proto-Greater Luhyia speakers had restricted the meanings they associated with this root to emphasize those of wealth and being wealthy, people speaking Lunyole expanded its meanings. In addition to retaining the meanings of wealth (*obuŋiinda*) and rich person (*omuŋiinda*), they developed a concept of numerical largeness that they expressed by changing the final vowel of the nominal form to yield *ehiŋiindi*, which is glossed in the dictionary as "abundance, crowd, herd, group, mass, multitude, collection; many people or domestic animals in one place."²⁵ As we saw in chapter 2, in Proto-Great Lakes Bantu, the same root was used to refer to power and authority, from which Proto-Greater Luhyia speakers derived one of their concepts of wealthy person. Among the Banyole, by contrast, we see a greater emphasis on the material (including in human form) expression of wealth: to be rich was to have many people, many animals, many belongings. And the perception of the quantity of wealth held by the rich led to the use of *-hind-* to refer to anything that existed in large amounts.

A different, albeit related, idea of wealth was expressed through the adoption of *-hind-* to talk about a particular form of agricultural land, notably "an old field where cowpeas have recently been harvested," also in the form of the noun *ehiŋiindi*.²⁶ Cowpeas (*Vigna unguiculata*) are an ancient African crop that are important for their nutritional value and because they fix nitrogen in the soil.²⁷ Thus, someone who had recently harvested a field of cowpeas had wealth in food, even if that wealth was nondurable. They also had newly enriched soil in which to grow other crops. This emphasis on wealth in particular kinds of land was likely connected to stress over population density and land conflicts with neighboring communities.²⁸ At the same time, Lunyole speakers held on to their concept of the wealthy as those with influence, something we see clearly in their derivation of the verb *ohuŋindigirisa*, meaning to influence or to persuade, from the same root.²⁹

Reflecting their preoccupation with economic difference, Lunyole speakers developed six new roots to talk about wealth and the wealthy in addition to ones they inherited. Three of these are particularly informative with regard to their conceptualization and reconceptualization of wealth. The first is the noun *omuhombe* that they used to refer to an extremely wealthy person.[30] Banyole coined this meaning from a root that has been reconstructed to Proto-Bantu, *-kómb-*, with the glosses "scrape, dig; lick (food) with finger."[31] Proto-Greater Luhyia speakers used the root with the same range of meanings that it held in Proto-Bantu. The semantic extension to wealth was done by speakers of Lunyole and may have referenced the perceived ability of the wealthy to eat without restraint. Implicit in this innovation is Lunyole speakers' use of the metaphor of eating to offer a criticism of those who were very wealthy because they scraped up every last piece of food for themselves, rather than leaving some for others to consume.[32]

A different concept again, that of the potential for wealth to be acquired through violence, was expressed by Lunyole speakers when they took *-yaay-*, a root used to talk about hunting, plunder, and loot in Proto-Greater Luhyia, and gave it the meaning prosperity through the noun *omuyaaya*.[33] The derivation of *omuyaaya* from a root that referenced the acquisition of wealth through warfare or through hunting reflects the reality that wealth could be obtained through means other than agricultural work. Hunting offered some men a way to become wealthy. Writing about South Central Africa, Kathryn de Luna has shown how expert hunters could obtain wealth and fame through their skill. What is more, this was a form of wealth and reputation that was only available to men.[34] Warfare, too, held the potential for some to acquire wealth, in the form of people and livestock. The association between wealth and military plunder was present, as we saw in chapter 2, in Proto-West Nyanza, and was expressed through the root *-yaand-*. Speakers of Proto-Greater Luhyia and the languages descended from it did not, however, use words derived from *-yaand-* in this way. When Lunyole speakers sought to communicate this concept of wealth acquired through violence (even if skillful), they turned instead to *-yaay-* and its more limited meanings of hunting and plundering. Combined with the idea that homesteads needed protection, in the form of sons as fences and as guards, the derivation of the noun *omuyaaya* suggests a certain level of conflict, whether among Banyole or between Banyole and their neighbors. Such conflict would have intensified feelings of precarity, even among those who were relatively wealthy as they sought to protect their accumulated wealth in an unstable environment. But while the concept of prosperity expressed through *omuyaaya* had its etymology in warfare and hunting, the noun's meanings also connected prosperity with peace, perhaps reflecting the benefits that accrued to victors in the aftermath of war or as the result of a successful hunt. In a further twist, Lunyole speakers used the same root to derive the verb *ohuyaaya* meaning "greedily grab food at a communal meal."[35] We can read a criticism of the wealthy in this etymology as those who accumulated and held on to their wealth by not sharing—an accusation that is also present in the noun *omuhombe*.

Because of the gendered nature of labor and the predominance of men in hunting and warfare, *omuyaaya* spoke to gendered concepts of wealth, of the wealthy, and of the means of becoming so. But Lunyole speakers did not understand only men to be capable of the possession of wealth. In fact, they developed a word specifically to describe a rich woman, *omugerama*. The word was a North Luhyia innovation in the form **omukelema*, where it was used to refer to women of honor and respectability.[36] Its translation into Lunyole to refer to the economic status of a woman suggests that women could and did hold wealth of their own and did not simply access it through their husbands. This reflected the widespread practice in sub-Saharan Africa of wives maintaining property separate from their husbands (in contrast to the general European and North American model where property is combined at marriage) and retaining control over their surplus crops or wealth from trade.[37] But this does raise the question of why Banyole women and men innovated a word to describe a wealthy woman, separate from the gender-neutral terms for a wealthy person. To have a noun referring specifically to a rich woman stands out as an unusual development in the Greater Luhyia languages and Bantu languages more generally. The word may have been used to emphasize the distinctiveness of a wealthy woman in Nyole society (with either positive or negative connotations).

The people who spoke Proto-Lunyole and modern Lunyole were sufficiently concerned about economic and social difference and about the economic precarity of households and individuals that they developed an extensive vocabulary to talk about poverty and wealth and about the poor and the rich. Their continued association of poverty with bereavement reflected the vulnerability of dependents in particular, but also the critical role played by networks of support in tiding people over periods of hardship. Those unable to call on a network would have been at particular risk. The ambivalent attitude of Lunyole speakers who had greater economic stability toward those without it comes across clearly to us, in their use of the root *-gad-* and its suggestion that the poor engaged in deceit. A tangible consequence of poverty—hunger—was, on the one hand, recognized by Banyole and, on the other hand, inverted to describe the wealthy as those who were sated, but who perhaps achieved satiation at the expense of others.

Proto-North Luhyia and Its Speakers

The communities that spoke Proto-North Luhyia, until approximately five hundred years ago after which it diverged into Lumasaaba, Ludadiri, and Lubukusu, had moved away from the homeland of their ancestors who had spoken Proto-Greater Luhyia. They created new communities and settlements in the foothills and slopes of Mount Elgon-Masaaba and the smaller neighboring volcanic peaks of Sekukulu and Nkokonjeru, some 95 to 130 kilometers (60 to 80 miles) north of the Victoria Nyanza. This was a sharply different landscape to the lowlands closer to the lake. Sir Harry Johnston, the British Special Commissioner to Uganda from 1899 to 1901, described the northern side of the mountain as composed of "foot-hills of fertile soil, which would be covered by rich tropical vegetation were not the place of this bush and forest taken for the most part by plantations of bananas and native cereals."[38]

Once members of the Proto-North Luhyia speaker community had adapted to their new home, they benefited from being able to grow perennial crops, including bananas, due to regular rainfall across the agricultural year.[39] Banana cultivation is a long-standing practice on and around the mountain, although the area is less famous in the historiography for banana cultivation than the Baganda communities who lived further west across the Nile.[40] As was true elsewhere, bananas required supplementing with other foods given their relatively poor nutritional value.[41] Proto-North Luhyia speakers would thus have eaten wild animals that they hunted and trapped, in addition to obtaining necessary protein from keeping small livestock. Farmers also benefited significantly from the fertile soil in their new homeland, composed as it was of volcanic ash and agglomerate that supplied a high nitrogen content.[42] The steep mountain slopes posed a challenge and the dangers of destructive landslides were all too real, especially after people cleared vegetation to open up land for cultivation. But in other places streams created natural terraces ideal for cultivation.[43] Johnston was struck by the fertility of the farms, noting the "foot-hills up this Alpine valley are much cultivated ... and are glistening green with bananas."[44] It would, however, have taken some time for the community of Proto-North Luhyia speakers to adapt to this unfamiliar environment and its particular climate, and stresses related to this period of adaptation are reflected in their development of new ideas about the wealthy and the poor.

The people who spoke Proto-North Luhyia articulated a view of poverty as intimately connected to both selfishness and lack through their use of the root

*-tak-. Even while they changed its meaning and connotations, they continued to use the root when they talked of the poor, although they changed their pronunciation of it to *-tax-.⁴⁵ The range of meanings Proto-North Luhyia speakers gave to *-tax- reflected their new articulation of poverty as not value-neutral. They used it as the basis of one noun, *omutaxa, to mean both a poor person and a selfish person and as the basis of another noun, *obutaxa, to mean avarice, selfishness, and meanness, as well as poverty and lack. This marked a shift away from the older meanings found among speakers of Proto-Greater Luhyia that emphasized the meaning lack in their usage of this root. Furthermore, we can identify this change in attitude toward the poor more broadly within the Proto-North Luhyia speaker community. For example, when they described a selfish person or selfishness and meanness, they used a compound root, *-lyasi.⁴⁶ Proto-North Luhyia speakers created this compound from the verb *-lya meaning eat and the adverb *-si meaning entirely, all. A selfish person, in this conceptualization, was someone who ate all the food and, hence, did not share. Such behavior was in direct violation of norms in favor of communal eating of quotidian meals in the household. It also went against the ideology underpinning larger communal feasts that, by the nineteenth century at least, marked important events such as marriages, the initiation and circumcision of boys (*imbalu*), and the end of harvest.⁴⁷

The ethnographic evidence is illuminating here, even though it describes practices in the early twentieth century, because it gives us some insight as to why an individual's decision to eat alone was condemned in such strong terms by speakers of Proto-North Luhyia. John Roscoe, the Anglican missionary turned ethnographer, offered his readers an egalitarian vision of the family evening meal among the Bamasaaba in the early twentieth century: "The family dines together, husband, wife and children sitting in a circle round a common vessel from which each person takes the food until it is finished."⁴⁸ The violation of this norm of sharing was encapsulated in the noun *omulyasi, someone who eats all the food. When Proto-North Luhyia speakers expanded the meaning of *omutaxa to include "selfish person," they were reflecting the reality that a poor person was not in a position to readily share food with neighbors and extended family members. Thus, someone seeking to conserve what little supplies of food she or he had by eating alone, or even within the narrowly defined household, could be perceived as acting selfishly. This perception held even if the action was the result of a genuine lack of provisions.⁴⁹ The change in meaning also reflected the difficulty a poor man would have faced in marrying and establishing a household and family. Although not his choice, his poverty and inability to marry would have negative consequences for the community through his lack of reproduction.⁵⁰ The conceptual connection with *omuyaaya* in Lunyole and its suggestion that people became wealthy through snatching up for themselves that which should be shared with others suggests a common condemnation of a refusal to share—something also present in the Ateso speaker community, as we will see in chapter 5. The particular framing of a poor person as selfish could also reflect a concern about the behavior of those who were not destitute, but who feared becoming so and sought to stave off destitution through restricting access to what they had.

Speakers of Proto-North Luhyia inherited the root **-tamb-* with its meanings of poverty, poor person, and bereavement from Proto-Greater Luhyia.[51] Even as they held on to those older meanings, they began to use the root to refer to someone disturbing, troubling, and even torturing another person. In order to convey these meanings of disturbance and torture, Proto-North Luhyia speakers coined new verbs and nouns from **-tamb-*. This use of the root was therefore distinct from simply expanding the meaning of existing words as happened with poverty and bereavement. Nonetheless, that they deliberately chose the root for poverty when they innovated new vocabulary to talk about disturbing, troubling, and torturing indicates that they perceived a strong connection between the two sets of meanings. The poor in their midst created deep discomfort for other members of the Proto-North Luhyia speaker community, perhaps because the poor turned to them for aid or because the poor were disruptive to the well-being of others.[52] The poor may have been especially disturbing to those around them who had enough to survive, but who did not have a significant surplus to give away. This may have been the very group whose selfishness was flagged through the noun *omutaxa*. In this case, then, limited socioeconomic differentiation within the community may have led to a hardening of attitudes toward the poor, as well as a recognition of different degrees of poverty in the community.[53] In a further sign of anxiety about the presence of poor people in their communities, Proto-North Luhyia speakers innovated additional vocabulary to talk about them from the root **-tali*: **ubutali* meaning poverty and **umutali* meaning poor person.[54]

Together with changes in how they conceptualized poverty, innovations in the ways in which Proto-North Luhyia speakers talked about the wealthy underscore a preoccupation with socioeconomic status in the community. Some of the changes point to a positive view of the wealthy. One change centered on the root **-hind-*, which was used by speakers of Proto-Greater Luhyia to speak about wealth and the wealthy.[55] Proto-North Luhyia speakers used the passive extension **-ifu* to derive the meaning respected from the root, yielding, for example, the noun **umuhindifu* meaning respected person.[56] In using the passive extension, speakers of Proto-North Luhyia emphasized that the act of respecting was directed toward the subject—other people respected her or him and when they did so, they acted upon her or him. A literal translation into English would be: a person who is respected (by somebody). In this innovation, we see the repeated reinvention—rather than simply retention across millennia—of an association between wealth and respect or honor. This association has been reconstructed to the Proto-Bantu-speaking community and their use of the root *-kum- when they spoke of both being honored and being rich.[57] Rather than an unbroken thread, however, this concept of the rich as worthy of honor had to be reinvented at different moments. It was, thus, a space of contestation in Bantu-speaking and other communities in the past. People did not naturally or automatically connect wealth and honor or wealth and respect; the connection had to be asserted over and over again. When enough people in a community felt the wealthy were not honorable or respectable, the association could drop away.

Particular ideas about different forms of wealth among people speaking Proto-North Luhyia found expression through the changes they made to the meanings associated with the root *-yaand-, which they also inherited from Proto-Greater Luhyia.[58] In Proto-Greater Luhyia, as we saw in chapter 2, the root referred both to material forms of wealth and to gendered dynamics through its meaning of bridewealth, with the latter meaning having been inherited from speakers of Proto-Great Lakes Bantu. In contrast to speakers of Lunyole, Proto-North Luhyia speakers retained only the relatively newer meanings of material wealth that their predecessors who had spoken Proto-Greater Luhyia had innovated. They stopped using the root to refer to bridewealth. In addition to this change in the meanings of *-yaand-, Proto-North Luhyia speakers coined a new noun, *butihi, to speak of riches or of a great wealth in things.[59] The etymology remains to be fully traced for this noun, but it may have been derived from the Proto-Bantu verb *-dip-, which Bastin and her colleagues glossed as "pay, compensate."[60] Alongside this, Proto-North Luhyia speakers may have developed a concept of prosperity as something expressed through growth and accumulation, using the root *-losela.[61] The evidence from Lubukusu is not consistent on this and so it may also have been that, after the breakup of Proto-North Luhyia, Lumasaaba or Ludadiri speakers developed this meaning for the root and it spread to the other language as an areal form. Through these words, the Proto-North Luhyia speaker community emphasized the material nature of wealth, suggesting a concern with material accumulation. When they used the words that they derived from these roots, Proto-North Luhyia speakers referenced a specific kind of wealth that took the form of property or possessions, rather than more expansive notions of wealth that included having dependents and being held in high regard.

In another move away from older concepts of wealth, the Proto-North Luhyia speaker community changed the meaning of an existing word to describe a particular kind of wealth, namely that of abundant wealth in the form of livestock. This was the root *-bayi* that appears to have been borrowed by members of the Proto-Greater Luhyia speaker community from a Southern Nilotic language, where it meant "to keep cattle."[62] The timing here is difficult to be sure of because of the distribution of the root with this meaning in the Greater Luhyia languages. It is found in all four subbranches, suggesting it was borrowed during the time that Proto-Greater Luhyia was spoken—that is, until around fifteen hundred years ago. Christopher Ehret has reconstructed the root with the form *pai* to Proto-Kalenjin. According to John Distefano, Proto-Kalenjin gradually diverged into Proto-Northern Kalenjin and Proto-Elgon-Mau Kalenjin over the second half of the first millennium.[63] Thus the timing is plausible, although of course, the chronology may well change with further research and better correlations with archaeological evidence. The key development, however, in terms of the concept of wealth occurred in the Proto-North Luhyia speaker community, which changed the pronunciation to *-bahi* and expanded its meaning to include the more specific meaning of "great wealth in livestock," alongside the wider-held meaning of "keep cattle."

Proto-North Luhyia speakers also talked about the intersection of wealth and status and innovated a new vocabulary for wealth to do so. To create these new meanings, they drew on an old root, *-kác-*, that has been reconstructed to Proto-Bantu with the meanings "dry up, coagulate, be hard."[64] By the time Proto-Greater Luhyia was spoken, the root was used to refer to brass and copper jewelry in the form of the noun *mukasa*, presumably in reference to the process in which the molten metal coagulated and hardened as it cooled. In Proto-North Luhyia, however, it came to mean wealth, honor, and leadership through the noun *obukasa*, and wealthy person, respected person, and leader through the noun *omukasa*.[65] This was a direct connection between wealth, power, and social standing that did not invoke the same kinds of tensions that are apparent through semantic changes after the divergence of Proto-North Luhyia, as we will see below. Nonetheless the complex and, at times, contradictory nature of Proto-North Luhyia speakers' ideas about wealth and the rich, as well as of poverty and of the poor, is apparent to us through the changes they made to their vocabulary for these concepts, not least in the framing of the poor as selfish.

Lumasaaba Speakers

Over time, the community that spoke Proto-North Luhyia expanded its settlements. As the communities became more dispersed so their dialects diverged until, by the mid-second millennium, they had become distinct languages, no longer readily mutually intelligible, but nonetheless still closely related. From this point on, people grew up in households where the primary language was Lumasaaba if they lived on the southwest slopes of the mountain, Ludadiri if they lived on the northwest slopes, and Lubukusu if they lived on the east and southeast slopes. Here they grew bananas, grains, and other crops, raised livestock, and hunted and trapped wild animals and birds. Roscoe reported in the early twentieth century, after visiting Lumasaaba-speaking communities, that they settled on a patrilineal clan basis, taking care to avoid infringing on the land of other clans. "The cultivated tracts of land are regarded by members of a clan as freehold property and are jealously guarded against any encroachment."[66] That said, he also noted that "the sides of the mountain have many natural terraces which afford ample space for a village, with land for cultivation both in the valleys and up the sides of the ridges," thereby presumably reducing the likelihood of conflict over agricultural land. Water, too, was a plentiful resource, as "copious streams of excellent water, gushing from springs on the mountain, supply the needs of the people and irrigate the land through which they flow."[67] Alongside agricultural work, Roscoe wrote that Bamasaaba households raised "small herds of cattle and a few goats and sheep, and each village has its fowls. These herds and flocks are left to the children to guard as they graze on the mountain sides, their elders being thus set free to labour in the fields."[68]

When they spoke of poverty and of wealth, Lumasaaba speakers drew on vocabulary they inherited from Proto-North Luhyia and Proto-Greater Luhyia and they innovated new words themselves. Through this we see conceptual continuities, including the continued association of poverty and bereavement in the root *-tamb-, which took forms such as the noun *umutambi* with the dual meaning destitute person and bereaved person, and *umudambiro*, which served as a greeting given to a bereaved person. They also held on to an association between poverty and helplessness expressed through this root that had been made by speakers of Proto-North Luhyia. Thus, *khutàmbà* meant to be poor, to be bereaved, and also to be helpless.[69] The poor, in this concept, were recognized as deserving of sympathy, but whatever sympathy speakers of Lumasaaba held for the poor was tempered by other perceptions.

Lumasaaba speakers retained the conceptual association between the poor and acts of disturbing, interrupting, and even torturing others that speakers of Proto-North Luhyia had held. They also expressed this through their use of the root *-tamb- in the verb *khutámbísà* with the meanings disturb, interrupt, trouble a person, make trouble, torture, or interrupt a person who is working. This highlights the existence of tensions around socioeconomic difference. Such tensions might come to the fore at times such as the communal marking of initiation, especially the ceremonies and feasts that accompanied *imbalu* (male initiation and circumcision) and which required significant resources in terms of meat and millet beer.[70]

Despite early twentieth-century depictions of Masaaba communities as relatively egalitarian—inasmuch as the gap between the wealthiest and poorest members of a village was not vast—Lumasaaba speakers were sufficiently worried about the poor that they had a number of different words to talk about them. In addition, they took care to name different degrees of impoverishment through old and new vocabulary. A conceptual history approach, thus, allows us to see historical tensions and socioeconomic realities that might not otherwise be apparent. Speakers of Lumasaaba stopped using the root *-tak- to talk about the poor but continued to use the Proto-North Luhyia innovations *ubutali* meaning poverty and *umutali* meaning poor person.[71] They coined *umurasyi* to mean destitute person and *burasyi* to refer to destitution. And they used *natang'wali* to mean a very poor person. Later still, and almost certainly no earlier than the nineteenth century, Lumasaaba speakers borrowed the Kiswahili phrase *maskini wa mungu* (lit. God's poor) to refer to a very poor person.[72] It is most likely that the latter was borrowed after Bamasaaba came into contact with traders from the coast who expanded their activities into eastern Uganda in the second half of the nineteenth century, with complicated consequences, as we will see in chapter 6.

The Lumasaaba speaker community had a wide-ranging vocabulary for wealth that covered conceptualizations of particular kinds of wealth and also the regard in which rich people were held by others in their communities. Cattle were an important form of wealth, as reflected in the continued use of the noun *bubwáhi* to mean great wealth in livestock; a noun that Bamasaaba inherited from people speaking Proto-North Luhyia.[73] Roscoe downplayed the significance of cattle in Bamasaaba households, but nonetheless noted that "more wealthy people keep a few cows, and a village may have from ten to twenty in it, though it seldom has fifty."[74] The Anglican missionary J. B. Purvis, however, who arrived in the area in

1903, highlighted the role of cattle ownership in political status: "The strongest patriarch, or chief, is the man who has been able to procure the most cattle, and with them buy the largest number of wives, for each of which he would have to pay from two to ten head of cattle, according to age and condition."[75]

In the early twentieth century, cattle were primarily used for bridewealth and so can be understood as a gendered form of wealth, even though access to them was not necessarily along gender lines.[76] At that time, according to Roscoe, bridewealth could commonly reach "six cows and a number of goats, from six to twelve, and a few fowls," while Purvis had the upper limit at ten cows.[77] While it is impossible to know for sure, it is not unreasonable to assume similar numbers for earlier centuries, especially because the bovine pleuropneumonia and rinderpest epidemics that affected cattle in the late 1890s would have resulted in smaller livestock holdings in the following decade and thus would have constrained inflationary pressures on bridewealth. In a context where people kept small herds of cattle, accumulating six to give as part of bridewealth would have been a significant burden. Roscoe observed that this was "a large sum for a man to obtain and it often takes eighteen months or even two years to realise the amount, and during this time he trades in various ways, or begs and borrows when possible."[78] The need to do so would likely have generated tensions between wealthier and poorer men in the community and, in particular, between wealthy, older, married men and poor, younger, unmarried ones. Such tensions would have fluctuated along with the fortunes of livestock holders, including the impact of droughts and outbreaks of animal diseases.

In other ways, however, Bamasaaba people worked to mitigate the hardships caused by differences in economic standing. Poverty, for example, did not restrict a person's access to healers in their community. The *Namwangala*, who was both a medium and priest for the deity Mwanga (who took the form of a snake), would, in the early twentieth century, accept smaller offerings, such as a chicken, from poor people seeking therapy, whereas wealthier supplicants would have to offer a goat. A similar practice was followed by the mediums of other deities and spirits.[79]

To talk about material property, Lumasaaba speakers used the noun *kúmùhàndù*, while the related noun *kimihándù* described possessions. Both of these were derived from the Proto-Great Lakes Bantu root *-yand-* discussed in chapter 2 and above.[80] For the Lumasaaba speaker community, the root had significantly narrower meanings than those attributed to it by their more distant linguistic ancestors, with wealth as described by this root limited to material goods. This material conceptualization of wealth was spoken about differently according to the quantity of possessions. Thus, to talk about great wealth in things, Bamasaaba drew on the root their Proto-North Luhyia ancestors coined, *-tihi, to form the noun butihi.[81] Finally, with reference to the material aspect of wealth, the concept of prosperity was expressed in terms of accumulation through the noun inzilò(o)sèlà, which was closely related to the verb khulò(o)sèlà meaning add, increase, develop.[82] As noted above, it is not clear if this was a concept of prosperity that they inherited from speakers of Proto-North Luhyia or if it was an innovation that they shared with speakers of Ludadiri.

The Lumasaaba speaker community conceived of the wealthy as worthy of respect or honor. They expressed respect for the wealthy through their continued use of the ancient root *-hind- in the forms buhindifu meaning wealth and respect, and umuhindifu with the meanings respected person and wealthy person.[83] A similar high esteem for the wealthy was expressed through words derived from the Proto-North Luhyia root *-kasa-, such as umukásyà meaning respected person, wealthy person, and leader and bukásyà meaning wealth, respect, and honor.[84] In her *Masaaba Word List*, Berthe Siertsema emphasized the connection between respect and wealth and between honor and wealth as expressed through this root:

HONOUR n. bu-kas(y)a (= wealth)
RESPECT n. lu-koosi, bu-kas(y)a (= wealth), bu-hindifu (?);
-[respect]ed p[erson]: umu-hindifu, umu-kas(y)a (= wealthy p[erson])[85]

Purvis's early twentieth-century account of chiefs being those with the most wealth in Masaaba society underscores this concept of wealth as bringing respect and honor as well as positions of leadership.[86] This understanding of the wealthy contrasts starkly with the concept of the poor as potentially problematic for the community. This contrast is especially strong with regard to leaders who gained their positions by virtue of their wealth and so for whom wealth determined political power and responsibility.

Lubukusu Speakers

Speakers of Lubukusu lived on the east and southeast side of Mount Elgon-Masaaba, in a landscape broadly similar to that on the mountain's north side. In contrast to their Lumasaaba-speaking linguistic siblings, they continued to use both *-tamb- and *-tak- with reference to the poor and to poverty. And with both roots, they expressed their negative views of poverty and of the poor. The associations between poverty, helplessness, bereavement, and punishment expressed through the root *-tamb- that we saw in Lumasaaba were similarly present in Lubukusu. In addition, Babukusu added a new association with women's sexual behavior that contravened social norms. They did this by using the noun *omutaamba* that is translated as harlot or prostitute in English.[87] It is likely that this occurred in the nineteenth century or later as Catholic and Anglican missionaries worked to introduce new moralities around sexual behavior. But it is also possible that this noun was used much earlier to refer to women who did not conform to social expectations, such as widows who were not inherited by their deceased husbands' heirs, whether from their own volition or not, and found other ways to survive.[88]

Speakers of Lumasaaba and Ludadiri dropped the meaning of poverty that the root *-tak- had held in Proto-Greater Luhyia and kept only the innovation of speakers of Proto-North Luhyia to use it to mean avarice and selfishness. In Lubukusu, however, people used the root to talk about poverty and lack and also to describe selfish or avaricious behavior. For example, the noun *buutakha* meant avarice, selfishness, meanness, lack, poverty, and want.[89] Lubukusu speakers also coined new words to talk about poverty and the poor, indicating that they perceived poverty to be a fact of consequence in their communities. They used the noun *butami* to refer to the condition of being poor and the noun *sisa* to refer to poverty but also to suffering for any reason.[90] The latter resembled the Nilotic concept of poverty and general suffering expressed through the root *-can-. In addition, Babukusu borrowed from Luyia speakers the noun *ómunyelele* with the meanings someone who is thin (but not as a result of illness) and poor person.[91] In Proto-Great Lakes Bantu the adjective *-nyerere meant narrow or thin. In the various languages that emerged from Proto-Great Lakes Bantu, the root has taken on different meanings that all contain within them the idea of thinness or narrowness. Thus, in the West Nyanza languages it is used to talk about thin copper bracelets but also to name a mongoose. In the Luyia languages it came to mean both a narrow path and a thin person. Lubukusu speakers, with their close connections with those speaking Luyia languages, borrowed the latter meanings. In so doing, they also borrowed a material conceptualization of poverty that included a connection between physical want of food and economic need.

Lubukusu speakers shared much of their vocabulary for wealth with their linguistic siblings speaking Lumasaaba. They used the noun *búbwaayi* to refer to great wealth in livestock and *kúmwáandu* to refer to property or possessions. They associated wealth with honor and leadership through the noun *omukasa* meaning respected person, wealthy person, and leader, and related forms such as *bukasa* meaning wealth, honor, and leadership.[92] Clear tensions over socioeconomic standing, however, are apparent in the vocabulary they derived from the root *-hind-.[93] On the one hand, we see similar usages as in Lumasaaba and, indeed, in Proto-North Luhyia. For example, the noun *omuyiinda* referred both to a wealthy person and to a respected person. On the other hand, Lubukusu speakers expressed a very different concept of the wealthy using the same root, but in verbal form: *khuuyiinda* meaning to squeeze through, to displace, and to take someone's space. Here then was an idea of wealth resulting from the displacement of others and an implicit criticism of the behavior of the wealthy. That Lubukusu attached both meanings to the same root speaks to social tensions around wealth and its absence just as much as does the older concept of the poor as those who disturbed others. Wealthy Proto-North Luhyia speakers and their Lubukusu-speaking linguistic descendants may have used *-hind-* to assert their claim to be respected, but other Lubukusu speakers used that very same root to assert that the wealthy had behaved in disrespectable, perhaps even violent, ways to acquire their riches. A final conceptual change in this speaker community was the explicit linking of prosperity with chance or luck through the root *-kabi*. Thus, we find the noun *eekhabi* meaning good luck, blessings, fortune, prosperity and the verb *khunyola zikhabi* with the meanings be fortunate, be prosperous.[94] Wealth, in this conceptualization, was not necessarily the result of industriousness or social standing, but rather a product of chance or good fortune.

Proto-Gwe-Saamia Speakers

Communities speaking Proto-Gwe-Saamia lived on the shores of the Victoria Nyanza and in its hinterland. Because this was likely the same landscape settled and inhabited by Proto-Greater Luhyia speakers, they benefited from inherited knowledge about the land and the best ways to cultivate it, where to collect wild plants for food and medicine, where to hunt wild animals, and how to navigate and fish on the lake. They would also have been the families that had successfully laid claim to households and land at moments of inheritance and conflict in contrast to those who settled elsewhere from choice or necessity. Perhaps because of this—because they were not faced with the challenges of adapting to a new homeland—they innovated less in the semantic fields of poverty and wealth than their linguistic siblings that spoke pre-Lunyole and Proto-North Luhyia. Nonetheless, they did make some important changes. The first of which is that they stopped using the root *-tamb-* to refer to poverty or bereavement. Instead, they began using it as a verb that referred to working hard without resting (*-*tamba*) and as a noun to mean hard worker (*omutambi).[95] The reality of poverty and the existence of the poor in these communities, however, is evidenced by their ongoing use of the roots *-*paat*- and *-*tak*- to talk about them.[96] While they used the former to create nouns meaning poor person (*omwaati) and poverty (*obwaati), they used the latter to talk about need and about being in want (*-*daha*). These are closely related senses, but with *-*tak*-, speakers of Proto-Gwe-Saamia highlighted the material conditions of poverty, while they used *-*paat*- to speak of it in more general terms.

When it came to wealth, this speaker community both held on to terminology developed by their Proto-Greater Luhyia ancestors and developed new words, reflecting a process of reconceptualization during the centuries that Proto-Gwe-Saamia was spoken. They, thus, continued to use words derived from the root *-*hind*-, such as *omuyiinda for a rich person and *ohuyiindiyala for becoming wealthy.[97] They also used the root *-*yaand*- to refer to both wealth and a wealthy person.[98] In addition to this inherited vocabulary, speakers of Proto-Gwe-Saamia adapted two roots to expand their ability to talk about these concepts. They took a root that can be reconstructed back to Proto-Bantu in the form *-*kúd*-, meaning grow up, and began using it to mean prosper (*ohuhulahulana) and prosperity (*ehulahulana).[99] In deriving these two words from the root *-*hul*- (grow), speakers of Proto-Gwe-Saamia used two different processes of derivation. They reduplicated the stem to yield *-*hulahula*, a process that in this case indicated repetition, a continual process of growing. They also added a reciprocal or associative extension to the reduplicated stem: -*an*-. While the most common meaning of this extension is to make the verb reciprocal (e.g., to see each other versus to see) and thus require two or more agents, it also has other semantic effects. These include "'chaining,' 'intensive/extensive,' 'iterative,'" and "anti-passive," among others.[100] One reading of this derivation then is an iterative growing together of age and wealth as a person moved toward elderhood. In Proto-Great Lakes Bantu the root included the meaning "rights of elderhood."[101] During the time that Proto-Greater Luhyia was spoken, the primary meaning of *-*hul*- was still connected to being an adult member of society and the responsibilities and rights that that entailed. In the Proto-Gwe-Saamia innovation, therefore, there is an implicit conceptualization of wealth as something that belonged to or accumulated to the elders rather than to the youth in the community. This concept complements the Proto-West Nyanza concept of poor people as not fully adult, although the two emerged independently of each other.

During the time that Proto-Gwe-Saamia was spoken, we can see a conceptual mapping of wealth and power onto the same roots. Thus, Proto-Gwe-Saamia speakers took the root *-nyal-, which, for Proto-Greater Luhyia speakers, meant power, and used it to speak of wealth in the form *obunyali, of a wealthy person in the form *omunyali, and of becoming wealthy in the form *ohunyalira.[102] This suggests a development, during these centuries, of a concept of the wealthy as powerful and of the powerful as wealthy. It is hard to disentangle these two meanings in order to understand whether one was seen as the basis of the other or whether they were perceived to grow together. What is likely is that the small-scale nature of political authority among communities speaking Proto-Gwe-Saamia, along with their longer history of settlement in the same area, created space for wealthier people to assert themselves in the community. In their very brief ethnographic overview of Basaamia and Bagwe societies, Richard Nzita and Mbaga-Niwampa argue that a rainmaker, or *Nalundiho*, could threaten the economic viability of individual households by withholding rain.[103] This is a useful illustration of how a powerful person—in this case one who could control rainfall—could ensure her or his own wealth and threaten the wealth of others.

Lusaamia Speakers

The community speaking Lusaamia has lived, from around five hundred years ago, in the area along the northeasternmost corner of the Victoria Nyanza, straddling what is today the border between Uganda and Kenya. In the early twentieth century, Johnston described the region around the northeast of the lake as composed of "extremely fertile land."[104] Noting the limited extent of woodland, he wrote, "nevertheless, there is still a fringe of fine trees along every watercourse, and the country is so splendidly clothed in fine grass and luxurious herbage—to say nothing of the flourishing crops of an agricultural people." Indeed, according to Johnston, the whole region "is most grateful to the eye." It consisted at that time "of rolling downs (though there is a little marsh in the valley of the Nzoia) covered with the greenest of grass, and made additionally beautiful by the blending with the green of fleecy white, shining mauve, or pale pink, effects which are caused by the grass being in flower or fluffy seed."[105]

This appealing landscape was home to many people. In 1883, the Scottish geologist and imperial explorer Joseph Thomson was sufficiently struck by the population density in Busaamia that he underscored it in his publication about his journey: "The extraordinary density of the population was to us a matter of great wonder. They streamed forth in thousands to see us."[106] The Mill Hill missionary stationed in "Kavirondo" in the early twentieth century, Father N. Stam, posited population density as the cause of conflict in the nineteenth century and earlier.¹⁰⁷ Indeed, Stam wrote in 1919: "When these families increased, then these different feuds came about [. . .] The *Banyalla* family lived South of the Nzoga river near the lake, separated from the Nilotic by the Yala swamps. They became too numerous, crossed the river and drove the *Samia* on, the *Samia* pressed on the *Bakhekhe* and so on."¹⁰⁸ The land may have been exceptionally fertile, but that did not preclude economic and political tensions.

The reality of conflict and insecurity manifested physically in the architecture of settlements. In his 1962 outline of land tenure in Busaamia, the anthropologist R. W. Moody noted that prior to the imposition of British colonial rule, people lived in "walled or moated villages called 'engoba' (sing: olukoba) which were sited on ridges or slight rises in the ground called 'engongo' (sing: olukongo)." Furthermore, wrote Moody, "cultivation of land around the 'olukoba' was limited to the area that could safely be protected by the warriors, and thus the women could not go very far away for their land."¹⁰⁹ Basaamia women and men, like most of their neighbors, have long practiced mixed agriculture, growing grain crops like millet alongside other crops and keeping small herds of livestock, especially goats. In 1885, Thomson described the general "Kavirondo" region as both remarkably fertile and intensively cultivated: "Almost every foot of ground was under cultivation. Yet the people seem to have some idea of the value of a rotation of crops, for they allow land to lie fallow occasionally, such parts being used as pasture-ground for the cattle and flocks."¹¹⁰

For those communities located close to the rivers that flowed into the Victoria Nyanza or located on the shores of the lake, fishing was also part of their economy. In a paper on fishermen in Busaamia, Moody wrote, "It would seem that Samia, ever since their incursion into the present area they occupy, have been engaged in fishing of some kind."¹¹¹ Boat fishing is a long-established practice on the Victoria Nyanza and, according to Moody, "it is evident that there have always been boat fishermen here."¹¹² Until the twentieth century, fishermen used drag traps called *ekoholo* that they pulled behind their boats on ropes. This work was done exclusively by men, but fishing in rivers and on accessible lake shores could be performed by women using baskets.¹¹³

In addition to agriculture, pastoralism, and fishing, a central feature of the Saamia economy was iron smelting and smithing. The Basaamia traded their iron ore and iron goods across the region and "the Samia Hills were a centre for its [iron's] production."¹¹⁴ Thomson was struck by the scale and skill of the smelters and smiths, highlighting their "astonishing dexterity" and the quality of the result: "The iron thus produced is first class, and the Wa-kavirondo, especially those of Samia, are remarkably clever blacksmiths."¹¹⁵ Once the iron had been extracted from the ore, blacksmiths worked it into jewelry, tools, and weapons.[116] The tools and skill needed suggest that Basaamia blacksmiths owned and acquired significant wealth. The scale of production, at least toward the end of the nineteenth century, also suggests that there was substantial demand among Basaamia and neighboring communities for iron goods and that people had the capacity to purchase them.

These positive depictions of the economic situation of Busaamia in the late nineteenth and early twentieth centuries capture a particular moment in time rather than a constant reality. This region was one of high soil fertility and reliable rainfall across the two rainy seasons, but also a region with high population densities that are remembered in oral traditions as being of long standing.[117] Even with good conditions, economic prosperity was contingent on the rains falling when they were expected and on an absence of pests. In the late 1920s and early 1930s, historian Martin Shanguhyia has shown how in nearby Vihiga County in Kenya, the combination of locust invasions, "long dry spells and short, often destructive, wet seasons," with colonial limitations on subsistence root-crop planting to boost cash crop production led to "increased incidences of food insecurity and episodes of famine."[118] The prolonged period of severe droughts from circa 1560 until circa 1620 and then again from the late eighteenth century would have produced very different outcomes to those described by Thomson and Johnston. The tensions produced during those periods of stress as well as the unequal distribution of wealth in general, including in access to the most fertile land, meant that Basaamia continued to use a large vocabulary to talk about the poor and the wealthy and about poverty and wealth.

When it came to poverty, Basaamia used words derived from roots that they had inherited from Proto-Greater Luhyia speakers, ones innovated by Proto-Gwe-Saamia speakers, words borrowed from other languages, and ones they innovated themselves. One set of words, the nouns *obumanani* meaning poverty and *omumanani* meaning poor person, and the verb *ohumanana* meaning become poor, were derived from the Kalenjin loanword *-panan-*, which, as we saw previously, spread through several of the communities that spoke languages descended from Proto-Greater Luhyia.[119] Despite its origin in a non–Greater Luhyia language, Lusaamia speakers used the noun to refer to all poor people, without distinction as to origin. Alongside these general words for poverty, they also used ones that had been coined by speakers of Proto-Greater Luhyia: in particular, *omwaati* meaning poor person, *ohuwaata* meaning become poor, and *obwaati* meaning poverty.[120] As with those derived from *-panan-*, these did not signify particular ways of being poor or particular kinds of poor people.

Lusaamia speakers also innovated two new sets of words to talk about poverty, indicating that it was an issue of some significant concern for them, despite the general fertility of the soil. One of these sets also referred to poverty in general and was formed from the root -*sakandu*, which yielded *omusakandu* meaning poor person and *obusakandu* meaning poverty.[121] The second set of words, however, described severe poverty or destitution. Thus, the noun *yandaba* referred to a destitute person, someone almost reduced to begging, and *ohwandaba* referred to destitution when it was used as a noun and to becoming destitute when used as a verb.[122] The need to distinguish between the poor and the very poor or the destitute speaks to the reality that not all Basaamia thrived economically, even if conditions were generally favorable. This reality was also reflected in the decision by Lusaamia speakers to borrow the noun *lukyolo* from Lusoga. This holds within it both a derogatory classification of the poor and a naturalization of poverty; it is discussed in detail in chapter 4.[123]

The possibilities for at least some people to succeed and become wealthy, by contrast, can be seen through the fact that Lusaamia speakers retained a number of words to talk about wealth and the wealthy, including some that had been innovated by their immediate linguistic ancestors speaking Proto-Gwe-Saamia. We should not understand the retention of this vocabulary as merely reflecting stasis in people's concepts of wealth. Of the vocabulary their ancestors who had spoken Proto-Greater Luhyia had used to talk of wealth, Basaamia retained only two roots. The first of these were the words derived from the root *-hind-*.[124] In Lusaamia, these took the form of the nouns *omuyiinda* meaning wealthy person, *obuyiinda* meaning riches or wealth, and *obuyindifu* meaning prosperity. In addition, they used the verb *ohuyindiyala* to refer to prospering, becoming wealthy, progressing, and being able. If someone wanted to specify the form of a person's wealth, she could qualify the noun; for example, *muyiinda ali n'engombe* described a person whose wealth lay in cattle. The other word inherited from Proto-Greater Luhyia was derived from the root *-yaandu*, which meant wealth, including the more narrowly material meanings property and possessions and, also, specifically bridewealth.[125] Lusaamia speakers dropped most of these forms and kept only *emyaando* meaning riches or wealth, referring to all kinds of wealth: land, cattle, children, and wives.

Alongside this vocabulary inherited from Proto-Greater Luhyia, Lusaamia speakers used terms that they inherited from those speaking Proto-Gwe-Saamia and they borrowed vocabulary from neighbors speaking North Luhyia languages. Thus, they continued to use words derived from the root *-nyal-* to talk about wealth and wealthy people.[126] For example, we find the nouns *obunyali* meaning wealth or total collection of riches and *omunyali* meaning a rich person or a wealthy person and also a successful person. Alongside these was the verb *ohunyalira* that referred to becoming wealthy and being able to transact. The negative forms were used to refer to someone who was unable or helpless (*atenyala*) and to being unable (*-sanyala*). Even in this example of the inverse of wealth being invoked by a negative form, what is most striking is that the inverse is not poverty. Rather it refers to the ability to care for oneself, with the implication being that the wealthy were those who were able to do so, while those without wealth were those who were unable to care for themselves. This could refer to physical capacity to generate wealth, whether through skilled iron smelting or blacksmithing or through the ability to successfully navigate the waters of the Victoria Nyanza and bring back catches of fish.

Basaamia used two further roots when they talked about the wealthy in the centuries before the nineteenth century. The first is also one that they inherited from their immediate linguistic ancestors who spoke Proto-Gwe-Saamia—namely, the root *-hulahulana*, which yielded the verb *ohulahulana* in Lusaamia, meaning prosper and progress.[127] As we saw above, Proto-Gwe-Saamia speakers innovated this root from the much older verbal root *-kúd-* (grow up) that has been reconstructed to Proto-Bantu. There is here a sense of movement into the acquisition of wealth, or at least a sense of directionality, that is absent in some of the other roots available to Basaamia. Finally, they borrowed a noun from the root *-bayi*, which has its origins in Proto-Kalenjin with the meaning keep cattle, but which Proto-North Luhyia speakers adapted to refer specifically to a person wealthy in livestock. That latter meaning, attached to the form *omwayi*, and specifying a person wealthy in cattle, is the one that Lusaamia speakers adopted.[128] The transformational nature of wealth in the form of cattle is key to understanding this choice: wealth in cattle in particular could be translated through bridewealth into wealth in wives and children.

Conclusion

The Greater Luhyia speaker communities lived in relatively close proximity to each other, even as the languages they spoke became increasingly distinct. One consequence of that continued proximity was the borrowing of words from one another. We saw this with Lubukusu speakers, who borrowed the word *omunyerere*, with the dual meaning of someone who is thin (but not as a result of illness) and poor person, from speakers of a Luyia language. Speakers of Greater Luhyia languages also lived in proximity to speaker communities of other Great Lakes

Bantu languages and of Nilotic languages. They borrowed words from both, covering a range of semantic domains, including those relating to socioeconomic status. We saw this with both *omumanani* and *-bayi* borrowed from Proto-Kalenjin. People's ideas about what it meant to be poor or to be rich varied across time and space, and in order to express those different concepts they coined new words, repurposed old ones, and borrowed others from their neighbors. Some of these were freighted with negative emotional meanings, such as framing the poor as selfish and disruptive. Others showed empathy by emphasizing suffering and bereavement. And others, especially those for the wealthy, conveyed positive emotions. The material realities of socioeconomic difference were also critical, whether they were the lack of food associated with poverty or the abundance of it associated with wealth. Those material realities at times translated into social ones, as with the conceptualization of the wealthy as powerful.

CHAPTER FOUR

Gender and Honor

North Nyanza Concepts of Poverty and Wealth through the Nineteenth Century

B
Y THE EIGHTH CENTURY, the dialects of Proto-West Nyanza had diverged to the point of no longer being mutually intelligible. We call the languages that they became Proto-Rutara and Proto-North Nyanza. The former was spoken in the drier lowlands to the west and south, in what is now central and southern Uganda and northwestern Tanzania.[1] The latter, our focus here, was spoken by people who lived on the northwestern shore and hinterland of the Victoria Nyanza in an arc curving from the Nile River southwestward to the Katonga River. Their innovations in their vocabulary for poverty and wealth reflect the consolidation of new forms of wealth and the elaboration of monarchical rule. By the thirteenth century, Proto-North Nyanza had in turn diverged into Luganda and Proto-South Kyoga. Luganda was spoken in the area that had been the heartland of the Proto-North Nyanza speaker community. Proto-South Kyoga, however, was spoken by people who had settled to the east of the Nile River (see map 4.1). Faced with new ecological and social realities, the changes they made to their terminology for poverty and wealth reflect an emphasis on building networks of support that cut across generations.

The socioeconomic conceptual landscape created and inhabited by speakers of Proto-North Nyanza and its descendant languages reflected their changing physical and social worlds. The range of concepts captured in the words they used to talk about the poor and the wealthy and about poverty and wealth defies easy labeling. Nonetheless, their concepts for economic difference coalesced in ways that reflect material, emotional, and social concerns. From the material perspective, we see a new concept of wealth as acquired, alongside a concern to distinguish between gradations of poverty. There was an intensification of the concept of poverty as a natural phenomenon, rather than the result of human decisions, one with consequences for physical appearance, but also of poverty

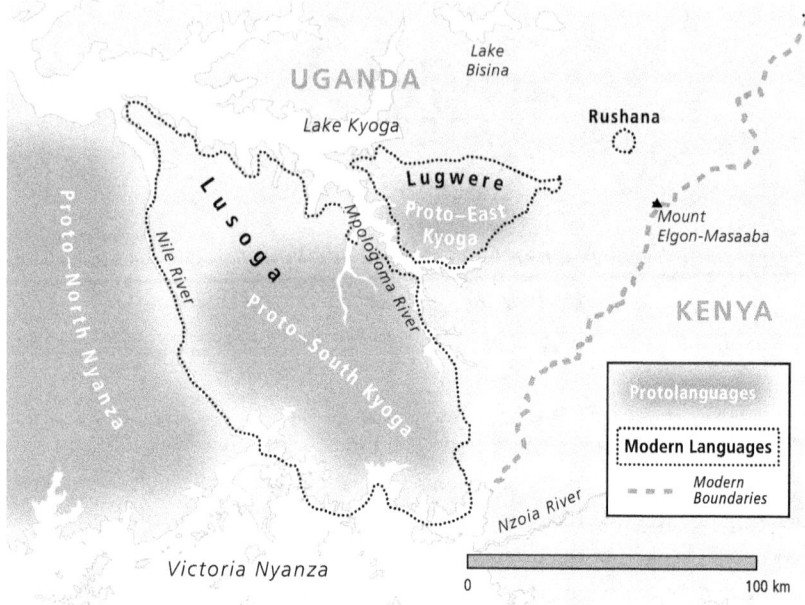

MAP 4.1. Map of Proto-North Nyanza, Proto-South Kyoga, Proto-East Kyoga, Lusoga, Lugwere, and Rushana. Map created by Nat Case.

as potentially a short-term or contingent condition. Emotional dimensions of poverty come across in joint conceptualizations of it with suffering and with evil. The deep social anxiety generated by socioeconomic difference within communities is apparent in the new concept of the poor as not fully human and in an emphasis on the individual failings of poor people. By contrast, the primary focus in Proto-North Nyanza speakers' concepts of wealth—and those speaking languages descended from it—was on gendered wealth, whether the transfer of wealth associated with women and the networks thereby created, or the transformation of material wealth into wealth in the form of women and children.

Proto-North Nyanza and Its Speakers

The changing economic, political, and environmental realities for speakers of Proto-North Nyanza were reflected in their development of new concepts for wealth and poverty. As well as establishing new communities ever further afield, they invested their resources in cultivating bananas, producing new cultivars of the fruit, including ones for cooking and brewing beer. As they increasingly specialized in banana cultivation, the land that Proto-North Nyanza speakers inhabited and worked acquired a different value for them. This value was based in the fact that, in contrast to millet fields that were harvested at the end of the growing season and planted with a new crop, bananas were a perennial crop. An established banana garden could provide fruit for a generation or more. Wealth, thus, inhered both in the lands best suited to banana cultivation, which became more highly sought after, and in banana plants themselves. The productive capacity of banana gardens allowed for the growth of larger populations on the hills around the lakeshore and for an expansion of the political power that centered in royal families.[2] The growing wealth that resulted was not shared equally, and consequent social tensions within these communities resulted in an increasingly negative view of the poor.

The people who spoke Proto-North Nyanza continued to draw on some of the vocabulary used by their linguistic ancestors who had spoken Proto-West Nyanza to talk about economic and social difference. They did so even as they innovated in their terminology for wealth and poverty and changed how they conceived of these socioeconomic statuses. They used the root *-jolo to refer to poverty and the poor, but emphasized the degree of poverty by expanding its meaning to include very poor person or destitute person (*omwolo).[3] At the same time, they stopped using *-jolo to mean soft or smooth, marking a break from the Proto-West Nyanza speaker community's concept of poverty as connected with being weak or soft. The root *-naku was also one which Proto-North Nyanza speakers inherited from Proto-West Nyanza.[4] As it had in the latter protolanguage, the root encapsulated a conceptual link for Proto-North Nyanza speakers between poverty, distress, and time. In particular, they emphasized emotional distress when they used *-naku to refer to misery and sorrow, as well as poverty and hardship. The association with time was more narrowly focused than it had been in Proto-West Nyanza, with speakers of Proto-North Nyanza using the root in the form *olunaku (pl. *ennaku) to mean day and no longer using it to talk about the larger time span of seasons.

This change in the meaning of *-naku suggests an important shift in the conceptualization of time, climate, and poverty. The climate data indicates that while Proto-North Nyanza emerged as a language during a period of higher rainfall, the centuries in which it was spoken were mostly part of a regional dry phase.[5] It is likely that this affected people's understanding of the seasons. David Schoenbrun has noted shifts in the vocabulary for the short rainy season of October and November that reflected climatic uncertainty.[6] Proto-North Nyanza speakers would have had to make sense of their changing climate, as well as adapt to it. The level of the Victoria Nyanza abruptly declined, reflecting a precipitous decline in rainfall, between twelve hundred and six hundred years ago. Those living on its shores, including the Proto-North Nyanza speaker community, would have had to adjust to this new reality and its consequences for socioeconomic difference. Reframing poverty as no longer necessarily a long-term condition may have been a response to the increased vulnerability of more of the population, those often described as the contingent poor, in this changed climate.

The community that spoke Proto-North Nyanza created a new vocabulary to reflect their ideas about the poor. To do so they used the root *-yavu.[7] They inherited this root from a Proto-Great Lakes Bantu root, *-yabu, that meant evil or filthy.[8] The etymology tells us that speakers of Proto-North Nyanza initially conceived of a connection between evil, filth, and poverty—perhaps with connections to witchcraft. Over time, however, its speakers moved away from this conceptualization and began using the root only to speak of poverty, no longer using it to refer to evil at all. As wealth began to be concentrated in the hands of those who controlled access to the best banana gardens, it may be that the initial exclusion from that land of those who were becoming poor led to accusations of witchcraft. Once the social stratification that resulted from the political and economic changes during this period had become established, what had previously needed to be explained as resulting from a rupture of social norms became the new social norm and thus no longer in need of explanation.[9] It may also be that the more widespread economic insecurity caused by the prolonged dry period removed some of the stigma of poverty over the centuries that Proto-North Nyanza was spoken.

A second noun coined by speakers of Proto-North Nyanza is somewhat more opaque in terms of its etymology than *-yavu. This is *lunkúpe, which they used to talk about a very poor person.[10] Unlike *mwavu, which was in the noun class for human beings (class one in the singular and class two in the plural), Proto-North Nyanza speakers placed this noun in class eleven, which encompasses several different categories, including languages, body parts, long, thin entities, implements, and utensils, and also natural phenomena.[11] Proto-North Nyanza speakers may have been invoking the emaciation of the very poor in choosing to put this new noun in this particular class. Alternatively—or additionally as the two are not mutually exclusive—they may have been invoking a framing of dire poverty as a natural occurrence, not the product of human action. Again, this was likely connected to the drier climate and the probability that it caused more widespread economic insecurity, with farmers less sure of being able to build up grain reserves to compensate for poor harvests. In either case, and clearly with a negative meaning, their choice of a nonhuman noun class suggests a dehumanization of the very poor. While more widespread poverty may, therefore, have led Proto-North Nyanza speakers to move away from supernatural explanations of poverty as caused by witchcraft, it also led them to adopt a conceptual framing of the very poor as less than human.

Finally, speakers of Proto-North Nyanza used the verb *-dooba* when they meant become destitute.[12] They innovated this, and the noun *-doobe*, meaning loincloth (worn by men), from a Proto-Bantu verb, *-dòb-*, "disappear; get lost."[13] In coining this verb, they articulated their understanding that poverty was a condition someone could move into, a person could become poor and not just be poor in a timeless manner. The particularly difficult climatic conditions in which they lived would have made this a more common reality for Proto-North Nyanza speakers. That they not only developed a new verb to talk about becoming destitute but used the same root to generate the meaning loincloth offers us insight into social perceptions of poverty and its consequences. Men who became poor could not afford bark cloth or skins for clothing and were instead reduced to near nakedness by wearing only a loincloth.[14] The Proto-North Nyanza speaker community's concepts of poverty thus ranged from a recognition of its emotional toll to a clear conceptual distancing of the very poor from the rest of society. One explanation for this is that as more people experienced contingent poverty, they may have wanted to distinguish themselves from those who lived in long-term destitution.

The existence of wealth and the wealthy in their communities was recognized by people who spoke Proto-North Nyanza in two main ways: one general and one explicitly gendered. To express the latter, they drew on the root *-yaandu*, which for speakers of Proto-Great Lakes Bantu held the meaning of gendered wealth.[15] As we saw in chapters 2 and 3, speakers of Proto-Greater Luhyia and its descendant languages used the root in diverging ways, while speakers of Proto-West Nyanza added the meanings plunder and loot to it. Those speaking Proto-North Nyanza continued to use it to refer to gendered forms of wealth, but they emphasized new aspects of this that referred to wealth specifically in the form of adult women. They used it to refer to widows in the form *namwandu*, with the *na-* prefix denoting that the noun referred to women only.[16] Schoenbrun has noted that this semantic extension was tied to the fact that a woman who was widowed was "often subject to the levirate"; that is, she was inherited by a brother or other male relation of her deceased husband.[17] Widows were thus a form of wealth that was passed on within the family, whether intra- or intergenerationally. Alongside this innovation, however, speakers of Proto-North Nyanza also coined *isemwandu* to refer to widowers, with the *ise-* prefix denoting that the noun referred only to men. This shifts the analysis somewhat, as a widower could simply remarry—or might even be able to claim a new bride from his deceased wife's family. The connection lies in an additional innovation—namely, the use of *-yaandu in the form *omwaandu to mean bridewealth, the transfer of which formalized the marriage between a wife and her husband. The form of wealth called *omwaandu was thus explicitly tied to women and their productive and reproductive capacities.

Socially approved marriage was not the only way men acquired wealth in the form of women. The Proto-North Nyanza speaker community used the root *-yaandu to refer to plunder and, in particular, to women and girls seized during warfare, retaining the innovation of their linguistic ancestors who had spoken Proto-West Nyanza. The choice to create new words for widow and widower from this root that was inextricably linked to wealth in the form of women and girls and wealth exchanged for women and girls in marriages gives us insight into the conceptual interweaving of marriage and wealth by Proto-North Nyanza speakers in these centuries. Thus, we can see during this period a pronounced focus on the gendered nature of at least some forms of wealth in these communities.

The new focus on control over particular plots of land and on royalty as the locus of political power at this time meant that there was a greater interest on the part of those with wealth and power to retain control over both wealth and power. For the community of Proto-North Nyanza speakers, that interest manifested itself through efforts to control women as a form of wealth and, especially, through efforts to control the transfer of women between households.[18] This was a process that became even more intense in the Luganda-speaking community after the dissolution of Proto-North Nyanza. Nonetheless, we can see the significance of this gendered form of wealth, one that could be inherited and transferred between households and which was embodied in women and girls, through the changes to *-yaandu during these centuries. But, in addition to its connection to the control of wealth, marriage—and especially the children anticipated to result from marriage—was critical in building networks that cut across patrilineal divides. A polygynous household in which the wives came from different clans and lineages, and perhaps different parts of the territory inhabited by Proto-North Nyanza speakers and beyond, would have a substantial network to turn to in time of need. That household could in turn support others in the network when they were in need. A focus on marriage as wealth during the prolonged dry period experienced by speakers of Proto-North Nyanza reflects the essential role played by networks that stretched beyond the immediate patrilineage or clan.

Alongside this elaboration in their vocabulary for this gendered form of wealth, Proto-North Nyanza speakers continued to use the root *-gaig- to refer to wealth in general (*obugaiga) and to those who were wealthy (*omugaiga, sing., *abagaiga, pl.).[19] They also used a verb derived from *-gaig- when they spoke of someone becoming wealthy: *-gaigawala. In contrast to *-yaandu, the words derived from *-gaig- were general and offer us little insight into how in particular people speaking Proto-North Nyanza conceived of the forms of wealth that they were referencing when they used them. What they do tell us, however, is that people speaking Proto-North Nyanza had an abstract concept of wealth alongside concepts that were grounded in particular forms of wealth. By contrast, when they used words derived from the inherited root *-fún-, Proto-North Nyanza speakers highlighted the acquisition of wealth.[20] In Proto-Bantu, the root had the form *-bún- and the meaning "break" or "snap."[21] Many Bantu-speaking communities used the root to create a verb that meant harvest. Proto-North Nyanza speakers, however, initially changed the meaning of the transitive verb *-fúna so that it meant get or obtain. They then expanded the meaning to include obtaining wealth in particular. When they used words derived from *-fún-, they were, therefore, specifying wealth as something one obtained or acquired, rather than as something that inhered in or simply happened to any particular individual. We see in the Proto-North Nyanza speaker community, therefore, different concepts of wealth, from that embodied by those who were gendered female and used to create new kinship networks through marriage and motherhood, to more material wealth that people could acquire.

Proto-South Kyoga and Its Speakers

As some families crossed the Nile to settle in new lands to the east and build new households and communities, the dialects that they spoke gradually diverged over several generations from that of the communities they had left behind. By the thirteenth century the two groups would no longer have found it easy to understand each other. One of the languages that emerged as a result of this process of gradual divergence was Luganda, spoken in the same area as Proto-North Nyanza, although expanding significantly over time, especially after the seventeenth century conquests by the Buganda kingdom. The other language, the focus here, was one we call Proto-South Kyoga, the ancestral language of Lusoga, Lugwere, and Rushana.

The landscape to the east of the Nile and closer to the Victoria Nyanza would have been generally familiar to the communities that spoke Proto-South Kyoga as it resembled that inhabited by speakers of Proto-North Nyanza. Those who settled further north, up toward Lake Kyoga, however, had to adjust to a flatter and rockier terrain and to rainfall that could fall violently, causing erosion on the lands they sought to cultivate. What is more, toward Lake Kyoga, rainfall was more sporadic across the agricultural year. This affected the economic choices made by Proto-South Kyoga speakers as they determined the best ways to thrive in their new settlements. In the southern half of this area, bananas could form the staple crop, supplemented as they would have been by fish, meat, and legumes. In the northern half, grain crops, especially millet, would have been more reliable, something borne out by the linguistic evidence for these crops in Proto-South Kyoga.[22] This settlement into the lands east of the Nile happened during a period in which the evidence from lake cores indicates, as we saw in the interchapter, more regular precipitation interspersed with several multidecadal episodes of reduced rainfall or drought, from the twelfth to fourteenth centuries.[23] Whether this was a key motivating factor for the communities that came to speak Proto-South Kyoga to establish themselves in new lands is unknown, but it likely contributed to their decisions. Once they had moved, the climatic conditions would certainly have complicated their efforts to build new households and communities.

For the most part, people speaking Proto-South Kyoga continued to use the same vocabulary as their linguistic ancestors who had spoken Proto-North Nyanza when they spoke of poverty and wealth or of paupers and rich people. They used nouns that they created from the roots *-jolo, *-yavu, and *-naku to name the poor.[24] But, living as they did in new linguistic as well as physical landscapes, they encountered people speaking languages descended from Proto-Greater Luhyia. In particular, they interacted with pre-Lunyole speakers and speakers of Proto-Gwe-Saamia. While their encounters would not always have been peaceful, and certainly the oral traditions reference violent conflict in more recent centuries at least, these communities also realized the benefits of building widespread networks through intermarriage and trade. We can see the mutual influence of these communities in the words their speakers borrowed from each other and passed on to their descendants. One such borrowing was the root *-tak-, which was used by Proto-Greater Luhyia speakers to talk about the poor and their poverty, as we saw in chapter 2.[25] Speakers of Proto-South Kyoga adopted this root, using it in the forms *ómútáki to describe a poor person and *óbútáki to describe poverty and need.

When they talked about wealth and the wealthy Proto-South Kyoga speakers continued to use the root *-gaig-.[26] They also continued to use the root *-fun- in the form *obúfuní*, meaning wealth and possession of property.²⁷ We see changes in their concepts through their emphasis on gendered forms of wealth, which they expressed by restricting the meanings of the root *-yàandu* to refer only to widows and bridewealth.²⁸ Thus, they no longer used words derived from the root to talk about the wealthy or about any form of wealth other than bridewealth. They also stopped using *-yàandu* to talk about plunder and booty. This may suggest that the Proto-South Kyoga speaker community engaged less in predatory raiding as a means of acquiring wealth, in particular wealth in people. As they remade their communities in a new context and contended with prolonged droughts, speakers of Proto-South Kyoga emphasized the peaceable networks formed through women, in particular through marriage, as a means of building and sustaining wealth in their households.²⁹ Their change in the use of *-yàandu* reflects this.

Lusoga Speakers

By around the start of the sixteenth century, Proto-South Kyoga had diverged into Lusoga and Proto-East Kyoga. Lusoga was spoken in the lands to the east of the Nile, west of the Mpologoma River, and south of Lake Kyoga, while Proto-East Kyoga was spoken to the east of the Mpologoma and Lake Kyoga (see map 4.1). The communities that spoke Lusoga lived in the same area as their linguistic ancestors who had spoken Proto-South Kyoga. Over time the language diverged into several dialects, including Lutenga, Lulamoogi, Lugabula, and Lusiki. Toward the end of the sixteenth century, Lusoga speakers would have encountered people speaking Southern Luo languages who migrated into the area from the north, having circumvented Lake Kyoga along its eastern shore, moving back westward into Busoga.³⁰ Eastern and northern Busoga were populated by Lusoga-speaking communities when Southern Luo migrants began to settle there, with "centres of intensive occupation in eastern Bukooli and at Kizenguli," but "scattered settlements and transient groups all across the interior and along the Mpologoma and Kyoga waterways."³¹ Drawing on Bethwell Ogot's work, David William Cohen noted that the "character of the migrations seems to have been dominated by certain persistent features." Notably, the "migration was not a flood, but rather a composition of small groups following disparate routes at various times over the several centuries of extensive migration." Furthermore, "the migrating Lwo groups were forever cleaving off into smaller units. Segments of larger groups broke off, leaving their camp for new lands over the horizon." This fission is remembered in the traditions as being caused by tensions within the group.³² The relations between the communities speaking Southern Luo languages and those speaking dialects of Lusoga (the borders of which were highly fluid, with overlaps between them) resulted in important changes in food production and exchange, political formations, and social life.

People in Busoga cultivated a number of staple crops, including bananas, millet, and sorghum.³³ Lusoga speakers, however, especially in the southern part of the region, increasingly focused on growing bananas, the result of which were the extensive banana groves described by Europeans in the 1890s that would likely have taken generations to develop.³⁴ The topographical and climatological differences between the area closer to the Victoria Nyanza and the area further north toward Lake Kyoga had significant implications for cultivation and the raising of livestock. Growing bananas and root crops in the north would have been especially challenging in drier years with precipitation falling off quite significantly with distance from the Victoria Nyanza. Here, millet and sorghum were more reliable crops. On the other hand, the areas further away from the lake were free of tsetse flies and the trypanosomiasis they transmitted. Basoga living in those areas "would have been able to incorporate livestock in their regime of food production, perhaps preferentially colonizing zones tending to be free of the sleeping sickness vector," in ways that were meaningful for their concepts of wealth and its absence.³⁵

In terms of social and political developments, the movement of people speaking Southern Luo languages into the area was significant in a number of ways. One of these was that several clans that went on to become prominent in Busoga into the twentieth century emerged from this process—namely, the abaiseMudoola, abaiseNaminha, abaiseBandha, abaiseKiruyi, abaiseWakooli, abaiseKiranda, and abaiseKibiga.³⁶ As Cohen noted, the "traditions indicate that families of Lwo origin were gradually leaving the core area of Lwo settlements and were, in several cases, assuming a dominant position among the Bantu-speaking groups with whom they came in contact."³⁷ Rather than imagine this as a straightforward process of immigration and domination, we need to pay attention to important clues that speak to the existence also of processes of integration and collaboration. One of these clues is in the names of the clans, which are Lusoga in origin. Indeed, at both the level of the clan and polity, the Southern Luo–speaking communities and their descendants (who adopted Lusoga as their primary language) depended heavily on preexisting Basoga clans and families. Even when some Luo lineages seized control of a number of kingdoms in northern Busoga, "their power was predicated on preexisting South Kyoga and Soga political ideologies that had motherhood at their core."³⁸

The gendered concept of wealth is apparent here expressed as it was through the continued use by speakers of Proto-South Kyoga of words derived from the root *-yaandu*.[39] This was evident in practices around marriage and the raising of children. One Southern Luo group, the Owiny Karuoth, "and their patrilineal descendants, restricted not only endogamic marriage (that is, within the Owiny Karuoth) but also marriages with groups that were, or once were, Luo-speaking."[40] This meant that the Luo-descended families gave bridewealth to Lusoga-speaking families in exchange for the reproductive and productive labor of their daughters. While some Lusoga-speaking families reciprocated, they did not restrict marriage in the same way and many women and men married the sons and daughters of other Lusoga-speaking families. When we consider socioeconomic difference, this practice of exogamous marriage by the Owiny Karuoth and other Southern Luo groups is of great significance. It meant that despite their relative wealth in terms of livestock when they arrived in Busoga and the political power they fairly rapidly acquired, they did not form a wealthy class or caste isolated from those among whom they settled. On the contrary, through the transfer of bridewealth and daughters, they continually redistributed some of their wealth to Lusoga-speaking households, a practice that continued across several generations.

Lusoga speakers inherited much of the vocabulary that they used to talk about poverty and wealth from the speaker communities of Proto-South Kyoga and Proto-North Nyanza. They elaborated on that vocabulary with new words that emphasized extremes of economic difference. Basoga continued to use the root *-jolo*, which has been reconstructed to Proto-Bantu as *-jódò*, to talk about a poor person, in the form of the noun *lukyóló*.[41] The form of this noun is unusual, and it differs from the forms of nouns derived from the root in other West Nyanza languages, as it has two noun class prefixes. Lusoga speakers first added the prefix for noun class seven, *ki-*. The nouns in this class are typically inanimate, but it can also be used to mark a noun as a derogative.[42] Thus in the same way that talking about someone in English as a poor thing creates distance between the speaker and the subject by dehumanizing the latter, but can also suggest compassion, so changing the prefix from that for the category of human beings, *mu-*, to that of things marked a shift in perception by the speaker toward the poor person in question. Lusoga speakers then added a second prefix, *lu-*, to the noun. This is the prefix for noun class eleven, which typically encompasses languages and body parts, but also includes natural phenomena, thin or narrow objects, and animals, as we saw above.[43] Having turned the noun into one derogatory toward the poor person being spoken about, Basoga women and men now suggested that their condition was a natural one as well as one that potentially gave the poor a new and undesired physical appearance. On the one hand, the framing of poverty as a natural phenomenon can be read positively, in that it did not include a judgment of the poor person. If so, it would have been a counterpoint to the use of the root *-tak- in Lusoga, which invoked social and spiritual failings, discussed below. On the other hand, invoking poverty as a natural phenomenon can be read negatively, as a framing which absolved others in the community of blame for the poverty of an individual. If poverty was a natural condition, then the selfishness or acquisitiveness of others, their unwillingness to give access to land or livestock or other resources, could not be held responsible. And the commentary on the undesirable emaciation of the destitute through the prefix *lu-* can also be read as critical or disparaging toward them.

When they used words that they had derived from the root *-naku, which they had also inherited from their Proto-West Nyanza linguistic ancestors, Lusoga speakers articulated a different concept of poverty.[44] This was one that closely resembled that held by speakers of Proto-Nilotic, expressed through the root *-can-, and inherited by speakers of Proto-Southern Luo and their linguistic descendants.[45] For Lusoga speakers, *-naku allowed them to articulate an idea of poverty as merely one among many forms of suffering. Thus, the noun *obúnakú* meant destitution, but it also meant affliction, anguish, misery, and grief. Similarly, *omúnakú* meant wretch, but also referred to someone without friends. The root *-naku and its new expressive possibilities for poverty and suffering appears to have resonated with speakers of Lusoga, who have coined a wide range of words from it, all with closely related meanings. This development is noteworthy because while *-naku had long held within it the joint conceptualization of poverty and grief, Lusoga speakers changed its meaning to encompass a much broader, almost comprehensive range of suffering. It seems highly likely that this resulted from the settlement in Busoga of people speaking a Southern Luo language and who developed, as we have seen, very close ties to the existing Lusoga-speaking population. Through their interactions, Lusoga speakers borrowed the Southern Luo concept of poverty expressed through the root *-can-, but transposed it onto their own root, *-naku, which already held some of the new meanings. Here, then, is an example of the borrowing of a concept of poverty across linguistic communities without the borrowing of the form of the word used to express that concept.[46] This suggests not only close interactions between the two speaker communities, but also high levels of bilingualism, meaning that there would have been significant overlap in the membership of the speaker communities, at least as long as the Southern Luo language continued to be spoken in Busoga.

Alongside *lukyôlo* and the words derived from **-naku* that had been used by speakers of Proto-West Nyanza, the Lusoga speaker community continued to use roots that their linguistic ancestors who had spoken Proto-North Nyanza had coined to talk about the poor and poverty. One of these was **-yavu*, derived from an older Proto-Great Lakes Bantu adjectival root that meant evil or filthy.[47] In Lusoga the meaning was, as in Proto-North Nyanza, restricted to only refer to poverty and being needy in the form of the noun *obwâvú* and to a pauper or poor person in the form of the noun *omwâvú*. The second retention from Proto-North Nyanza was the noun *lúnkúpe*, which Proto-North Nyanza speakers used to speak about a pauper or a very poor person.[48] As we have seen, and as with *lukyôló*, the *lu-* prefix of *lúnkúpe* places it in the category of natural phenomena or thin objects. In continuing to use the noun, alongside their derivation of *lukyôló* from **-jolo*, we can see Lusoga speakers emphasizing the physical appearance of the very poor and emphasizing that the destitute were an inevitable part of their world.

This sense that the very poor were a natural phenomenon, and so neither they nor others were to blame for their condition, did not carry over in the ways in which Basoga used the root **-tak-*. This they inherited from Proto-South Kyoga speakers, who had in turn borrowed it from their neighbors speaking Greater Luhyia languages.[49] In Lusoga, the nouns derived from the root took on highly freighted meanings. As well as referring to being poor and in need, Lusoga speakers came to use *óbútákí* to refer to a deficiency in conduct, manners, and etiquette or to a physical, social, and spiritual failing. This was a clear conceptualization of poverty as being the result of—or at least intimately connected with—the individual failing of the person who was poor. It is, as with all innovations during a single modern language, very difficult to date this, but it may well have been a development connected to the introduction of Christianity and its particular constellation of ideas about morality and immorality in the opening years of the twentieth century.[50]

Lusoga speakers felt the need to distinguish between degrees of poverty and in particular to distinguish the very poor or destitute from those who were "merely" poor. They used *lúnkúpe* as one means of doing so. But this was apparently insufficient, and they also innovated a new noun with the meaning very poor person—namely, *omúghédhére*.[51] They derived this from a Proto-Great Lakes Bantu verbal root that meant pant or wheeze. For example, in Luganda we find the verb *kùwe'jjera*, with the meanings breathe hard and gabble, and in Runyankore and Rukiga we find the verb *kuheijeera* with the meanings of wheeze and groan. In using this root to talk about the very poor, Basoga expressed a concept of destitution as a condition with physical manifestations, whether in actual difficulty breathing or in vocalization of the hardship being experienced.

The new—or renewed—distinctions of socioeconomic status in Soga society that were expressed through nouns describing those who were very poor or destitute also found expression through the fairly extensive vocabulary for the wealthy. Once more this vocabulary was a mixture of inherited terms, some with shifts in meaning in Lusoga, and new terms coined by Lusoga speakers or borrowed from neighbors speaking other languages. The oldest word that they used to talk about wealth was **omwandu*.[52] We have seen how in Proto-North Nyanza this meant bridewealth, in addition to meaning plunder taken in warfare, often in the form of women and girls, and inherited wealth, including the widows of the deceased male head of the household. In Lusoga the root took the form of nouns that continued these meanings of gendered wealth connected to marriage: *omwândú* meaning bridewealth, *namwândú* meaning widow, and *sémwándú* meaning widower. We can see in this a very strong association of wealth with the movement of women and girls between households, whether in exchange for livestock and other goods at marriage or as part of an inheritance. The importance of networks formed with powerful newcomers, like the Southern Luo speakers who took control of several polities in the area, in ensuring socioeconomic stability comes across through this concept of wealth. In marrying their daughters to Lusoga-speaking families, the Southern Luo speaker community and its descendants in Busoga both created networks of economic and political support and redistributed their own wealth in livestock to those outside their immediate lineages.

Lusoga speakers, like their linguistic ancestors who had spoken Proto-South Kyoga, did not use the root **-yaandu* to mean plunder and booty. From the seventeenth century, especially, the Lusoga-speaking communities were frequently targeted by their Luganda-speaking neighbors to the west. These military attacks were part of expansionary and predatory moves by the kingdom of Buganda that started after the accession of King Kateregga and his Queen Mother Nabuso Nabagereka in the early to mid-seventeenth century and continued through the nineteenth century.[53] The substantial loss of wealth, particularly in the form of women and girls, from the Soga kingdoms to Buganda may have caused them to change their conceptualization of wealth in relation to *omwaandu*. The result was that Lusoga speakers' concept of wealth as expressed through *omwaandu* focused only on legitimate transfers of gendered wealth, such as with the Luo lineages, and not that which was stolen through violent conflict.

The Proto-West Nyanza root *-gaig- that could mean rich person or wealth was also one that Lusoga speakers continued to use for both of these meanings.[54] For the most part, the latter retained the range of meanings that Proto-West Nyanza speakers attached to the root when they innovated it. But Lusoga speakers made one important change that spoke to their emphasis on gendered forms of wealth. Namely, they added the specific meaning of rich man with many wives to the noun *omúgaigá*. Underscoring their concept of wealth as wealth in people, Lusoga speakers also gave the meaning rich man with many wives to three further nouns: *omúfuní*, *ómúlokí*, and *omúkombé*, although the last of these needed qualifying as *omúkombé ow'ábákazí* (lit. a man wealthy in wives).[55] Beyond highlighting their concept of wealth as wealth in people, this change instigated by Lusoga speakers also modified their concept of wealth in people to explicitly specify that it was held by men. Thus, another way of talking about a wealthy man was to use the phrase *omúsaadha byági*, with the literal meaning of a man of granaries. In a polygynous household, each wife had her own granary that she would fill with crops from the fields she cultivated with the help of her children. A man with many granaries was, therefore, a man with many wives and hence, in the Soga conceptualization, a wealthy man.[56]

The noun *omúfuní* was derived from the Proto-North Nyanza root *-fún-*, which speakers of the language used to articulate the concept of acquired wealth.[57] For the Lusoga speaker community, the acquired wealth that they referenced with *omúfuní* took the form of wives and was thus restricted to men. By contrast, Lusoga speakers derived *ómúlokí* from a Proto-North Nyanza intransitive verb *-lóka*, meaning sprout.[58] The etymology points to the possibility for change in one's socioeconomic condition, as in the phrase *Yali mwavu aye buti yaloka* ("He was poor but now has become wealthy.")[59] The noun *omúkombé*, used in the phrase *omúkombé ow'ábákazí* (a man wealthy in wives), is from Lunyole, where it has the form *omuhombe* and the meaning an extremely wealthy person.[60] It was derived from the Proto-Bantu root *-kómb-*, with the glosses "scrape, dig; lick (food) with finger," as we saw in chapter 3.[61] When Lusoga speakers borrowed it from Lunyole, they shifted its meaning so that the degree of wealth was not specified, but its gendered aspect was.

Lusoga speakers, thus, made a number of important changes to their vocabulary for poverty and wealth, reflecting shifts in how they understood these concepts. They placed even greater emphasis on gendered wealth and the networks it generated. But they also increasingly conceived of wealth as belonging to men, especially wealth in people, whether women, children, or other dependents. Lusoga speakers conceived of dire poverty as a natural condition. And they borrowed from their Luo-speaking neighbors and in-laws the concept that poverty was merely one among many forms of suffering, highlighting how a concept could translate across linguistic boundaries, even when the form of the word did not.

Proto-East Kyoga and Its Speakers

When Lusoga emerged from Proto-South Kyoga, the other language that resulted was Proto-East Kyoga, the ancestral language of Lugwere and Rushana. The people who spoke Proto-East Kyoga lived to the east of their Lusoga-speaking linguistic siblings, moving back and forth across the Mpologoma River in response to political and climatic events into the nineteenth century. Across the Mpologoma, they lived in a region of great and growing linguistic diversity. To their immediate south and east were people speaking Greater Luhyia languages, including Lunyole and Lumasaaba. Families speaking Southern Luo languages moved through this area to Busoga in the west and southeastward to the northwestern shore of the Victoria Nyanza. By the end of the eighteenth century, speakers of Proto-East Kyoga increasingly encountered Ateso speakers who were moving into the area from the north and northeast.[62] This process continued well into the nineteenth century, after the divergence of Proto-East Kyoga into Lugwere and Rushana. While conflict was one aspect of living in a diverse and changing human landscape, other more peaceful interactions also occurred, including significant intermarriage between those who spoke Proto-East Kyoga as their mother tongue and those with other mother tongues. These relationships came to be reflected in the vocabulary of Proto-East Kyoga speakers, through words such as *kideero*, a noun meaning granary that they borrowed from a Southern Luo language.[63]

The physical landscape that Proto-East Kyoga speakers inhabited was similar to that of Busoga, with low hills and swampy valleys. Rainfall, although adequately distributed through the year for banana cultivation, was less reliable than in lands closer to the Victoria Nyanza to the south. Severe droughts were a fairly frequent occurrence for those who spoke Proto-East Kyoga and their descendants. As a result, East Kyoga women and men placed an emphasis on having a flexible and diverse economic basis to sustain them through the failures of grain or root harvests. Developing and maintaining knowledge related to gathering wild foods, hunting, and fishing was essential for them and shows that, while environmental stresses are an important factor for us to consider as historians, people drew on their existing skills and acquired new ones in order to adapt and thrive in different ecological contexts. A turn toward hunting, for example, in the context of drought and famine is remembered in a Gwere oral tradition that tells of the founding of a polity in the late eighteenth century.[64]

Proto-East Kyoga was spoken until around the 1830s, when a group of people who later came to call themselves Bashana fled the area due to conflict and settled to the east in Bulegenyi in the foothills of Mount Elgon-Masaaba.[65] They found themselves holding marginal status in a new linguistic and social landscape as a minority group between the larger and more powerful Bamasaaba and Sebei communities. In the 1920s several Bashana migrated to western Kenya in search of agricultural employment.[66] Given the relatively rapid degree of linguistic change in Rushana after its speakers settled in Bulegenyi, a function of their marginality, it is difficult to reconstruct the vocabulary that Proto-East Kyoga speakers innovated to talk about poverty and wealth. Nonetheless, we can identify the words that they inherited from Proto-South Kyoga and earlier ancestral languages.

When they wanted to talk about the poor and about poverty, people who spoke Proto-East Kyoga could use *obwavu, derived from the Proto-North Nyanza root *-yavu.[67] When they wanted to speak of someone who was very poor, they turned to another Proto-North Nyanza noun, *lùnkúpe.[68] And they also used the root *-tak-, which their forebears who had spoken Proto-South Kyoga had borrowed from Greater Luhyia–speaking neighbors.[69] Unlike in Lusoga, however, the nouns *óbútáki, meaning poverty, and ómútáki, meaning poor person, did not acquire freighted meanings of moral failure. In a change from Proto-South Kyoga, people speaking Proto-East Kyoga stopped using words derived from the roots *-naku and *-jolo to talk about poverty in an apparent narrowing of their conceptualization of poverty away from the emotional and temporal meanings of the former and the ideas of weakness and pliability of the latter.

When it came to talking about wealth, there was less innovation in vocabulary. This contrasts with more significant innovation across time in terms of the vocabulary for—and concepts of—poverty. This suggests that poverty and the poor, rather than the other extreme of wealth, were the primary focus of their anxieties around socioeconomic difference. Given the relatively limited accumulation of wealth, at least by the standards of the Buganda kingdom and more recent developments in the region, there may have been less focus on the wealthy and their riches. But that is not to say that there was no socioeconomic disparity or that the wealthy were not thought about and discussed. When the

Proto-East Kyoga speaker community talked about the wealthy, they used three roots. The first of these was the root *-gaig-, which had been innovated by people speaking Proto-West Nyanza.[70] In contrast to the developments in Lusoga, for those who spoke Proto-East Kyoga, the meaning remained only the general ones of wealth and wealthy person in the forms óbugáigá and ómugáigá. The second root was *omwandu, which again referenced gendered wealth in particular, both the wealth used to transact marriages, generally in the form of livestock given as bridewealth to the bride's family, and inherited wealth in the form of widows.[71] Finally, they used the root *-fun-, which had the general meaning get and the specific meanings wealth and get rich.[72] For those who spoke Proto-East Kyoga, therefore, wealth could be gendered and allowed people to build relationships across lineage and clan divides that could support them in times of hardship. And wealth was something that could be acquired. It was not, however, conceived as necessarily the basis for social or political standing. There was not, for example, any association between honor, respect, and wealth in their vocabulary, in contrast to the concepts of wealth in neighboring speaker communities.

Lugwere Speakers

Unlike the more usual and more gradual differentiation of dialects into distinct languages, Proto-East Kyoga abruptly split into Lugwere and Rushana in the 1830s as a result of famine and conflict. One group of Proto-East Kyoga speakers fled to the western foothills of Mount Elgon-Masaaba and became the Bashana, as noted above.[73] The Lugwere speaker community that stayed in the lands just east of the Mpologoma waterway had to contend with the prolonged dry period that had begun in the late eighteenth century and continued well into the nineteenth century. They also had to contend with continued insecurity as a result of conflict from political disputes and with the arrival of Iteso families from the north. But immigration was not without its benefits. The oral traditions remember a Teso man, Laki Omugobera, whose hunting skills allowed him to provide food for two mothers who were starving, and whose son went on to found the Balalaka polity.[74] The all too real consequences of the prolonged dry period are also present in the oral traditions, naming as they do individual famines that occurred during this time. There was, for example, the *matyama* famine of the 1780s, when people speaking Ateso moved into the area in search of relief, and the *bukwikwi* famine of the 1830s named for the wild plant that Bagwere ate to survive during this time of intense hardship.[75]

In this context, Lugwere speakers adapted their concepts of poverty and wealth as they sought to make sense of their particular socioeconomic situation and its tensions. The profound challenges they faced are reflected in a proliferation of words for poverty and the poor, in marked contrast to a far more limited vocabulary for wealth and the wealthy. The root *-tak-*, borrowed by speakers of Proto–South Kyoga from Lunyole, was used by Lugwere speakers in what might be seen as contradictory—or at least noncomplementary—ways.[76] The nouns *ómútáki* and *óbútáki* came to mean poor person and poverty, respectively, while the verb *ókutakíwálá* came to mean become poor. The verb *ókutaká* held the range of meanings we saw in chapters 2 and 3 with reference to Proto–Greater Luhyia and its descendant languages—namely, to want, need, or like. But in Lugwere it also came to mean wish, desire, intend, love, and adore. While the meaning of desire is one that Yvonne Bastin and her colleagues reconstructed to the Proto-Bantu form of the root, *-càk-*, the distribution of meanings in Great Lakes Bantu languages makes it unlikely that the Lugwere senses of the root were inherited rather than reinvented. Nonetheless, given the base meaning of *-tak-* as desire, it is not surprising to find such meanings reappear. The Lugwere extension of the root's meaning to include love, desire, and adore happened alongside the continued meanings of poverty, poor person, and being in need. Thus, on the one hand, Lugwere speakers used -*tak*- to express their recognition of the relationship between unmet needs and poverty and, on the other, they used it to express deep, positive emotions. This suggests a conception of poverty as a condition in which desires are unfulfilled, but also points to the strength of the feeling of need among the poor mirroring the strength of the feelings of desire and adoration.

Lugwere speakers chose not to keep many of the words their linguistic ancestors had used to talk about poverty and the poor. They did not use the roots *-jolo* or *-naku* with those meanings. And although they kept the root *-yavu*, they only used it in the form *bwavu*, meaning poverty, and did not use it to refer to the poor themselves.[77] They did, however, continue to use the words their Proto–North Nyanza–speaking linguistic ancestors developed to talk about becoming destitute using the root *-doob-*: *kudòòba* in Lugwere for become destitute and become poor, *budòobi* for destitution and poverty, and *kidoobi* for the adjective destitute.[78] They also retained the meaning loincloth associated with the root, in the form *muloobe*. Alongside these they continued to use the noun *lunkupe*, meaning very poor person, coined by Proto–North Nyanza speakers. Alongside these inherited forms, speakers of Lugwere coined two new words to talk about a poor person: *nairange*, meaning a person who is poor and lacking respect or a lowly person, and *nambadi*, with the sense irresponsible husband, but with the particular meaning of one who could not provide for his wife or wives and their children.[79]

In order to further express their concepts of poverty and the poor, Lugwere speakers borrowed words and meanings from their neighbors speaking other languages. A number of these were attached to the root *-tamb-*, which speakers of Proto-Greater Luhyia used to talk about poverty, as we saw in chapter 2.[80] For the Proto-Greater Luhyia speaker community, *-tamb-* conveyed their concept of poverty as entwined with bereavement. This idea of poverty was expressed by Lunyole speakers when they used the root in the form *-damb-*, although they also used it to refer to severe poverty or destitution. Bagwere borrowed *-damb-* from their Banyole neighbors, but they used it only to express the concept of severe poverty or destitution. Thus, we find *mudambi* in Lugwere with the meaning very, very poor person. This emphasis on extreme poverty complemented Lugwere speakers' use of *lunkupe* to refer to a destitute person. They did not borrow the concept of poverty as entwined with bereavement that Lunyole speakers also expressed through this root. They did, though, borrow the North Luhyia concepts of suffering and disturbance associated with the same root, in the forms of *kudambadamba*, meaning to suffer a lot, and *kudambya*, meaning to disturb, vex, or cause trouble. Lugwere speakers borrowed other words derived from the same root from the Greater Luhyia languages Lugwe and Lusaamia, but with a slightly different form, reflecting the phonological changes in Greater Luhyia languages after they diverged from each other. In Lugwe and Lusaamia, the root took the form *-tamb-* and referred to hard work and workers. In Lugwere we find the verb *kutamba* meaning work and the noun *mutambi* meaning worker. This was, then, a highly productive root for speakers of Lugwere, who used it to talk about suffering, intense poverty, and work, making an implicit connection between these different meanings.

The final root related to poverty that speakers of Lugwere borrowed from their Lunyole-speaking neighbors offers us insight, albeit indirectly, into their shifting concepts of the poor. Speakers of Proto-Greater Luhyia innovated the root *-paat-* to mean poor person, poverty, and become poor, as we saw in chapter 2.[81] It had the same meanings in Lunyole, making it a stable concept across centuries. But when speakers of Lugwere borrowed it from Lunyole in the form *mupaati*, they changed its meaning from poor person to nonrelative. In so doing, they drew a connection between the two senses. The root allowed them to demarcate those who could and could not make claims for assistance by marking a boundary between relatives and nonrelatives. This aspect of separating insiders and outsiders was further underscored when Lugwere speakers derived a new verb from the same root to express the meaning set a limit or set a boundary: *kupaatiika*.

The prolonged dry period, famine, and conflict that formed the backdrop to the emergence of Lugwere likely contributed both to the intellectual innovation in concepts of poverty and the lack of innovation in concepts of wealth. Speakers of Lugwere used words inherited from Proto-South Kyoga and their earlier linguistic ancestors when they talked about wealth and those who possessed it. For the general concept of wealth and a wealthy person they used words derived from the root *-gaig-*, which had been coined by speakers of Proto-West Nyanza.[82] In Lugwere we find *ómugáigá*, meaning rich person, *óbugáigá*, meaning riches, and *ókugaigáwála*, meaning become rich. For gendered wealth, they turned to the root *-yaand-*, coined by speakers of Proto-Great Lakes Bantu: *namwandu* meaning widow and *mwandu* meaning wealth in livestock, with the latter an essential part of bridewealth.[83] Finally, highlighting the acquisitional aspect of wealth, they used the innovation of their Proto-North Nyanza speakers, who took their verbal root *-fun-*, meaning get or acquire, and began using it to refer to wealth. In Lugwere this took the forms *ókusuná*, meaning prosper, and *bya kusuná*, meaning wealth.[84] In a parallel development, the Lugwere speaker community began using *ókusuná* when they talked about acts of marriage, thus *ókusuna mukalí* for marrying a woman (lit. get a woman) and *ókusuna musaizá* for marrying a man (lit. get a man). I have argued elsewhere that this may "suggest an easing of some of the formal processes of marriage."[85] Given the backdrop of multidecadal drought and repeated famine, it would likely have been necessary to adjust expectations for bridewealth exchange and marriage ceremonies in order to ensure continued social reproduction and the establishment of networks of support.

Conclusion

As they sought ways to cope with the challenges and opportunities of settling in new lands, interacting with strangers, and the fluctuations of the climate, people speaking North Nyanza languages adapted their concepts of what it meant to be poor or rich. In particular, they placed strong emphasis on gendered wealth, wealth in people, and the networks that were formed through marriage. They also created new words for distinguishing between the poor and the very poor or destitute, and in so doing tended to frame destitution as natural and the destitute as not fully human. But speakers of Proto-North Nyanza and the languages that emerged from it also underscored the hardships brought about by poverty in their conceptualization of it as a form of suffering and misery.

CHAPTER FIVE

Orphans and Livestock

Nilotic Concepts of Poverty and Wealth through the Nineteenth Century

After the speaker communities of Proto-Southern, Proto-Western, and Proto-Eastern Nilotic diverged in their gradual expansion south and east, speakers of some of the languages descended from each of them found themselves centuries later living in relative proximity to each other in eastern Uganda and western Kenya (see map 5.1). While pastoralism remained a core feature of many of their economies and cultures, speakers of the languages descended from Proto-Kalenjin, Proto-Ateker, and Proto-Southern Luo developed quite distinct ideas about social and economic difference. The major themes of emotion, materiality, and the social thread through their concepts of poverty and wealth. Emotional dimensions were limited to poverty and its conceptualization alongside bereavement and suffering. Material framings of poverty centered on the absence of cattle and the physical wasting that resulted from chronic hunger. For wealth, the focus was on the accumulation of livestock, but also, in the Ateso speaker community, on wealth in harvested crops. Concepts of poverty grounded in social relationships included ideas of poverty as social death and kinlessness, as well as of the poor as disruptive. Unusually, among the Nilotic speaker communities, Ateso speakers coined a word to specify the condition of poverty for women, highlighting differences in experiences of poverty along gendered lines. When it came to wealth, there were strong emphases across the speaker communities on the translation of wealth into social status through its distribution to others.

Proto-Kalenjin and Its Speakers

The Southern Nilotic language we call Proto-Kalenjin existed from the time of the breakup of Proto-Southern Nilotic into Proto-Omotik-Datooga and

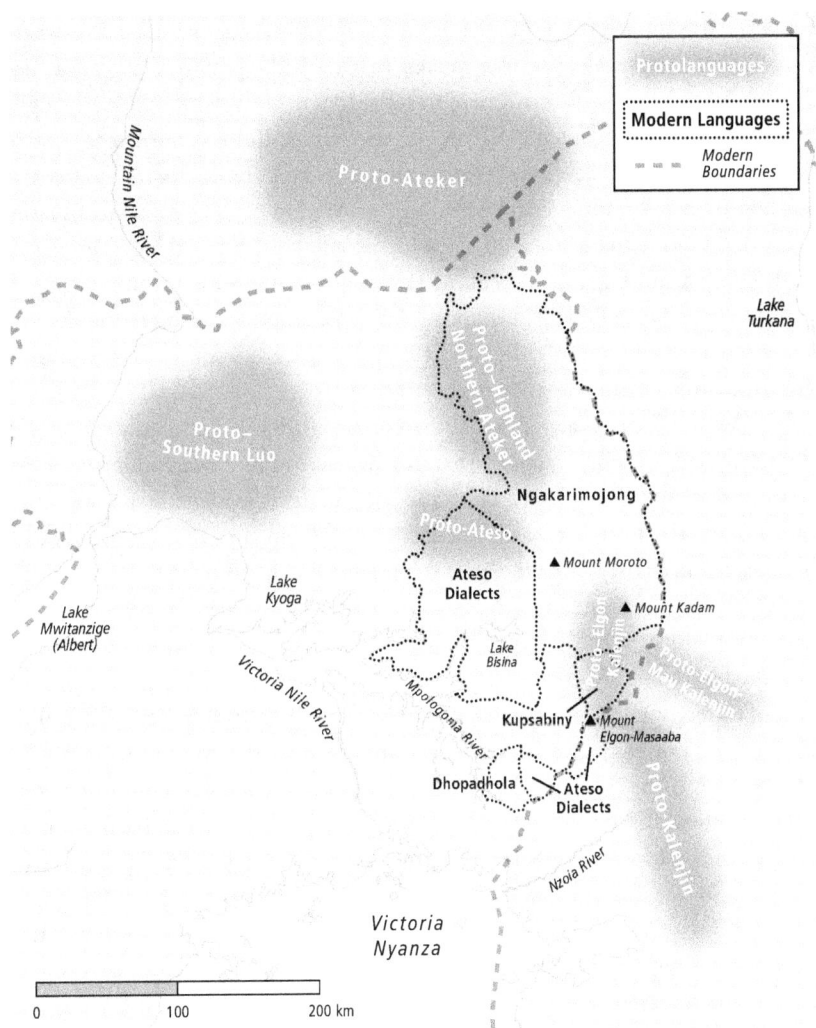

MAP 5.1. Map of Proto-Kalenjin, Proto-Elgon-Mau Kalenjin, Proto-Elgon Kalenjin, Proto-Ateker, Proto-Highland Northern Ateker, Proto-Ateso, Proto-Southern Luo, Kupsabiny, Kalenjin, Jie, Ateso Dialects, Ngakarimojong, and Dhopadhola. Map created by Nat Case.

Proto-Kalenjin until a little less than fifteen hundred years ago.[1] Its speakers lived between Mount Elgon-Masaaba and the eastern Rift Valley in Kenya.[2] Over the next five hundred years or so, Proto-Kalenjin-speaking communities in turn gradually changed the ways they spoke and what their words meant, until their dialects had diverged into two new languages. One, Proto-Northern

Kalenjin, was spoken to the north and east of the Cherangany Hills.[3] The other, Proto-Elgon-Mau Kalenjin, was spoken in an area largely similar to that inhabited by speakers of Proto-Kalenjin (see map 5.1).[4] As was the case for people speaking languages descended from Proto-Greater Luhyia and Proto-North Nyanza, the Proto-Kalenjin speaker community and its descendants had to contend with several multidecadal periods of reduced rainfall or drought. In later centuries, such climate stressors led some people speaking Kalenjin languages to seek refuge among Bantu-speaking farming communities. The borrowing of vocabulary between Proto-Kalenjin speakers and people speaking various Bantu languages in the region highlights the long-standing existence of reciprocal, if not necessarily equal, relationships between them.[5]

Speakers of Proto-Kalenjin combined pastoralism and grain cultivation, although for at least some it appears that they began to move toward more intensive cattle and small-livestock raising.[6] From the linguistic evidence, we know that they milked their cattle in addition to bleeding them, and that when they did butcher animals, they dried the meat to preserve it. Alongside their pastoralism, some members of this community—apparently predominantly women—grew grain crops such as millet. They brewed alcohol from both millet and honey, presumably a function of what ingredients were easiest to access but also a function of different tastes, with mead being quite distinct from millet beer. Young people were initiated into age sets, a group of people within their community and perhaps even wider district, with whom they collaborated and cooperated (albeit not without tensions) throughout their lives. Age set membership, thus, formed the basis of many social interactions.[7] But Proto-Kalenjin speakers also marked the transitions between life stages, at least for men, through the use of age grades. The *muren* age grade was for those classified as young men and the *payyan* age grade was for those classified as elder men.[8] Age grades were at the center of political decision-making, with men in the elder age grade holding the majority of power.[9] It was in these contexts that people speaking Proto-Kalenjin modified their thinking and ways of talking about poverty and wealth.

The Proto-Kalenjin speaker community kept the same word that their Proto-Southern Nilotic–speaking linguistic ancestors had borrowed from Proto-Iraqw, several centuries earlier, to talk about poverty and the poor. This was the root *-panan-*.[10] In Proto-Kalenjin it could be used to speak of poverty or destitution. When it was used to talk about a person, however, the meaning could be ambiguous between a poor person or an orphan, suggesting that Proto-Kalenjin speakers may not have distinguished between these categories of person. At the very least, it suggests that they associated kinlessness and vulnerability with poverty. In a break with the Proto-Southern Nilotic concept of the poor expressed through the root *-panan-, Proto-Kalenjin speakers also began to use it to refer to begging. In so doing, they appear to have been articulating an understanding that orphans—and the poor more generally—could not depend on their kin to help them automatically. Instead, the poor and the orphaned had to plead for help and faced the intense vulnerability that we associate with begging, a vulnerability that emerges from the fact that no one was obliged to assist a beggar unlike the social norms that would require members of a household to help one among them who needed it.

This extension of *-panan- to include the meaning begging points to tensions over the presence of poor people in Proto-Kalenjin-speaking communities, tensions that may have been related to a greater emphasis on pastoralism both economically and culturally. Such tensions are apparent in another word that Proto-Kalenjin speakers used to talk about the poor and that referenced, in particular, the lack of social standing that was consequent upon being poor. This is a root that they innovated to refer to a specific form of lack—namely, a lack of wealth in cattle. It took the form of the noun *me:i-, which meant a person without cattle, and which they derived from a Proto-Southern Nilotic verb, *mɛ:R, meaning to die.[11] In deriving the word for a person without cattle from the verb to die, the Proto-Kalenjin speaker community directly connected a lack of cattle to death and bereavement and to a markedly lower social status.

The range of meanings for this root in the modern Kalenjin languages highlights that, for those who spoke Proto-Kalenjin, the kind of material wealth one had mattered and that it was especially important to own not just any kind of livestock, but to own cattle in particular. In later centuries, as we will see below, this privileging of cattle over all other forms of wealth became increasingly salient for some Kalenjin-speaking communities as well as for those speaking Eastern Nilotic languages, most famously the Maasai. But this particular innovation tells us that conflicts over modes of economic production, the different forms of wealth that they generated, and their cultural significance were already emerging as much as fifteen hundred years ago. It also points to economic production and social and cultural identity being increasingly tightly interwoven by this period. The derivation of this root from an older verb meaning to die reflects, in particular, a perception that men without cattle experienced social death, or at least social exclusion. This is a notion that has been neatly encapsulated more recently through the Maasai (and thus Eastern, rather than Southern, Nilotic) phrase "the poor are not us."[12] But the word *me:i- further highlights—as with *-panan- the central role played by family networks in ensuring the economic as well as social security of young people in its overlapping meanings of a person without livestock and orphan. An orphan, especially a boy whose parents died before he was of age to be given his own livestock, would find himself marginalized in his community, both socially and economically.

Elgon-Mau Kalenjin Languages and Their Speakers

Proto-Elgon-Mau Kalenjin emerged from Proto-Kalenjin by the turn of the millennium after a process of differentiation that began a few centuries earlier.[13] Integral to that process was a fairly intense engagement with other communities, notably with hunter-gatherer communities. The end result of this engagement was the adoption of Proto-Elgon-Mau Kalenjin by these communities of hunter-gatherers.[14] Speakers of some dialects of Proto-Elgon-Mau Kalenjin moved far from what might be termed the core area of the language from around the ninth to fifteenth century, including into what is today southern Maasailand in Tanzania. Those who came to speak Proto-Elgon Kalenjin, however, lived "all around Mount Elgon, from the plains surrounding the mountain up to the elevations above the tree line."[15] In part as a result of interactions with speaker communities of other languages, especially Greater Luhyia Bantu languages, Proto-Elgon Kalenjin began to differentiate into distinct dialects and then languages fairly early on, with a split into Proto-Pok-Ong'am and Proto-Sapiny-Kony by around the thirteenth or fourteenth century. These protolanguages were spoken until around the sixteenth century or perhaps more recently still.[16] Since the emergence of Kupsabiny and Kony as distinct languages, there has been further dialectal variation. Speakers of Kupsabiny belong to a cluster commonly known as Sebei that also includes Sor and Mbai communities.[17]

As had their Proto-Kalenjin-speaking linguistic ancestors, the Proto-Elgon-Mau Kalenjin speaker community and the subsequent Proto-Elgon Kalenjin speaker community combined pastoralism and grain cultivation. For some Kalenjin speakers, however, the archaeological evidence points in particular to intensive cattle and small-livestock raising in the second millennium. Archaeological research on the Sirikwa Holes in western Kenya reflects this shift. The Sirikwa Holes "are saucer-shaped hollows occurring in numerous groups on the hillsides throughout most of the highland region west of the rift valley, as well as in the higher parts of the rift itself around Nakuru, and certain areas further east."[18] These hollows served as cattle pens. They were surrounded by a stockade with a house attached and were constructed from as early as the twelfth century until this mode of living was abandoned at some point in the eighteenth century. Over this period, several thousand such homesteads were constructed. The archaeologist John Sutton noted that "each family would have needed a new cattle-pen every five or so years—as the fence timbers rotted, and the house structures deteriorated, or the dung-heap reached an uncomfortable size" and the large number of homesteads reflected that reality across six or so centuries.[19]

Sutton initially argued that "people who take the most elaborate precautions to guard their livestock are often those who possess the fewest" and thus concluded that the Sirikwa were likely sedentary mixed-farmers rather than exclusively or predominantly pastoralist.[20] His subsequent excavations, however, suggested that "the original, perhaps the 'ideal,' Sirikwa life was more uncompromisingly pastoral."[21] Excavations on Hyrax Hill revealed what Sutton described as "a decidedly pastoral economy, with small, probably zebu, cattle, apparently with a strong emphasis on milk, and flocks of goats and sheep." Absent from the site were "signs of cultivated plants or the cooking of vegetables."[22] By the twelfth century, then, at least some Kalenjin-speaking communities appear to have embraced an almost exclusively pastoralist economy, with important implications for their concepts of socioeconomic difference. At the same time, from the archaeology "there is little evidence for socioeconomic differentiation within Sirikwa or surrounding communities."[23] The archaeologist Matthew Davies noted that "all sites are relatively standardized in the levels and qualities of artefacts found, and structures and faunal remains seem to vary in relation to moderate specialization and familial size rather than formal social differentiation."[24]

The lack of archaeological evidence for formal social differentiation does not, however, mean that these societies were entirely egalitarian as is evident from the linguistic record. People speaking Proto-Elgon-Mau Kalenjin developed a new vocabulary for talking about being wealthy. This vocabulary was grounded in the root *mokor-*, from which the speaker community coined nouns to refer to wealth or riches and to a wealthy person or to wealthy people.[25] The structure of this root indicates that it is a loanword.[26] Another clue about its etymology comes from the first syllable, *mo-*, and the fact that the root is used to form person nouns, such as wealthy person. The most plausible source for the root is therefore a Bantu word with the singular person class prefix **mo-* and the root **-kor-* that means grow or age. Because of the phonology in the Kalenjin reflexes and because of the geographical distribution of the relevant languages, it would seem that an East Nyanza protolanguage was the original source.[27]

From all this we can infer that **mokor-* likely derives from the East Nyanza noun *omokoro*, meaning elder. When Proto-Elgon-Mau Kalenjin speakers began using the noun, they dropped the final vowel and instead added the Southern Nilotic noun suffixes *-io* and *-ion*. The association of wealth with elderhood is one we have already encountered and so its appearance here is not altogether surprising. It is noteworthy, however, that in contrast to their Eastern Nilotic–speaking linguistic cousins, Proto-Elgon-Mau Kalenjin speakers did not associate wealth with livestock or cattle in the words that they used to talk about it. At the same time, the absence of ownership of livestock was clearly conceptualized as poverty. Given their association of poverty with lack of livestock through the root **me:i-*, which they inherited from speakers of Proto-Kalenjin, it is possible that the idea that wealth took the form of livestock was so dominant and taken for granted that it did not need to be marked linguistically.

Kupsabiny and Its Speakers

People speaking Proto-Sabiny-Kony and its descendant languages, including Kupsabiny, had a range of economic practices. Some members of the speaker community engaged predominantly in agriculture on the mountain, while others engaged predominantly in pastoralism on the plains. Those living above an elevation of 2,700 meters (or around 8,900 feet), in more recent times at least, combined agriculture, pastoralism, and gathering wild honey. Distefano posited that this, in addition to differences in architecture, may point to them being a distinct group that adopted Proto-Sabiny-Kony as a result of the settlement of its speakers on the mountain.[28] In common with Proto-Sabiny-Kony speakers, those who came to speak Kupsabiny were primarily focused on pastoralism but also grew grains. Through increased contact with North Luhyia–speaking communities on Mount Elgon-Masaaba and in its foothills, they adopted the cultivation of bananas and root crops, with their communities becoming increasingly sedentary.[29]

According to the anthropologist Walter Goldschmidt, before the twentieth century "the economy was a dual one. The men cared for the animals and the women milked the cows and cultivated small garden plots using iron hoes."[30] Wealth, however, consisted of livestock among the Sebei (that is, Kupsabiny, Mor, and Sok speakers). "If a man was to be a successful Sebei, he had to build up his personal possession of livestock." This led to the potential for violence. Raiding the herds of others was the quickest way to build up one's own herd, but "raiding of this kind could escalate into warfare."[31] The accumulation of wealth through raiding others was complicated by efforts to avoid predation through the branding and marking of cattle and other livestock to connect them to their owner. "Since the cattle were branded (with cuts on their ears) and were individually known in the local area, they could not be taken from neighbors." Theft from neighbors or other members of the community "was punishable, as well as morally reprehensible."[32] As a result, young men raided for cattle further afield, but such actions, while mitigating the potential for intracommunal tensions, could result in retaliation and escalation leading to more serious intercommunal violence.

At the same time, the accumulation of wealth in livestock as the result of raiding other communities resulted in high social status for those men who were successful. "A man who had many cattle among the Sebei had prestige, whether it was because of the cattle themselves or whether it was because people believed that his having them showed that he had the qualities of courage, ability, and astuteness." Furthermore, wealth in the form of livestock, and cattle in particular, translated into other forms of social status: "Having wealth meant that he could get the things that are important, which . . . meant having wives and children and ultimately grandchildren, and which meant also having influence and leadership."[33] This conceptualization of wealth was one that was directly expressed through the vocabulary that Kupsabiny speakers used to talk about the wealthy.

In comparison to the extensive lexicons speakers of Bantu languages in eastern Uganda, in particular, developed to talk about the wealthy and the poor, it is striking that Kupsabiny speakers and their linguistic forebears who had spoken Proto-Elgon-Mau Kalenjin restricted themselves to a much more limited vocabulary. When it came to talking about the wealthy, Kupsabiny speakers used only words derived from the loaned root *mokor-* that Proto-Elgon-Mau Kalenjin speakers had borrowed from people speaking an East Bantu language.[34] In Kupsabiny these words took the form of the nouns *mokoriondet* for wealthy person and *mokoriondit* for wealth, alongside the verb *mokoron* for prosper. Reflecting the association made between wealth and status, the noun *mokoriondet* came to be used also to refer to a leader. Other nouns that meant leader, however, such as *kandoindet*, could not be used to talk of wealth, suggesting that there were other ways to conceive of leadership. Although the noun *mokoriondit* did not describe a particular form for wealth, it could be modified to specify or emphasize wealth in the form of livestock: *mokoriondit toga*. And while *mokoriondet* could be used for women or men, the greater recognition of and possibilities for men to hold wealth (as we saw in the ethnographic descriptions above) come across in the use of the noun to refer to a polygynous man.[35]

Just as they used only one root to talk about wealth, so Kupsabiny speakers used only one root when they spoke of poverty. This was the root *-panan-* that they inherited from Proto-Elgon-Mau Kalenjin speakers and was borrowed by

Proto-Southern Nilotic speakers, from speakers of Proto-Iraqw.[36] For those speaking Kupsabiny, the root could be used to talk about both poor people and orphans. As was the case for their Proto-Kalenjin-speaking forebears, when they chose to use the noun *pánáne:t*, Kupsabiny speakers expressed an understanding of poverty and orphanhood as interwoven and overlapping, rather than as distinct categories. Poverty, for them, was a condition of being without kin as much as it was a condition of being in material need.

It is unclear what we might conclude from the fact that the vocabulary for socioeconomic difference—at least as expressed in terms of wealth and poverty—is highly limited in Kupsabiny. We cannot use it to conclude that wealth was not considered important or that Sebei society was egalitarian. The ethnographic data shows that this was certainly not the case in the twentieth century and there is nothing to indicate that it was true for earlier centuries either. Quite the opposite could be asserted given the centrality of the acquisition of a particular form of wealth—cattle—to the social reproduction of the community. Some wealth, at least, was essential for any individual young man and, by extension, young woman (who could not otherwise marry or become a socially recognized mother) to move into the life stages of marriage, parenthood, and elderhood. What is more, a poor man was also one who had failed to prove himself by raiding for livestock and so faced not only a lonely future, but one in which he was held in low regard by his community. Despite this, Kupsabiny speakers did not express these ideas through the words that they used to talk about wealth and poverty. This is an important reminder that while a conceptual history of oral societies that draws on the lexicon used to talk about particular concepts can tell us a great deal, as we have seen in other contexts, it does not hold all the answers and there is much it cannot tell us.

Proto-Ateker and Its Speakers

People speaking Proto-Ateker are understood to have inhabited areas across what is today the border between northern Uganda and South Sudan between around 2,500 and 1,000 years ago.[37] They practiced pastoralism and cultivated grain crops, including finger millet (*Eleusine coracana*)—which they inherited from predecessors who had spoken Proto-Eastern Nilotic—and sorghum (*Sorghum bicolor*).[38] Over subsequent centuries, and in fits and starts, people speaking Proto-Ateker gradually settled lands to the north and northeast of Lake Kyoga, between Mounts Moroto and Elgon-Masaaba, and eventually to the south of Mount Elgon-Masaaba (see map 5.1). William Fitzsimons, in his recent classification of Ateker, drawing on extensive fieldwork, identified an early divide between the Atcso languages on the one hand and the Northern Ateker languages on the other. Based on this, he posited that Proto-Ngikatapa, or pre-Teso, speakers moved southward from around 900 CE in response to a drying climate that threatened their ability to successfully grow grain crops further north.[39] As people speaking Ateker languages settled further afield from each other, the dialects they spoke diverged into distinct languages. Into the present, however, there is significant dialect chaining, with neighboring dialects being more similar to each other than to those further apart in space.

People speaking Proto-Ateker expanded and adapted the vocabulary used by their linguistic ancestors who had spoken Proto-Tung'a and Proto-Eastern Nilotic to talk about economic difference. They continued to use the root *-can- in this regard.[40] This root, as we saw in chapter 2, was used by speakers of Proto-Eastern Nilotic, as well as their linguistic forebears speaking Proto-Nilotic, to talk about poverty and the poor while not distinguishing poverty from other forms of suffering. For Proto-Ateker speakers, *-can- allowed them to place poverty alongside grief, something apparent in the plural noun *ŋican that glossed as poverty, grief, and adversity. But they shifted their conceptual framework for poverty and suffering by adding a new meaning to the root *-can-: punishment. We can see this in the modern Ateker languages. Thus, in Ateso, the causative verb *aitican* means maltreat and punish, while the noun *aiticanet* means punishment, penalty, and inconvenience.[41] Similarly, in Ngakarimojong, we find the causative verb *akisican* meaning afflict and punish.[42] These meanings of punishment in relation to *-can- are not present in Turkana, but the Turkana noun *ŋican* does have the meaning torture alongside the meanings noted above. The transitive nature of the verbs meaning punish, maltreat, and afflict tells us that speakers used them to describe events with two participants (e.g., the afflicter and afflicted) who were "clearly distinct." This clear distinction between the two participants was partly based on physical distinctiveness, but also referred to the understanding that they played "maximally distinct roles in the event in question."[43] While my reading of this semantic development is that it was poor people who were seen as inconveniencing, even punishing, those less destitute, it is possible to invert that reading in the case of speakers of Ateker languages. Regardless, what is apparent from this innovation is that it reflected a strong social distinction between the poor and others, a social distinction that spilled into other aspects of life, although it did not translate into political hierarchies along the lines of wealth.[44]

During the time that Proto-Ateker was spoken, its speaker community elaborated its concept of and vocabulary for wealth. The Proto-Ateker speaker community coined the root *-jak- to jointly express being wealthy and having power.⁴⁵ The root may be derived from an older meaning of extraction, reflecting the ability of some to extract wealth from land and livestock and from people.⁴⁶ It is also possible that the association between wealth and power was older, or differently constituted. In the Western Nilotic language Shilluk, *jak* means to govern or to rule, while *jago* is a ruler or leader. This raises the possibility that the root *-jak- may have been used by speakers of Proto-Nilotic to make the conceptual connection between wealth and power, but further research across the Nilotic languages spoken in South Sudan is needed to confirm this possibility.

Wealth was conceived of in other ways too. Proto-Ateker speakers also used the root *-bar- when they talked about wealth, one they inherited from Proto-Tung'a.⁴⁷ When they spoke words derived from the root *-bar-, however, Proto-Ateker speakers made an important change from its usage among their linguistic ancestors who had used it with a general meaning of wealth. For Proto-Ateker speakers, *-bar- specified wealth in the form of livestock. This marked an important turning point in Ateker concepts of wealth toward specifying certain forms of wealth and, in particular, toward livestock as the most socially and culturally valued form of wealth. In so doing, Proto-Ateker speakers excluded from their concept of the wealthy those without livestock, whether due to age, gender, or other reasons.

Ateker Languages and Their Speakers

The turn of the first millennium was, as we have seen, a prolonged period of reduced rainfall across East Africa. For the Proto-Ngikatapa Teso speakers in the Proto-Ateker homeland, who depended on grain cultivation, this extended era of reduced rainfall posed a profound threat to their existence. While those speaking Proto-Northern Ateker adapted to the drier climate by shifting to transhumant pastoralism, early Ateso speakers instead moved further south into a region with more reliable rains. By the start of the seventeenth century, there was an established Proto-Ateso speaker community in the Usuku region of eastern Uganda.⁴⁸ The historian J. B. Webster wrote that, at times, "the movement was slow as people moved unhurried in search of new land and prosperity, sometimes there were almost hordes of people, destitute and fleeing from famine, cattle and human diseases or the destruction of war." He posited that the migrations in the early sixteenth century were likely by people searching for new land and prosperity.⁴⁹ Fitzsimons, drawing on linguistic innovations, has shown the role of climate events in helping to prompt these movements. In addition to the droughts that occurred during the Medieval Climate Anomaly and lasted to the late thirteenth century, further multidecadal droughts occurred at the turn of the fifteenth century and in the second half of the sixteenth century.[50] After settling in Usuku, the speakers of Proto-Ateso gradually diverged, and new dialects emerged, around three hundred years ago: Tesyo, spoken in Tororo south of Mount Elgon-Masaaba, and Proto-Kyoga-Bisina Teso. The latter then yielded the three varieties of Ateso spoken in Pallisa, Usuku, and Ngora around two hundred years ago.[51]

Proto-Ateso was one language to emerge from Proto-Ateker at the end of the first millennium. The other was Proto-Northern Ateker, spoken in South Sudan until the mid-thirteenth century, when two new languages emerged from it: Proto-Lowland Northern Ateker and Proto-Highland Northern Ateker. The first gave way, by the eighteenth century, to the dialects of Toposa, Nyangatom, and Turkana, spoken in South Sudan, Ethiopia, and northwestern Kenya, respectively. Proto-Highland Northern Ateker yielded, by the seventeenth century, Ngakarimojong, Jie, and, likely, Dodos. While distinct dialects, they are mutually intelligible.[52]

Ateso and Its Speakers

In the oral histories collected and used by J. B. Webster, D. H. Okalany, C. P. Emudong, and N. Egimu-Okuda, Iteso men gave a number of reasons for their ancestors' migrations.[53] Common to many were economic concerns, with the majority citing a search for better land as a major impetus.[54] Conflict—warfare and domestic—were also reasons for migration. Domestic conflict could have its roots in economic circumstances. Webster offered examples of this, such as a man having to move away if he was "too poor to either provide a feast as a memorial (apunya) to a deceased father or pay a bull for his initiation into manhood."[55] Yakobo Isamat, for example, recalled that his grandfather, Angodingodi, had to move "because his clan hated him because he was poor."[56]

While most of those interviewed for the Teso Historical Texts project said that "the rich" were the most likely to migrate—at least in the late nineteenth century period which was their reference point—the oral histories themselves told a different story, one in which the vast majority of migrants were poor. Webster noted that poor migrants either had "no cows and a few goats or one to five head of cattle." Their relative poverty was also evidenced by the fact that they were usually either single men or a man with one wife and their children. "Seldom did you find a man who had two wives as a pioneer."[57] Here, then, we can see economic status, and poverty in particular, acting as a catalyst for the migration of people into new areas. This echoes narratives about the dispersal of Nilotic-speaking communities centuries earlier, as noted in chapter 2. It also speaks to the realities facing people who relied on rain-fed agriculture under conditions of prolonged aridity.

When they talked about poverty, Ateso speakers drew on two main roots, one of which was ancient, *-can-, and one that they innovated themselves, -bak-. They also innovated a new gender-specific noun, *amule*, for when they talked about a poor woman. As we have seen, *-can- can be reconstructed back to Proto-Nilotic, for whose speakers it held a general meaning of suffering.[58] Poverty was one form of suffering alongside many others. In Proto-Ateker, the root expressed a concept of poverty as coexisting with—or existing on the same scale as—grief and adversity. For the Proto-Ateker speaker community it came to also mean punishment and the affliction of punishment on others. Ateso speakers elaborated on this further: *ecanit* means poverty, while *aiticanet* means punishment or penalty and also inconvenience. Poverty and those experiencing it, thus, came to be conceived of not only in highly negative terms, but also as highly disruptive.

This very negative framing of poverty extended in material directions as well as emotional ones. Ateso speakers began to use the root *-can- to connect poverty directly with scarcity though the adjective *icana* which could either describe a person as poor or destitute or could describe anything as being scarce or rare. This association with scarcity—and its physical consequences—also began to be expressed with the root -can- in the form of the verb *aicanicanun*, meaning to become wasted away, as in the phrase: *ecanican akekuwan* ("her body is wasting away.")[59] People speaking Ateso thus conceived of poverty as an experience that had severe consequences for those who suffered it as well as for those around them. Significantly, they came to express their conceptions of the physical experience of poverty as including severe malnutrition through this ancient root. This marked a real break from the past and from other communities speaking Ateker languages.

The notion that poverty was a miserable condition to live in was expressed both through the root *-can- and through the new root innovated by speakers of Ateso. This was the root -bak-, which yielded the noun *ibakor*, meaning both poverty and misery, and also yielded the adjective *lo-na-ibakor*, meaning destitute.[60] It is clear that Ateso-speaking women and men did not view poverty as a positive condition by any means. They did, however, view it as having particular gendered connotations, or rather as having particular implications for women, as is apparent in their innovation of the noun *amule* to describe a poor woman as distinct from poor people in general. In order to talk about poor men specifically, by contrast, Ateso speakers had to qualify the noun *ican*—for example, *akilokit lo ican*. That they felt the need to coin a new noun only for poor women suggests that Iteso women and men came to understand female poverty as of a different quality or nature from male poverty. Ethnographic descriptions from the early to mid-twentieth century speak to the existence of different experiences of poverty along gender lines. One example comes from the *ainyonyo* (smearing) ceremony performed to initiate a new wife "into the clan taboos of her husband."[61] The ceremony, in which her mother-in-law and other older women smeared the wife with ghee, might be performed on the day of the marriage or as late as after the birth of the first child to ensue from it. It required, among other things, the slaughtering of an ox and so entailed considerable expense. The colonial official and ethnographer J. C. D. Lawrance noted that "if the smearing ceremony is not performed owing to poverty or absence of relatives, a woman's children must not be seen by her relatives until she has been smeared or until they have grown up."[62] For married women living in poverty, then, social norms could isolate them from their kin and the support that they might otherwise expect from their natal relatives.

The Teso Historical Texts illustrated some of the ways in which poverty prompted people speaking Ateker languages to move in search of new land and opportunities. But wealth could also be a factor in such moves. One of the Texts, an interview with Omoding of Ogooma in Nyero about his grandmother, Atengorit, narrates the story of a wealthy woman who migrated:

> Her huband was Okede ... the family was wealthy before Okede died. Following his death, Atengorit remained unmarried, she was not given over to a brother of Okede. She had many children. She lived in Adok Aderun but migrated and died in Ogooma. Atengorit was very rich and she entertained lavishly. She was rich in food, had many cattle, sheep and goats. She became wealthy through hard work. She was mainly a cultivator, exchanging food for goats and goats for cattle.
>
> Adok became over-populated. Ejajuwai [Atengorit's son] (father of the speaker) came to Ogooma and Atengorit and all her children followed him, the old home in Adok was abandoned and strangers of another clan took it over. Atengorit moved looking for more land. Rich people often migrated when their herds became too large for their land.[63]

This narrative not only captures the motivations for migration—and hence the settlement of Ateso speakers in eastern Uganda—but also some of the concepts of wealth held by Iteso women and men. Atengorit was rich in food, *amio*, but she took care to translate her *amio* into wealth in livestock, *ibaren*, and, in particular, into wealth in cattle.[64] The narrative also highlights the importance of sharing wealth, in this case, by entertaining lavishly. Wealth was not something to be hoarded and hidden, but rather was to be used in building and maintaining relationships beyond the immediate family group.[65] This particular aspect can be found in widely divergent communities across the world and across time. The "puzzle" of the Ghana Living Standards Survey in which households spent similar proportions of their income on food regardless of their economic situations, as discussed by Jane Guyer, was a result of this.[66] The imperative of translating wealth into social standing can also be seen in the potlatch ceremonies of Native American communities in northwest North America and in big-man exchange systems of Melanesia.[67]

Speakers of Ateso expressed different concepts of wealth depending on the root they chose. Some were ones that Ateso speakers themselves innovated. One was inherited from those who spoke Proto-Ateker: *-bar-*. The root *-bar-*, innovated by the Proto-Ateker speaker community, encapsulated a concept of wealth as indistinguishable from livestock, in contrast to the older Proto-Tung'a meaning of *-bar-* that described wealth in general terms.[68] The Proto-Ateker concept continued into Ateso where we find *abar*, meaning wealth, and *abaran*, meaning rich person, alongside *ibarasit*, meaning head of cattle, and *ibaren*, meaning wealth in livestock, as well as the adjective *ebarit* for someone wealthy in livestock. As seen in the narrative about Atengorit who migrated to Ogooma, *ibaren* was the form of wealth that marked a person as truly wealthy and was the form of wealth that could be passed on to successors, ensuring wealth in subsequent generations.

Alongside this ancient root, Proto-Ateso speakers took another old root and gave it a new meaning for talking about wealth and those who possessed it. This was the root *-rian-*, which Fitzsimons has reconstructed to Proto-Ateker, with the meaning equal (in size, height, and so on).[69] Speakers of Proto-Ateso added a causative prefix, -*ke*-, and changed the meaning to prosperity, wealth, be rich, and be skillful.[70] This is a somewhat counterintuitive derivation, at least for speakers of English. Fitzsimons noted that Proto-Ateso speakers understood "prosperity in terms of equality" and points to the metaphorical use of the name of a poisonous plant (*ejungula*) to describe becoming rich as a critique of excessive inequality.[71] In addition to the conceptualization of prosperity and wealth as a leveling force, by elevating people out of dependence, Ateso speakers connected wealth with being skillful. Thus, the intransitive verb *akerianut* meant both to be rich and to be skillful. For example, *ekeriaka kesi* can mean they are rich and they are skillful.[72] By combining these meanings onto a single verb, Ateso speakers presented a concept of wealth as deserved; wealth was the result of a person's knowledge and actions.

Ateso speakers specified another form of wealth other than wealth in livestock and coined a new word to do so. This was the root *-mio* which yielded the nouns *amio*, meaning wealth in food, and *amion*, meaning one who is wealthy in food, with the plural *amiiok*.[73] It also yielded the intransitive verbs *aimi*, meaning be rich in crop products, and *amiyo*, meaning be wealthy or have plenty of anything, especially food. Finally, the root yielded an adjective that referred to a person, *emiyono*, meaning tending to be wealthy in crops. While the interviewees in the Teso Historical Texts agreed that the Iteso "were farmers before they acquired cattle," Webster noted that the nineteenth century, "when the ancestors of the Iteso were settling their present homeland in large numbers," was "a century of unusual agricultural progress and development."[74] Iteso women and men who engaged in farming began using iron hoes and cultivating new crops. So large was the demand for hoes that Basoga traders brought them to Teso communities where they received ivory tusks in exchange.[75] Not coincidentally, given the close relationship between the accumulation of wealth in crops and wealth in cattle, this was also a time in which "the cattle population greatly expanded."[76] Lawrance, too, noted that cultivation was central to the success of the Iteso during their settlement of what came to be Teso District.[77] The ability of Iteso families to not only survive but to generate wealth through agriculture was critical. They could then translate it into *ibaren* wealth (wealth in livestock) that they could use to create the essential networks formed through marriages. This is reflected in their innovation of this new root, which contrasts to developments among people speaking other Ateker languages.

This distinction in forms of wealth, between wealth in livestock and wealth in food or crops, was an important reconceptualization by Ateso speakers. Nonetheless, wealth in cattle retained a higher prestige than wealth in food.[78] *Amio* or wealth in food referred to the grain crops of millet and sorghum and the legume crop of groundnuts, but it particularly referred to millet, which as Webster noted, "became the most prestigious food" in Iteso society.[79] Millet and the other crops could, as we have seen, be translated into wealth in the form of livestock. Thus, at least in the nineteenth century, men seeking to build up bridewealth could accumulate wealth in food through industriousness that they could then convert into bridewealth. We see this in the case of Papa Eunyat of Moruita: "Out of his cultivated crops he secured goats and exchanged the goats for cows so that he could marry."⁸⁰ Another example comes from Mr. Oboi of Agurut in Nyero whose grandfather, Emelet, "came alone from Magoro and settled in Ariet (Nyero) where he died. (In Ariet) he had worked very hard, got much food which he exchanged for cattle ... he became so successful that he was able to marry five wives and produced five children."⁸¹ In so doing, these men each obtained a large household, called *ojakait* (big home), and each became an *ejakait* (head of ojakait), with each of their wives being an *ajakait* (wife of ejakait).⁸² In coining these words, Ateso speakers drew on the Proto-Ateker root *-jak-* that meant to be wealthy and to have power.⁸³

Wealth in livestock or *ibaren* was, thus, an important means of gaining social and political status. But livestock, especially smaller livestock such as goats, also offered Iteso households a buffer against hunger during times of scarcity: "In almost any year many farmers were compelled to exchange goats for food in the months just prior to harvest, having depleted their own stores."⁸⁴ This combined approach appears to have been a productive one for Iteso people. "As a result of preoccupation with agriculture the Ikumama as a whole became very wealthy by the standards of the 'fathers' in Karamoja. While it is easy to see pastoralists with their cattle and agriculturalists with their granaries this was inaccurate. The Iteso were able to boast far larger herds of cattle than the Karimojong. This was true of the colonial period and there is no reason to doubt that it was true of the asonya as well."⁸⁵

While people speaking Proto-Ngikatapa Teso had long lived in eastern Uganda, the eighteenth and nineteenth centuries were ones of change with the arrival of new families expanding the population significantly. At times, such as for much of the nineteenth century, people speaking Ateso generally experienced economic security as they built up wealth in crops and livestock. The importance of wealth in crops was expressed through the root *-mio*, but the cultural dominance of wealth in livestock was expressed through the root *-bar*. The translation of material wealth into other forms of social and political capital was also expressed through their vocabulary. The entwined nature of material wealth and social standing meant that the poor suffered across multiple registers. The developments in Ateso vocabulary for poverty highlight this reality of physical, emotional, and social suffering caused by scarcity.

Highland Northern Ateker and Its Speakers

People speaking Ngakarimojong and Jie have lived for the past few centuries in what is today northeastern Uganda. While the total area known as Karamoja is vast (some 27,000 square kilometers or 10,600 square miles), the population density is very low.[86] The area is mostly composed of plains, which "are interrupted by isolated mountains."[87] Average annual rainfall varies from around 600 to 900 millimeters (24 to 36 inches) and "daytime temperatures usually fluctuate between 25 and 40°C [77 to 104°F]."[88] While rainfall levels historically have been high enough to support agricultural production in theory, the distribution of rain across the year has been such that it could be difficult for crops to survive the wind and sun.[89] As a result, the amount of land used for agricultural production historically has been low and has required extended periods of fallow after three to six years of cultivation.[90]

Despite this, women did grow crops and the anthropologist P. H. Gulliver reported, in the 1950s, being told that, for the Jie, "sorghum is the cattle of women," and "men own cattle, women own gardens," reflecting ideas about the division of labor and access to particular kinds of resources along gender lines.[91] Based on fieldwork in the mid-twentieth century, but with evidence for earlier periods, the anthropologist Neville Dyson-Hudson noted that among the Karimojong, "a considerable part of their food, most particularly that of women and children, is provided by garden produce."[92] Sorghum was the main staple, but other crops such as cucumbers, marrows, and beans were also grown.[93] Gulliver argued that agricultural crops, especially sorghum, were as important to the Jie as animal products and that "this had been the case for many generations."[94] Furthermore, he noted that both the Jie and Karimojong "would starve without their agricultural produce."[95] Fitzsimons has reconstructed this mode of production to the time when early Proto-Highland Northern Ateker was spoken and traced its evolution for speakers of Ngakarimojong and Jie, offering clear evidence in support of Gulliver's argument.[96] The potential reward from agricultural labor was uncertain, with reports from the 1950s that in about "two years out of five the rainfall is either too small or badly distributed, so that crops are severely damaged. Soils are generally poor.... On the whole agriculture is a rather precarious occupation."[97] The historian John Lamphear wrote that the burden of labor fell exclusively on women, who were in charge of cultivating "the plots surrounding the homestead."[98] Women bore "the responsibility for providing labour for every phase of the cycle," banding "together to work communally on each others' plots at tilling times."[99] In addition to being a source of food, sorghum could be brewed into beer, which had both social and ritual importance.[100]

Political and other forms of identification in Karamoja underwent significant reimagining during colonial rule and in the decades after independence. Before colonialism, speakers of Highland Northern Ateker were divided into three main communities, speaking distinct, but mutually intelligible dialects: Dodosŏ, Jie, and Karimojong.[101] The theologian Ben Knighton has described these as politico-religious communities, while Fitzsimons has described them as republics or ritual confederacies.[102] Each was further divided into sections and clans, with specific political and social norms. The various sections of the Karimojong, for example, could raid each other for cattle, but they could not raid other members of their section. Cattle raiding was similarly "not sanctioned within the tighter political communities: the Dodosŏ, the Jie and each of the 11 Karimojong territorial sections."[103] For young men, rapid accumulation of wealth through cattle raiding depended on venturing beyond the community.

Ideas about wealth and belonging and about poverty and exclusion or othering come across from the linguistic evidence. Before the division of Proto-Northern Ateker into its Highland and Lowland branches, its speakers innovated a root, *-ka-yar-an*, with the meaning servant, from an older Proto-Ateker root, *-jar-*, which meant to be alive or to subsist. Fitzsimons, who reconstructed this root, noted that "as a last resort to avoid death, these *-ka-yar-an* may have pawned themselves or perhaps their families as servants to wealthier herders in order to access livestock from which they could sustain life."[104] The iteration of this ancient noun in the modern language of Ngakarimojong suggests that people with this status were not afforded respect: *akayaran* "one who lives on someone (not working)."[105]

Speakers of Ngakarimojong continued using the ancient root *-can-* to talk about poverty and about the poor.[106] They gave a similar range of meanings to words derived from this root as in Ateso. Thus, we have the nouns *ŋican*, meaning trouble, affliction, hardship, suffering, grief, poverty, adversity, and calamity, and *acanaanu*, meaning poverty. Alongside them are the verbs *akicana*, meaning to lack or be lacking; *akicanut*, meaning to trouble, disturb, annoy, molest, afflict, or cause to be sad; and *akisican*, meaning to afflict or punish. The long-standing Eastern Nilotic concept of poverty as a condition of suffering clearly continued for Ngakarimojong speakers alongside the Proto-Tung'a expansion of the concept to include trouble and disturbance.

Ngakarimojong speakers also continued to use a more recent root, likely innovated by speakers of Proto-Northern Ateker, sometime around the turn of the first millennium. This is the root *-kulyak-*, which was used to mean poverty or destitution as well as a poor or destitute person.[107] It was expressed in Ngakarimojong through the nouns *akulyako*, meaning poverty or abject poverty, *akulyakanut*, meaning poverty due to lack of cattle, *ekulyakana*, meaning poor person, and *ekulyakit*, meaning pauper. But it also came to be the name given by Ngakarimojong and Jie speakers to speakers of Rub languages, such as Ik and So, who are understood to be the firstcomers in the region and who were displaced and marginalized as a result of the expansion of Ateker speakers. According to oral traditions collected by Lamphear, "The Ngikuliak are magic. If any misfortune befalls them, it will also befall the Jie. That is because they are the oldest people in Najie. God put them here. Orwakol (the leader of one group of Paranilotic-speaking Jie) found them here when he came. They were the first."[108] The description of them as poor people that is inherent in the name, perhaps because they were lacking in cattle, suggests disdain on the part of Ngakarimojong speakers. Lamphear noted, however, that the Jie and Ngikuliak had a symbiotic relationship that was crucial in the eighteenth and nineteenth centuries when the Ngikuliak were able "to provide an all-important refuge for impoverished Jie."[109] It may have been precisely their reliance on the Ngikuliak that led Jie and Ngakarimojong speakers to describe them as the people of poverty in an attempt to create a distance of status that did not necessarily or consistently exist in material terms.

For those who were fellow Karimojong, being so poor as to be dependent on others was marked as a particular status and their patron was "referred to as 'the owner' of the dependent client."[110] While not a condition of slavery, despite the language, it was an exchange of only shelter and food for labor in the cattle camp by the destitute.[111] Furthermore, the wealthy patron could "unhesitatingly call on [the dependent client's] services as long as the relationship lasts."[112] Given the disdain shown toward the very poor in their own communities, it is not hard to imagine Ngakarimojong and Jie speakers seeking to distance themselves from those, such as speakers of Ik and Rub, who had helped them survive but who did not hold the same concepts of wealth as them.

The Ngakarimojong speaker community had a relatively extensive vocabulary for wealth, but despite their dependence on agriculture in addition to pastoralism, they did not specify a form of wealth in crops, in contrast to speakers of Ateso. Instead, they emphasized wealth in the form of livestock and the conceptual linkages between wealth and power. Thus, the Proto-Ateker root *-bar- yielded in Ngakarimojong, among other forms, the plural noun *ŋibaren*, meaning livestock, wealth, and good luck, and the intransitive verb *ebarar*, meaning be plenty or numerous. Both of these highlighted the concept of wealth as taking the form of livestock and the potential for that wealth to reproduce and be numerous.[113] Wealth in livestock did not accrue to a single individual. Rather, "a herd (*esipan*) is a property unit: it is associated with, and defines by the criterion of common interest, a group of kin who have rights in and subsist from the animals of the herd."¹¹⁴ Thus, the head of the household, who controlled the herd and its disposal, such as for bridewealth, held significant power over the women, men, and children who composed the household.

This conceptualization of wealthy people as leaders and of leaders as wealthy people was further articulated by speakers of Proto-Highland Northern Ateker through the roots *-jak- and *-polo-. In Proto-Ateker, *-jak- referred to wealth and being wealthy, as well as referring to power of some kind.¹¹⁵ In Ateso, as we have seen, the root came to specify a large household and those who were heads of such households. In Ngakarimojong, the root *-jak- retained both meanings of wealth and power, such as through the verb *ajakaania*, meaning become wealthy; the adjective *ejakaana*, meaning wealthy, well off, or rich; and the noun *ejakait*, meaning chief. Although the specific meaning chief is almost certainly a product of colonial rule in the twentieth century, its adoption for that particular context appears to have grown out of the older associations between wealth and power.

The root *-polo- also reflected the overlain meanings of wealth and power.¹¹⁶ It was originally borrowed by Proto-Ateker speakers from speakers of a Western Nilotic language, likely Proto-Lwo. In its original language, the root was used to mean many or numerous. That meaning was retained as can be seen with the Ngakarimojong adjective *epol*, meaning big, great, or large. But Proto-Ateker speakers added a new meaning to use the root "to speak about standing and leadership."¹¹⁷ The Proto-Northern Ateker speaker community used it to convey their concept of wealth as connected to power and of power as connected to wealth. In the modern Northern Ateker languages we find, for example, the meanings chief (*akapolon*) and honor (*apolou*) in Turkana, and the meaning to prosper (*apoloor*) and to be in charge of (*apolokin*) in Ngakarimojong.

Ngakarimojong speakers were all too aware of the contingency of their economic security and of the real possibility that they could be tipped into the suffering of poverty that they expressed through the root *-can-*. Rada Dyson-Hudson, who carried out the research among Karimojong farming women that was drawn on by her husband in his publications, reported that between 1919 and 1958, they experienced total crop failure on average once every four years. Beyond catastrophic failure, they had only "one chance in three that the crop will just save them from hunger" and "a less-than even chance that the work of cultivation will be rewarded by a good crop or better."¹¹⁸ The same forces that led to crop failure would also have affected the well-being of livestock, especially cattle, which are more vulnerable to drought than goats and sheep.¹¹⁹ The importance they placed on livestock as the wealth of the household and of the good management of that wealth in the face of such precarity was expressed through the roots -*bar*- and -*jak*-. Wealth, leadership, and power were inseparable concepts for this speaker community.

Southern Luo: Dhopadhola and Its Speakers

People speaking the Southern Luo language Dhopadhola live today in Budama in easternmost Uganda and, according to their own oral traditions, settled in the region between the early sixteenth and late nineteenth centuries.[120] Bethwell Ogot, the foremost historian of the Luo-speaking peoples, has noted that the process by which modern Dhopadhola speakers came to live there was complex. As with other processes of migration and settlement, they did not move into land unoccupied by other people. Japadhola thus had early encounters and interactions with Lunyole speakers in particular, with whom they clashed over land.[121] Despite this, the lands in which Dhopadhola speakers settled were more sparsely populated than was often the case for other Luo-speaking migrants. One result of this was that "unlike the Kenya Luo whose land rights are based on the right of conquest, in Padhola the right to property in land is derived from first occupation. By clearing the forest for purposes of cultivation, they thereby established permanent rights over the area so cleared."[122] Wealth was something acquired through the hard work of cutting bush and turning it into productive fields.

It is in this context that we can understand Dhopadhola speakers' use of only one root when talking about poverty, the Proto-Nilotic *-*can*-.[123] As in other Nilotic languages, in Dhopadhola -*chan*- could be used to refer to suffering in general as well as to poverty in particular. Thus, we find the nouns *chandirok*, meaning sufferings or trouble, *chandi*, meaning poverty or misery, and *jachandi*, meaning poor person. Dhopadhola speakers, like their linguistic ancestors and cousins, conceived of poverty as one among many forms of suffering. They also conceived of it as problematic. The transitive verb *chandò*, for example, could be used to mean punish, make miserable, torment, and annoy. The meaning here is productively ambiguous. On the one hand, it could mean that poor people tormented those around them in their community by making demands on their resources or by failing to ensure proper social reproduction by transferring bridewealth and contributing to funerals. On the other hand, it could be a recognition that poverty was a form of torment for those suffering it. Individually and jointly, these framings of poverty make clear that Dhopadhola speakers understood it in highly negative terms.

Wealth, by contrast, had much more positive connotations. Two roots in Dhopadhola refer to wealth. One is of Proto-Southern Luo origin, **lim*-, and the other, -*ŋang'*-, is an innovation in Dhopadhola. As we saw in chapter 2, when they used the root **lim*-, Proto-Southern Luo speakers conceived of wealth as intertwined with visiting.[124] These overlapping meanings of wealth, visiting, and gift exchange are also evident in Dhopadhola, where *lím* came to mean gift or present, as well as wealth, and where *límó* came to mean receive, as well as pay a visit. Like their Proto-Southern Luo–speaking linguistic ancestors, Dhopadhola speakers emphasized sociability and redistribution as part of their concept of wealth. While this fits with many theoretical models of wealth in sub-Saharan Africa, it is not one that regularly comes across from the linguistic evidence. It may be that Dhopadhola speakers—and their predecessors who had spoken Proto-Southern Luo—felt the need to remind the wealthy that this was the expectation. It may also be that this conceptualization of wealth and its social implication was so widely agreed upon that the two meanings converged onto a single root.

Speakers of Dhopadhola conceived of wealth as inherently social. But they also understood it as something that varied in its quantity. To express this understanding, they used the root, -*ŋang'*-.[125] Thus, we find that *aŋang'o* means rich, while *ngango* means wealth, riches, or immense wealth. Similarly, *jaŋang'o* or *ja ngango* refers to a rich person but also more specifically to a very rich person. And this could be qualified to specify the age and gender of the person with wealth: *dhako jaŋang'o* or *dhako mu ngang* to specify a rich woman and *jichwo jaŋang'o* to specify a rich man. While less etymologically insightful than **-can*-, the innovation of -*ŋang'*- tells us two things. One, that the presence of wealthy, indeed very wealthy, people in the Dhopadhola speaker community was significant enough that the community coined a new vocabulary for talking about them. And two, the fact that there is no overlap in the meanings of the words derived from this root with specific forms of wealth—for example, wealth in livestock or in grain—nor with power tells us that these were likely not their primary concerns when it came to wealth.

Conclusion

Nilotic-speaking communities are paradigmatically associated with pastoralism in the literature on East Africa. They are often understood to measure all their wealth in cattle and other livestock. There is a truth to that. But as with all single narratives, it is only a partial truth.[126] It is also not a timeless truth. People speaking Southern and Eastern Nilotic languages did develop concepts of wealth that specified its form in livestock and concepts of poverty as the lack of ownership of livestock, and of cattle more particularly. But some communities, including those speaking the Western Nilotic language Dhopadhola, did not conceive of wealth in these terms and others had competing material concepts of wealth in food crops. A more prevalent concept of wealth across these centuries was its equation with leadership and power and the complementary concepts of poverty as kinlessness or social death. And while the poor may have faced hostility, as when they were conceived of as being disruptive and troublesome, the ancient concept of poverty as a form of suffering persisted, reflecting an understanding in the wider community of their plight.

CHAPTER SIX

Wealth, Poverty, and the Colonial Economy

Nineteenth and Early Twentieth Centuries

B Y THE START OF the nineteenth century, almost all of the speaker communities of the modern languages of eastern Uganda were established in the region. The only exception among African languages was the division of Proto-East Kyoga (or pre-Lugwere) into Lugwere and Rushana. That happened when a group of Proto-East Kyoga speakers fled conflict and drought in the 1830s, and settled in Bulegenyi, in the foothills of Mount Elgon-Masaaba. They came to identify themselves as Bashana and their language as Rushana, while those they left behind came to identify themselves as Bagwere and their language as Lugwere.[1] Since the early nineteenth century, new languages have arrived from outside the region and eastern Ugandans have borrowed from them as they long had from each other's languages. This is as true for concepts of poverty and wealth as for other semantic fields. Many speaker communities adopted, for example, the Kiswahili noun *maskini* to talk about the poor and their poverty. Kiswahili speakers had themselves in turn borrowed the word from Arabic, where it has the form *miskīn*. While some concepts of poverty—and of wealth—were grounded in particular local contexts, others traveled more readily along trade routes and across boundaries of language and economics.

The kinds of interactions between people that led to the borrowing of new words and concepts were ancient in eastern Uganda, as we have seen. There was, however, something of an acceleration or intensification of those interactions as the region was increasingly incorporated into global trade networks and as colonial conquest and rule were violently imposed. This led to speaker communities developing new concepts of poverty and wealth, alongside their existing concepts. These new concepts were ones that reflected the changing economic, political, and cultural environments that speakers of eastern Ugandan languages inhabited. Christian missionaries, for example, brought moralistic and patriarchal attitudes toward poor women and the strategies some of

MAP 6.1. Map of eastern Uganda in the early twentieth century. Map created by Nat Case.

them turned to in order to survive—or even transcend—the poverty that they experienced. The imposition of British rule brought about economic dislocation through violence; the removal of livestock and people, especially women, from communities that resisted colonial rule; and disruption to existing modes of subsistence and trade. Simultaneously, it introduced new concepts of wealth, such as the possession of a bicycle or a government position, and poverty, including poverty as expressed through the absence of clothing, alongside new means of acquiring wealth and status. This was, then, another period of disruption for the region—across multiple vectors—but it did not mark a rupture in people's conceptualizations of poverty and wealth. Rather, eastern Ugandans drew on their existing concepts as they made sense of the profound changes that they experienced. In doing so, they adapted their concepts of poverty and wealth as they had time and again in the past.

Disruption: Natural and Social

The nineteenth century in eastern Uganda began amid a severe multidecadal drought that lasted from around 1780 to 1830.[2] Such a long climatic event would necessarily have had a profound impact on the ability of communities to sustain themselves through agriculture and herding. At the same time, the drought's impact would have varied in different places, based on a whole range of factors from microclimates to soil quality and the water table. Furthermore, there would not have been a single individual or collective response to the challenges posed by prolonged drought or aridity. Communities, households, and families would have made different decisions in the face of repeated crop failures or the death of livestock. And the kinds of decisions made after three, four, or five years of drought would have been different to those made after twenty or thirty years of aridity. According to the available paleoclimatological data, this period of pronounced aridity lasted half a century, spanning two or more generations of a family. The change in rainfall would have appeared to be permanent and irreversible. As such, people would have shifted from short-term reactions to a drought expected to last one or two growing seasons to an adaption to their new reality of consistently reduced rainfall.

The memory of continual settlement and resettlement of communities in eastern Uganda in this period is surely related to this long period of pronounced aridity. The historian Gideon Were dated the growth and expansion of Iteso settlement south of Mount Elgon-Masaaba to these decades.[3] The disruption this settlement caused was profoundly felt by the Babukusu communities displaced by the Iteso. Babukusu recalled this as a time of "great hardship" in which their "homes were burnt, villages abandoned, crops and property looted and destroyed, and the country left desolate."[4] As they fled south, they paid a high price for refuge, one that was disproportionately paid by Babukusu women and girls. "A typical example of this was Bunyala (Port Victoria) where their hosts are said to have behaved in a most indecent and injudicious manner by violating the marital status of the female refugees by forcefully marrying them; young female fugitives were also forcefully married."[5] This violent acquisition of women and girls by men in host communities reflects the continuing gendered concept of wealth as embodied by women and expressed through the root *-yaand-.[6]

Communities speaking Greater Luhyia languages did not use this root to mean plunder or loot, in the way that those speaking West Nyanza languages did. Still, in their use of words derived from this root, speakers of Greater Luhyia languages retained a strong conceptualization of women and girls both as wealth and as the generators of wealth.

The instability caused by these population movements and their accompanying violence was one impetus for several Greater Luhyia–speaking communities to live in fortified villages or hamlets, with large walls and moats surrounding them.[7] The anthropologist R. W. Moody noted of the Basaamia that cultivation of land around the *olukoba* (walled or moated village) was limited to the area that could be safely protected by the village's warriors. Women, who in Saamia communities were those primarily engaged in agricultural labor, were thus restricted in their movement and work to fields near the *olukoba* and thereby faced limitations on the amount of food they could produce.[8] This insecurity compounded what would have almost certainly been poorer harvests during the prolonged drought. The continued conceptualization of poverty as resulting in emaciation among these speaker communities, while not an innovation in the nineteenth century, would have gained renewed significance under these conditions. And at least one term making this conceptual connection may well have been innovated during this time of insecurity. This is the root *-ŋat-*, which Lunyole speakers coined from a Proto-Greater Luhyia root. They gave it the meanings suffer in exile and be ostracized, as well as using it to talk about lacking everything and living a life of poverty.[9] Because of the antiquity of Lunyole as a language, it is—as I noted in chapter 3—impossible to date such innovations, but the continued salience of this concept well into the nineteenth century is nonetheless apparent. Similarly, while the Greater Luhyia root *-nyerere* predated this period, its emphasis on emaciation as a result of poverty would have held renewed meaning as people faced chronic food insecurity.[10]

Slave and Ivory Trades

The nineteenth century saw significant new external pressures on communities in the region. Greater Luhyia–speaking people living closest to the Victoria Nyanza became the targets of an expansionist and increasingly maritime Buganda.[11] The Scottish geologist and colonialist Joseph Thomson learned after reaching Busaamia in 1883 that one of his porters, a man called Mambruki, was in fact the brother of Uchen, the "principal chief of Samia." Mambruki "had been captured when a boy, and sold as a slave to the traders." When they arrived in Busaamia, Mambruki was "recognized and welcomed as one who had been lost and found. Before he was allowed to enter the walls of the village, a goat had to be killed and the blood sprinkled on the door and posts."[12] Were argued that it was most likely raiders from Buganda who had enslaved Mambruki and then sold him to the coast in the mid-nineteenth century.[13] Raiding for slaves by Baganda and others to sell into the caravan trade introduced profound new challenges for households, which experienced the loss of members, as well as wider disruptions of social and economic life.

Slavery was by no means a new phenomenon in East Africa in the nineteenth century.[14] The increased slave raiding that communities experienced at this time, however, would have intensified forms of poverty conceived of as entwined with bereavement and need. Family members were lost, usually as completely as if they had died. Slave raiding increased at a time when households in eastern Uganda were recovering from the prolonged dry period that likely ended in the 1830s. While anxieties over food insecurity faded in this time of more plentiful rains, this new development in slave raiding threatened the economic security of households by removing productive members. It, along with population movements and conflict, also forced people to live in defensive and constrictive patterns.

Traders from the East African coast and the Indian Ocean networks were a new factor in eastern Uganda in the nineteenth century. Based on the oral histories he collected from Abawanga elders, Were estimated the first arrival of Swahili traders to have been in the mid-nineteenth century (circa 1841 to circa 1868). They established a base at Elureko in Western Kenya. This was the settlement that would become known as Mumias during the era of colonial competition and conquest, named for the Muwanga chief, Mumia. The arrival of the coastal traders affected communities differently depending on whether those communities were able to mobilize to effectively protect themselves against slave raiders or had goods to trade, especially ivory.[15] As was the case with Mambruki, a small number of those taken away and enslaved in this violent manner may have been able to return. The vast majority, however, would not have come back to their communities, creating real trauma and loss for their families and a profound sense of bereavement. In Greater Luhyia–speaking communities, bereavement and poverty had long been conceptualized together and expressed through roots such as *-tamb-.[16] The slave trade of the nineteenth and early twentieth centuries would have only accentuated this sense that the two were intimately entangled.

The arrival of outside traders was not uniformly negative for communities in eastern Uganda. Further north, the Jie initially viewed with distrust those they called Habaci and who came from what is today southern Ethiopia around

1880. "When the first *Habaci* began coming here, the Jie thought they were very strange people indeed. We had not seen 'red' people like them before. We didn't understand why they had come here and at first the people were afraid they had come here to kill us."[17] But they soon established positive relations, as they also did with the Swahili traders, whom they called Acumpa, who arrived later in the 1880s. Both groups of traders were interested in ivory and tended to hunt the elephants themselves, thus inadvertently rendering a service to Jie farmers whose fields were at risk of being trampled.[18] Lamphear was emphatic that all of his interlocutors were clear that neither the Habaci nor the Acumpa engaged in slave raiding among the Jie. "The *Acumpa* came here from the south-east when the Ngikosowa were initiating. They only wanted to shoot elephants, and they brought beads, wire, and other things to trade," recalled one group of Jie interviewees.[19] Other interviewees narrated, "Those who came here to shoot elephants and trade things never caused any trouble, except once, when there was that fight at Nalingakan. Other than that, they were peaceful. They never killed any of the Jie or took away any of our women or children."[20] These reports from members of the Jie communities contrast with colonial depictions of Swahili and Ethiopian traders in Jie and Karimojong lands that emphasized violence and theft.[21]

In terms of wealth and their concept of it as taking the form of livestock, the Jie people's positive relations with the Habaci and Acumpa were critical. Those relations enabled Jie households to rebuild their cattle herds after the devastations of the 1890s, discussed further below. "The first relief to the shattered communities of Karamoja was provided by the elephant-hunting strangers (especially the *Acumpa*, it would seem)," wrote Lamphear, "who enterprisingly bought up large herds of cattle in areas unaffected by the diseases, and drove them to Karamoja, in order to trade them to the impoverished Karimojong, Jie and Dodos."[22] Over time, Jie men themselves took up elephant hunting on behalf of the outsiders, while others "accompanied the traders as guides and porters." They were paid in livestock for their labors, with "a pair of large tusks fetching as much as thirty cattle."[23] Spurred by this success, they increasingly engaged in trade as middlemen, taking iron goods to Turkana communities in northwestern Kenya and livestock to the Labwor Acholi communities in northern Uganda, accumulating further wealth.[24]

From this position of renewed wealth, Jie men turned to raiding and warfare to further enrich themselves in livestock and shore up their position vis-à-vis their neighbors. They did this under the leadership of the hereditary war-leader Loriang who innovated military formations and strategies that resulted in a series of successes, including in battles with enemies using firearms against the Jie spears.[25]

By the end of the first decade of the twentieth century, British visitors to the area described the Jie community as "small but very compact, rich, and independent"[26] and as "so rich in cattle and sheep as to be indifferent to other sources of meat supply."[27] Although the wider context in which this rebuilding of wealth occurred was rapidly changing—and indeed the British did their best to put an end to the raiding that undergirded it—the continuity in the concept of wealth is important to highlight. Despite the profound disruptions of the last decade of the nineteenth century (or indeed perhaps because of it), Jie and Karimojong concepts of wealth remained firmly grounded in possession of livestock as expressed through the use of words derived from the root *-bar- to mean both wealth and livestock.[28]

Catastrophe

Colonial conquest in East Africa, as we well know, coincided with drought, famine, and epidemics of human and animal diseases, some new and some old. These years of crisis came after a half century of relative abundance. The prolonged period of reduced rainfall at the end of the eighteenth and start of the nineteenth centuries was followed by generally increased rainfall that lasted until the last quarter of the nineteenth century. The level of the Victoria Nyanza, for example, peaked in 1878, at a height that has not since been surpassed.[29] Five years later Thomson traveled through the region. He wrote that he and his caravan "passed along a perfect lane of people, all carrying baskets of food which they were dying to dispose of for beads. There were honey, milk, eggs, fowls, beans, &c., &c."[30] Thomson was "most impressed" by "the surprising number of villages, and the generally contented and well-to-do air of the inhabitants."[31] As they continued toward the Victoria Nyanza, this image of prosperity continued. "Food," he reported, "was surprisingly cheap and apparently inexhaustible. Four men's food in flour was got for one string of beads, eight men's food of sweet potatoes for the same, a sheep for fifteen strings, and a goat for twenty strings."[32]

In the closing decades of the nineteenth century, however, people in eastern Uganda experienced catastrophic drought, even if its duration was shorter than the drought that opened the century. The 1880s and 1890s witnessed a period of deep drought across much of East Africa, during which "lake levels fell and glaciers receded."[33] Between the late 1870s and early 1890s, rainfall was below mean levels for thirteen consecutive years. While not amounting each year to drought levels, the cumulative effect of persistently low rainfall was devastating for many communities.[34] But across the region, people did not experience the drought and its consequences at exactly the same time or in the same ways.

The Victoria Nyanza in the south, for example, exerted different forces on the climate than did the plateaus of the north, leading to distinct levels and distributions of precipitation.

British and other travelers through the southern part of the region in these years continued to emphasize the abundance of food and other resources. The Mill Hill bishop, Henry Hanlon, wrote about Busoga in 1898 during his visit to the polity of Luuka. "The country is less hilly, lies slightly lower, and is more moist and fruitful than Uganda [Buganda]. This northern part, being the home of the elephant, is a common hunting ground for tusks of ivory. Flocks and herds are more numerous and larger than in Uganda." Among other derogatory and racist explanations, Hanlon blamed the wealth of Luuka, and of Busoga more generally, for the limited success of the Mill Hill Mission there. "Their wealth in cattle, sheep, and goats, and in ivory, and the rich productiveness of their land in plantains, their simple food," he wrote, "are obstacles to their speedy conversion."[35]

By the opening years of the twentieth century, however, the drought had brought catastrophe to the southern part of eastern Uganda. Another Mill Hill Father, Anthony Vanterm, wrote about Busoga in 1900: "Famine gets very bad out here, and we regularly meet with some corpses lying in the high grass when we are on our missionary journeys." Tacitly acknowledging the disruptive presence of missionaries and the encroachment of colonialism, he noted that Basoga women and men accused them "of being the cause of the long drought, and many a petition has been made to me to let the rain fall." He was dismissive of this request, as he was of the performance of a ceremony on the shores of the Victoria Nyanza "with the intention of obtaining rain from the spirits."[36] A few months later the consequences of the drought continued to be felt, with Father Drontman reporting that "the harvest reaped here at Lubas is still scanty." By then the drought had broken and "heavenly rain has now come down in a torrent."[37] The arrival of torrential rains, however, prolonged the famine by washing away topsoil and seedlings.[38]

Where Bishop Hanlon had blamed the wealth of the Basoga for their indifference to Christianity, Father Drontman placed the blame for the famine on the supposed "vices of all kinds" of the Basoga.[39] For the Catholic missionaries, wealth resulted in lack of faith and immorality caused poverty and famine. These were new concepts in Busoga at the start of the twentieth century. While the first notion, that wealth was a hindrance to Christianity, did not get incorporated into Lusoga terms for wealth, the second, that immorality caused poverty, did. We saw this in chapter 4 with the root *-tak-, which in Lusoga acquired the meaning of spiritual failing alongside the older meaning of poverty.[40]

Further east, Christian notions of morality also likely affected the meaning of the Lubukusu noun *omutaamba* that is today translated into English as harlot, prostitute, or whore, and which Lubukusu speakers used to name a woman whose behavior contravened social expectations. As we saw in chapter 3, they derived this from the root **-tamb-*, changing the final vowel to *-a* in order to distinguish it from the noun *ómutaambi*, meaning poor person.[41] A poor woman who engaged in extramarital sex in exchange for economic and social security of some kind was thus marked out for condemnation.

Further north, unreliable and reduced rainfall in the late nineteenth century had devastating effects, leading pastoralist communities, in particular, to seek refuge among the farming communities that they otherwise tended to disparage.[42] In interviews in the 1960s and 1970s with Lamphear, Jie elders remembered in cataclysmic terms the situation in the mid-1890s, when drought was followed by swarms of locusts and an outbreak of smallpox. One man named Amuk recalled that "most Jie were left with no food at all. Nothing. They went up towards Kapeta and gathered wild fruits."[43] Another, called Longoli, said that "nearly all the cattle in Najie died. Only one bull, belonging to Lokalong of Panyagara, was left in all of Najie . . . I remember that my father had only two cows left out of his entire herd. Many people went to the bush and hunted wild animals."[44] Among the Iteso of Usuku, people ate the bulbs of water lilies to survive. The famine was catastrophic and "death from starvation was widespread." The impacts of the failed rains were compounded as drought was "followed by a cattle disease followed yet by swarms of locusts."[45] An estimated two-thirds of the cattle in Teso died.[46] People were pushed to desperation. "The rain-making ceremonies were performed in greater and greater panic," and "the pillaging of granaries and the stealing of children for sale for food turned society into almost total anarchy."[47]

The famine also saw a rupture in the concept of wealth and power as mutually constitutive and generally (albeit not always) positive, a concept discussed in chapter 5. The story of Okadaro illustrates this rupture. He was perhaps the first *emuron* among the Iteso (a foreteller and "probably the most influential individual in Iteso society"[48]) in what is today Katakwi District. He became wealthy and powerful as a result of his ability to foretell the outcome of battles during war with Karimojong communities. Okadaro demanded payment in cattle or labor in exchange for a prediction and, as a result, amassed large reserves of grain and livestock. His actions during the famine of 1894 to 1896, however, led to his downfall. Despite the fact that he performed the rainmaking ceremony *elelekeja*, the drought persisted, an outcome that undermined Okadaro's status as a skilled *emuron*. But it was his exploitation of his wealth, alongside his friend Olokotum, during the famine that most aggravated his community, the members of which expected him to share his wealth to alleviate their suffering.[49]

When the famine came, both Olokotum and Okadaro possessed large stores of food from the previous years when they had had many people working for them. Okadaro and Olokotum now became very rich by selling their food to people who were starving. People became jealous of this surplus food which they worked to produce. So they destroyed the homes of the two men in order to get "their" food. Since Okadaro's elelekeja repeatedly failed to bring rain, the people believed that he was purposely killing rain in order that he and his friends might amass wealth.[50]

Critically, for thinking about conceptualizations of the wealthy, it was the exploitative behavior of these two rich men during a time of catastrophe that led to the attack, not their wealth in and of itself nor the power that they wielded. Another *emuron*, Orwatum, was not blamed for the situation because "he was not getting wealthy as a result of the famine."[51] William Fitzsimons has argued that an understanding of economic equilibrium was central to Teso society and politics long before this and that those who became too rich or used their wealth to exploit others were condemned by their peers.[52]

For pastoralist societies, the situation in the 1890s was profoundly aggravated by repeated outbreaks of bovine pleuropneumonia followed by the rapid spread of rinderpest. Bovine pleuropneumonia was present in Maasai herds by "the second half of 1883, when its effects were witnessed by Thomson north of Nakuru."[53] By itself, this outbreak of bovine pleuropneumonia did not "seriously disrupt the stock economy," noted the historian Richard Waller, as there was enough livestock in the region for pastoralists to be able to make up their losses through raiding.[54] The impact of such raiding by Maasai on neighboring communities, including those of the Ngakarimojong and Sapiny, was not insignificant, but those who had been raided could, in turn, raid others beyond the reach of the Maasai to restock. The epidemic, thus, disrupted stability and instigated physical and economic violence across communities, even as it left the basis of the economy largely intact. The arrival of rinderpest, however, threatened the economic and social viability of pastoralists. Having been introduced by Italian soldiers in the Horn of Africa, this new (or at least new strain of) disease laid waste to herds throughout eastern and southern Africa. "It finished the cattle and swept the land."[55] Starting in 1891, rinderpest wiped out up to 90 percent of the cattle in parts of East Africa. Some communities saw entire herds—or close to entire herds—die in the course of a couple of months, weeks, or simply days.[56]

The scale of loss was absolutely devastating. Faced with the destruction of their wealth and the basis of their identity, pastoralist communities increased their raids on others, in a desperate attempt to restock, and in turn they experienced counterraids from communities seeking to do the same. "Raids grew more violent," because so many cattle had been lost.[57]

The devastation of herds and the loss of wealth that this entailed had direct consequences for social reproduction and the ways in which wealth was translated into social status and into networks of reciprocal support. Among the Iteso, for example, families no longer had cattle to use as bridewealth in their sons' marriages. "It is stated," wrote J. C. D. Lawrance, the colonial official and amateur ethnographer, "that after the rinderpest outbreak of 1890 bride-price fell as low as one head of cattle and thirty goats."[58] Because the bridewealth acquired for a daughter could usually be used for the marriage of a son in the household, as well as for growing the size of the household herd, the consequences of the dramatically smaller number of cattle in the region rippled across communities. But the stigma of marrying with few or no cattle forming the bridewealth appears to only have been remembered in association with women. The Iteso men who shared their histories with the historian J. B. Webster told him that "in the drought and rinderpest epedemic [sic] of 1894–1896 the cattle were again wiped out and the mothers of the present generation had to be married with the exchange of goats rather than cows."[59] Poverty was gendered in memory as well as in reality, with women carrying its shame in their marriages.[60]

Colonial Rule

The people of eastern Uganda experienced a dramatic transformation in their political status in the last decade of the nineteenth century, as did so many others on the continent. British colonial rule had real and profound consequences for the lives of those in the region and for how they conceived of poverty and, especially, wealth. These transformations were accentuated in eastern Uganda by its residents' relative isolation from Europe and Europeans prior to this point. The arrival of a different kind of foreigner in eastern Uganda, the kind who sought not only to trade but to impose their rule over the region, began in the 1880s. Among the first of these foreigners to arrive was Joseph Thomson, who led a Royal Geographic Society expedition to map a new trade route from the Indian Ocean to the Victoria Nyanza. He traveled through Kenya and into eastern Uganda in 1883, staying at Mumias for some of his time in the region. Six years later, Frederick Jackson traveled there on behalf of the Imperial British East

Africa Company, with the explicit imperial ambitions of "opening up" the area that Britain claimed as within its sphere of influence. Jackson went on to intervene in the politico-religious conflict in Buganda, against orders from London.[61] Overlapping with Jackson, Carl Peters arrived in the region as an agent of the German Empire. Peters was reportedly initially welcomed by Greater Luhyia–speaking communities in 1890, as he promised to aid them in their conflicts with Iteso communities.[62] The German flag was briefly raised over Mumias, much to Jackson's consternation, given his conviction that the British had a prior imperial claim. The Heligoland Treaty of 1890 strengthened that claim, by demarcating the boundaries of Tanganyika, claimed by Germany, from the rest of East Africa, which Germany recognized as British territory. In 1894, the competing European powers declared the region, including much of what is now Kenya, to be part of the British Protectorate of Uganda.[63]

Despite this diplomatic and political change, the British had neither the capacity nor the will in the late nineteenth century to invest the resources that would be needed to make that change felt in any significant way on the ground. According to the historian Michael Twaddle, "The Sebei and Gisu clans occupying the northerly and western slopes of [Mount Elgon-Masaaba] ... remained independent of British colonial control throughout the 1890s, and their perceptions of British intentions appear to have remained most hazy."[64] Toward the end of the decade, in 1898, the British colonial administration sent an expedition to the area, under the command of J. R. L. Macdonald, with the aim of securing the territory and establishing British rule through "treaties with local chiefs."[65] Camped out on Mount Elgon-Masaaba for months, the expedition came under repeated attacks by those living there and eventually retreated to Nairobi, defeated in its mission. Areas inhabited by speakers of Ateso, Jie, and Ngakarimojong also remained outside of effective British command into the twentieth century. Eastern Uganda became "a refuge for objectors to British protectorate rule," because it was not under colonial authority on the ground.[66]

The colonial administration in the Uganda Protectorate, under the leadership of Special Commissioner Harry Johnston, thus decided to award Semei Kakungulu the task of bringing "the unruly Kedi or Lango people under control, and further to keep the district clear of mutineers."[67] Kakungulu, from the province of Koki south of Buganda, had made his name as a military leader during the conflicts within Buganda and in the British campaign against *Mukama* (King) Kabareega of Bunyoro. Kakungulu had already set his sights on eastern Uganda, launching raids in the region, but now had "much stronger British backing for his and his followers' attempts to conquer Bukedi and to incorporate it within the Uganda Protectorate."[68] Most relevant, perhaps, for concepts of poverty and wealth, he was also tasked with acting "as a collector imposing a hut and gun tax" on those under his control.[69] For the British, taxation was a key means by which they sought to extract material wealth from the Protectorate and its people.[70] But taxation also offered those charged with collecting it new justification for acquiring wealth from those they governed or administered.

Kakungulu's strategy was military and not diplomatic when, in 1900, he sent armed expeditions to conquer swathes of territory from Bugwere in the west to Mount Elgon-Masaaba in the east. He accomplished this goal by the end of the year. But his predatory tactics and willingness to use excessive violence made him unpopular in the region and, ultimately, with the British colonial administration, which was forced to address complaints about his behavior. The anthropologist Joan Vincent wrote about the violence of his strategy in conquering Teso:

> Reliable witnesses wrote of Kakungulu's "scorched earth" policy; Iteso elders spoke of the conquest in terms of pillage and rape. The troops, they said, would enter a village, round up old people and womenfolk, and hold them hostage for the surrender of fighting men. Cattle would be seized and food crops plundered. In localities where the Iteso offered no resistance, homesteads remained unmolested; but the troops lived off the countryside, leaving, in these postfamine years, little behind.[71]

Kakungulu and his soldiers were acting on the Luganda concept of wealth as plunder and loot, encapsulated in the root *-yaand-, that Luganda speakers had inherited from those speaking Proto-West Nyanza.[72] In Luganda, *omwandu* referred to "plunder, booty seized in war," and was especially used to talk about women who had been taken in this way.[73] In seizing cattle and food crops from Iteso households, Kakungulu's troops targeted their two primary forms of wealth. As we saw in chapter 5, these were *ibaren* (from the root *-bar-), which described the concept of wealth in livestock, and *amio*, which described the concept of wealth in food crops.[74]

Kakungulu sought both the power of a king in eastern Uganda and vast wealth. He conceptualized the two as inseparable. He confiscated cattle from the communities he now governed, claiming that this was punishment for armed attacks by members of those communities.[75] So effective was he at extracting this wealth that news reached Buganda of the opportunities available in Bukedi and ambitious men traveled east to join him and make their own fortunes.[76] For the most part they made those fortunes through the heavy taxation of those over whom Kakungulu appointed them as chiefs, as well as through punitive fines for legal infractions and disputes.[77] The resentment and poverty this generated among the Iteso, Bagwere, Bamasaaba, and others being taxed was so great that the British were forced to intervene.[78] By February 1902, the British colonial administration had negotiated a settlement with Kakungulu in which he would resign from his official colonial appointment, but would be granted twenty acres of personal property at Mbale.[79] Despite this, the British acknowledged that "Kakunguru was practically the king, and remained so up to the end of 1904."[80] By then, Kakungulu embodied a concept of wealth in which political leaders had riches that were on a vastly different scale to what Bamasaaba and others in the region had known previously. He had also introduced centralized political authority, on behalf of the British colonial state, with a clear emphasis on taxation; an introduction that would further shift concepts of wealth in the area.

Colonial Work, Taxation, and New Forms of Power

The imposition of British rule in eastern Uganda brought about economic dislocation through violence, the removal of livestock and people, especially women, from communities that resisted colonial rule, and disruption to existing modes of subsistence and trade. Simultaneously, it introduced new concepts of wealth and poverty, including poverty as expressed through the absence of clothing, alongside new means of acquiring wealth and status. For example, by 1901, a colonial report noted that in some Greater Luhyia–speaking communities, "the great aim and ambition of the men, after that of obtaining large families, is to join the ranks of the Police Force."[81] Joining the colonial police force offered men a means to acquire funds to purchase cattle for bridewealth that was outside of the constraints of familial or community ties. Young men might, thereby, be able to marry sooner than if they had to rely on their fathers to provide the bridewealth cattle. Already married men who wanted to marry an additional wife, but did not have the economic means or the social standing to acquire the necessary cattle, could use their colonial salaries to purchase them. The division between the new forms and conceptions of wealth and the old ones was thus fluid from the outset.

We see this conceptual fluidity in the case of Bubukusu. Babukusu communities not only resisted the imposition of British overrule, but actively organized to attack the fort at Mumias. They bought rifles from deserting porters in exchange for cattle, building up a sizable arsenal. Frederick Spire, the British representative at Mumias in 1894, decided they should be disarmed and sent twenty-five Sudanese soldiers to take them by force. This backfired. The Sudanese soldiers were all killed and their weapons added to the Bukusu arsenal. On arriving at Mumias, having been deputed to replace Spire, Charles W. Hobley, who would go on to be the provincial commissioner of Kavirondo Region, determined that the humiliation had to be avenged. He assembled a massive force of Sudanese, Baganda, and Maasai troops, alongside those of Chief Mumia. Faced with a force of over a thousand soldiers and a maxim gun, the Babukusu were defeated, despite inflicting significant losses on the colonial troops.[82] The troops "took with them back to Mumias a great herd of Bukusu cattle and a large group of women." Chief Mumia then called Babukusu elders to "parley."

> One of the elders whom Mumia invited was Namajanja of the Bukhoone clan, who was a son-in-law of Mumia's uncle, Sakwa. Mumia instructed Namajanja to come with cattle, hoes and goats as a ransom for the arrested women. Namajanja did so, and got a fortune for himself, for the British were eager to place someone over South Bukusu as chief, and a panel of Babukusu suggested the name of Namajanja, who had secured the return of their women. That is how Namajanja gained ascendency in Bukusu.[83]

The colonial soldiers, many of whom were Baganda and thus had a concept of wealth as plunder (*òmwandù*), were working according to existing ideas of warfare and wealth. The ransoming, organized by Mumia but presumably with the approval of Hobley, also fit into this existing concept. But we can see a new concept of wealth in Namajanja's appointment as chief by Hobley. Although chosen by Babukusu elders, his power was predicated on the support—political and military—of the colonial administration. And he acquired wealth through that new position. Both his wealth and the chiefship were inherited by his son Sudi, who was named for the slave raider Sudi of Pangani, who was infamous in the region.[84] While we cannot know Namajanja's motivations in selecting a name for his son, his decision to name him Sudi serves as an effective metaphor for the violence underpinning new forms of wealth at the end of the nineteenth century.

The introduction of taxation at the start of the twentieth century imposed a heavy burden on people, many of whom were still suffering from famine and epidemics of disease, both human and animal. It also promoted a concept of individual wealth and ownership, because "the payment of taxes was deemed an individual matter for each adult male."[85] And it created a new means for some Ugandan men to acquire wealth and power as colonial tax collectors.[86] The British colonial administration saw taxation as a means to generate material wealth in two ways. One was as a means to cover the costs of governing the Protectorate. The other, emerging from their racist views of the residents of Uganda, was as a means of "stimulating a people, not inclined to over-exertion, to better their condition, and make their country contribute its share to the world's prosperity."[87] This was a common refrain from the British administrators, with Special Commissioner Harry H. Johnston contrasting what he perceived as the potential wealth of the Uganda Protectorate with his racist beliefs that it was laziness that prevented that wealth being realized. He wrote of his hope "that the negro will awake to an idea of the wealth which lies in his untilled soil, and realize that he may become a wealthy man if he will only be reasonably industrious."[88]

To that end, Johnston included a hut tax in the 1900 Uganda Agreement signed with the Buganda kingdom, but which applied across the whole Protectorate: "The native taxes are fixed at 3 rupees (4s.) per house or dwelling-hut per annum."[89] Because of the limited availability of currency in the economy, people were initially permitted to pay their tax in labor or in kind. A detailed list of equivalences was sent to the tax collectors in each district. This list distinguished between unskilled labor and skilled labor. Unskilled labor was further divided between that of "able-bodied men," valued at three rupees for a month's work, and that of "able-bodied women," valued at only two rupees. Skilled labor, such as boat-building or carpentry, was "to be appraised according to local rates of pay," but must not exceed nine rupees for a month's work. If they were paying in kind, people could use agricultural products, such as sorghum (valued at 40 lb. to the rupee—and so requiring 120 lb. of sorghum each year to cover the tax per dwelling place) and groundnuts (valued at 30 lb. to the rupee—and so requiring 90 lb. of groundnuts to cover the tax). Livestock was also accepted, with valuations ranging from one-fifth of a rupee for a fowl to forty-five rupees for a cow and her calf. These options notwithstanding, the desire of the colonial administrator to introduce a cash economy was underscored with the instruction that "every encouragement is to be given to the natives to pay, if possible, in cash."[90]

When, in 1905, the colonial administration introduced a poll tax on adult males, it stipulated payment in cash and began "forcibly encouraging," in Teso at least, the cultivation of cash crops, especially cotton and coffee, to generate the necessary currency.[91] Missionaries supported this effort. "The government wanted a crop introduced which would permit its growers to pay their taxes in cash rather than kind," noted Vincent, and "the missionaries wanted to inculcate the work ethic in order to modernize those whom they considered primitive and to clothe the heathens."[92] Cotton production grew dramatically from its introduction in the first decade of the twentieth century, before declining steeply by 1917. Farmers in Kumi district increased their cotton production from one million pounds in 1909–1910 to 6.3 million pounds in 1911–1912, after the importation of ploughs and a "ploughing school."[93] This did not, however, immediately translate into consistent payment of taxes. Frederick Jackson, who was by then governor of Uganda, wrote to London—using familiar racist tropes—that the people of Bukedi "though they may be wild, savage and difficult to control have been taught to cultivate cotton . . . and though many of the natives as yet pay no hut or poll tax, they assuredly will."[94]

British colonial rule and the imposition of taxation created new forms of power and new means of accumulating significant wealth for a small minority of Ugandan men. Women were excluded from this opportunity for the duration of colonial rule. That exclusion may have changed ideas about who could be an owner, shifting it toward a gendered conceptualization that only men could be wealthy. William Fitzsimons has shown that Proto-Ateker speakers innovated vocabulary that specified that both women and men could be owners, with women owning the crops that they grew and thus having the possibility of accumulating wealth.[95] We also saw in chapter 5 examples of Teso women like Atengorit who "was very rich . . . in food, had many cattle, sheep and goats."[96] But with the arrival of Kakungulu, his troops, and the Baganda men he appointed as chiefs in eastern Uganda, the introduction of centralized power and taxation shifted this dynamic.

There had been no chiefs in Teso prior to colonial rule. The creation of this new political and administrative office, and with it the power to accumulate wealth through taxation, resulted in a new concept of wealth. Baganda men who were appointed as tax collection agents in Teso were remunerated with 10 percent of the tax that they collected, while the chiefs of those areas received 5 percent.[97] Consistent complaints against the Baganda and the compliance of the chiefs, whose positions were the creation of colonial rule, led the British administration to gradually remove the Baganda agents from 1909.[98] With the removal of the Baganda agents, the Iteso colonial chiefs received 10 percent of the taxes they collected. As had been the case with the Baganda men they replaced, the goal was to incentivize chiefs to collect as much tax as possible. This seems to have been effective with tax revenues from Teso District increasing 240 percent from 1910 to 1914.[99] Vincent pointed out that this change also meant that "by 1912, seven Iteso chiefs, all from the southern counties, had begun to acquire large and official cash incomes that far exceeded anything available to other Iteso at the time."[100] Whereas Iteso people had previously conceived of wealth primarily in terms of livestock (*ibaren*), especially cattle, and in terms of food crops (*amio*), wealth was now being accumulated in currency, first in rupees and, after 1920, in shillings.

Missionary Education

Missionary education and colonial administration created new means of social advancement and shifted the conceptualization of wealth in the process. Having had missions in Busoga in the late 1890s, Protestant missionaries of the Church Missionary Society and Catholic missionaries of the Mill Hill Fathers turned their attentions further east in the opening years of the twentieth century. Semei Kakungulu granted the Catholic Mill Hill Fathers land at Budaka in Bugwere in September 1901, although the relationship between Kakungulu and the Catholics quickly soured.[101] Reverend William Crabtree and his wife Mrs. Crabtree established an Anglican Church Missionary Society (CMS) mission station further east at Nabumali (also known as Mpumudde), opening a school there in 1903.[102] While the numbers of both students and Christians remained very small initially, Vincent argued that it was demand from chiefs for an education for their sons that pushed the Mill Hill Fathers to give instruction in reading and writing, however limited. The preference of the missionaries was to train students in vocational skills such as brickmaking, carpentry, and tailoring.[103] Despite their hesitation, mission education proved to be central to new ways of becoming wealthy and, consequently, of how wealth was understood.

The detailed life story of R. J. N. Madaba is illustrative of some of the ways in which social, economic, and political life changed in the time of colonial rule and missionary education. He was born early in the twentieth century, approximately 1904, in Butandiga on the northwest slopes of Mount Elgon-Masaaba, in what is today Sironko District. When Madaba was six or seven (approximately 1910), while out herding cattle with his older brother, he was kidnapped by ivory and slave traders from the East African coast. They walked from Bumasaaba to Mogadishu in Somalia, a distance of over twelve hundred miles. There he was sold to a Somali man, who took him to the island of Pemba and, after some four months, sold him to a woman Madaba described as Arab. Madaba remembered that experience as particularly harsh: "It was at this place that I realized I had been sold over as a slave because I had seen how lots of people were sold as slaves. The Arab woman treated me very cruelly indeed." In 1914, she took Madaba to Zanzibar and, when she died, he was inherited by her brother, Ahmisi Bin Saidi, who took him to Mombasa. There, he learned Arabic, having at some point converted to Islam.[104]

Unfortunately, Madaba glossed over what happened next, but likely due to the abolition of slavery on the Kenyan coast in 1907, it appears that Ahmisi turned him over to the CMS, although he may have first found himself with Catholic missionaries. From 1915 to 1920, he attended Buxton High School, the CMS school in Mombasa founded in the 1890s.[105] Importantly for Madaba's later career, the curriculum at Buxton High School was taught through the medium of English rather than Kiswahili.[106] Having completed his education and converted to Anglicanism, he trained as a teacher. In 1921, he met a visiting reverend and reported telling him "that I was a Gisu Karamojong of Butandiga." This information was relayed up to Archdeacon Mathers in Mbale, who in 1927 arranged Madaba's appointment as a teacher at Nabumali High School, the CMS school in Mbale. Madaba did not stay long at Nabumali, transferring first "to Buwalasi Primary School then Simu as Coffee buyer."[107]

Madaba used his skills of literacy and fluency in English and "became a clerk and interpreter at the D.C.'s [District Commissioner's] Office at Bubulo." He rose steadily through the ranks of colonial administration. By 1934 he had been appointed *muluka* (parish) chief; in 1939 he was promoted to *gombolola* (subcounty) chief; and in 1948 he became *ssaza* (county) chief of North Bugisu. Madaba still held this position in 1957 when he was nominated by the district commissioner to go on a "Chief's tour to England" and was asked to write a summary of his career from which we are able to learn his story.[108] While Madaba's case is exceptional, it nonetheless illustrates some of the profound transformations in eastern Uganda over the course of his life. In Madaba's time, education and conversion to Christianity became essential to social mobility, and wealth was most reliably acquired through cash crops and a government appointment, particularly as a chief.

For other men in eastern Uganda, missionary education and employment in the colonial administration offered opportunities to acquire wealth and power without Madaba's traumatic experience of abduction and enslavement. Leo Wakida was the son of Lyada, who ruled the Balalaka polity in Bugwere in the late nineteenth century and who had significantly expanded its borders during his reign.[109] Lyada successfully negotiated with Kakungulu to retain power under the new regime.[110] In a further sign that he was able to navigate the new political situation, Lyada sent Wakida to study with the CMS missionaries at Namilyango in Buganda. On completing his education there in 1915, Wakida was immediately appointed as a *ssaza* chief by the British, a high-level appointment for someone so junior. The existing *ssaza* and *gombolola* chiefs in Bugwere "feared Leo Wakida" and "they thought that he would look at them as uneducated and would not recognize the older chiefs who were not educated."[111]

Other boys in Bugwere similarly benefited from missionary education. Alex Pokino, for example, went to school at Namilyango in 1914, was appointed as clerk to the district commissioner in 1920, and then became a *muluka* chief, before changing careers and becoming head teacher at the CMS boys' school in Dabani, Busaamia.[112] Ezekeri Kageni similarly moved between teaching and colonial administration. Born around 1896, he attended school in Mbale from 1908, becoming a teacher at the CMS school at Nabumali. In 1915 he "became a clerk of poll tax" at Iki Iki in Bugwere. He made his way up through the hierarchy of colonial administration, becoming in turn a *muluka* chief in 1918, a *gombolola* chief in 1919, and a *ssaza* chief in 1935.[113] For these men, missionary education was a new means to accumulate wealth, something that fit into the acquisitional concept of wealth expressed through the Lugwere verb *ókusuná*.[114] This was a fundamentally new—and heavily gendered—way to become wealthy, with wealth acquired in the form of cash, but it could nonetheless fit into the older concept of *ókusuná*.

Material Poverty, Material Wealth

As new forms of material goods arrived in eastern Uganda and grew in prevalence, the possession or lack of possession of some of them in particular came to be integrated into concepts of wealth and poverty. New forms of clothing not only covered much more of the body but also marked a person's status in the shifting political economy of the region. At the start of the twentieth century, most people still dressed their bodies largely as they and their ancestors had done in the nineteenth century and earlier, albeit not without changes. An intelligence report from 1902 described the "Kavirondo" (roughly the Greater Luhyia- and Luo-speaking communities who lived around the northeast shores of the Victoria Nyanza) as "unclothed, the young women and the men are usually absolutely nude with the exception of a few strings of beads or wire round their necks arms and ancles [sic] etc. The married women sometimes wear a short fringe of beads in front and a short tail of some sort of fibre at the back."[115] Writing about Luyia and Luo communities in western Kenya, but broadly applicable to both the Greater Luhyia and Nilotic communities further west, the historian Margaret Jean Hay noted:

> Conceptions of proper dress in the early 1900s centered around the minimal forms of clothing (usually constructed from hides), together with paint and adornment (of plaited fiber, beads, wire, and carved bone), appropriate

for specific situations: attending funerals, meeting one's in-laws, going to market, or traveling some distance from home.[116]

Social status was clearly marked through differences in dress, whether that was to distinguish between those who were married and those who were not, or to distinguish between those who were wealthy and powerful and those who were not. One important change, as Hay remarked, that had taken place by the early twentieth century was the greater availability of and significant increase in "use of beads and wire by both men and women." This was "one result of expanding trade contacts with the coast and the greater presence of imported goods."[117]

At the same time, by the end of the first decade of the twentieth century, changes in clothing had spread. While missionaries and colonial officials preferred to publish photographs of eastern Ugandans with the minimal clothing that had previously been the norm, photographs of groups of people clearly show that, by 1910, many men had begun to wear either a white cotton wrapper or the coastal white gown known as a kanzu.[118] "As early as 1908," in western Kenya, "the provincial commissioner reported a growing tendency among the men living near Kisumu, the provincial capital, to wear Western-style clothes," in the form of trousers and a tunic.[119] But access to these new forms of clothing was limited and they thus, initially at least, served to mark wealth and status. Colonial officials reinforced this by using clothing to mark the status of certain people. "In 1909 Chief Mumia and a few other western Kenyan leaders recognized as paramount chiefs were issued a dark cloak trimmed with embroidery (to be worn over a *kanzu*)." Photographs offer further evidence that "the official uniform of white kanzu with dark robes" had been adopted by Luo and Luyia chiefs.[120]

As clothing came to mark high social status and wealth among Lunyole speakers and others, so its absence came to be part of the conceptualization of poverty, a marked break from the past when kanzu or Western-style clothing were not present in the region. We see this, for example, in a root Banyole borrowed from speakers of North Nyanza languages, *-dooba*.[121] In Lunyole it yields the verbs *ohudooba*, meaning become a pauper or be in abject poverty, and *ohudobaana*, meaning waste away in poverty and toil, as well as the nominal form *endoobe*, with the meanings of loincloth and sanitary pad. These meanings remained connected with the root when Lunyole speakers borrowed it from Lusoga. Proto-North Nyanza speakers innovated *-*dooba*, meaning become poor, and *-*doobe*, meaning loincloth, from a Proto-Bantu verb, *-*dòb*-, that meant disappear or get lost.[122] In Luganda, *kùdoòba* has the dual meanings be stripped of everything and be destitute. Given the importance in Ganda society of clothing made from bark cloth, skins, and, from the late eighteenth century, cotton as a marker of status, we can read a semantic mapping of poverty, nakedness, and minimal clothing onto this root.[123] Banyole, by contrast—as with their other Greater Luhyia–speaking neighbors, only embraced more extensive clothing well into the twentieth century. Their borrowing of this root points to Lunyole speakers adopting a new conceptualization of poverty in which one's inability to dress appropriately was paramount.

Conclusion

The nineteenth century in eastern Uganda opened in an exceptionally long and severe drought and ended in a shorter, but nonetheless serious, drought, and with the imposition of alien, centralized government. During and in between these moments, people living in the region created, found, and adapted to new opportunities and challenges, whether the extended period of good rainfall from around the mid-1830s to the late 1870s, the expansion of coastal trade, or the intensified threat of slave raiding. Many of the developments of this period touched on people's concepts of poverty and wealth. The periods of drought reinforced ideas among speakers of Greater Luhyia languages that associated poverty with emaciation, while the violence and loss caused by slave raiders underscored the concept of poverty as bereavement. The massive disruption to pastoralist economies caused by the combination of drought and livestock diseases toward the end of the nineteenth century impacted the composition of bridewealth, with women who married into newly impoverished households being remembered as those who married without cattle. The advent of Christian missionaries and their particular forms of morality introduced a new concept of poverty as the result of personal moral failing and a new—or renewed—emphasis on the particular moral failing of poor women who sought some social and economic security through extramarital sex. Christian morality regarding the clothing of bodies likely also fed into the concept of poverty as the inability to adequately clothe oneself, although the advent of new forms of clothing and of status as expressed by those forms of clothing was key. Ganda concepts of wealth and status shaped the adoption of this concept in eastern Uganda as much as did European ones.

Eastern Ugandans retained and reworked their concepts of wealth over the nineteenth and early twentieth centuries, using them to help make sense of some of the changes they were experiencing. The concept of wealth as livestock was in play as people exchanged ivory tusks for cattle, building up substantial herds during a time of more plentiful rains. The drought and epidemics of livestock disease at the end of the nineteenth century profoundly threatened this concept and the social reproduction through bridewealth that cattle underpinned. Conflicts over land associated with the growth and expansion of communities saw women and girls being forcibly married, in a violent expression of the gendered concept of wealth as women and girls. Colonial conquest continued this violence and reinforced the concept of wealth as plunder—plunder both by colonial troops and by those deputized to conquer and govern on behalf of the British. Prolonged drought and the abuse of power by the wealthy could pose a challenge to the concept of wealth as power, but the possibilities for the accumulation of significant wealth by colonial chiefs through taxation and punitive fines gave it new, instrumental meaning. And possibilities for individual accumulation through the colonial state and the new markets it created shored up the concept of wealth as accumulation, even as women were excluded from those opportunities.

CONCLUSION

After this long journey through time and through the many different concepts of poverty and wealth that people in eastern Uganda have held on to, adopted, and discarded over the centuries, it is useful to return to the prayer that a group of Banyole men made to their ancestors in the 1970s.

> We are begging here for wealth, we are begging that the children here may study and learn, here we also would like a motorcar to drive. Wherever we plant millet, wherever we plant sesame, wherever we plant sorghum, may it come quickly and soon. Here let us elope with women, we are begging here for facility in getting wives, here we beg for reproduction, may we strike two by two so that we may have a twin ceremony everyday. Let us be well, you give us life and let us be free from cold.[1]

In their prayer, the men juxtaposed concepts of wealth that can be reconstructed back to the Proto-Greater Luhyia speaker community, some two thousand years ago, with ones that could only have come into being in the twentieth century, and with others from the intervening millennia. They prayed for a successful harvest in millet, which would feed them and their families, but which could also be traded to create other forms of wealth. For these men's ancestors, that trade might have been for livestock or a copper armlet. In the 1970s, the trade might have been for cash to pay school fees or to buy seeds for a cash crop, such as sesame. They prayed for wealth in women and children—and for a way to obtain these that did not involve dependence on their fathers or other elders. As we have seen, the root *-yaandu has been reconstructed back to Proto-Great Lakes Bantu, as much as 2,500 years ago, when it already explicitly referenced wealth in women, as well as heritable wealth. The people in the different speaker communities that existed between then and the 1970s and who spoke words derived from this root to express a concept of wealth mobilized several variations of meaning when they did so. Sometimes speaker communities expanded it to include plunder in warfare and at others they narrowed it to refer to only one form of wealth, such as material possessions. But the gendered concept of wealth it expressed continued to hold significance, and so across centuries, even millennia, the root endured, along with the tensions its meanings held within them. For the Lunyole-speaking men who made this prayer to their ancestors, however, *omwandu* meant bridewealth.

Colonial conquest and, perhaps especially, colonial rule and the market forces of twentieth-century capitalism brought important changes to eastern Uganda and to the ways in which people living there conceived of poverty and wealth, and what it meant to be poor and to be rich. The nineteenth century opened into a multidecadal drought that would have challenged farmers' ideas about what a growing season was and what they might expect to harvest. As in earlier times of profound climate stress, such as during the Medieval Climate Anomaly, people sought new lands in which to grow grains and other foodstuffs, or sought temporary refuge until they could farm their old lands again. Faced with chronic food insecurity, people associated poverty with emaciation and hunger. After the rains returned, people in eastern Uganda benefited from more reliable harvests, but found themselves engaged in new trade networks. As traders from outside the region sought elephant tusks and enslaved people, so some households found themselves in the position of having newfound wealth and others found themselves in positions of intense vulnerability. Those who acquired wealth through trading ivory tusks sought to translate it into other, more salient, forms of wealth, such as livestock, using words derived from the root *-bar-* to refer to the latter. While new economies opened, people held on to older concepts of wealth and poverty. Those older concepts came into play during colonial conquest, with British and African troops plundering for women, children, and livestock as they sought to gain wealth as well as impose defeat. In so doing they, too, acted on the ancient concept of wealth, expressed through the root *-yaandu*.

Colonialism also brought Christianity and with it a new and moralistic concept of poverty as the result of individual failing and of wealth as resulting in moral degradation. But the education offered by Christian missionaries alongside the new opportunities for wage labor on behalf of the colonial state created radically different ways of obtaining wealth. Young men with Protestant or Catholic educations could take on positions of power over their elders and obtain wealth without the need to maintain relationships with their fathers and their fathers' peers. Furthermore, the colonial state explicitly tied together power and wealth through the right of chiefs to retain a portion of the taxes they collected. As I have shown, the conceptualization of wealth and power as entwined was by no means a new phenomenon in eastern Uganda, but the extremes of economic disparity between those with power and those without, and the violent force of the colonial state behind chiefs, shifted the reality and meaning of the relationship between wealth and power. It was chiefs who first had access to the new material markers of wealth—clothing, bicycles, and other consumer goods. Owning and displaying ownership of these goods was a marker of power, as well as wealth, and others increasingly sought access to them. As a result, the absence of ownership of clothing, in particular, came to be part of the conceptualization of poverty, at least among the Banyole. And sixty or so years later, men prayed for wealth, for money for school fees, and for motorcars. When they did so, they invoked the material conceptualizations of wealth—and of poverty—that had long been held by their linguistic ancestors in eastern Uganda, albeit in changed form.

A *longue durée* approach to writing the conceptual history of poverty and wealth in eastern Uganda allows us to see the ways in which the concepts invoked by these Banyole men in the 1970s, and by others across the region in the twentieth and twenty-first centuries, are new and the ways in which they draw on much older ways of thinking about social and economic difference. Taking an interdisciplinary approach to this work, and drawing in particular on the methods of historical linguistics, brings to light much that would otherwise be hidden from view as a result of the limited material evidence and the relatively recent adoption of writing in the region. It also demonstrates that even in contexts of relative material equality between households, people still invested intellectual energy in creating new ways to talk about the poor and the rich, suggesting that even limited economic difference was an issue of concern and was expressed through language. Through all this, I have shown the tremendous diversity in the ways people conceived of poverty and the poor, as well as wealth and the wealthy—a diversity and creativity that stretches deep into the past.

I have also been able to show that, long before the developments of the nineteenth and twentieth centuries, people in eastern Uganda changed their concepts of poverty and wealth as they adjusted to living in new places alongside people speaking different languages, to new climates, and to changes in their own societies. The complexity of eastern Ugandans' intellectual engagements with these concepts stands out as a powerful reminder that colonialism and capitalism did not introduce economic thought to this region. That complexity is reflected in, for example, their concepts of wealth as gendered, as creating honor and respect, and as the result of violence. It is also reflected in the range of material forms of wealth, whether livestock, food, harvested fields, or women and girls. In their intellectual work of conceptualizing poverty, eastern Ugandans allowed for it to be a form of suffering as well as a condition that imposed harm, and they drew a direct connection between poverty and bereavement. They recognized the material lack that marked poverty, and the physical consequences on the human body of living in poverty. But they also condemned the poor for their poverty, whether by tying it to deceit or to women's behavior that contravened social norms. For some, poverty meant having a junior status, for others it resulted in their disparagement, and for others still, it resulted in social death.

The range of concepts of poverty and wealth held by people in eastern Uganda, and their innovativeness in conceiving and reconceiving of these statuses, also underscores the benefit of an approach that foregrounds indigenous meanings, rather than drawing on external theories and concepts. My hope is that in this way, the intellectual work of eastern Ugandans on the questions of what it meant to be poor or rich, over the past two thousand years and more, challenges our assumptions about economic difference, both in eastern Uganda and elsewhere. I hope to have shown that societies in the region were neither egalitarian nor eternally destitute, but instead experienced differences in wealth and in degrees of poverty, in a variety of forms, social and emotional, as well as material. Rich and poor people in those societies took the time to craft a dynamic intellectual and robust tradition about what those differences meant for them. We can learn much from paying attention to that tradition.

APPENDIX

Reconstructed Vocabulary

This appendix contains the evidence that forms the basis of my comparative historical linguistic reconstructions of vocabulary that I draw on in this book. The modern attestations come from 105 interviews that I conducted in Uganda and from published and unpublished lexicographic materials. Please see the bibliography for all references. Note that for reasons of space, this is not a comprehensive listing of all attestations and meanings in all languages. Where I have reconstructed a root to a particular protolanguage, I give the full range of meanings in relevant languages. When there are borrowings and wider distributions of relevance, I also give those.

Abbreviations

*	reconstructed form, not attested
adv.	adverb
adj.	adjective
caus.	causative
cl.	noun class
excl.	exclamation
lit.	literally
n.	noun
n.f.	noun feminine
n.m.	noun masculine
n.p.	noun phrase
pl.	plural
v.	verb
var.	variant
v.i.	intransitive verb
v.p.	verb phrase
v.t.	transitive verb

Entries

1. ***-tak-**, n. cl. 1/2, cl. 14; Gloss: poor person, poverty, lack
   Protolanguage: Proto-Greater Luhyia
   Etymology: from Proto-Bantu *-càk- "desire, wish; search for"[1]
   Greater Luhyia
   Lunyole: *obutahi* n. bereavement; situation of having lost a loved one
   Lumasaaba: *umutaki* n. poor person; *umutakha* n. selfish person; *-takha* adj. avaricious, selfish; *butakha* n. avarice, selfishness, meanness; *khutakha khumanya* v. be ignorant
   Ludadiri: *-takha* adj. avaricious, selfish; *butakha* n. avarice, selfishness, meanness; *khutakha khumanya* v. be ignorant; *umutakha* n. a selfish person
   Lubukusu: *omutakha* n. selfish person, poor person; *buutakha* n. avarice, selfishness, meanness, lack, poverty, want; *khuutakha* v.t. be without, not have, lack; *-takhani* adj. few, scarce; *-takha* adj. avaricious, selfish; *butakha* n. avarice, selfishness, meanness; *khutakha khumanya* v. be ignorant; *khúútakha khúkhwiiyikina* v. be unreliable (lack being confident); *khúútakha khuumanya* v. be ignorant (lack knowing); *xuutaxa* v. menstruate, start menstruation (euphemism)
   Lugwe: *ohudaha* v. want, need; *ohudaha* n. needing, wanting
   Lusaamia: *mubudahano* n. being in need; *ohudaha* v. like, want, need; *omudahani* n. needy person; *obudahano* n. destitution, need
   Lukisa: *okutakha* v. be without, lack, be poor, needy; *omutakha* n. poor person, needy person
   Luwanga: *obutakha* n. lack, poverty, want; *okhutakha* v.t. be without, lack
   Lutsotso: *obutakha* n. lack, poverty, want
   Lulogooli: *umudaka, avadaka* n. poor person, one who lacks, one who has no possessions nor home, beggar; *-daka* adj. poor, destitute, needy; *uvudaka* n. poverty, poorness; *kudaka/khudakha* v. be poor, be without, to lack
   North Nyanza
   Lusoga: *óbútáki* [Lulamoogi only] n. misery, degradation; *butaki* n. be in need; deficiency in conduct, manners, money, etiquette; physical, social, and spiritual ineptitude; *ómútáki* n. poor person, miserable, dejected, degraded
   Lugwere: *óbútáki* n. poverty, abject poverty; *ókutakíwálá* v.i. to become poor; *ókutaká* v.i. to want, need, like, wish, desire, intend, love; *ómúntu*

ómútáki n. poor person; *mutaki* n. poor, destitute person; *kutakirya* v. wish something for somebody

East Nyanza

Chijita: *omutaka* n. poor person

2. *-**tamb**-, n. cl. 1/2, cl. 14, v.i.; Gloss: poor person, poverty, be poor
Protolanguage: Proto-Greater Luhyia
Etymology: Proto-Bantu *-támb- "call; take; receive; walk; play"²

Greater Luhyia

Lunyole: *omudambi* n. bereaved person, orphan, helpless person; *ohudamba* v. be poor, have nothing, be bereft of things; *ohudambadamba* v. get into trouble and roam about in a poor state; *ohudambisania* v. toil, work hard so as to get rid of poverty; *ohudambya* v. cause misery that makes somebody suffer; *ohudamba* v. be bereaved, suffer; *obudambi* n. destitution, pauperism, state of being in abject poverty

Lumasaaba: *bútàmbì/budambi* n. poverty; *umutambi/umudambi* n. poor person, destitute person, helpless person, bereaved person; lack, deficient, few; poor man; *khutàmbà* v. be poor, destitute, be helpless, be bereaved, lack; *khutàmbà* n. lack, deficiency; *khútàmbà* v.t., n. lack; *khutambe* n. being poor; *-tambi* adj. poor, destitute, helpless; *khutàmbísà* v.t. disturb, interrupt, trouble a person, make trouble, torture, interrupt a person working, punish; *kumutambo/khumutambo* n. grief, bereavement, pity; *umudambiro* greeting given to bereaved person; one bereaved; *umutambisa* n. person who disturbs others; *syitambiso* n. punishment; *khitambiso* n. punishment, torture

Ludadiri: *umutambi* n. destitute person, helpless person, bereaved person; lack, deficient, few; poor person, poor man; *-tambi* adj. poor, destitute, helpless, few; *kumutambo* n. grief, sorry, bereavement, pity; *nakhatambi!* excl. never! not at all!; *butámbí* n. smallness

Lubukusu: *omutambi/umutambi* n. poor person, destitute person, helpless person, bereaved person, poor man; lack, deficient, few; *khutàmbà/khútaamba* v. be poor, be destitute, be helpless, be bereaved, lack; *khútàmbà* n. lack, deficiency; *khutambe* n. being poor; *-tambi* adj. poor, destitute, helpless, few; *umutamba/omutamba* n. whore, harlot, prostitute; *omuxhasi omutambi* n. poor woman; *omusani omutambi* n. poor man; *omwana omutambi* n. poor child; *atamba enju* v.p. s/he doesn't have a home; *atamba badeba* s/he doesn't have relatives; *bútàmbì/bhutambi* n. poorness, poverty; smallness; *kumutambo/khumutambo* n. grief, suffering, bereavement, pity, sorrow, poverty; *umutambisa* n. person who disturbs others; *syitambiso/ siitambisyo* n. punishment, torture; *khitambiso* n. punishment, torture; *khúútaambya* v.t. disturb (interrupt), trouble a person, make trouble, torture, cause to be poor; *khutàmbísà/khutambisya* v.t. disturb, interrupt, trouble a person, make trouble, torture, interrupt a person working, punish; *na-xa-tambi!* excl. not at all!, never!

Lugwe: *-tamba* v. work vigorously without resting; *omutambi* n. hard worker

Lusaamia: *-tamba* v. work vigorously without resting; *omutambi* n. hard worker

Lukisa: *omutamba* n. harlot, prostitute

Luwanga: *omutamba* n. harlot, prostitute; *omutambi* n. a needy person; *okhutamba* v.t. need, be lacking in, lack

Lutsotso: *omutamba* n. harlot, prostitute; *omutambi* n. needy person

Luidakho: *mutamba* n. harlot, prostitute; *mutambi* n. needy person; *-tamba* v.i. need, be lacking in, lack; *-tambakhatia* v.t. bungle, make a mess of

Lulogooli: *umudaambi, avadaambi* n. person who is in need or want or trouble, person who's always lacking what to eat or do; *kudaambiza* v. cause trouble, distress, or unhappiness; *daamba* v. to be in need or want or in trouble, to be always lacking what to eat or do; *ikidaambale* n. bad manners, mannered, gross misconduct

Lutirichi: *khutaamba* v. moving anyhow with no direction, especially of a woman leaving a marital home to go to another

North Nyanza

Lusoga: *ókudambá* (Lulamoogi) v. to suffer; *ókudambyá* v. to make someone suffer

Lugwere: *mudambi* n. very, very poor person; *budambi* n. lack, neediness, deficiency, deprivation; *kudamba* v. lack, be in need, be deficient, be without something, labor, toil, struggle, suffer; *kudambadamba* v. suffer a lot; *kudambamu* v. suffer a bit; *kudambya* v. disturb, vex, cause trouble, inconvenience or make somebody suffer; *mudambo* (pl. *midambo*) n. travail, struggle; *kutamba* v. work, act of doing something; *mutambi* n. worker, employee, laborer

East Nyanza

Chijita: *-tambulya* adj. a few, not much

3. *-**paat**-, n. cl. 1/2, v.i.; Gloss: poor person, be poor
Protolanguage: Proto-Greater Luhyia
Etymology: from Proto-Bantu *-pát- "hold"[3]

Greater Luhyia
   Lunyole: *omupati* n. poor person
   Lugwe: *omwaati* n. poor person; *ohuwaata* v. become poor
   Lusaamia: *omwaati* n. poor person; *omuwaati* n. poor person; *ohuwaata* v. become poor; *obwaati* n. poverty; *obuwaati* n. poverty
   Luwanga: *-hara* v.i. be very poor, needy, destitute
North Nyanza
   Luganda: *òmùpaati* n. person whose behavior is uncouth
   Lugwere: *mupaati* (pl. *bapaati*) n. nonrelative, somebody not related to you; *kupaatiika* v. set a limit, boundary regulation; impose a requirement

4. *-yaand-*, n. cl. 3/4; 14; Gloss: wealth, bridewealth, property, possessions
   Protolanguage: Proto-Great Lakes Bantu *-jàandu n. "wealth, property (in women or concerning the transfer of women), heritable, durable wealth (ritual, material, spiritual)"[4]
   Etymology: innovation in Proto-Great Lakes Bantu
   Greater Luhyia
      Lunyole: *omwandu* n. bridewealth; *namwandu* n. widow
      Lumasaaba: *kimyaandu/kimiaandu* n. wealth; *kúmùhàndù* n. property; *kimihándù* n. possessions; *khuhàndà* v. pay (fine, old debt, rent)
      Ludadiri: *khuhàndà* v. pay (fine, old debt, rent)
      Lubukusu: *kimyaàndù/kimihándù* n. property, possessions, goods, belongings, luggage; *kumuandu/kúmwáandu* n. property, possessions
      Lugwe: *namwandu* n. widow; *semwandu* n. widower
      Lusaamia: *emyaando* n. wealth; *musacha ali n'emyaando* n. wealthy man; *muyiinda ali n'emyaando* n. man wealthy in land, cattle, children, wives
      Lukisa: *omwandu* n. chattel, possession, property, article of luggage or personal belonging; *emyandu* n. goods, belongings, luggage
      Luwanga: *omwandu* n. chattel, possession, property, article of luggage or personal belonging; *emyandu* n. goods, belongings, luggage
      Lutsotso: *omwandu* n. chattel, possession, property, article of luggage or personal belonging; *emyandu* n. goods, belongings, luggage
      Luidakho: *mwandu* n. chattel, possession, property, article of luggage or personal belonging
      Lulogooli: *umwaandu, imyaandu* n. wealth or possessions, the homestead of a person, property in general, especially that paid in marriage dowry; *kuzya mu mwaandu* v.p. inherit a woman whose husband has died; *kuha mwandu* v.p. bequeath

North Nyanza
   Luganda: *omwandu* n. royal storehouse for booty; booty of women, slaves, and goods; harem; riches; `*nnamwandú* n. widow; `*ssemwandu* n. widower
   Lusoga: *omwândú* n. bridewealth; *okúkwa omwândú* v.p. pay bridewealth; *namwándú* n. widow
   Lugwere: *mwandu* n. wealth in livestock; *námwándu* n. widow; *sémwándu* n. widower
Rutara
   Runyoro: *omwandu* n. plunder, booty seized in war, generally consisting of women; property left by dead person
   Rutooro: *omwandu* n. plunder, booty seized in war, generally consisting of women; property left by dead person
Western Lakes
   Kinande: *ómwandu* n. inheritance
   Kitembo: *múánda* n. king's servant, unmarried person; *búánda* n. state of servitude; tip given to a servant when sent on an errand; *mwandzu* n. inheritance, large quantity, a lot
East Nyanza
   Chijita: *omwandu* n. inheritance
Western Nilotic
   Luo: *mwandu* n. wealth, riches; *jamwandu* adj. rich, from a wealthy family

5. *-**hind**-, n. cl. 1/2, cl. 14, adj.; Gloss: rich person, riches, wealth, wealthy
   Protolanguage: Proto-Greater Luhyia
   Etymology: from Proto-Bantu *-pìnd- "fold, hem, plait"; "turn, invert, change"[5]
   Greater Luhyia
      Lunyole: *omuɲiinda* n. rich person, rich man; *obuɲinda* n. wealth; *obuɲiinda w'emmere* adj. wealthy in food; *obuɲiinda w'engombe* n. wealth in cattle; *ehiɲindi, ebiɲindi* n. abundance, crowd, herd, group, mass, multitude, collection; many people or domestic animals in one place; year in school; *ehiɲindi* n. old field where cowpeas have recently been harvested; *ehy'obuɲinda* n. wealth, e.g., estate, assets, property; *ohuba omuɲinda* v. be rich, wealthy; state of having much money; *ohuɲindigana* v. stampede; *ohuɲindigania* v. cause a stampede; *ohuɲindigirisa* v. influence, persuade; *ohuɲindiha* v. push; *ohuɲindihira* v. send, push, or direct something toward somebody; *ohuɲindihiha* v. be possible; *ohuɲinduluha* v. be extremely wealthy

Lumasaaba: *buyiindifu/buhiindifu* n. wealth, respect, affluence (concrete), treasure; *omuyiindifu/omuhiindifu* n. wealthy person; *umuhiindifu* n. wealthy person, affluent person, respected person; *khuhiindira* v. to prosper; *buyiinda/buiinda/buhiinda* n. wealth, riches; *umuyiinda/umuhiinda/umuiinda* n. wealthy person; *khúhindìlà* v.i. become wealthy; *-hinda* adj. rich; *-hindifu* adj. affluent, rich, wealthy; *buhindile* n. affluence (abstract), richness; *uwoʾmuhinda* n. prince, princess; *khuhindukha* v. exclaim

Ludadiri: *buhindifu* n. wealth, respect, affluence (concrete), treasure; *khúhindìlà* v.i. become wealthy

Lubukusu: *khuhindala* v. become rich, become wealthy, live long, be permanent; *-inda* adj. rich; *buhìndà/bwiinda/buuyiinda* n. riches, wealth, affluence, treasure; *omuyiindifu* n. rich person; *omwiinda/omuyiinda* n. rich person, wealthy person, respected person; *khuyiinda* v. to squeeze through, to displace, take someone's space; *búúyiindile* n. being rich, affluence; *khúúyiindila* v. become rich; *khuuyiindira* v.i. live very long; *khúuyiindyaala* v.i. become rich, wealthy; *ómuyiindila* n. one who has lived very long

Lugwe: *owuyiinda* n. wealth; *ohuyiindiyala* v. become wealthy; *omwiinda* n. wealthy person, rich person

Lusaamia: *obuyiinda* n. riches, variety of riches; *omuyiinda* n. wealthy person, prosperous person; *muyiinda ali nʾengombe* n. wealthy person with cattle; *muyiinda ali nʾemyaando* n. wealthy person with riches (land, cattle, children, wives); *omuhasi omuyiinda* n. wealthy woman; *omusacha omuyiinda* n. wealthy man; *ohuba omuyiinda* v. become rich; *ohuyindiyala* v. to prosper, progress, be able; *om(u)yìinda* n. prosperous person; *om(u)yíinda* n. basket for flour (wicker basket smeared with cow dung)

Lukisa: *obuhinda* n. wealth, riches; *okhuhindahala* v. become rich, wealthy; *okhuhindahasya* v. enrich, make wealthy; *omuhinda* n. rich person

Luwanga: *omuyindira* n. one who has lived long; *-yindira* v.i. live very long; *-yindifu* adj. aged, long-lived; *obuyinda* n. wealth, riches; *okhuyindasia* v.t. enrich, make wealthy; *okhuyindiala* v.i. become rich, wealthy; *okhuyindira/okhuiindira* v.i. live very long; *omuyinda* n. rich person; *omuyindiri* n. regularly recurring sound, rhythm, beat

Lutsotso: *obuyinda* n. wealth, riches; *okhuhindahala* v. become rich, wealthy; *okhuhindahasya* v. enrich, make wealthy; *omuyinda* n. rich person

Luidakho: *-hindahala* v.i. become rich, wealthy; *-hindahasia* v.t. enrich, make wealthy; *buhinda* n. wealth, riches; *muhinda* n. basket used as a measure; *muhinda* n. rich person; *muyindira/muhindira* n. one who has lived long

Lulogooli: *kihinda* n. basket; *kuhinda* v. push, to jostle, to crowd; *kuhindahala* v. have plenty, to be rich; *kuhindagiridza* v. send a person against their will, push (e.g., a cart); go in the face of advice, orders, etc.; push on in the face of opposition difficulty; *kuhindana* v. crowd each other, jostle each other, press against each other; *kuhindira* v. continue to be permanent, be durable, live to a very old age; *muhindiri* n. elderly person; *ubuhindiri* n. continuance, durability; *kuhiinda* v. swell, bloat, heap up; *kwiihiinda* v. hit hard; *kuhiindika* v. soften, be easily movable; *umuhiinda* n. rich person, wealthy individual; *hiindahala* n. wealth, riches, possessions; *kuhiinduula* v.t. stretch or heave upward something heavy, shift from one place to another, especially heavy logs of wood or rods of iron; *kuhiindyuuka* v. shout with a loud or shrill voice

North Nyanza

Lugwere: *muyinda* n. rich, wealthy person; *buyinda* n. riches, wealth, affluence, prosperity; *kiyindi* n. crowd; *kiyindiyindi* n. dry cowpea stalk or field after harvest

6. *-**jolo**, n. cl. 1/2, cl. 14, adj.; Gloss: poor person, soft person, poor, soft

Protolanguage: Proto-Bantu *jódò* n. cl. 1 "weak; smooth; poor"[6]

Etymology: Proto-Bantu meanings continued in Proto-West Nyanza, but in Proto-Greater Luhyia meaning of poverty not retained

West Nyanza

Luganda: *òmwôlò* n. very poor/poverty-stricken person, destitute wretch, poor wretch, beggar; *òbwôlo* n. poverty, indigence, destitution

Lusoga: *lukyôló* n. pauper

Lugwere: *omwolo* n. age mate, peer, people having approximately the same age; age group; generation; *b'omwolo gumo* n. contemporaries; age mates

Runyoro: *obworobi* n. softness, tenderness; *obworoba* n. softness; *omworoozi* n. guardian, nurse; *mpora* adv. softly; *kworobya* v. soften; *ekirukwaroba* adj. soft

Rutooro: *obworobi* n. softness, tenderness; *obworoba* n. softness; *omworoozi* n. guardian, nurse; *mpora* adv. softly; *kworobya* v. soften; *ekirukwaroba* adj. soft

Runyankore: *obwôro* n. poverty; *kutèèra óbwôro* v.p. become poor; *obwórozi* n. guardianship; *omwôro* n. poor person; *omwórozi* n. guardian; *omwoyóyo* n. lack; *okwó:roba* v. to be tender (e.g., meat), easy (e.g., exam), etc.; *okwó:robya* v.caus. to make soft, etc.; *obwórozi* n. guardianship, husbandry

Rukiga: *obwôro* n. poverty, laziness; *kutéèra óbwôro* v.p. become poor; *obwórozi* n. guardianship, husbandry; *omwôro* n. poor person, lazy person; *omwórozi* n. guardian; *omwoyóyo* n. lack

Ruhaya: *omwóòro* n. poor person; *obworo* n. poverty

Runyambo: *omwôro* n. poor person; *obwôro* n. poverty

Luzinza: *obworo* n. traditional powder

Western Highlands

Rukoonzo: *ómwólo* n. weak person; *óbwólo* n. weakness, docility; *eryólóba* v.i. to weaken; *eryóloberéra* v.i. weaken, weaken a great deal, be too ripe (e.g., a banana); *eryólobyâ* v.t. make cheaper

Kinande: *ómwólo* n. weak person; *óbwólo* n. weakness, docility; *eryólóba* v.i. weaken; *eryóloberéra* v.i. weaken, weaken a great deal, be too ripe (banana); *eryólobyâ* v.t. make cheaper

Kirundi: *umwôro* n. poor person, unhappy person, miserable person, indigent person, beggar; *akanyámworo* n. portion for poor people; *rwôro* adv. poorly, humbly; *ubwôro* n. poverty, misery, destitution, indigence, need, penury, necessity; *kwôroha* v. be light, supple, soft; soften, ease, calm, moderate, be easy

East Nyanza

Chijita: *oBuwóro* n. peace, calm

Eciruuri: *yoorobha* v.i. soften; *yoorofya* v.t. soften

Ekegusii: *omworo* n. lazy person, lax person; *-oro* adj. lazy; *-ororo* adj. yielding, gentle, calm and kind, tame, quiet, easily managed, not stormy, mild, tender, soft, simple, plain, uncomplicated, straightforward, mindless, limp, lacking strength or energy, pliable, flexible, supple, easily influenced, pliant, slack, loose, smooth, pleasant, soft, docile, ease, effortless, elementary: *ororoba* v. (of people) soften one's firm belief, be soft in attitude, relax, slacken; *ororobia* v. ease, simplify, slacken, soften

7. *****-naku**, n. cl. 1/2, cl. 9/10, cl. 14; Gloss: poor person, sorrow, misery, season, time
Protolanguage: Proto-West Nyanza
Etymology: possible connection to Proto-Nilo-Saharan root *$nàk^h$, "to reject," or *-$nàk'w/nà:k'w$ "to suck," but further research is required[7]

North Nyanza

Luganda: *òlùnakù* n. day (pl. *ènnakù*), trouble, sorrow, vexations, sadness; *-nakù* adj. troubled, distressed, wretched, miserable, sorrowful, poor; *kùnakùwala* v.i. be sorry, be troubled, be disturbed, be sorrowful, be miserable, be poor/in great need; *kùnakuwalira* v.t. be troubled, sorry because of, be in misery at; *kùnakùwaza* v.t. afflict, make trouble, make sorrow, make miserable, make wretched, make poor; *obunaku* n. distress, misery, poverty; *obunakuwavu* n. sadness, sorrow, unhappiness; *omunaku* n. poor person, person in misery/wretchedness, disturbed/troubled person; *nakuwavu* adj. sad, sorrowful, unhappy; *ekyennaku* adv. unfortunately

Lusoga: *obúnakú* n. affliction, anguish, destitution, misery, misfortune, depression, grief; *olúnakú* n. day; *omúnakú* n. a wretch, friendless; *omúnakuwavú* n. melancholy; *omúnakughavú* n. miserable, dejected; *énaku* n. adversity, anguish, depression, misery, grief, hardship, hapless, distress, needy, suffering, days (pl. of *olúnakú*), indigent, misfortune; *okúséndá énakú* v. put with misery; *okúnakughálá* v. be unhappy, be indignant, be angry, be miserable, be bereaved, deplore, be desolate, be depressed, be distressed, be downcast, fret, be gloomy, be displeased; *obúnakughavú* n. chagrin; *okúnakugházá* v. upset, disappoint, bereave, depress, distress, displease; *okúnakuwálá* v. become sad, bewail

Lugwere: *naku* n. sadness, sorrow; *ólunáku* n. day; *naku ginu* adv. nowadays; *bunakuwali* n. sorrowfulness, grief, sadness; *kunakuwala* v. grieve, be sad, sorrowful, show remorse

Rutara

Runyoro: *enaku* n. need, trouble, grief, sorrow, misery, poverty, type of small caterpillar; *obunaku* n. poverty; *omunaku* n. poor person, one in trouble or distress, one badly off, man who has no wife to cook for him

Rutooro: *enaku* n. need, trouble, grief, sorrow, misery, poverty, type of small caterpillar; *obunaku* n. poverty; *omunaku* n. poor person, one in trouble or distress, one badly off, man who has no wife to cook for him

Runyankore: *obunáku* n. time, season, period, trouble, chronic misery; *obunáku* n. the poor ones; *omunáku* n. wretch, poor man, destitute; *enáku* (pl.) n. troubles, sorrows, needs, suffering, grief; *kureeba enáku* v. suffer, be in trouble; *kutééra énáku* v. mock; *enáku* n. person, animal, or object of exceptional (good or bad) qualities; *-nakuhara* v.i. become destitute or desolate

Rukiga: *obunáku* n. time, season, period, trouble, chronic misery; *obunáku* n. the poor ones; *omunáku* n. wretch, destitute, poor man; *enáku* (pl.) n. troubles, sorrows, suffering, grief, needs; *kureeba enáku* v. suffer, be in trouble; *kutééra énáku* v. mock; *enáku* n. person, animal, or object of exceptional (good or bad) qualities; *-nakuhara* v.i. become destitute or desolate; *-nakura* v.t. cause someone to be poor and depressed

Ruhaya: *enâku* n. hardship, misery, poverty; *obunâku* n. poverty; *omunâku* n. poor person

Runyambo: *obunáku* n. poverty, time, season; *omunáku* n. poor person; *enáku* n. hardship; *orunáku* n. a single day as a measure of work done

Kikerewe: *olunaku* n. day

Luzinza: *enaku* n. grief, sorrow

Greater Luhyia

Lunyole: *olunaku* (pl. *enaku*) n. day

Lugungu

Lugungu: *bunaku* n. aloneness, state of being with few/no relatives/children; *munaku* n. poor person; somebody who has few/no possessions/relatives, name of a person; *naku* n. orphanhood

8. *-**tung**-, v., n. cl. 1/2, cl. 14; Gloss: be wealthy, wealth, wealthy person

Protolanguage: Proto-Great Lakes Bantu

Etymology: from Proto-Bantu *-túng- "put through; thread on string; plait; sew; tie up; build; close (in)"[8]

North Nyanza

Luganda: *kùtúnga* v.t. sew, thread on string, thread, pin, attach, put on a spit/skewer; *kwetunga* v.i. attach oneself (to), join; *kùtunguka* v.i. become unsewn, become detached/unstuck, come apart, slip off, protrude; *kùtungula* v.t. undo, unstring (beads, old-fashioned holed money), detach (meat from a skewer); *entungiro* n. patches of bark cloth; *omutunzi* n. sewer, tailor

Lusoga: *okútungá* v. to sew, to lace; *omútunzí* n. tailor

Lugwere: *ókutungá* v. sew, stitch, knit, weave, plait; *ókutungá ékísámpa* v. put a hem on a mat; *ómútúngi* n. tailor, weaver, knitter; *ókutungirira* v. do something in succession, straight, in a row, running or alternating; *ókutungulula* v. unpick, unsew; *lutungo* n. series, sequence, progression, queue, chain/course of events, loom; *-tungatunga* adv. alternately, sequentially, in series, in succession, in a row

Rutara

Runyoro: *okutunga* v.t. have, get, acquire, obtain, hold in slavery; *okutunga* v.t. thread on a string or stick; *omutungi* n. man of acquired wealth, rich man; *obutungi* n. wealth; *kutungurra* v.t. flowering of millet, unthread; *kutungukuruka* v.i. become unthreaded, come out of a swamp or forest; *omutungi w'ente* n.p. cattle keeper

Rutooro: *okutunga* v.t. have, get, acquire, obtain, hold in slavery; *okutunga* v.t. thread on a string or stick; *omutungi* n. man of acquired wealth, rich man; *obutungi* n. wealth; *kutungurra* v.t. flowering of millet, unthread; *kutungukuruka* v.i. become unthreaded, come out of a swamp or forest; *omutungi wénte* n.p. cattle keeper

Runyankore: *kutúnga* v. have, get, keep for oneself; thread; *kutúngisa* v. enrich; *kutúnguuka* v.i. develop; *kutúngurura* v.t. develop, enrich, promise, encourage; *omutúngi* n. rich man; *obutúngi* n. riches, property, possessions

Rukiga: *kutúnga* v. have, get, keep for oneself; thread; *kutúngisa* v. enrich; *kutúnguuka* v.i. develop; *kutúngurura* v.t. develop, enrich, promise, encourage; *omutúngi* n. rich man; *obutúngi* n. riches, property, possessions

Ruhaya: *kutúnga* v.t. pierce, pass something through something else; *kutúnga* v.t. keep animal(s), tame; *kutúnga* v.i. become rich, be wealthy; *kutúnga* v.t. give someone something; *omutúngi* n. rich man

Runyambo: *kutúnga* v. prosper, become rich; give wealth to; keep/look after; put something on a stick by piercing it; arrange beads on a string; *kutúnga ebigúnju* v. keep animals; *kutúnga orukúmu* v. point; *omutúnji* n. rich man

Kikerewe: *kutuunga* v. govern, keep animals; *kutuundula* v.t. pierce

Luzinza: *kutunga* v. tie together things on the stick/rope, become rich, point a finger to something/someone; *omutungi* n. rich man

Greater Luhyia

Lunyole: *ohutunga* v. sew, stitch, do needlework, string fish together through gills; *omutungi* n. tailor

Lumasaaba: *khurúngà* v. weave (cloth), sew; *umurungi* n. weaver, tailor, dressmaker; *khurúngà* v. pay a person for something

Ludadiri: *khurúngà* v. weave (cloth), sew (also on machine); *umurungi* n. weaver, tailor, dressmaker

Lubukusu: *khúúruunga* v. pay, join, thread, insert; *khúúruunga* v. weave (cloth), sew, compensate, pay someone for something; *khúúruungira* v. pay for; *khúúruungya* v.t. cause to pay, charge; *kúmuruungi* n. bribe, present brought to powerful person to win their good will; *kúmuruungo* n. payment, fine, compensation, sacrifice, bribe, wages, salary; *ómúruungi* n. payer, weaver, tailor, dressmaker

Lukisa: *okhurunga* v. pay, thread, insert; *okhurungwa* v. be paid; *omurungo* n. payment, sacrifice, fine, compensation

Luwanga: *okhurunga* v.t. pay; *okhurunga* v.t. thread, insert; *omurungo* n. payment, sacrifice, fine, compensation

Lutsotso: *okhurunga* v. pay, thread, insert; *omurungo* n. payment, sacrifice, fine, compensation

Luidakho: *murungo* n. payment, sacrifice, fine, compensation; *-runga* v. pay, thread, insert

Lulogooli: *-tuunga* v. pierce, repay a debt, thread a needle; *ubutungi* n. payment; *kutungira* v. pay for, set a stake at a definite place; *mutungiri* n. one who pays for; *butungiri* n. payment for; *kitungu* n. price, penalty, fine; *kutunguka* v. be pierced or stuck on stick

Lugungu

Lugungu: *kutunga* v. receive, get, obtain, acquire, possess, own, have something that may make you rich; *mutungi* n. rich, wealthy person; *itungu* n. wealth, property, riches, assets

Western Lakes

Kinande: *omṵtsṵngị* [cedilla = high vowel] n. guardian (of children, animals)

Kitembo: *kútsungá* v. thread; *kútsungúlá* v.t. remove (beads) from thread, undo a necklace

Kinyarwanda: *-tûung-* v. have domestic animals, raise animals, possess, be rich, have property in abundance, assure the subsistence of someone, look after someone

Kirundi: *itûnga* n. riches, possession, abundance; *gutûnga* v. possess, have, be the owner of; *kwîtunga* v. look after oneself; *umutûngo* n. property

East Nyanza

Ecejiita: *ebitungwa* (pl.) n. cattle; *kutunga* v.t. pierce, tame, thread; *omutuungi* n. cattle keeper

Eciruuri: *-túgá* v. tame

Ekegusii: *-to:onga* v. pin, impale; *-tuga* v. rear, bring up, raise, tame, raise animals as one's property, nurture, domesticate, breed; *omotugi* n. person who keeps or rears animals, successful animal farmer, foster parent; *obotugi* n. art of animal keeping or rearing

Ikikuria: *omotongo* n. pieces of meat on a skewer, beads on a string; *-tonga* v. to put in series, line up, thread, string, outstrip (someone in a race);

orotongo n. row, line of any crop; *-tungia* v. to string or tighten (bow), string or tune (stringed instrument)

9. ***-gaig-**, n. cl. 1/2, cl. 14; Gloss: rich person, riches, wealth
Protolanguage: Proto-West Nyanza
Etymology: innovation in Proto-West Nyanza
North Nyanza

> Luganda: *òbùga'gga* n. wealth, riches; *-ga'gga* adj. rich, wealthy, plutocrat; *kùga'ggawala* v.i. be rich, become rich; *kùga'ggawaza* v.t. enrich, make wealthy; *òmùga'gga* n. rich person; *omusolo gw'obugagga* n. income tax; *-gaggawala* v.i. be or become rich/wealthy; *òmùnnagagga* n. very rich person; *nnagagga* n. very wealthy person; *ssegagga* n. very rich man
> Lusoga: *obúgaigá* n. affluence, luxury, wealth, fortune, means, riches; *obúgaigá obw'ómuntú* n.p. estate; *omúgáigá* n. rich/wealthy person, rich man with many wives, affluent person, magnate; *okúgaigághálá/okúgaigáwálá* v. become rich; *okúgaigágházá* v. enrich
> Lugwere: *óbugáigá* n. riches; *ókugaigáwála* v.i. become rich; *(ómúntu) ómugáigá* n. rich person; *kusuna óbugáigá* v. get wealth
> Rushana: *mugaaga* n. rich person

Rutara

> Runyoro: *obugaiga* n. riches, wealth; *omugaiga* n. rich person; *kugaigahara* v.i. become rich, become very rich
> Rutooro: *obugaiga* n. riches, wealth; *omugaiga* n. rich person; *kugaigahara* v.i. become rich, become very rich
> Runyankore: *obugáiga* n. riches; *omugáiga* n. rich person, rich man
> Rukiga: *obugáiga* n. riches, wealth; *omugáiga* n. rich person, rich man
> Ruhaya: *obugáiga* n. wealth; *kugáigaara* v.i. become rich, be wealthy; *omugáiga* n. wealthy person, rich person
> Runyambo: *omugéiga* n. rich man
> Kikerewe: *kugaga* v. go bad; *kugagahala* v. become extremely rich
> Luzinza: *omugeega* n. wealthy person

Greater Luhyia

> Lunyole: *obugaaga* n. riches, wealth; *ohuyaba eby'obugaaga* v. mine; *eby'obugaga ebyomwiroba* n. minerals

Lugungu

> Lugungu: *mugaiga* n. rich person

East Nyanza
　Ecejiita: *okugaga* v.i. spoil, go bad; *omugaga* n. rich man; *kugagaala* v. prosper
　Ikikuria: *omogaaka* n. an elder, the head of a homestead or family

10. *-can-, n, v.i.; Gloss: poor person, poverty, being poor, suffer
　Protolanguage: Proto-Nilotic
　Etymology: innovation in Proto-Nilotic; Fitzsimons has reflexes across all branches of Ateker, although, as here, Eastern Nilotic reflexes appear limited to Ateker[9]
　Eastern Nilotic
　　Ngakarimojong: *ŋican, ngican* n. trouble, affliction, hardship, suffering, grief, poverty, adversity, calamity; *akican* v. trouble, disturb, annoy, molest; *acanaanu* n. poverty; *akicana* v.i. lack, be lacking, poor; *akicanut* v.t. trouble, disturb, annoy, molest, afflict, cause to be sad; *akisican* v.t. afflict, punish; *acananut* v. be lacking, poor
　　Ateso: *ican* n. poverty, trouble, misery, distress; *aican* v.t. trouble, vex, pester, annoy, trouble; *aicana* v.i. be poor; *ecanit* n. poverty; *aicanakin* v.i. become poor, suffer; *aicanican* v.t. spoil, waste; *aicanicanun* v.i. to become wasted, spoiled; *aitican* v.t. maltreat, punish, inflict misery/sadness, pester, disturb; *aiticanet* n. punishment, penalty, inconvenience; *aiticanio* n. punishment; *araut na ican* v.p. being poor; *icana* adj. (of person) poor, destitute; (of anything) rare, scarce; *itunganan yeni ican, itunganan yeni ican adepar, itunganan yeni ican noi* n. poor person; *aberu na ican* n. poor woman; *akilokit lo ican* n. poor man; *ikoku yen ican* n. poor child
　　Turkana: *ngican* n. adversity, grief, grievance, hardship, misery, misfortune, poverty, torture, trouble; *akican* v.t. annoy, disturb, grieve, trouble; *akisicanakin* v.t. grieve; *akicane* v.i. lack; *akicanakin* v.t. trouble, v.i. lack; *acanakinet* n. lack, poverty; *akicanut* n. poverty; *icana* adj. destitute, miserable, needy, poor; *icanana* adj. disturbing, troublesome
　Western Nilotic
　　Acoli: *can* n. poverty, need, misery, plate; *can* v. pile, arrange; *canne* n.p. her/his poverty or misery; *canne* v. struggle, suffer; *canno* v.t. arrange, pack, pile up, set in order; *denno can* v.i. suffering, [lit. "he borrowed suffering"]; *lacan* n. poor person, needy person, bachelor

Lango: *càn* n. poverty, want, indigence, misery, death in homestead, helplessness, accident, trouble; *can adot* n. misery; *cane* v. suffer privation, be poor, suffer hardship, want, suffer penury, endure pain; *cano* v. arrange, set in order, line up, list, enumerate, trouble, mistreat; *acan* adj. poor; *acan adot* n. very poor person

Dholuo: *chan* n. want, indigence, poverty; *chando* v.t. lack, need, be in want, be without, harass, bother, trouble, inconvenience; *chandore* v.i. be poor, be in need, suffer, overstrain oneself, overexert oneself, inconvenience oneself; *chandruok* v.t. bother, harass, v.i. suffer privation, suffer hardship, want, suffer penury; *chano* v.t. arrange, set in order, plan, organize, make arrangement, intend to; *chano* n. poverty, want; *chanruok los* n. arrangement; *gima ochan* n. list; -*chan* adj. poor; *mochando* adj. poor; *chanore* v.t. be in line, form a line (as for a parade), form a pattern; be organized; *chanruok* n. arrangement, classification, grouping, plan; *jachan* n. poor person

Dhopadhola: *chan* n. planning, layout, order, poverty, destitution; *chandirok* v. suffer, be in trouble; *chandirok* n. suffering, trouble, destitution; *chandi* n. misery, poverty, destitution; *chandò* v.t. punish, mistreat, make miserable, torment, annoy; *chandò* v.i. be in need of, be poor in; *chanirok* v. take position in rows, ranks, sorting out; *chanò* v. put in order, rows, arrange; *candere* v.i. suffer (e.g., due to poverty); *candere* v.t. subject children to suffering; *cando* v.t. punish; *jacandi* n. poor person, very poor person; *dhano ma ja cand* n. poor person; *dhano ma ja cand saw* n. very poor person; *dhako jacandi* n. poor woman; *dhako ma ja cand* n. poor woman; *jichwo jacandi* n. poor man; *jal ma ja cand* n. poor man; *nyathi jacandi* n. poor child; *nyathi ma ja cand* n. poor child

Lango: *càn* n. poverty, want, indigence, misery, death in the homestead, helplessness, accident, trouble; *can adot* n. misery; *cane* v. be poor, suffer privation, suffer hardship, want, suffer penury, endure pain; *cano* v. arrange, set in order, line up, list, enumerate, trouble, mistreat; *acan* adj. poor; *acan adot* n. very poor person

11. *-**panan**-, n.; Gloss: pauper, orphan
    Protolanguage: Proto-Southern Nilotic
    Etymology: loan from Proto-Iraqw[10]; later borrowed from Proto-Southern Kalenjin into Greater Luhyia languages
    Iraqw
        Iraqw: *panmo* n. orphan; *paanimoo* n.m. (pl. *paneemoo*) orphan; *pan'uuma* n.f. orphanhood

Kalenjin
  Kupsabiny: *pánánɛːt* n. poor person, orphan; *pananci* v. beg; *pananiadit* n. poverty, destitution; *panan* adj. poor; *pananiet ngat* n. very poor person; *chesiet pananiet* n. poor woman; *pondeti pananiet* n. poor man; *lekwet pananiet* n. poor child; *panan* n. poor person, beggar; *panan nyobo mi chan* n. destitute person; *chuto nyo pananat* n. poor person; *panandit* n. poverty; *panan nyobo mi chan* n. destitute person; *bananet* n. orphan
  Nandi: *banan* n. poorness; *bananda* n. poorness, insufficiency; *ke-banan* v.i. look uncared for, lack something; *ke-bönön-ji* v. plead for someone, appeal, beg; *bananet/kɪpánáɲât* n. poor person, orphan; *panan* n. poor man (no relations and no property)
  Pok: *pánánɛːt* n. poor person, orphan
  Päkot: *pananɛ* n. poor person, orphan
  Kipsikiis: *kɪpánánâːt* n. poor person, orphan; *keːpanan* v. be poor
  Keyo: *pánăn* n. poor person, orphan
  Tuken: *pánan, pánanaːn* n. poor person, orphan
  Markweta: *pánân* n. poor person, orphan
  Kony: *pánánɛːt* n. poor person, orphan
  Bong'om: *panăn* n. poor person, orphan
  Terik: *kɪpánáɲâːt* n. poor person, orphan
  Sogoo: *pánanĕːt* n. poor person, orphan
  Akie: *pananɛ* n. poor person, orphan

Great Luhyia
  Lubukusu: *khúumanana* v.i. become poor; *ómumanani* n. poor person; *búúmanani* n. poverty; *omubanani* n. destitute person; *bhubanani* n. (extreme) poor(ness)
  Lugwe: *omumanani* n. poor person; *ohumanana* v. become poor; *owumanani* n. poverty
  Lusaamya: *obumanani* n. poverty; *omumanani* n. poor person; *ohumanana* v. become poor
  Lukisa: *obumanani* n. poverty; *okhumanana* v.i. be poor, needy, destitute, become poor, need, be lacking in, lack
  Luwanga: *omumanani* n. poor person; *okhumanana* v.i. be very poor, needy, destitute; *obumanani* n. poverty; *okhumanna* v.i. become poor
  Lutsotso: *omumanani* n. poor person; *obumanani* n. poverty; *okhumanana* v.i. be poor, needy, destitute, become poor, need, be lacking in, lack
  Luidakho: *-manana* v.i. become poor; *bumanani* n. poverty; *mumanani* n. poor person

Lulogooli: *mumanani* n. poor person; *ubumanani* n. poverty; *uvumanani* v. lack, be poor and needy, be in need

12. **-bar-*, v., n.; Gloss: get rich, be rich, wealth, riches
    Protolanguage: Proto-Tung'a; in Proto-Ateker shift in meaning to specify wealth in livestock
    Etymology: from Proto-Nilotic "increase in size"[11]
    Eastern Nilotic
    Ngakarimojong: *abaru* n. riches, wealth; *ekabaran* n. wealthy person, rich man, capitalist; *akibar* v. get rich, become wealthy; *ibarasit* n. domestic animal, cattle; *ebarit* adj. wealthy; *abarit* adj. rich, wealthy; *abarun* v. become rich; *ngibaren* n. livestock (pl.), riches, good luck; *ebarar* v.i. be plenty, numerous
    Turkana: *abar(u)* n. affluence, prosperity, wealth; *ibarasit* n. cattle, livestock; *ngibaren* n. prosperity, livestock (pl.); *akibar* v.i. prosper; *ebarit* n. prosperity, riches, wealth; *ebarit* adj. affluent, wealthy, rich; *abaran* adj. affluent; *ekabaran* n. affluent person
    Ateso: *ibarasit* n. a cow, goat, sheep, etc., as wealth; *ibaren* n. livestock; *aitabar* v.t. make rich, wealthy; *ebarit* adj. (of person) wealthy, rich in livestock, money, etc.; *ebarara* adj. (of livestock, birds, etc.) be many; *ekabaran* n. rich man, wealthy man; *abar* n. wealth, treasure; *abarit noi* n. riches; *ibaren* (pl.) n. livestock as wealth; *abaran* n. rich man; *itunganan yeni ebarit* n. rich person; *aberu na abaran* n. rich woman; *akilokit lo abaran* n. rich man
    Maa: *abar* v. profit

13. **-lim-*, n., v.; Gloss: wealth, riches, visit
    Protolanguage: Proto-Southern Luo
    Etymology: Proto-Southern Luo semantic innovation, from older Western Nilotic or Nilotic root
    Southern Luo
    Acoli: *lim* n. visit, money, wealth especially in livestock, property; *lim* adj. sweet; *limo/limmo* v.t. visit, visiting for inspection; *citto ka limmo* vp. going to visit your friend; *limu* n. graveyard; *limuk* adv. totally, completely; *alimma* n. slave
    Dholuo: *limo* v.t. visit, call on

Dhopadhola: *lím* n. gift, present, wealth, immense wealth, earnings; *ólimo lim (ongang)* v.p. he is rich; *límó* v. receive, pay a visit, check (crops in the garden, food when cooking)

Lango: *lim* n. riches, wealth; *lim* adj. sweet; *limo* n. visitation, cemetery; *limo* v. visit, receive

Nuer-Dinka

Dinka: *lim* v. beg, look for; *lim* n. servant

14. **-gad-**, n. cl. 1/2, cl. 14; Gloss: poor person, poverty

Protolanguage: Lunyole

Etymology: from Proto-Greater Luhyia *-gad- v. deceive, cheat; n. deceiver, cheat

Greater Luhyia

Lunyole: *omugadi* n. poor person; *obugadi* n. poverty, destitution, pauperism, abject poverty

Lubukusu: *buukati* n. deceit

Lukisa: *obukati* n. deceit, cunning, craftiness, cheating, particularly in trade; *okhukatilisya* v.t. coax, wheedle, deceive with fair words, flatter; *omukati* n. liar

Luwanga: *okhukatia* v.t. deceive, cheat, lie, tell untruths; *obukati* n. deceit

Lutsotso: *obukati* n. deceit, cunning, craftiness, cheating, particularly in trade

Luidakho: *bukati* n. deceit; *-kata* v.t. lie, tell untruths, deceive, cheat

Lulogooli: *kugada/kugaada* v. lie, cheat, say untruths, deceive, practice deceit, beguile; *kugadahala* v. be lazy, idle, shiftless, wander about; *mugadi* n. deceiver, cheat; *kugadira* v. deceive; *ubugadi* n. deceit; *khugata* v. to deceive; *ubugati* n. deception

15. **-ŋat-**, v.i.; Gloss: suffer, live a life of poverty

Protolanguage: Lunyole

Etymology: from Proto-Greater Luhyia *-ŋat- v.i. become emaciated, ill

Greater Luhyia

Lunyole: *ohuŋata* v. suffer in exile, be ostracized, lack everything and suffer, live life of poverty

Lumasaaba: *khung'aha* v.i. become thin

Ludadiri: *khung'aha* v.i. become thin

Lubukusu: *khung'aha/khúúng'aa* v.i. become thin, weak, ill; *-ng'ahu* adj. thin
Lukisa: *okhung'aha* v.i. become weak and tired, become thin, become soft
Luwanga: *-ng'aha/okhung'aa* v.i. become thin, weak, ill
Lutsotso: *okhung'aa* v.i. become thin, weak, ill
Luidakho: *-ng'aha* v.i. become thin, weak, ill
Lulogooli: *-ng'aha* v. become slim, thin, wear out, emaciate, slender

16. **omuhombe**, n. cl. 1/2; Gloss: extremely wealthy person
Protolanguage: Lunyole
Etymology: from Proto-Bantu *-kómb-* v. "scrape, dig; lick (food) with finger"[12] via Proto-Greater Luhyia
Greater Luhyia
Lunyole: *omuhombe* n. extremely wealthy, rich person; *ohuhomba* v. lick; *ohuhombaho* v. find taste of something by licking; *ohwehomba* v. lick lips or fingers when eating; *ehitahombehaho* n. unattainable thing, unachievable thing, impossible thing, something bland, tasteless
Lumasaaba: *khukómbà* v. lick; *khukhwíkòmbà* v. wish, long for, desire, cover; *bubwikómbi, lil'ikómbi* n. wish, desire
Ludadiri: *khukómbà* v. lick; *khukhwíkòmbà* v. wish, long for, desire, covet, crave; *bubwikómbi, lil'ikómbi* n. wish, desire
Lubukusu: *khúúkhoomba* v.t. lick, suck (e.g., a sweet), taste, sip, clear a plate clean; *khukhwíkòmbà* v. wish, long for, desire, covet, crave; *khúúkhoombákhô* v. lick on something, drink alcohol; *khúúkhoombelesya* v.t. cause to lick clean, deceive, flatter, toady; *líikhoombana* n. act of licking each other, kiss; *búúkhoomba* n. porridge, that which is sipped; *imakómbè* n. shrine; *bubwikómbi* n. wish, desire; *oweekomba* n. admirer; *liliikoomba* n. admiration; *béémwiikóómbe* n. circumcision candidates, those who have just been circumcised; *líikóombe* n. hut where circumcised boys go to live until healed
Lukisa: *okhukhomba* v.t. lick, suck, taste something; *okhukhomberesya* v.t. lick clean, deceive, flatter, toady
Luwanga: *okhukhomba* v.t. lick, suck, taste something; *okhukhomberesya* v.t. lick clean, deceive, flatter, toady
Lutsotso: *okhukhomba* v.t. lick, suck, taste something; *okhukhomberesya* v.t. lick clean, deceive, flatter, toady
Luidakho: *khomba* v. eat meat or other relish without staple food, or out of proportion to the staple food; *khomba* v.t. lick, suck (e.g., sweet); *khomba* v.t. lick clean, deceive, flatter, toady

Lulogooli: *khukhomba* v. lick, taste

North Nyanza

Lusoga: *omúkombé* n. rich/wealthy person, magnate; *omúkombé ow'ábákazí* n. polygamous man; *okúkombá* v. lick, taste (food), lap; *okúkombáku* v. to sip, to kiss. Note: meaning of rich person is a loan from Lunyole

17. **-yaay-**, n. cl. 3/4; Gloss: prosperity, peace, blessing

Protolanguage: Lunyole

Etymology: possibly from Proto-Great Lakes Bantu, via Proto-Greater Luhyia, *-yaay-* n. hunt, plunder, loot; v. hunt, plunder; or an areal form between Greater Luhyia and West Nyanza[13]

Great Luhyia

Lunyole: *omuyaaya* n. prosperity, peace, blessing, luck; *ohuyaaya* v. greedily grab food at a communal meal

Lumasaaba: *biyaaya* n. plunder, take quickly and greedily, loot; *khuyaaya* v. plunder; *bibintu biyaaye* n. booty

Lubukusu: *biyaaya* n. plunder; *khuyaaya* v. plunder, take quickly and greedily, loot; *bíbiindu bííyaaye* n. booty; *biiyaaya* n. those that have been taken; *biiyaaye* n. booty; *búúyaaya* n. new food, recently harvested food

Lukisa: *okhuyaya* v.t. snatch, take by force

Luwanga: *okhuyaya* v.t. snatch, take by force, despoil

Lutsotso: *okhuyaya* v.t. snatch, take by force

Luidakho: *-yaya* v.t. snatch, take by force, despoil

Lulogooli: *kuyaaka/kuyaaga* v.t. ambush, snatch from, plunder; *kwiyaya* v. go about at will, conquer, overcome

West Nyanza

Luganda: *kwâya/kuyaya* v.t. pillage (food), plunder, forage, steal food in a greedy manner; *obwayi* n. sacking, pillage, expropriation of property by force; *òmwâyi* n. marauder, plunderer, pillager; *-âyè* adj. stolen by pillage; *òlwâyo* n. loot, plunder, food taken as offering to *lubaale* shrine; *kwayira* v.t. forage for; *kwayirira* v.t. forage for constantly; *kùyayùka* v.i. be frayed, wear out

Runyoro: *okwaya* v.t. raid, pillage, cut down food plants, loot; *omwayi* n. marauder, raider

Rutooro: *okwaya* v.t. raid, pillage, cut down food plants, loot; *omwayi* n. marauder, raider

Runyankore: *kwaya* v. plunder (food); *omwayo* n. plunder (esp. food)

Rukiga: *kwaya* v. plunder (food); *omwayo* n. plunder (esp. food)
Runyambo: *kwaya* v. loot, plunder, take away everything

18. **omugerama**, n. cl. 1/2; Gloss: rich woman, wealthy woman
    Protolanguage: Lunyole
    Etymology: loan from Proto-North Luhyia **-kelema* n. respected woman, woman of high rank
    Greater Luhyia
    Lunyole: *omugerama* n. rich woman, wealthy woman
    Lumasaaba: *omukelema* n. married woman of rank; lady or respected woman; also used to refer to "wife of" e.g., *omukelema wa*
    Ludadiri: *omugyelema* n. lady or respected woman, woman of honor and respectability; also used to refer to "wife of" e.g., *omugyelema wa*
    Lubukusu: *ómukelema* n. married woman of rank, queen; *nábúkéléma* n. beloved one (female), queen, last wife in a polygynous family

19. **-lyasi*, adj.; Gloss: selfish, mean
    Protolanguage: Proto-North Luhyia
    Etymology: compound word from **-lya* v. "eat" and **-si* adv. "entirely, all"
    Greater Luhyia
    Lumasaaba: *umulyasi* n. selfish person; *ubulyasi* n. selfishness, meanness
    Ludadiri: *umulyasi* n. selfish person; *ubulyasi* n. selfishness, meanness
    Lubukusu: *umulyasi* n. selfish person

20. **-tali*, adj. n. cl. 1/2, cl. 14; Gloss: poor, poor man, poverty
    Protolanguage: Proto-North Luhyia
    Etymology: unclear, but possibly a compound from the negative infix *-ta-* and the verbal *-li* to be
    Greater Luhyia
    Lumasaaba: *-tali* adj. poor; *butali* n. poverty; *umutali* n. poor man
    Ludadiri: *-tali* adj. poor; *butali* n. poverty; *umutali* n. poor man
    Lubukusu: *-tali* adj. poor; *bu(u)tali* n. poverty; *umutali/omutali* n. poor man

21. **-tihi*, n. cl. 14; Gloss: riches, great wealth in things, prosperity
    Protolanguage: Proto-North Luhyia
    Etymology: possibly from Proto-Bantu **-dip-* v. "pay, compensate"[14]

Greater Luhyia
Lumasaaba: *butihi* n. great wealth in things; *khutiya* v. prosper
Ludadiri: *butihi* n. great wealth in things
Lubukusu: *butii* n. riches

22. *-**bayi**, n. cl. 1/2, cl. 14; Gloss: person wealthy in livestock, great wealth in livestock
Protolanguage: Proto-North Luhyia
Etymology: loan from Proto-Kalenjin (*pai) into Greater Luhyia with meaning "keep cattle"; independent innovations in Proto-North Luhyia and Lusaamia with expansion of meaning to "great wealth in livestock" and "a person wealthy in livestock"[15]

Greater Luhyia
Lunyole: *ohubaya* v. rear animals; *obwayi* n. animal husbandry, payment made to a herdsman for looking after one's animals (usually in form of an animal); *omwayi/omubayi* n. herdsman; *ehyayo* n. area where grazing of animals is done

Lumasaaba: *bubwáhì* n. grazing, great wealth in livestock; *bubáhì* n. great wealth in livestock; *umwáhì* n. shepherd, herdsman, reaper; priest, Protestant; *khukhwahílìsà* v. look after, take care of (animal, child, thing); *bubwahílìsì* n. care (good care); *kamàhílò/lilyàhílò* n. pasture; *khukhwàhísà* v.t. herd, graze

Ludadiri: *bubwáhì* n. grazing, great wealth in livestock; *bubáhì* n. great wealth in livestock; *umwáhì* n. shepherd, herdsman, reaper; priest, Protestant; *khukhwahílìsà* v. look after, take care of (animal, child, thing); *kamàhílò/bwàhílò* n. pasture; *khukhwàhísà* v.t. herd, graze

Lubukusu: *bubwahílìsì* n. care (good care); *búbwaayi* n. grazing, tending cattle, great wealth in livestock; *ómwaayi* n. shepherd, cowherd, herdsman, herder, reaper, priest, Protestant; *kámaayílwe* n. grazing ground, pasture; *khúkhwaaya* v. graze, herd (sheep, cattle, etc.); *khúkhwaayilisya* v. look after, take care of; *khúkhwaayisya* v.t. cause to herd, graze; *bibyayo* n. domesticated animals; *sisyayo* n. (a head of) cattle; *omubaayi* n. person with many animals

Lusaamia: *omwayi* n. person wealthy in cattle; *omwayi byayo* n. herder with many cattle

Lukisa: *okhwaya* v.i., v.t. graze, herd (sheep, cattle, etc.), gather vegetables; *omwayi* n. shepherd, herder (of cows, goats, sheep, etc.); *obwayiro* n. grazing ground; *eshyayo* n. goat or sheep, the herd while grazing

Luwanga: *okhwaya* v.i., v.t. graze, herd sheep, cattle, etc., gather vegetables; *omwayi* n. shepherd, herder (of cows, goats, sheep, etc.); *obwayiro* n. grazing ground; *eshyayo* n. goat or sheep, the herd while grazing; *efwayo* n. flocks

Lutsotso: *okhwaya* v.i., v.t. graze, herd (sheep, cattle, etc.), gather vegetables; *omwayi* n. shepherd, herder (of cows, goats, sheep, etc.); *obwayiro* n. grazing ground; *eshyayo* n. goat or sheep, the herd while grazing; *ebyayo* n. flocks

Luidakho: *-khwaya* v.t. graze; herd (sheep, cattle, etc.), gather vegetables; *shiayo* n. flock, herd, crowd; *shyayo* n. goat, sheep, herd while grazing; *shayo* n. grazing ground; *mwayi* n. shepherd, cowherd, etc.

Lulogooli: *kwa(a)ya* v. herd, shepherd, tend sheep, goats, cattle in field, feed (an animal); *mwayi* n. shepherd; *ubwayi* n. herdsmanship, turn to herd; *kyayo* n. flock, herd

North Nyanza

Lusoga: *okwâyá* v. rear, graze; *omwâyi* n. shepherd; *ebyâyó* n. livestock, herd

Lugwere: *ókubayá* v. keep (domestic animals); take care of domestic animals; look after domestic animals

Kalenjin

Nandi: *ke-bai* v. feed, keep cattle; see another person in an irregular relationship (man and woman); *kebai tuga* v. keep cattle; *ke-bai kei* v. have one another in a common-law relationship

23. *****-kasa**, n. cl. 1/2, cl. 14; Gloss: wealthy person, respected person, leader, wealth, honor, leadership

Protolanguage: Proto-North Luhyia

Etymology: from Proto-Greater Luhyia **mukasa* n. brass jewelry, copper jewelry; from Proto-Bantu **-kác-* v.i. "dry up; coagulate; be hard";[16] but there is also a Proto-West Nyanza and Proto-Greater Luhyia areal or Proto-Great Lakes Bantu root **-kasa* v. be useful, good, suitable

Greater Luhyia

Lunyole: *omwene mugasa* n. (idiom) owner; *ohugasa* v. be useful, beneficial, fruitful; *omuuta atagasa* n. nobody, somebody having no influence; *omugasa* n. bangle

Lumasaaba: *-kás(y)à* adj. rich, wealthy; *bukás(y)à* (pl.) n. wealth, riches, respect, honor, leadership; *bubwikásyà* n. great riches; *umukás(y)à* n. respected person, wealthy person, leader, chief of county, formerly also the judge; *umugasya* n. traditional ruler, god, lineage head

Ludadiri: *-kás(y)à* adj. rich, wealthy; *bukás(y)à* n. wealth, riches, respect, honor, leadership; *bubwikásyà* n. great riches; *umukás(y)à* n. respected person, wealthy person, leader, chief of county, formerly also the judge

Lubukusu: *umukás(y)à* n. chief justice; *bukasa* n. wealth, riches, honor, leadership; *buukasa* n. chiefdom, kingship; *khúúkaliisya kumukasa* v. increase wealth, status; *kùmùkàsà* n. gold, brass, brass ornament, copper; *omukasa* n. respected person, wealthy person, leader, clan elder, county chief, judge, village headman; *owekumukasa* n. king; *bubwikasa* n. great riches

Lukisa: *omukasa* n. brass, brass ornament; *okhukasa* v.i. be suitable, appropriate, fitting, in good order, pleasing, beautiful, become sweet, nice, good, right, etc.

Luwanga: *omukasa* n. brass, brass ornament; *okhukasa* v.i. be suitable, seemly, appropriate, fitting, in good order, pleasing, beautiful

Lutsotso: *okhukasa* v.i. be suitable, appropriate, fitting, in good order, pleasing, beautiful, become sweet, nice, good, right, etc.; *omukasa* n. brass, brass ornaments

Luidakho: *-kasa* v.i. be suitable, seemly, appropriate, fitting, in good order, pleasing, beautiful; *mukasa* n. brass; brass ornament

Lulogooli: *mugasa* n. brass; *kugasa* v. be well, be good, be prosperous; *kugasira* v. be good for, suitable to, be fit; *ubugasu* n. prosperity, blessing, well-being; *-gasu* adj. well, good, gentle

24. *-losela, n. cl. 1/2, cl. 9/10, v.t.; Gloss: old woman; prosperity; prosper, develop, increase

Protolanguage: Proto-North Luhyia

Etymology: Proto-North Luhyia innovation with semantic overlap between increase and develop on the one hand and old age for women, only, on the other; with semantic extension to "prosperity" in Lumasaaba and Ludadiri; the latter may be a Proto-North Luhyia development but the Lubukusu sources are not consistent

Greater Luhyia
- Lumasaaba: *inzilò(o)sèlà* n. prosperity; *khulò(o)sèlà* v.t. add, increase, develop; *khukhwiló(ó)sèlà* v. continue, proceed, maintain, improve, develop, be prosperous, multiply (of living beings); *khulosela(kho)* v. give extra; *khuloselayo* further(more); *lililóósèlèlà* n. improvement; *umulóòsi* n. old woman, witch
- Ludadiri: *inzilò(o)sèlà* n. prosperity; *khulò(o)sèlà* v.t. add, increase, develop; *khukhwiló(ó)sèlà* v. continue, proceed, maintain, improve, develop, be prosperous, multiply (of living beings); *khulosela(kho)* v. give extra; *khuloselayo* further(more); *lililóósèlèlà* n. improvement; *-lóòsi* adj. old (of women)
- Lubukusu: *khukhwiló(ó)sèlà* v. continue, proceed, maintain; *khulosela(kho)* v. give extra; *eeloosela* n. prosperity; *xuuloosya* v. follow (as in birth order), explain, talk; *xuxwiloosela/xuxwiloosya* v. continue, proceed, maintain, keep following; *xuulosela(xo)* v. give extra; *xuuloselayo* further(more); *liilooselela* n. improvement; *omulóòsi* n. old woman, witch; *khúúloosyaala* v. become old and wise (of a woman); *omuloosi omukhulu* n. big woman
- Lulogooli: *umuloosya* n. mature person, reasonable person

25. **munyerere**, n. cl. 1/2; Gloss: thin person, poor person
Protolanguage: Lubukusu
Etymology: loan from Luyia languages; in Proto-Luyia we find **munyerere* n. "someone thin (not due to illness), poor person"; and in Proto-Great Lakes Bantu we find **-nyerere* adj. "narrow, thin"
Greater Luhyia
- Lumasaaba: *namunyélè* n. very long beer banana (knee-high)
- Lubukusu: *siinyèlélè* adj. thin; *bunyelele* adj. narrow; *ómunyelele* n. naturally thin person (not due to illness), poor person
- Lukisa: *omunyerere* n. naturally thin person (not due to illness), poor person; *obunyerere* n. narrowness (e.g., of a path), thinness (e.g., of a person)
- Luwanga: *omunyerere* n. person who is normally thin (not result of illness), poor person; *-nyerere* adj. narrow, thin
- Lutsotso: *omunyerere* n. naturally thin person (not due to illness), poor person; *-nyerere* adj. narrow, thin
- Luidakho: *munyelele/munyerere* n. naturally thin person (not due to of illness), poor person

Lulogooli: *-nyerere* adj. thin, lean, slim, young, youthful; *munyerere* n. young person
West Nyanza
Luganda: *olunyere* n. wire; *akanyere* n. (wire) bracelet; *kinyere* n. large bracelet/earrings
Lusoga: *akánhéré* n. bracelet; *ekínhéré* n. necklace
Runyoro: *ekinyeerre* n. thin, copper wire bracelet; *orunyeerre* n. thin twisted copper wire bracelet; *omunyerre* n. a mongoose
Rutooro: *ekinyeerre* n. thin, copper wire bracelet; *orunyeerre* n. thin twisted copper wire bracelet; *omunyerre* n. a mongoose
Runyankore: *orunyerére* n. bangle
Rukiga: *orunyerére* n. bangle
Ruhaya: *enyérere* n. metal bracelet, bangle
Runyambo: *ekinyerere* n. long, straight hair; *enyerére* n. copper wire worn on legs and arms
East Nyanza
Ikikuria: *-nyerre* adj. thin, slender, narrow

26. **eekhabi**, n. cl. 9; Gloss: prosperity, fortune, blessings, good luck
Protolanguage: Lubukusu
Etymology: semantic extension from Proto-Greater Luhyia *-kabi* n. luck, blessing; with loans into Lugwere and Lusoga
Greater Luhyia
Lunyole: *ekabi* n. luck, chance, good fortune; *ohusuna ekabi* v. be fortunate; *ow'ekabi* n. lucky person, fortunate person; *ekabi* n. ground beetle, insect believed to bring good luck (*sp. Calosoma sycophanta*)
Lumasaaba: *inkhàbi* n. good luck, blessing, opportunity; *inkhabi 'mbi* n. bad luck; *-e'nkhabi'mbi* adj. unfortunate; *khunyola zinkhabi* v. be fortunate; *bukabi* n. beneficence, charity, providence, good luck; *umukabi* n. benefactor
Ludadiri: *ikakhàbi* n. good luck, blessing, opportunity; *inkhabi 'mbi* n. bad luck; *-e'nkhabi'mbi* adj. unfortunate; *khunyola zinkhabi* v. be fortunate; *bukabi* n. beneficence, charity, providence, good luck; *umukabi* n. benefactor
Lubukusu: *inkhàbi* n. good luck, blessing; *ikhabi* n. prosperity; *inkhabi 'mbi* n. bad luck; *-e'nkhabi'mbi* adj. unfortunate; *khunyola zikhabi* v. be fortunate, be prosperous; *bukabi* n. beneficence, charity, providence,

good luck; *umukabi* n. benefactor; *kumukabwa* n. good luck, blessing, opportunity, prosperity

Lukisa: *ikhabi* n. luck, fortune, blessing, bless you (after someone sneezes); *ikhabi mbi* n. bad luck; *tshikhabi* excl. bless you

Luwanga: *ikhabi* n. luck, fortune, blessing; *ikhabi imbi* n. bad luck

Lutsotso: *ikhabi* n. luck, fortune, blessing, bless you (after someone sneezes); *ikhabi mbi* n. bad luck

Luidakho: *ikhabi* n. luck, fortune, blessing; *ikhabi mbi* n. bad luck

Lulogooli: *inkavi/ingavi* n. good fortune, good luck, bad luck, blessing, curse

West Nyanza

Lusoga: *enkábí* n. blessing, blessedness, good luck, chance, luck, big weevil (in banana plantation)

Lugwere: *énkábi* n. luck

27. **-hulahulana-*, v.i., n. cl. 15; Gloss: prosper; prosperity
Protolanguage: Proto-Gwe-Saamia and Lunyole areal form
Etymology: Proto-Bantu **-kúd-* v. "grow up"[17]
Greater Luhyia

Lunyole: *ohulahulana* v.i. prosper; *ohuhulahulania* v. develop, progress, modernize

Lugwe: *ohuhulahulana* v. to prosper; *ehulahulana* n. prosperity

Lusaamia: *ohulahulana* v. to prosper, progress; *ohulahulana munganga eye* v. progressing in her/his business

28. **-nyal-*, n. cl. 1/2, 14, v.; Gloss: wealthy person, wealth; become wealthy
Protolanguage: Proto-Gwe-Saamia
Etymology: from Proto-Greater Luhyia **-nyal-* n. "power"
Greater Luhyia

Lumasaaba: *bunyali* n. ability, success; *búnyàlà* n. power, energy, authority, capability; *khunyàlà* v. can, be able to, may, succeed, cope with, manage, control, govern, compel

Ludadiri: *bunyali* n. success; *búnyàlà* n. power, energy, authority, capability; *khunyàlà* v. can, be able to, may, succeed, cope with, manage, control, govern, compel

Lubukusu: *búúnyali* n. power, ability, energy, authority, capability; *khúúnyala* v.i. can, have opportunity to, have ability to, be able to, may, succeed, cope with, manage, control, govern, compel; *senyalata* n. helpless person

Lugwe: *owunyali* n. wealth; *omunyali* n. wealthy person, rich person

Lusaamia: *obunyali* n. total collection of riches, wealth; *ohunyalira* v. ability to transact, become wealthy; *omunyali* n. successful person; rich, wealthy person; *atenyala* n. helpless person, someone unable; *-sanyala* v. be unable

Lukisa: *okhunyala* v.i., v.t. satisfy, be enough for; *okhunyalikha* v.i. suffer, be possible

Luwanga: *okhunyala* v.i., v.t. satisfy, be enough for, be able, have opportunity; *okhunyala* v.t. disembowel; *okhunyalikha* v.i. suffer, be possible; *obunyali* n. power, ability

Lutsotso: *okhunyala* v.i., v.t. satisfy, be enough for; *okhunyala* v.t. disembowel; *okhunyalikha* v.i. suffer, be possible; *obunyali* n. power, ability

Luidakho: *-inyalikha* v.i. suffer; be possible; *-nyala* v.t. disembowel; *-nyala* v.i., v.t. satisfy; be enough for, be able, have opportunity; *bunyali/obunyali* n. power, ability

Lulogooli: *kunyala* v. be able, have power, have strength, manage; *linyala* n. strength, power; *munyali* n. one who is able; *ubunyali/uvunyali* n. authority, strength, power, might; *kunyalidza* v. to strengthen; *kunyalika* v. be possible, overcome; *kunyalikidza* v. overcome, beat severely, excessively

29. ***-yavu**, n. cl. 14, cl. 1/2; Gloss: poverty; poor person
Protolanguage: Proto-North Nyanza
Etymology: from Proto-Great Lakes Bantu root *-yabu* adj. evil, filthy[18]
North Nyanza
Luganda: *-avù* adj. poor, impoverished, destitute; *òbwavù* n. poverty, destitution, indigence; bald patch on head caused from carrying many headloads (i.e., indicative of poverty); *kwàvùwala* v.i. become poor; *kwavùwaza* v.t. make poor, impoverish; *òmwavù* n. poor person

Lusoga: *obwâvú* n. poverty, poor, destitution, indigence, needy, pauperism; *omwâvú* n. poor person, pauper; *okwâvúwálá* v. become poor

Lugwere: *bwavu* n. poverty, state of being poor
Rutara
Rukiga: *-aaju* n. difficulty caused by jealousy

Luzinza: *-fu* adj. evil, wicked
Greater Luhyia
Lunyole: *omwafu* n. poor person; *owaafu* n. poverty
Lugungu
Lugungu: *bu̱habu̱* n. carelessness, irresponsibility

Western Lakes
    Kinande: *ekyábu̧* n. garbage dump
    Kirundi: *umwavu* n. sweepings; misfortune
    Kinyarwanda: *umwaavu* n. dirt, filth; *icyaavu* n. rubbish dump, trash heap, latrine

30. ***lunkupè**, n. cl. 11; Gloss: indigent, very poor person
Protolanguage: Proto-North Nyanza
Etymology: unclear
North Nyanza
    Luganda: *lùnkupè* n. indigent, very poor person
    Lusoga: *lúnkúpe* n. pauper, needy person, disadvantaged person, deprived person, wretch, poor person, penniless person, penurious person; *omwavu lunkope* n. pauper, very poor person
    Lugwere: *lunkupe* n. very poor person

31. *-**doob**-, v.i., n. cl. 1/2; Gloss: become poor, poor person
Protolanguage: Proto-North Nyanza
Etymology: Proto-Bantu *-*dòb*- "disappear; get lost"[19]
North Nyanza
    Luganda: *kudóòbá* v.i. be stripped of everything, be destitute, suffer greatly; *èndoòbe* n. loincloth
    Lusoga: *okúdoobá* v. suffer; *okúdoobádóóbá* v. be houseless, homeless, dispossessed, on the street, down and out, destitute, penniless, needy, impoverished; *endóobé* n. loincloth
    Lugwere: *kudooba* v. lose wealth, become poor, destitute, impoverished, needy, poverty-stricken; *kidoobi* adj. destitute; *muloobe* n. loincloth; *budòobi* n. poverty
Greater Luhyia
    Lunyole: *ohudooba* v. become a pauper, be in abject poverty; *ohudobaana* v. waste away in poverty, toil; *endoobe* n. loincloth

32. *-***fun***-, v., n. cl. 14; Gloss: prosper; wealth, riches
Protolanguage: Proto-North Nyanza
Etymology: semantic extension from Proto-North Nyanza *-*fun*- "get, acquire"

North Nyanza
    Luganda: *kufúná* v.t. get, obtain, procure; *kufúnìrá* v.t. get for, obtain for; *kufunamu* v. profit from, benefit from
    Lusoga: *obúfuní* n. possession of property, wealth; *omúfuní* n. wealthy person, rich, well-off, well-to-do, affluent, prosperous, rich man with many wives, with good luck; *okúfuná* v. obtain, attain, get, achieve, acquire, earn, receive; *enfúni* n. plant used in rituals in order to obtain wealth; *okúfunirá* v. obtain for; *énfuná* n. income
    Lugwere: *ókufuná/ókusuná* v. get, receive, earn, prosper, gain, obtain, acquire; *byensuna* (var. *byenfuna*) n. economics; *bya kufuna* n. riches, wealth
Rutara
    Runyambo: *kufúna* v. gain, profit
Lugungu
    Lugungu: *kufuna* v. receive, get, obtain, acquire [noted as loan from Luganda]

33. **mughedhere**, n. cl. 1/2; Gloss: very poor person
    Protolanguage: Lusoga
    Etymology: from Proto-West Nyanza verb *-heijeera* "wheeze" or "pant," in turn from Proto-Great Lakes Bantu *-jeera* "breathe"
West Nyanza
    Luganda: *kùwe'jjera* v.i. breathe hard, gabble, talk incessantly; *kùwe'jjeza* v.t. make out of breath, tire out, importune; *kùwejjerera* v.i. gabble at, to; *kùwe'jjawejja* v.i. pant, be out of breath; *òlùwe'jjowejjo* n. puffing, panting, hard breathing; *kùwe'zzawezza* v.t. make out of breath
    Lusoga: *omúghédhéré* n. poor, wretch; *okúhééra* v. breathe; *okúghéérúúká* v. gasp
    Lugwere: *ókuyeelá* v. breathe; *ókuyeelá énza* v. exhale; *ómúyéélo* n. sigh; *kuyeeruuka* v.i. be out of breath, puffed; *buyeerero* n. breather; *kuyeeresya* v.t. cause breathlessness; *kutaweera* v.i. be breathless
    Runyoro: *okuhiihira* v.i. pant, breathe with difficulty, make noise like that of an owl, be ready to flower (millet); *okuhiija* v.i. pant
    Rutooro: *okuhiihira* v.i. pant, breathe with difficulty, make noise like that of an owl, be ready to flower (millet); *okuhiija* v.i. pant

Runyankore: *kuheijeera* v. wheeze, groan
Rukiga: *kuheijeera* v. wheeze, groan
Runyambo: *kuhéijera* v. groan in pain

34. ***omuloki***, n. cl. 1/2; Gloss: rich man with many wives
    Protolanguage: Lusoga
    Etymology: derived from Proto-North Nyanza verb **-loka* "sprout"
    North Nyanza
        Luganda: *kulókà* v.i. start growing, sprout, take root; *èndokò* n. slip, shoot for transplanting; *endokwa* n. seedling, cutting, sprout, shoot
        Lusoga: *ómúlokí* n. rich man; rich man with many wives (Lulamoogi dialect only); *okúloká* v. become rich, survive, sprout; *éndokwá* n. seedling, sprout
        Lugwere: *kuloka* v. germinate, sprout, shoot, produce buds, branches, take root

35. ****meːi***, n.; Gloss: poor person without cattle
    Protolanguage: Proto-Kalenjin
    Etymology: from Proto-Southern Nilotic **mɛːr* "to die"[20]
    Nandi: *meiwöt* n. agricultural person, person living without cattle; *meiwaget* n. do-nothing, discourteous person, inferior person; killjoy, spoilsport
    Päkot: *mèeywɔ̀ndén* n. poverty, indigence; *mèeywɔ̀ndé ŋù* n. your poverty; *mèeywɔ̀n* n. poor person; *meei* n. poor person
    Datooga: *mɛːw* v. die
    Omotik: *mɛy* v. die

36. ****mokor-***, n.; Gloss: rich person, wealth, riches
    Protolanguage: Proto-Kalenjin or areal form in Kalenjin languages
    Etymology: from Proto-Bantu *-kòdò* n. cl. 1/2 "adult, important person, master, elder brother (sister), old person";[21] borrowed into Proto-Kalenjin from Proto-East Nyanza or later loan from Ekegusii
    Kalenjin
        Nandi: *ke-mögören* v. to be wealthy; *mögörnötet* n. wealth, capital; *mögöriöt* n. rich person
        Päkot: *mókɔ́síyà* n. wealth, richness; *moŋgɔrnán* n. wealth; *mòkɔ́ɔ̀s* adj. rich, wealthy; *mòkɔséc* adj. rich, wealthy; *moŋgɔriyɔ́n* n. rich man; *mɔ́ɔŋgɔɔr* n. rich man

Kupsabiny: *mokoriondit* n. wealth, riches; *mokoriondit ngat* n. immense wealth; *mokoriondet* n. rich person; *mokoriondet ngat* n. very rich person; *chesiet mokoriondet* n. rich woman; *pondeti mokoriondet* n. rich man; *lekweti mokoriondet* n. rich child

Southern Luo
Dholuo: *jamoko* n. self-made man, rich man, one who lacks for nothing; note this is a loan word from Kalenjin languages

East Nyanza
Ekegusii: *omokoro* (pl. *abakoro*) n. aged person, old person, person advanced in years, pioneer, elder, older person, elderly person

Ikikuria: *-koro* adj. mature, adult, fully grown, senior, old, ancient, former; *-koroha* v. have lasted, be old, be worn out; *omonto omokoro* n. adult, elder, ancient person; *omokoro* n. ancestor, forebear

37. *-**jak**-, v., n.; Gloss: become wealthy; rich person, leader
    Protolanguage: Proto-Ateker
    Etymology: possibly by semantic extension from "extract"; reflexes in Shilluk raise possibility that the overlapping meanings of wealth and power are much older in Nilotic languages

Eastern Nilotic
Ngakarimojong: *ejakait* n. chief; *ejakaana* adj. rich, well off; *ajakaaniar* v. become rich; *ajakaanut* n. wealth, kingdom

Turkana: *ejok* adj. rich

Ateso: *ajakaanut* n. chieftaincy, reign, administration, management; *ajakait* n. mistress, madam, Mrs.; *ejakait* n. mister, Mr., master, councillor, gentleman; *ejakaana* adj. dignified, stately; *ajakun* v.t. extricate, force open toward the speaker; *ajakun aunoi* v.p. ease the ropes; *ajakun akiro* v.p. break the silence; *ajakun amisiri* v.p. clean a bushy plot; *ojakait* n. big home; *ejakait* n. head of ojakait; *ajakait* n. wife of ejakait

Western Nilotic
Shilluk: *jak* (*jäk*), *jyak* v. govern, rule, reign, judge, oversee; *jago* (*jaago*) (pl. *jäki*) n. chief, foreman, ruler, leader

38. *-**kerian**-, v., n.; Gloss: be rich, skillful, wealthy; prosperity
    Protolanguage: Proto-Ateso
    Etymology: from Proto-Ateker *-*rian-* "equal" with addition of causative prefix[22]

Ateker

> Ngakarimojong: *ariyan* adj. equal; *erian* adj. correct
>
> Ateso: *akerianut* adj. successful (especially in business); *akerianut* n. wealth, prosperity, affluence, economy; *akerianut* v.i. be rich, skillful; *akerianar* v.i. prosper; *arian* n. equality in size, length, or height; *arian* v.i. be equal, the same in size, length, or height; *arianikin* v.i. become equal, the same size, etc.; *eirian* adj. equal

39. -**mi(y)o**-, v., n.; Gloss: be wealthy in food; wealth in food, someone wealthy in food
    Protolanguage: Ateso
    Ateker

    > Ateso: *amio* n. wealth in food; *amion* n. one who is wealthy in food; *aimi* v.i. be rich in crop products; *amiyo* v.i. be wealthy, have plenty of anything, especially food; *emiyono* adj. (of person) tending to be wealthy in crops

40. *-**kulyak**-, n.; Gloss: poverty, destitution, poor or destitute person
    Protolanguage: Proto-Northern Ateker
    Etymology: unclear; see also *-kulyak-it[23]
    Ateker

    > Ngakarimojong: *akulyako* n. poverty, abject poverty; *akulyakan* v. become poor; *ekulyakana* adj. poor; *ekulyakane* n. euphemism for penis; *ekulyakit* n. pauper, poor man; *ekulyakit* adj. poor; *akulyakanut* n. poverty (e.g., because of no cattle)
    >
    > Turkana: *ekulikit* adj. destitute

41. *-**polo**-, n.; Gloss: wealth, power
    Protolanguage: Proto-Northern Ateker
    Etymology: from Proto-Ateker loan from Western Nilotic[24]
    Northern Ateker

    > Ngakarimojong: *apoloor* v.i. prosper; *apolou* adj. importance; n. greatness; *apoloun* v. grow; *epol* (pl. *epolok*) adj. big, great, large; *ekapolon* n. chief, boss, Lord; *akitopol* v. cause to be great; *akitopoloor* v. be proud, take pride in; *apolokin* v. be in charge of, supervise; *apolou* n. greatness, authority; *apolou akou* n. pride; *apolounet* n. age; *ekapolon* n. chief, king; *akapolon* n. chief's wife, queen
    >
    > Turkana: *akapolon* n. chief; *apolou* n. honor

42. **-ngang'**, n.; Gloss: wealth, riches, wealthy person
   Protolanguage: Dhopadhola
   Etymology: unclear
   Southern Luo
   Dhopadhola: *aŋang'o* adj. rich; *ngango* n. wealth, riches, immense wealth; *jaŋang'o, ja ngango* n. rich person, very rich person; *dhano mu ngang swa* n. very rich person; *dhako jaŋang'o, dhako mu ngang* n. rich woman; *jichwo jaŋang'o* n. rich man; *nyathi jaŋang'o, nyathi mu ngang swa* n. rich child

NOTES

Introduction

1. Jane I. Guyer has pointed out how recently it is that this happened, in Guyer, "Pauper, Percentile, Precarity: Analytics for Poverty Studies in Africa," *Journal of African History* 59, no. 3 (2018): 437–48.

2. Poverty in Welsh is *tlodi*, a poor woman is a *tlodwraig*, while a poor man is a *tlodwr*. The noun *angen* is also occasionally used for poverty but has the primary meaning "need." Bruce Griffiths and Dafydd Glyn Jones, *Geiriadur yr Academi: The Welsh Academy English–Welsh Dictionary Online* (Bangor University on behalf of the Welsh Language Commissioner, 2012), https://geiriaduracademi.org.

3. World Bank, "Poverty Headcount Ratio at $1.90 a Day (2011 PPP) (% of Population) – Sub-Saharan Africa," https://data.worldbank.org/indicator/SI.POV.DDAY?locations=ZG; World Bank, "GDP (Current US$) – Sub-Saharan Africa," https://data.worldbank.org/indicator/NY.GDP.MKTP.CD?locations=ZG; World Bank, "Gini Index (World Bank Estimate)," https://data.worldbank.org/indicator/SI.POV.GINI. Any reading of World Bank or other statistics on African economies should be read alongside critiques of the underlying data. See, for example, Morten Jerven, *Africa: Why Economists Get It Wrong* (London: Zed Books, 2015). In January 2021, the *Monitor* reported that the Ministry of Finance estimated a ten percentage-point increase in the poverty rate to 28 percent in Uganda due to COVID-19, with eastern Uganda especially hard hit with an increase in its poverty rate from 28.8 percent to 53.3 percent. "Reduce Rising Level of Poverty in Uganda," *Monitor*, January 30, 2021. https://www.monitor.co.ug/uganda/oped/editorial/reduce-rising-level-of-poverty-uganda-3211864.

4. Nakanyike B. Musisi, "Women, 'Elite Polygyny,' and Buganda State Formation," *Signs* 16, no. 4 (1991): 757–86.

5. A point also made in the following, among others: Steven Serels, *The Impoverishment of the African Red Sea Littoral, 1640–1945* (Cham, Switzerland: Palgrave Macmillan, 2018), 10; Morten Jerven, "The History of African Poverty by Numbers: Evidence and Vantage Points," *Journal of African History* 39, no. 3 (2018): 449–61.

6. The categorization of poverty into conjunctural and structural, at least in the African context, can be attributed to John Iliffe in *The African Poor: A History* (Cambridge: Cambridge University Press, 1987). For a recent example showing how the colonial state

created structural poverty in one community, see Serels, *Impoverishment*. This is not, however, a simple narrative, as recent research on living standards has indicated; see Ewout Frankema and Marlous van Waijenburg, "Structural Impediments to African Growth? New Evidence from Real Wages in British Africa, 1880–1965," *Journal of African Economic History* 72, no. 4 (2012): 895–926.

7. For a good summary of the latter, see Corrie Decker and Elisabeth McMahon, *The Idea of Development in Africa: A History* (New York: Cambridge University Press, 2020), 166–68. For a counter perspective, see Rhiannon Stephens, "Poverty's Pasts: A Case for Longue Durée Studies," *Journal of African History* 59, no. 3 (2018): 399–409.

8. These are *dàndá* n. cl.14 'poverty' and *kúm* v. "be honored, be rich," with the asterisk denoting a reconstructed form. Yvonne Bastin, André Coupez, Evariste Mumba, and Thilo C. Schadeberg (eds.), *Bantu Lexical Reconstructions 3/Reconstructions lexicales bantoues 3* (Tervuren, Belgium: Musée Royale de l'Afrique Centrale, 2003), Main 858, Main 2113, https://www.africamuseum.be/en/research/discover/human_sciences/culture_society/blr/.

9. Susan Reynolds Whyte, "Men, Women and Misfortune in Bunyole," in *Women's Religious Experience*, ed. Pat Holden (London: Croom Helm, 1983), 183. Whyte notes that while there was no fixed structure for these prayers, they "always cover certain points such as 'getting wealth,' 'getting children,' and 'getting wives.'"

10. Jane Guyer noted, "The concept of wealth-in-people was developed in the 1970s, mainly by Miers and Kopytoff, as a less theoretical, more descriptive, looser and therefore more open concept to encapsulate established observations that no one disputed: that human beings could be explicitly valued in material terms in Africa, and that many of the person–thing conversions have been about acquiring and consolidating direct controls over people in a context where indirect controls through land, capital and the threat of superior force are either absent altogether or only intermittently realizable." Jane I. Guyer, "Wealth in People, Wealth in Things – Introduction," *Journal of African History* 36, no. 1 (1995): 86. On elopement and bridewealth in the history of neighboring North Nyanza–speaking communities, see Rhiannon Stephens, "'Whether They Promised Each Other Some Thing Is Difficult to Work Out': The Complicated History of Marriage in Uganda," *African Studies Review* 59, no. 1 (2016): 127–53.

11. Nasanairi Arugai, Omodoi, Toroma, Teso Historical Texts no. 16; quoted in J. B. Webster, "Usuku: The Homeland of the Iteso," in J. B. Webster, C. P. Emudong, D. H. Okalany, and N. Egimu-Okuda, *The Iteso during the Asonya* (Nairobi: East African Publishing House, 1973), 24.

12. Nasanairi Arugai, Omodoi, Toroma, Teso Historical Texts no. 16; quoted in Webster, "Usuku," 24.

13. On the ivory trade from East Africa at the time, see Edward A. Alpers, *Ivory and Slaves: Changing Patterns of International Trade in East Central Africa to the Later Nineteenth Century* (Berkeley: University of California Press, 1975); Abdul Sheriff, *Slaves, Spices, and Ivory in Zanzibar: Integration of an East African Commercial Empire into the World Economy, 1770–1873* (London: James Currey, 1987); Jeremy Prestholdt,

Domesticating the World: African Consumerism and the Genealogies of Globalization (Berkeley: University of California Press, 2008), 79–80.

14. Elsewhere on the continent, Toby Green has reminded us of the need to think of forms of wealth as having multiple purposes, which include the entwining of "economic accumulation and religious power," in Igbo communities in Nigeria. Green, *A Fistful of Shells: West Africa from the Rise of the Slave Trade to the Age of Revolution* (Chicago: University of Chicago Press, 2019), 19. He draws on the earlier work of Jane I. Guyer on currency in particular to make the point. Guyer, *Marginal Gains: Monetary Transactions in Atlantic Africa* (Chicago: University of Chicago Press, 2004).

15. This section draws extensively on Rhiannon Stephens and Axel Fleisch, "Introduction: Theories and Methods of African Conceptual History," in *Doing Conceptual History in Africa*, rev. ed., ed. Axel Fleisch and Rhiannon Stephens (2016; Oxford: Berghahn Books, 2018), 1–20; and Rhiannon Stephens, "'Wealth,' 'Poverty' and the Question of Conceptual History in Oral Contexts: Uganda from c. 1000 CE," in *Doing Conceptual History in Africa*, rev. ed., ed. Fleisch and Stephens, 21–48.

16. Melvin Richter, "*Begriffsgeschichte* and the History of Ideas," *Journal of the History of Ideas* 48, no. 2 (1987): 255.

17. Stephens and Fleisch, "Introduction," 1.

18. Terence O. Ranger, "Towards a Usable Past," in *African Studies since 1945: A Tribute to Basil Davidson*, ed. Christopher Fyfe (London: Longman for the Centre of African Studies, Edinburgh, 1976), 26.

19. Friedrich Nietzsche, "Second Essay: 'Guilt,' 'Bad Conscience,' and the Like," in *The Genealogy of Morals: A Polemic*, trans. Horace B. Samuel (New York: Boni and Liveright, 1918), 70.

20. See chapter 1 for a fuller discussion of the method and other scholarship drawing on it.

21. Historical archaeologists have, however, started to explore the archaeology of poverty; see the special issue "Poverty in Depth: New International Perspectives," *International Journal of Historical Archaeology* 15, no. 4 (2011).

22. There are studies that look at concepts of poverty in Africa, but they usually are not historical. See, for example, Elizabeth Amoah, "African Traditional Religion and the Concept of Poverty," in *Religion and Poverty*, ed. Peter J. Paris (Durham, NC: Duke University Press, 2009), 111–27.

23. K. O. Diké, *Trade and Politics in the Niger Delta, 1830–1885: An Introduction to the Economic and Political History of Nigeria* (Oxford: Clarendon Press, 1956), 28–30.

24. A. G. Hopkins, *An Economic History of West Africa* (London: Longman, 1973).

25. Robin Palmer and Neil Parsons, eds., *The Roots of Rural Poverty in Central and Southern Africa* (Berkeley: University of California Press, 1977).

26. Iliffe, *The African Poor*.

27. Samir Amin, "The Class Struggle in Africa," in *Classes and Class Struggle in Africa*, by Samir Amin and Robin Cohen (Lagos: Afrografika, 1977), 28–52; Walter Rodney, *How Europe Underdeveloped Africa* (Washington: Howard University Press,

1972). A useful overview of the literature to 1990, alongside his own analysis, is offered in Zeleza's sweeping survey, Paul Tiyambe Zeleza, *A Modern Economic History of Africa Volume I: The Nineteenth Century* (Dakar: CODESRIA, 1993). For a more recent intervention, see Green, *Fistful of Shells*.

28. Jan Vansina, *How Societies Are Born: Governance in West Central Africa before 1600* (Charlottesville: University of Virginia Press, 2004), 29.

29. Robin Palmer and Neil Parsons, "Introduction. The Roots of Rural Poverty: Historical Background," in *The Roots of Rural Poverty in Central and Southern Africa*, ed. Robin Palmer and Neil Parsons (Berkeley: University of California Press, 1977), 10.

30. Julius K. Nyerere, "Socialism and Rural Development," in *Freedom and Socialism/ Uhuru na Ujamaa: A Selection from Writings and Speeches, 1965–1967* (Dar es Salaam: Oxford University Press, 1968), 337.

31. Amoah, "African Traditional Religion," 119.

32. John Lonsdale, "The Moral Economy of Mau Mau: Wealth, Poverty and Civic Virtue in Kikuyu Political Thought," in *Unhappy Valley: Conflict in Kenya and Africa. Book Two: Violence and Ethnicity*, by Bruce Berman and John Lonsdale (Oxford: James Currey, 1992), 340.

33. Steven Feierman, "Reciprocity and Assistance in Precolonial Africa," in *Philanthropy in the World's Traditions*, ed. Warren F. Ilchman, Stanley N. Katz, and Edward L. Queen II (Bloomington: Indiana University Press, 1998), 3–24. See also the discussion in chapter 5 of this work on the nature of the relationship between the wealthy and the poor in Jie and Karimojong communities.

34. Pierre de Maret, "Histoires des croisettes," in *Objets-signes d'Afrique*, ed. Luc de Heusch (Tervuren, Belgium: Musée Royale de l'Afrique Centrale, 1995), 133–45; Nicolas Nikis and Alexandre Livingstone Smith, "Copper, Trade and Politics: Exchange Networks in Southern Central Africa in the 2nd Millennium CE," *Journal of Southern African Studies* 43, no. 5 (2017): 895–911; Colleen E. Kriger, *Cloth in West African History* (Lanham, MD: AltaMira Press, 2006); Kriger, *Pride of Men: Ironworking in 19th Century West Central Africa* (Portsmouth, NH: Heinemann, 1999); Andrea Felber Seligman, "Wealth Not by Any Other Name: Material Aesthetics in Expanding Commercial Times, ca. 16th–20th Centuries," *International Journal of African Historical Studies* 48, no. 3 (2015): 449–69; see also Jane I. Guyer, ed., *Money Matters: Instability, Values and Social Payments in the Modern History of West African Communities* (Portsmouth, NH: Heinemann, 1995).

35. This literature is far too extensive to list here, but it is worth noting that the author of *The Periplus of the Erythraean Sea* wrote, around the first century CE, that the primary exports from East Africa were ivory, rhinoceros horn, tortoiseshells, and palm oil. *The Periplus of the Erythraean Sea: Travel and Trade in the Indian Ocean by a Merchant of the First Century*, trans. Wilfred H. Schoff (New York: Longmans, Green, 1912), 285.

36. Christopher Ehret, *An African Classical Age: Eastern and Southern Africa in World History, 1000 B.C. to A.D. 400* (Charlottesville: University Press of Virginia Press, 1998), 19.

37. Guyer, "Wealth in People," 89. Guyer offers her own answers to these questions, such as in her discussion of the centrality of the possession of titles to being an Igbo man of rank. Guyer, *Marginal Gains*, 68–82.

38. Ogbu U. Kalu, "Poverty in Pre-colonial and Colonial West Africa: Perceptions, Causes and Alleviation," in *Themes in West African History*, ed. Emmanuel Kwame Akyeampong (Athens: Ohio University Press, 2006), 163.

39. Suzanne Miers and Igor Kopytoff, eds., *Slavery in Africa: Historical and Anthropological Perspectives* (Madison: University of Wisconsin Press, 1977); Caroline Bledsoe, *Women and Marriage in Kpelle Society* (Stanford, CA: Stanford University Press, 1980). See Guyer, "Wealth in People."

40. Jane I. Guyer and Samuel M. Eno Belinga, "Wealth in People as Wealth in Knowledge: Accumulation and Composition in Equatorial Africa," *Journal of African History* 36, no. 1 (1995): 92.

41. Joseph C. Miller, *Way of Death: Merchant Capitalism and the Angolan Slave Trade, 1730–1830* (Madison: University of Wisconsin Press, 1988), xx.

42. Guyer and Eno Belinga, "Wealth in People as Wealth in Knowledge."

43. Kathryn M. de Luna, *Collecting Food, Cultivating People: Subsistence and Society in Central Africa* (New Haven: Yale University Press, 2016), 115.

44. Parker Shipton, *The Nature of Entrustment: Intimacy, Exchange, and the Sacred in Africa* (New Haven: Yale University Press, 2007); Shipton, *Mortgaging the Ancestors: Ideologies of Attachment in Africa* (New Haven: Yale University Press, 2009).

45. Shipton, *Mortgaging the Ancestors*.

46. Margaret Atkins and Robin Osborne, eds., *Poverty in the Roman World* (Cambridge: Cambridge University Press, 2006); Peter Brown, *Treasure in Heaven: The Holy Poor in Early Christianity* (Charlottesville: University of Virginia Press, 2016); Michel Mollat, *The Poor in the Middle Ages: An Essay in Social History*, trans. Arthur Goldhammer (New Haven: Yale University Press, 1986).

47. Neville Morley, "The Poor in the City of Rome," in *Poverty in the Roman World*, ed. Atkins and Osborne, 31.

48. Mollat, *The Poor in the Middle Ages*, 2. See also his list of Latin keywords related to poverty that were most frequently used in medieval texts in appendix 3 of Michel Mollat, *Études sur l'histoire de la pauvreté (Moyen-Age – XVIe siècle)*, vol. 2 (Paris: Publications de la Sorbonne, 1974), 841–42.

49. Christel Freu, *Les figures du pauvre dans les sources italiennes de l'antiquité tardive* (Paris: De Boccard, 2007); Mollat, *The Poor in the Middle Ages*.

50. Among others, see Jan Vansina, *Paths in the Rainforests: Toward a History of Political Tradition in Central Africa* (Madison: University of Wisconsin Press, 1990); Ehret, *African Classical Age*; Edda L. Fields-Black, *Deep Roots: Rice Farmers in West Africa and the African Diaspora* (Bloomington: Indiana University Press, 2008); David L. Schoenbrun, *A Green Place, A Good Place: Agrarian Change, Gender, and Social Identity in the Great Lakes Region to the 15th Century* (Portsmouth, NH: Heinemann, 1998); Rhiannon Stephens, *A History of African Motherhood: The Case of Uganda,*

700–1900 (New York: Cambridge University Press, 2013); de Luna, *Collecting Food, Cultivating People.*

51. Lonsdale, "Moral Economy of Mau Mau"; Jan Kuhanen, *Poverty, Health and Reproduction in Early Colonial Uganda* (Joensuu, Finland: University of Joensuu Publications, 2005); Prestholdt, *Domesticating the World.*

52. Laura Fair, *Pastimes and Politics: Culture, Community, and Identity in Post-Abolition Urban Zanzibar, 1890–1945* (Athens: Ohio University Press, 2001), 7–8.

53. Prestholdt, *Domesticating the World*, 53.

54. Stephanie Wynne-Jones, *A Material Culture: Consumption and Materiality on the Coast of Precolonial East Africa* (Oxford: Oxford University Press, 2016), 5.

55. In 2019–2020, for example, the devastation from locust swarms across not only East Africa, but also across the Middle East and the Indian subcontinent, was readily connected with climate change. Abubakr A. M. Salih, Marta Baraibar, Kenneth Kemucie Mwangi, and Guleid Artan, "Climate Change and Locust Outbreak in East Africa," *Nature Climate Change* 10, no. 7 (2020): 584–85.

Chapter One : Methodologies and Sources for a Conceptual History of Economic Difference over the *Longue Duree*

1. Historians also grapple with the challenges of writing postcolonial history in the absence of orderly and accessible archives. For an early discussion of this, see Stephen Ellis, "Writing Histories of Contemporary Africa," *Journal of African History* 43, no. 1 (2002): 1–26. For a more recent example of the need to pull together sources from multiple locations, see Jean Allman, "Phantoms of the Archive: Kwame Nkrumah, a Nazi Pilot Named Hanna, and the Contingencies of Postcolonial History-Writing," *American Historical Review* 118, no. 1 (2013): 104–29.

2. For a particularly innovative example of this in African history, see David Lee Schoenbrun, "Pythons Worked: Constellating Communities of Practice with Conceptual Metaphor in Northern Lake Victoria, ca. A.D. 800 to 1200," in *Knowledge in Motion: Constellations of Learning across Time and Place*, ed. Andrew Roddick and Ann Stahl (Tucson: University of Arizona Press, 2016), 216–46.

3. The research articles in the journal *Contributions to the History of Concepts* are a good example of this, as well as of the range of conceptual history as it increasingly moves beyond European history.

4. For examples of some of the possibilities beyond archives, see the contributions to Axel Fleisch and Rhiannon Stephens, eds., *Doing Conceptual History in Africa*, rev. ed. (2016; Oxford: Berghahn Books, 2018).

5. Pamela Khanakwa, "Male Circumcision among the Bagisu of Eastern Uganda," in *Doing Conceptual History in Africa*, ed. Fleisch and Stephens, 115–37; Ana Lúcia Sá, "The Concept of 'Land' in Bioko: 'Land as Property' and 'Land as Country,'" in *Doing Conceptual History in Africa*, ed. Fleisch and Stephens, 138–61.

6. Wyatt MacGaffey, "A Note on Vansina's Invention of Matrilinearity," *Journal of African History* 54, no. 2 (2013): 272.

7. Kathryn M. de Luna, *Collecting Food, Cultivating People: Subsistence and Society in Central Africa* (New Haven: Yale University Press, 2016), 42.

8. Kathryn M. de Luna, "Hunting Reputations: Talent, Individuals, and Community in Precolonial South Central Africa," *Journal of African History* 53, no. 3 (2012): 279–99.

9. Edda L. Fields-Black, *Deep Roots: Rice Farmers in West Africa and the African Diaspora* (Bloomington: Indiana University Press, 2008). While her research area was in many ways an even harder place to do this kind of work than eastern Uganda in terms of source material, Fields-Black's ability to draw on written texts by outsiders was key in making her study possible.

10. On forms of political and social complexity in Africa, see Susan Keech McIntosh, "Pathways to Complexity: An African Perspective," in *Beyond Chiefdoms: Pathways to Complexity in Africa*, ed. Susan Keech McIntosh, 1–30 (Cambridge: Cambridge University Press, 1999).

11. Fa-Digi Sisòkò and John William Johnson, *Son-Jara: The Mande Epic* (Bloomington: Indiana University Press, 1986); Ralph A. Austen, ed., *In Search of Sunjata: The Mande Oral Epic as History, Literature, and Performance* (Bloomington: Indiana University Press, 1999); Alexis Kagame, *La poésie dynastique au Rwanda* (Brussels: Institut royal colonial belge, 1951); Claudine Vidal, "Alexis Kagame entre memoire et histoire," *History in Africa* 15 (1988): 493–504.

12. Compare, for example, M. S. M. Semakula Kiwanuka, *A History of Buganda from the Foundation of the Kingdom to 1900* (New York: Africans Publishing, 1972); Benjamin Ray, *Myth, Ritual, and Kingship in Buganda* (New York: Oxford University Press, 1991); Christopher Wrigley, *Kingship and State: The Buganda Dynasty* (Cambridge: Cambridge University Press, 1996); Holly Elisabeth Hanson, *Landed Obligation: The Practice of Power in Buganda* (Portsmouth, NH: Heinemann, 2003); Neil Kodesh, *Beyond the Royal Gaze: Clanship and Public Healing in Buganda* (Charlottesville: University of Virginia Press, 2010).

13. A. E. Afigbo, *Ropes of Sand (Studies in Igbo History and Culture)* (Nsukka: University of Nigeria Press, 1981); Akinwumi Ogundiran, *Archaeology and History in Ìlàrè District (Central Yorubaland, Nigeria), 1200–1900 A.D.* (Oxford: Archaeopress, 2002); Derek Nurse and Thomas Spear, *The Swahili: Reconstructing the History and Language of an African Society, 800–1500* (Philadelphia: University of Pennsylvania Press, 1985); Chapurukha M. Kusimba, *The Rise and Fall of Swahili States* (Walnut Creek, CA: AltaMira Press, 1999); Innocent Pikirayi, *The Zimbabwe Culture: Origins and Decline of Southern Zambezian States* (Walnut Creek, CA: AltaMira Press, 2001); de Luna, *Collecting Food, Cultivating People*.

14. The "Sirikwa Holes" in Kenya are an exception to this and are discussed in chapter 5.

15. Jan Ifversen, "About Key Concepts and How to Study Them," *Contributions to the History of Concepts* 6, no. 1 (2011): 66.

16. David Schoenbrun, "Mixing, Moving, Making, Meaning: Possible Futures for the Distant Past," *African Archaeological Review* 29, no. 2 (2012): 300.

17. There are several works that offer detailed descriptions of the methodologies of comparative historical linguistics and how to apply them. For books by linguists, see, for example, Lyle Campbell, *Historical Linguistics: An Introduction*, 2nd ed. (Cambridge, MA: MIT Press, 2004); Gerrit J. Dimmendaal, *Historical Linguistics and the Comparative Study of African Languages* (Amsterdam: John Benjamins, 2011); Brian D. Joseph and Richard D. Janda, *The Handbook of Historical Linguistics* (Malden, MA: Blackwell, 2005). These books are useful in setting out the fundamental principles, but it is worth remembering that historical linguists have different intellectual goals to historians as they are interested in language for its own sake and not as an archive for writing history. For a book by a historian of Africa, see Christopher Ehret, *History and the Testimony of Language* (Berkeley: University of California Press, 2011). See also the methodological discussions in David Lee Schoenbrun, *A Green Place, A Good Place: Agrarian Change, Gender, and Social Identity in the Great Lakes Region to the 15th Century* (Portsmouth, NH: Heinemann, 1998), 37–52, 265–69.

18. Thus, while recent research on genetics can offer useful insights into Africa's deeper past, it has proven complicated to develop a robust methodology that accounts for the reality that genes, languages, and ethnicity are not a single package. Indeed, as soon as someone learns to speak a language different to that of her parents, she moves outside of any simple genetics-language-ethnicity model. For helpful overviews of genetics in African history that span the recent dramatic changes in the field, see Scott MacEachern, "Genes, Tribes, and African History," *Current Anthropology* 41, no. 3 (2000): 357–84; MacEachern, "States and Their Genetic Consequences in Central Africa," *Proceedings of the National Academy of Sciences of the United States of America* 116, no. 2 (2019): 356–57.

19. Harald Hammarström, Robert Forkel, Martin Haspelmath, and Sebastian Bank, *Glottolog 2.7* (Jena: Max Planck Institute for the Science of Human History, 2016), http://glottolog.org.

20. See, for example, Ranko Matasovic, *Etymological Dictionary of Proto-Celtic* (Leiden: Brill, 2009), http://dictionaries.brillonline.com/proto-celtic.

21. Hammarström, Forkel, Haspelmath, and Bank, *Glottolog 2.7*. There is no standard nomenclature for Bantu protolanguages, with the result that some protolanguages have two or more labels. A useful overview of the different nomenclature to the end of the twentieth century is offered in Derek Nurse and Gérard Philippson, "Towards a Historical Classification of the Bantu Languages," in *The Bantu Languages*, ed. Derek Nurse and Gérard Philippson (London: Routledge, 2003), 164–81.

22. See, for example, Derek Nurse, *Swahili and Sabaki* (Berkeley: University of California Press, 1993); Raevin F. Jimenez, "Rites of Reproduction: Gender, Generation and Political Economic Transformation among Nguni-Speakers of Southern Africa, 8th–19th Century CE" (PhD diss., Northwestern University, 2017).

23. Morris Swadesh, "Lexico-Statistic Dating of Prehistoric Ethnic Contacts: With Special Reference to North American Indians and Eskimos," *Proceedings of the American*

Philosophical Society 96, no. 4 (1952): 452–563. For his original list, see 456–57. Swadesh developed the list for a northern North American context, hence the inclusion of "ice" and "snow."

24. For more on lexicostatistics, see Brett Kessler, *The Significance of Word Lists* (Stanford, CA: CSLI Publications, 2001); April McMahon and Robert McMahon, *Language Classification by Numbers* (Oxford: Oxford University Press, 2005).

25. McMahon and McMahon, *Language Classification*, 6; Christopher Ehret, "Subclassifying Bantu: The Evidence of Stem Morpheme Innovation," in *Bantu Historical Linguistics: Theoretical and Empirical Perspectives*, ed. Jean-Marie Hombert and Larry M. Hyman (Stanford, CA: CSLI, 1999), 43–147.

26. Gérard Philippson and Rebecca Grollemund, "Classifying Bantu Languages," in *The Bantu Languages*, 2nd ed., ed. Mark Van de Velde, Koen Bostoen, Derek Nurse, and Gérard Philippson (London: Routledge, 2019), 335–54, here 343–47. For early examples and discussion of this work, see Clare J. Holden and Russell D. Gray, "Rapid Radiation, Borrowing and Dialect Continua in the Bantu Languages," in *Phylogenetic Methods and the Prehistory of Languages*, ed. Peter Forster and Colin Renfrew (Cambridge: McDonald Institute for Archaeological Research, 2006), 19–32; Lutz Marten, "Bantu Classification, Bantu Trees and Phylogenetic Methods," in *Phylogenetic Methods and the Prehistory of Languages*, ed. Forster and Renfrew, 43–56.

27. Philippson and Grollemund, "Classifying Bantu Languages," 344.

28. Rebecca Grollemund, "Nouvelles approches en classification: Application aux langues Bantou du Nord-Ouest" (PhD diss., Université Lumière Lyon 2, 2012).

29. Since Joseph Greenberg's work, a number of scholars have made the case for Nilo-Saharan as a genetic family with the Nilotic languages forming a subbranch: Joseph H. Greenberg, "Studies in African Linguistic Classification: IV Hamito-Semitic," *Southwestern Journal of Anthropology* 6 (1950): 47–63; M. Lionel Bender, *The Nilo-Saharan Languages* (Munich: LINCOM Europa, 1996); Christopher Ehret, *A Historical-Comparative Reconstruction of Nilo-Saharan* (Cologne: Rüdiger Köppe, 2001). But as Pascal Boyeldieu notes, a number of important questions remain about its integrity as a language phylum, including regarding the consequences of linguistic interference from other languages. Further research on groups such as Nilotic may result in a stronger classification at deeper levels, but that work remains incomplete; Pascal Boyeldieu, "Les langues nilo-sahariennes," in *Dictionnaire des langues*, ed. Emilio Bonvini, Joëlle Busuttil, and Alain Peyraube (Paris: Presses universitaires de France, 2011), 185–90, here 188.

30. This classification is very sound. It was first proposed in 1950 and has been reconfirmed by researchers working in the decades since; Gerrit J. Dimmendaal, "Reconstructing the Historical Development of Nilotic: A Testcase for Cladistic and Rhizotic Models of Genetic Affinity," *Sprache und Geschichte in Afrika* 19 (2008): 31–66. Lionel Bender preferred to use what he termed a "neutral" terminology of E9a, E9b, and E9c, rather than Eastern, Southern, and Western, because "the geographical locations are overlapping"; M. Lionel Bender, "Nilo-Saharan," in *African Languages: An Introduction*, ed. Bernd Heine and Derek Nurse (Cambridge: Cambridge University Press, 2000), 46.

31. The Tung'a subbranch is also known as Lotuko-Maa-Teso-Turkana.

32. William Fitzsimons, "Distributed Power: Climate Change, Elderhood, and Republicanism in the Grasslands of East Africa, c. 500 BCE to 1800 CE" (PhD diss., Northwestern University, 2020). I am indebted to Will for his generosity in sharing this classification with me before the dissertation was complete. See also Bender, *Nilo-Saharan Languages*, 31–32; Ehret, *Nilo-Saharan*, 70–71; Rainer Vossen, *The Eastern Nilotes: Linguistics and Historical Reconstructions* (Berlin: Dietrich Reimer, 1982), 295–96; Dimmendaal, "Historical Development of Nilotic," 35; Hammarström, Forkel, Haspelmath, and Bank, *Glottolog 2.7*. Please note that in the 2016 version of Rhiannon Stephens, "'Wealth,' 'Poverty' and the Question of Conceptual History in Oral Contexts: Uganda from c.1000 CE," in *Doing Conceptual History in Africa*, ed. Fleisch and Stephens, 28, Toposa is mistakenly listed under Lotuko-Maa. This is corrected in the 2018 version. As Vossen notes, there is inadequate data but Toposa should belong to the Ateker subbranch along with other languages that are underdocumented such as Jie and Dodos. William Fitzsimons's research confirms this.

33. This is derived from John Albert Distefano, "The Precolonial History of the Kalenjin of Kenya: A Methodological Comparison of Linguistic and Oral Traditional Evidence" (PhD diss., University of California, Los Angeles, 1985), 96–97. See also Bender, *Nilo-Saharan Languages*, 32; Bender, "Nilo-Saharan," 46; Ehret, *Nilo-Saharan*, 71; Dimmendaal, "Historical Development of Nilotic," 38; Hammarström, Forkel, Haspelmath, and Bank, *Glottolog 2.7*.

34. This is derived from Bender, *Nilo-Saharan Languages*, 29–31; Bender, "Nilo-Saharan," 46; Ehret, *Nilo-Saharan*, 70; Dimmendaal, "Historical Development of Nilotic," 39–40; Fitzsimons, "Distributed Power," chapter 2; Hammarström, Forkel, Haspelmath, and Bank, *Glottolog 2.7*.

35. For the classification of Great Lakes Bantu, see David L. Schoenbrun, "Great Lakes Bantu: Classification and Settlement Chronology," *Sprache und Geschichte in Afrika* 15 (1994): 39–72.

36. A useful overview of some of these debates, as well as the presentation of one view of the genetic classification of Bantu languages, can be found in Thilo C. Schadeberg, "Historical Linguistics," in *The Bantu Languages*, ed. Derek Nurse and Gérard Philippson (London: Routledge, 2003), 143–63; Derek Nurse and Gérard Philippson, "Towards a Historical Classification of the Bantu Languages," in *The Bantu Languages*, ed. Nurse and Philippson, 164–81. For an update that crucially includes recent phylogenetic classifications, see Philippson and Grollemund, "Classifying Bantu Languages." See Hammarström, Forkel, Haspelmath, and Bank, *Glottolog 2.7*, "Narrow Bantu" for a visualization of the classification. For a recent effort to integrate human genetic evidence with linguistic evidence, see Cesare de Filippo, Koen Bostoen, Mark Stoneking, and Brigitte Pakendorf, "Bringing Together Linguistic and Genetic Evidence to Test the Bantu Expansion," *Proceedings of the Royal Society B: Biological Sciences* 279, no. 1741 (2012): 3256–63.

37. Rhiannon Stephens, *A History of African Motherhood: The Case of Uganda, 700–1900* (New York: Cambridge University Press, 2013), 24. See also Rhiannon Stephens,

"A History of Motherhood, Food Procurement and Politics in East-Central Uganda to the Nineteenth Century" (PhD diss., Northwestern University, 2007), 30–58.

38. The Greater Luhyia classification is my own based on data collected during fieldwork and from numerous dictionaries and wordlists. It also draws on the following earlier classifications: Martin Mould, "Greater Luyia," in *Studies in the Classification of Eastern Bantu Languages*, by Thomas H. Hinnebusch, Derek Nurse, and Martin Mould (Hamburg: Helmut Buske, 1981), 181–261; Rachel Angogo Kanyoro, *Unity in Diversity: A Linguistic Survey of the Abaluyia of Western Kenya* (Vienna: Afro-Pub, 1983); Evelyne Kisembe, "A Linguistic Analysis of Luyia Varieties Spoken in Western Kenya" (MA diss., Memorial University of Newfoundland, 2005). Much of the research on Greater Luhyia languages has focused on those spoken in Kenya, although research by Michael Marlo is remedying that. As with the Nilotic languages, significant gaps remain in our knowledge and it is to be anticipated that new research will improve and even significantly change the classification proposed here.

39. See Ehret, *History and the Testimony of Language*, 105–32.

40. Dimmendaal, *Historical Linguistics*, 71–73.

41. Schoenbrun, *A Green Place*, 32–37, 46–48.

42. Fitzsimons, "Distributed Power," chapter 2.

43. Specifically, it involves voicing dissimilation in contexts where a voiceless stop is immediately followed by a syllable containing another voiceless stop. Mould, "Greater Luyia."

44. William O'Grady, "Semantics: The Analysis of Meaning," in *Contemporary Linguistics: An Introduction*, ed. William O'Grady, Michael Dobrovolsky, and Francis Katamba (London: Longman, 1996), 283.

45. Elizabeth Closs Traugott and Richard B. Dasher, *Regularity in Semantic Change* (Cambridge: Cambridge University Press, 2002), 3.

46. For specific examples of these particular developments, see Schoenbrun, *A Green Place*.

47. Andreas Blank, "Why Do New Meanings Occur? A Cognitive Typology of the Motivations for Lexical Semantic Change," in *Historical Semantics and Cognition*, ed. Peter Koch and Andreas Blank (Berlin: De Gruyter Mouton, 1999), 70–82.

48. Blank, "Why Do New Meanings Occur?," 74.

49. Blank, "Why Do New Meanings Occur?," 77.

50. Blank, "Why Do New Meanings Occur?," 79.

51. Blank, "Why Do New Meanings Occur?," 80.

52. Blank, "Why Do New Meanings Occur?," 80–81.

53. This paragraph draws extensively on Stephens, "'Wealth,' 'Poverty,'" 27.

54. O'Grady, "Semantics," 276.

55. O'Grady, "Semantics," 276.

56. Dirk Geeraerts, *Diachronic Prototype Semantics: A Contribution to Historical Lexicology* (Oxford: Clarendon Press, 1997), 113.

57. For more on Bantu noun classes, see Francis Katamba, "Bantu Nominal Morphology," in *The Bantu Languages*, ed. Nurse and Philippson, 103–20; Jouni Maho, *A*

Comparative Study of Bantu Noun Classes (Gothenburg, Sweden: Acta Universitatis Gothoburgensis, 1999); Mark Van de Velde, "Nominal Morphology and Syntax," in *The Bantu Languages*, ed. Van de Velde, Bostoen, Nurse, and Philippson, 2nd ed., 237–69.

58. See Katamba, "Bantu Nominal Morphology," 109 for a full listing of these noun classes.

59. For an excellent overview of the history of interactions between the two disciplines and a model of how better and better-informed collaboration can work, see Kathryn M. de Luna and Jeffrey Fleisher, *Speaking with Substance: Methods of Language and Materials in African History* (New York: Springer, 2018).

60. For a useful summary of this, see Ceri Z. Ashley, "Towards a Socialised Archaeology of Ceramics in Great Lakes Africa," *African Archaeological Review* 27, no. 2 (2010): 137.

61. For East Africa specifically, see, for example, Paul Lane, "The 'Moving Frontier' and the Transition to Food Production in Kenya," *Azania: Archaeological Research in Africa* 39, no.1 (2004): 243–64; Paul Lane, Ceri Ashley, and Gilbert Oteyo, "New Dates for Kansyore and Urewe Wares from Northern Nyanza," *Azania: Archaeological Research in Africa* 41, no. 1 (2006): 123–38; Paul Lane et al., "The Transition to Farming in Eastern Africa: New Faunal and Dating Evidence from Wadh Lang'o and Usenge, Kenya," *Antiquity* 81, no. 311 (2007): 62–81; Darla Dale and Ceri Z. Ashley, "Holocene Hunter-Fisher-Gatherer Communities: New Perspectives on Kansyore Using Communities of Western Kenya," *Azania: Archaeological Research in Africa* 45, no. 1 (2010): 24–48. For earlier work that brought together scholars working across the continent, see J. Desmond Clark and Steven A. Brandt, eds., *From Hunters to Farmers: The Causes and Consequences of Food Production in Africa* (Berkeley: University of California Press, 1984).

62. Dale and Ashley, "Holocene," 26. The sedentary nature of these communities is also suggested "by the recovery of part of a Giant Elephant Shrew (*Rhynchocyon chrysopygus*) mandible in the faunal assemblage" because the shrew "may well be indicative of settled communities." Lane, Ashley, and Oteyo, "New Dates," 130.

63. Dale and Ashley, "Holocene," 25.

64. Ashley, "Towards a Socialised Archaeology," 144, citing M. D. Leakey, W. E. Owen, and L. S. B. Leakey, *Dimple-based Pottery from Central Kavirondo, Kenya Colony*, Occasional Paper no. 2 (Nairobi: Coryndon Memorial Museum, 1948).

65. Ashley, "Towards a Socialised Archaeology," 147.

66. Dale and Ashley, "Holocene," 40–41.

67. Dale and Ashley, "Holocene," 41.

68. G. W. B. Huntingford, "Introduction," in *The Periplus of the Erythraean Sea, by an Unknown Author: With Some Extracts from Agatharkhides "On the Erythraean Sea,"* trans. and ed. G. W. B. Huntingford (London: Hakluyt Society, 1980), 1–15, here 12.

69. See, for example, Jan Vansina, *Oral Tradition: A Study in Historical Methodology* (London: Routledge and Kegan Paul, 1965); and Vansina, *Oral Tradition as History* (Madison: University of Wisconsin Press, 1985).

70. Most famously, Bethwell A. Ogot, *History of the Southern Luo, Volume I: Migration and Settlement* (Nairobi: East African Publishing House, 1967).

71. Renée L. Tantala, "Verbal and Visual Imagery in Kitara (Western Uganda): Interpreting 'The Story of Isimbwa and Nyinamwiru,'" in *Paths Toward the Past: African Historical Essays in Honor of Jan Vansina*, ed. Robert W. Harms, Joseph C. Miller, David B. Newbury, and Michele D. Wagner (Atlanta: African Studies Association Press, 1994), 223–43.

72. Gideon S. Were, *Western Kenya Historical Texts: Abaluyia, Teso and Elgon Kalenjin* (Nairobi: East African Literature Bureau, 1967); Were, *A History of the Abaluyia of Western Kenya* (Nairobi: East African Publishing House, 1967); F. E. Makila, *An Outline History of the Babukusu of Western Kenya* (Nairobi: Kenya Literature Bureau, 1978).

73. The Masaaba M. R. Association, "The History of Bugisu," unpublished manuscript (1973), shared with author by Pamela Khanakwa.

74. Ronald R. Atkinson, ed., "Bugwere Historical Texts," Ronald R. Atkinson Private Collection; David William Cohen, ed., "Collected Texts of Busoga Traditional History," David William Cohen Private Collection; Cohen, *Towards a Reconstructed Past: Historical Texts from Busoga, Uganda* (Oxford: Oxford University Press, 1986); John Lamphear, *The Traditional History of the Jie of Uganda* (Oxford: Clarendon Press, 1976); Ogot, *History of the Southern Luo*; J. B. Webster, D. H. Okalany, C. P. Emudong, and N. Egimu-Okuda, *The Iteso during the Asonya* (Nairobi: East African Publishing House, 1973).

75. For example, Erika Higenyi, "The History of the Banyole," trans. Elley Wesana-Chomi, unpublished manuscript (1968), shared with author by Susan Reynolds Whyte; original manuscript written in Luganda (1936); Y. K. Lubogo, *A History of Busoga*, trans. Eastern Province (Bantu Language) Literature Committee (Jinja: East African Literature Bureau, 1960). See also several essays in the *Uganda Journal*.

76. A Report by Major E. H. Gorges on the Wa-Kavirondo, 20-8-1901 pp. 66–69, here 67; FO2/804, Foreign Office: Political and Other Departments: General Correspondence before 1906, Africa, National Archives, UK.

77. Solange Ashby, "Dancing for Hathor: Nubian Women in Egyptian Cultic Life," *Dotawo: A Journal of Nubian Studies* 5, no. 1 (2018): 63–90.

Chapter Two: Excavating Early Ideas about Poverty and Wealth

1. The earliest date for Late Stone Age Kansyore Ware around the Victoria Nyanza is from the site of Luanda in Kenya, calibrated to 7819–6590 BCE. Darla Dale and Ceri Z. Ashley, "Holocene Hunter-Fisher-Gatherer Communities: New Perspectives on Kansyore Using Communities of Western Kenya," *Azania: Archaeological Research in Africa* 45, no. 1 (2010): 28; see also Paul Lane et al., "The Transition to Farming in Eastern Africa: New Faunal and Dating Evidence from Wadh Lang'o and Usenge, Kenya," *Antiquity* 81 (2007): 62–81. Both cite, in relation to the earliest date available, Peter Robertshaw et al., "Shell Middens on the Shores of Lake Victoria," *Azania* 18 (1983): 1–43. Robertshaw et al. noted the need for confirmatory dating and that the Luanda date (precalibration) of 8240 ± 245 before present (BP) was "possibly much too old." "Shell

Middens," 35. The calibrated date is more in line with dates from excavations conducted by Dale and Ashley.

2. David Lee Schoenbrun, *A Green Place, A Good Place: Agrarian Change, Gender, and Social Identity in the Great Lakes Region to the 15th Century* (Portsmouth, NH: Heinemann, 1998), 43.

3. For a discussion of the importance of water transportation and of networks connecting people across and on the lake (on islands), as well as the long-term settlement of islands, see Andrew Reid and Ceri Ashley, "Islands of Agriculture on Victoria Nyanza," in *Archaeology of African Plant Use*, ed. Chris J. Stevens et al. (Walnut Creek, CA: Left Coast Press, 2014), 179–88. Some of the oral traditions that Gideon Were collected in 1964 among the Greater Luhyia–speaking communities explicitly referenced their ancestors crossing the lake in order to arrive in eastern Uganda and western Kenya. Gideon S. Were, *Western Kenya Historical Texts: Abaluyia, Teso and Elgon Kalenjin* (Nairobi: East African Literature Bureau, 1967). For a history centered on the lake, see David Lee Schoenbrun, *The Names of the Python: Belonging in East Africa, 900 to 1930* (Madison: University of Wisconsin Press, 2021).

4. Igor Kopytoff, ed., *The African Frontier: The Reproduction of Traditional African Societies* (Bloomington: Indiana University Press, 1987).

5. Schoenbrun, *A Green Place*, 65–90.

6. Dale and Ashley, "Holocene," 40–41. For linguistic records, see, for example, Christopher Ehret, *Southern Nilotic History: Linguistic Approaches to the Study of the Past* (Evanston, IL: Northwestern University Press, 1971), 144–49.

7. This was the case despite the fact that speakers of Proto-Great Lakes Bantu had their own vocabulary for poverty. For example, David Schoenbrun has reconstructed the root *-keni* (n. cl. 1/2) to Proto-Great Lakes Bantu with the meaning "poor person." David Lee Schoenbrun, *The Historical Reconstruction of Great Lakes Bantu Cultural Vocabulary: Etymologies and Distributions* (Cologne: Rüdiger Köppe, 1997), 134.

8. See root 1 in the appendix for reflexes, meanings, and distributions.

9. In a reversal of the direction of semantic change for this root in Bantu languages, in English the original meaning of the verb want was "lack" from which speakers first derived the additional meaning "need" and then "desire." Andrew L. Sihler, *Language History: An Introduction* (Amsterdam: John Benjamins, 2000), 118. See also the *Oxford English Dictionary*, where the earliest quotation for want as *desire* is from 1707, whereas the earliest quotations for want as *lack* date to the thirteenth century. "want, v." OED *Online*, December 2015, Oxford University Press, http://www.oed.com/view/Entry/225527?rskey=qo7EkG&result=3.

10. Schoenbrun, *Historical Reconstruction*, 64, no. 80; Yvonne Bastin, André Coupez, Evariste Mumba, and Thilo C. Schadeberg, eds., *Bantu Lexical Reconstructions 3/Reconstructions lexicales bantoues 3* (Tervuren, Belgium: Musée Royale de l'Afrique Centrale, 2002), Main 418, https://www.africamuseum.be/en/research/discover/human_sciences/culture_society/blr. There is also a variation or variant form *-tàk-* "desire, lack," VAR 9606.

11. Rob Marchant et al., "Drivers and Trajectories of Land Cover Change in East Africa: Human and Environmental Interactions from 6000 Years Ago to Present," *Earth Science Reviews* 178 (2018): 339.

12. See root 2 in the appendix for reflexes, meanings, and distributions.

13. Bastin, Coupez, Mumba, and Schadeberg, eds., *Bantu Lexical Reconstructions 3*, Main 2746, 2747, 2751, 2754, 2757.

14. Schoenbrun, *Historical Reconstruction*, 66, no. 86; 239, no. 365.

15. Gender is a significant factor in the vulnerability of bereaved households to poverty as studies on the particular vulnerabilities of widows show. This gender dynamic is difficult to reconstruct for the deeper past because the language is often gender-neutral. Kenda Mutongi's work on colonial and postcolonial Maragoli in Western Kenya is exemplary in showing how bereavement shaped the social and economic lives of widows and their children: Kenda Mutongi, *Worries of the Heart: Widows, Family, and Community in Kenya* (Chicago: University of Chicago Press, 2007), especially 95–159. For other more contemporary examples, see Paul C. Rosenblatt and Busisiwe Catherine Nkosi, "South African Zulu Widows in a Time of Poverty and Social Change," *Death Studies* 31, no. 1 (2007): 67–85; Dominique van de Walle, "Lasting Welfare Effects of Widowhood in Mali," *World Development* 51 (2013): 1–19.

16. On histories of emotion and affect in precolonial Africa, see Kathryn M. de Luna, "Affect and Society in Precolonial Africa," *International Journal of African Historical Studies* 46, no. 1 (2013): 123–50. On the history of death in Africa, see the special issue, *Journal of African History* 49, no. 3 (2008), in particular the historiographical overview by Rebekah Lee and Megan Vaughan, "Death and Dying in the History of Africa since 1800": 341–59; Walima T. Kalusa and Megan Vaughan, *Death, Belief and Politics in Central African History* (Lusaka: Lembani Trust, 2013). Work on orphans also highlights the importance of material *and* affective dimensions of bereavement. For example, Rachel E. Goldberg and Susan E. Short, "'The Luggage That Isn't Theirs Is Too Heavy . . .': Understandings of Orphan Disadvantage in Lesotho," *Population Research and Policy Review* 31, no. 1 (2012): 67–83. Brad Weiss's work on Buhaya explores the relationship between commodification, memory, and death. See, for example, Brad Weiss, "Forgetting Your Dead: Alienable and Inalienable Objects in Northwest Tanzania," *Anthropological Quarterly* 70, no. 4 (1997): 164–72.

17. See root 3 in the appendix for reflexes, meanings, and distributions.

18. Bastin, Coupez, Mumba, and Schadeberg, eds., *Bantu Lexical Reconstructions 3*, Main 2414.

19. Jane Guyer discusses the contemporary framing of poverty as a condition of being stuck, in Jane I. Guyer, "Pauper, Percentile, Precarity: Analytics for Poverty Studies in Africa," *Journal of African History* 59, no. 3 (2018): 437–48, here 447. For the derived root, see Bastin, Coupez, Mumba, and Schadeberg, eds., *Bantu Lexical Reconstructions 3*, Derived 2415.

20. I am grateful to Kathryn M. de Luna for helping me make this connection.

21. See root 4 in the appendix for reflexes, meanings, and distributions.

22. David L. Schoenbrun, personal communication, March 2017. See also Rhiannon Stephens, *A History of African Motherhood: The Case of Uganda, 700–1900* (New York: Cambridge University Press, 2013), 84. For the history of marriage in the region and the role of women within it, see Rhiannon Stephens, "'Whether They Promised Each Other Some Thing Is Difficult to Work Out': The Complicated History of Marriage in Uganda," *African Studies Review* 59, no. 1 (2016): 127–53; Schoenbrun, *A Green Place*.

23. In this, the root comes close to capturing what Guyer has described as the "composition of assets crucial to resilience to shock and also to onward growth." Guyer, "Pauper, Percentile, Precarity," 446.

24. See root 5 in the appendix for reflexes, meanings, and distributions.

25. Bastin, Coupez, Mumba, and Schadeberg, eds., *Bantu Lexical Reconstructions 3*, Main 2520 and DER 2522.

26. In the Ruvuma languages in Tanzania, for example, it took on the meanings to buy and to trade alongside other meanings of to twist, to overturn, to revolutionize. Andrea Felber Seligman, "Encircling Value: Inland Trade in the Precolonial East African-Indian Ocean World, ca. 1st–17th Centuries" (PhD diss., Northwestern University, 2014), 40. I am grateful to Yaari Felber Seligman for our conversations about this root which have helped shape and clarify my thinking.

27. Schoenbrun, *Historical Reconstruction*, 251, no. 385.

28. For example, we find in Kinande, *erihinúka* (to change); in Kitembo, *kúíndáálá* (to tumble); in Kirundi, *guhindigana* (threaten to rain), *ihindagu* (inconstancy, continual change); in Luganda, *kuyinda* (approach with a show of strength); in Runyankore-Rukiga, *kuhindúka* (change, turn, be transformed), *omuhinzi* (spirit provoker, rouser); and in Runyambo, *kuhinduka* (alter, change; deflect, turn against).

29. Schoenbrun, *A Green Place*, 45–46.

30. Schoenbrun, *A Green Place*, 72–74.

31. Schoenbrun, *A Green Place*, 188.

32. See root 6 in the appendix for reflexes, meanings, and distributions.

33. Bastin, Coupez, Mumba, and Schadeberg, eds., *Bantu Lexical Reconstructions 3*, ID Main 6938; ID (no label) 6924; see also ID Derived 3524 and ID Derived 6940.

34. I am grateful to Abosede George for helping me make this connection.

35. Schoenbrun, *A Green Place*, 99.

36. Schoenbrun, *Historical Reconstruction*, 109–10, no. 156; 133, no. 196.

37. Schoenbrun, *A Green Place*, 177.

38. On the more recent meanings connected to slavery, see David Schoenbrun, "Violence, Marginality, Scorn and Honour: Language Evidence of Slavery to the Eighteenth Century," in *Slavery in the Great Lakes Region of East Africa*, ed. Henri Médard and Shane Doyle (Oxford: James Currey, 2007), 43–44.

39. Stephens, *A History of African Motherhood*, 48–50.

40. See root 7 in the appendix for reflexes, meanings, and distributions. There may be a connection to the Proto-Nilo-Saharan root *nàkʰ, "to reject," or *-nàk'w/nà:k'w "to suck," but further research is required to clarify this question. Christopher Ehret, *A Historical-Comparative Reconstruction of Nilo-Saharan* (Cologne: Rüdiger Köppe, 2001), 313, no. 251 and no. 252.

41. Elias Mandala has written powerfully about the need to appreciate Malawian peasants' conceptualization of time as both cyclical and linear in order to understand the history of seasonal hunger in the Tshiri valley of Malawi and its relationship to poverty and episodic famine. Elias C. Mandala, *The End of Chidyerano: A History of Food and Everyday Life in Malawi, 1860–2004* (Portsmouth, NH: Heinemann, 2005).

42. Ferdinand Walser, *Luganda Proverbs* (Berlin: Reimer Verlag, 1982), 1449, no. 1457; my translation, which varies slightly from the original. This proverb is also cited in Père Le Veux, *Premier essai de vocabulaire luganda–français d'après l'ordre étymologique* (Maison-Carrée, Algeria: Imprimerie des missionaires d'Afrique [Pères Blancs]), 1917), 706; and R.A. Snoxall, *Luganda–English Dictionary* (Oxford: Clarendon Press, 1967), 236.

43. John Iliffe, *The African Poor: A History* (Cambridge: Cambridge University Press, 1987).

44. See root 4 in the appendix for reflexes, meanings, and distributions.

45. On the more recent history of slavery and warfare in Buganda, see Richard Reid, "Human Booty in Buganda: Some Observations on the Seizure of People in War, c.1700–1890," in *Slavery in the Great Lakes Region of East Africa*, ed. Henri Médard and Shane Doyle (Oxford: James Currey, 2007), 145–60.

46. Bastin, Coupez, Mumba, and Schadeberg, eds., *Bantu Lexical Reconstructions 3*, Main 3081.

47. See root 8 in the appendix for reflexes, meanings, and distributions.

48. For more recent examples of creativity in the composition of wealth from Equatorial Africa, see Jane I. Guyer and Samuel M. Eno Belinga, "Wealth in People as Wealth in Knowledge: Accumulation and Composition in Equatorial Africa," *Journal of African History* 36, no. 1 (1995): 91–120; Florence Bernault, *Colonial Transactions: Imaginaries, Bodies, and Histories in Gabon* (Durham, NC: Duke University Press, 2019).

49. See root 9 in the appendix for reflexes, meanings, and distributions.

50. The place of Lugungu within the classification of Great Lakes Bantu is the least well established due to the limited research on the language when Schoenbrun was working on this. More recent linguistic work on Lugungu has focused primarily on description and lexicography. Currently it forms an independent branch of the Great Lakes Bantu languages.

51. We find, for example, *bugagga* (wealth) in Lumasaaba and *omugagga* (rich person) in Lugwe. The long—or geminate—consonant "gg" at the start of the final syllable clearly marks the nouns as relatively recent loans from Luganda, rather than inherited forms.

52. The dating here is provisional and based on research by Ehret some decades ago. He himself noted that relying on cognate counting for dating with such small numbers of cognates as exist for Proto-Nilotic is problematic, but, to date, there remains little archaeological research done that could be used for correlations. Ehret, *Southern Nilotic History*, 29. Recent work by William Fitzsimons has demonstrated the antiquity of Proto-Ateker and Proto-Tung'a, pushing the dating of Proto-Southern Nilotic further back. He posited that the dissolution of Proto-Nilotic could have been as early as 2000 BCE. William Fitzsimons, "Distributed Power: Climate Change, Elderhood, and Republicanism in the Grasslands of East Africa, c. 500 BCE to 1800 CE" (PhD diss., Northwestern University, 2020), 102.

53. See, for example, the herding and farming vocabulary Ehret has reconstructed: Ehret, *Southern Nilotic History*, 95; and Ehret, *Nilo-Saharan*, 380, no. 558.

54. See root 10 in the appendix for reflexes, meanings, and distributions. The following draws on and revises some of the arguments in Rhiannon Stephens, "'Wealth,' 'Poverty' and the Question of Conceptual History in Oral Contexts: Uganda from c. 1000 CE," in *Doing Conceptual History in Africa*, rev. ed., ed. Axel Fleisch and Rhiannon Stephens (2016; Oxford: Berghahn Books, 2018), 21–48.

55. Further research is needed on the Nilotic languages as a group, in addition to the work that has been completed on the Southern and Eastern Nilotic languages. See Franz Rottland, *Die Südnilotischen Sprachen: Beschreibung, Verglechung und Rekonstruktion* (Berlin: Dietrich Reimer, 1982); Ehret, *Southern Nilotic History*; Rainer Vossen, *The Eastern Nilotes: Linguistic and Historical Reconstructions* (Berlin: Dietrich Reimer, 1982). Fitzsimons's doctoral dissertation is an invaluable contribution and significantly expands our knowledge of the Ateker languages of Eastern Nilotic; Fitzsimons, "Distributed Power."

56. John Albert Distefano, "The Precolonial History of the Kalenjin of Kenya: A Methodological Comparison of Linguistic and Oral Traditional Evidence" (PhD diss., University of California, Los Angeles, 1985), 100.

57. Ehret, *Southern Nilotic History*, 33.

58. Ehret, *Southern Nilotic History*, 39.

59. Ehret, *Southern Nilotic History*, 29, 31; Rottland, *Südnilotischen Sprachen*, 254–56.

60. Ehret, *Southern Nilotic History*, 44–47.

61. See root 11 in the appendix for reflexes, meanings, and distributions.

62. Ehret, *Southern Nilotic History*, 114. Note, however, that the reflex of *pan* in modern Iraqw translates as orphan, but not as pauper. Maarten Mous, Martha Qorro, and Roland Kießling, *Iraqw–English Dictionary with an English and a Thesaurus Index* (Cologne: Rüdiger Köppe, 2002), 81.

63. In making this argument, he appears not to accept the reflex for *panan* in Datooga that Ehret offers as evidence of his reconstruction to Southern Nilotic. Rottland, *Südnilotischen Sprachen*, 400.

64. Fitzsimons, "Distributed Power," chapter 2. As noted above, Fitzsimons's dating pushes the existence of Proto-Ateker, Proto-Tung'a, and Proto-Eastern Nilotic further

back in time compared to earlier research: Vossen, *Eastern Nilotes*, 49; citing Christopher Ehret et al., "Some Thoughts on the Early History of the Nile-Congo Watershed," *Ufahamu* 5, no. 2 (1974): 85–112; and Christopher Ehret, "Cushites and the Highland and Plains Nilotes to A.D.1800," in *Zamani: A Survey of East African History*, ed. Bethwell A. Ogot (Nairobi: East African Publishing House, 1974), 150–69.

65. Vossen, *Eastern Nilotes*, 479–83.

66. See root 10 in the appendix for reflexes, meanings, and distributions.

67. This meaning is present in the Western Nilotic language Dhopadhola, but not in other Western Nilotic languages; it was borrowed into Dhopadhola from neighboring Eastern Nilotic languages rather than being an inherited gloss.

68. Marchant et al., "Drivers and Trajectories," 338.

69. See root 12 in the appendix for reflexes, meanings, and distributions.

70. Fitzsimons, "Distributed Power," 402–3, reconstruction PT1.

71. Christopher Ehret, *The Civilizations of Africa: A History to 1800* (Charlottesville: University of Virginia Press, 2002), 220; Ehret, *Nilo-Saharan*, 424, no. 762; 587–88, no. 1451.

72. See root 13 in the appendix for the full set of reflexes, meanings, and distributions.

Interchapter: Overview of Climate Developments

1. There is some data from Ethiopian tree rings that includes trees dated back to the mid-eighteenth century, but older evidence remains elusive. E. Gebrehiwot Gebregeorgis et al., "Historical Droughts Recorded in Extended *Juniperus procera* Ring-Width Chronologies from the Ethiopian Highlands," *International Journal of Biometeorology* 64, no. 5 (2020): 739–53.

2. Kathleen D. Morrison, "Provincializing the Anthropocene: Eurocentrism in the Earth System," in *At Nature's Edge: The Global Present and Long-Term History*, ed. Gunnel Cederlöf and Mahesh Rangarajan (New Delhi: Oxford University Press, 2018), 1–18. This Eurocentrism is evident in the periodization of past climate events, whether the Roman Warm Period (circa 250 BCE to 400 CE) or the Medieval Climate Anomaly (circa 950–1250 CE), that directly reference European history to the exclusion of other chronologies.

3. For a good overview that focuses on how this affects rainfall, see Sharon E. Nicholson, "Climate and Climatic Variability of Rainfall over Eastern Africa," *Reviews of Geophysics* 55 (2017): 590–635; Nicholson, "A Review of Climate Dynamics and Climate Variability in Eastern Africa," in *The Limnology, Climatology and Paleoclimatology of the East African Lakes*, ed. Thomas C. Johnson and Eric O. Odada, with Katherine T. Whittaker (Amsterdam: Gordon and Breach Science Publishers, 1996), 25–56. See also Rob Marchant et al., "Drivers and Trajectories of Land Cover Change in East Africa: Human and Environmental Interactions from 6000 Years Ago to Present," *Earth Science Reviews* 178 (2018): 322–78, here 326; and Jessica E. Tierney et al., "Late Quaternary

Behavior of the East African Monsoon and the Importance of the Congo Air Boundary," *Quaternary Science Reviews* 30 (2011): 798–807.

4. Edmond A. Mathez and Jason E. Smerdon, *Climate Change: The Science of Global Warming and Our Energy Future*, 2nd ed. (New York: Columbia University Press, 2018), 31.

5. Mathez and Smerdon, *Climate Change*, 33. Sharon Nicholson has recently argued that the ITCZ is not an adequate explanation for the pattern of bimodal rainfall, at least in equatorial West and Central Africa, noting that a complex range of processes are at play. Sharon E. Nicholson, "The ITCZ and the Seasonal Cycle over Equatorial Africa," *Bulletin of the American Meteorological Society* 99, no. 2 (2018): 337–48.

6. Nicholson, "The ITCZ and the Seasonal Cycle," 338. On the role of the ITCZ in the South Asian monsoon, see Sulochana Gadgil, "The Monsoon System: Land-sea Breeze or the ITCZ?," *Journal of Earth System Science* 127, no. 1 (2018): 1–29.

7. Mathez and Smerdon, *Climate Change*, 71.

8. Mathez and Smerdon, *Climate Change*, 71.

9. Nerilie J. Abram et al., "Palaeoclimate Perspectives on the Indian Ocean Dipole," *Quaternary Science Reviews* 237 (2020), https://doi.org/10.1016/j.quascirev.2020.106302.

10. Abram et al., "Palaeoclimate Perspectives on the Indian Ocean Dipole."

11. Naomi E. Levin, "Environment and Climate of Early Human Evolution," *Annual Review of Earth and Planetary Sciences* 43, no. 1 (2015): 419.

12. Marchant et al., "Drivers and Trajectories," 327 (quote), citing W. Nyakwada, L. A. Ogallo, R. E. Okoola, "The Atlantic-Indian Ocean Dipole and Its Influence on East African Seasonal Rainfall," *Journal of Meteorology and Related Sciences* 3 (2009): 21–35; Nicholson, "Climate and Climatic Variability," 594.

13. Marchant et al., "Drivers and Trajectories," 339.

14. Dirk Verschuren, "Reconstructing Fluctuations of a Shallow East Africa Lake during the Past 1800 Yrs from Sediment Stratigraphy in a Submerged Crater Basin," *Journal of Paleolimnology* 25, no. 3 (2001): 305; James M. Russell and Thomas C. Johnson, "A High-Resolution Geochemical Record from Lake Edward, Uganda Congo and the Timing and Causes of Tropical African Drought during the Late Holocene," *Quaternary Science Reviews* 24, no. 12–13 (2005): 1382 (quote); James M. Russell et al., "An 11 000-yr Lithostratigraphic and Paleohydrologic Record from Equatorial Africa: Lake Edward, Uganda–Congo," *Palaeogeography, Palaeoclimatology, Palaeoecology* 193 (2003): 42.

15. Marchant et al., "Drivers and Trajectories," 339.

16. J. Curt Stager, Brian F. Cumming, and L. David Meeker, "A 10,000 Year High-Resolution Diatom Record from Pilkington Bay, Lake Victoria, East Africa," *Quaternary Research* 59, no. 2 (2003): 180.

17. Stager, Cumming, and Meeker, "10,000 Year High-Resolution Diatom Record," 179–80.

18. Bronwen Konecky et al., "Impact of Monsoons, Temperature, and CO_2 on the Rainfall and Ecosystems of Mt. Kenya during the Common Era," *Palaeogeography, Palaeoclimatology, Palaeoecology* 396 (2014): 20.

19. Marchant et al., "Drivers and Trajectories," 339 (quote), citing Verschuren, "Reconstructing Fluctuations," see in particular 307–8.

20. Gijs de Cort et al., "Multi-basin Depositional Framework for Moisture-Balance Reconstruction during the Last 1300 Years at Lake Bogoria, Central Kenya Rift Valley," *Sedimentology* 65, no. 5 (2018): 1688.

21. Stager, Cumming, and Meeker, "10,000 Year High-Resolution Diatom Record," 180.

22. Maria Ryner, Karin Holmgren, and David Taylor, "A Record of Vegetation Dynamics and Lake Level Changes from Lake Emakat, Northern Tanzania, during the Last c. 1200 Years," *Journal of Paleolimnology* 40, no. 2 (2007): 583–601.

23. Mathez and Smerdon, *Climate Change*, 258; Stager, Cumming, and Meeker, "10,000 Year High-Resolution Diatom Record," 180.

24. Stager, Cumming, and Meeker, "10,000 Year High-Resolution Diatom Record," 180.

25. Marchant et al., "Drivers and Trajectories," 339.

26. Dirk Verschuren, Kathleen R. Laird, and Brian F. Cumming, "Rainfall and Drought in Equatorial East Africa during the Past 1,100 Years," *Nature* 403, no. 6768 (2000): 412.

27. de Cort et al., "Multi-basin Depositional Framework," 1689.

28. Marchant et al., "Drivers and Trajectories," 339 (quote), citing for Western Uganda: Immaculate Ssemmanda et al., "Vegetation History in Western Uganda during the Last 1200 Years: A Sediment-Based Reconstruction from Two Crater Lakes," *Holocene* 15, no. 1 (2005): 119–32; and for Lake Simbi and Naivasha: Dirk Verschuren and Dan J. Charman, "Latitudinal Linkages in Late Holocene Moisture-Balance Variation," in *Natural Climate Variability and Global Warming: A Holocene Perspective*, ed. Richard W. Battarbee and Heather A. Binney (Chichester, UK: Wiley, 2008), 189–231.

29. J. Curt Stager et al., "Solar Variability and the Levels of Lake Victoria, East Africa, during the Last Millennium," *Journal of Paleolimnology* 33, no. 2 (2005): 247.

30. Verschuren, Laird, and Cumming, "Rainfall and Drought," 412; de Cort et al., "Multi-basin Depositional Framework," 1689–90.

31. Aylward Shorter, *Chiefship in Western Tanzania: A Political History of the Kimbu* (Oxford: Clarendon Press, 1972), 250; cited in Gerald W. Hartwig, "Demographic Considerations in East Africa during the Nineteenth Century," *International Journal of African Historical Studies* 12, no. 4 (1972): 657.

32. Marchant et al., "Drivers and Trajectories," 339.

33. Stager et al., "Solar Variability," 244, 247.

34. Verschuren, Laird, and Cumming, "Rainfall and Drought," 412.

35. de Cort et al., "Multi-basin Depositional Framework," 1690.

36. Konecky et al., "Impact of Monsoons," 20.

37. Konecky et al., "Impact of Monsoons," 21–22.

38. Konecky et al., "Impact of Monsoons," 22.

39. Marchant et al., "Drivers and Trajectories," 340 (quote), citing Dirk Verschuren et al., "History and Timing of Human Impact on Lake Victoria, East Africa," *Proceedings of the Royal Society B: Biological Sciences* 269, no. 1488 (2002): 289–94; Ilse Bessems et al., "Palaeolimnological Evidence for Widespread Late 18th Century Drought across Equatorial East Africa," *Palaeogeography, Palaeoclimatology, Palaeoecology* 259 (2008): 107–20.

40. William Fitzsimons, "Distributed Power: Climate Change, Elderhood, and Republicanism in the Grasslands of East Africa, c. 500 BCE to 1800 CE" (PhD diss., Northwestern University, 2020).

Chapter Three: The Bereft and the Powerful

1. See root 11 in the appendix for reflexes, meanings, and distributions.

2. The modern Kalenjin languages are: Nandi, Kipsikis, Keyo, Tuken, Markweta, Sapiny, Kony, Bong'om, Pok, Terik, Kinare, Sogoo, Akie, and Päkot. Franz Rottland reconstructed *panan, "pauper, orphan," to Proto-Kalenjin, spoken until around 1,500 years ago, while Christopher Ehret found that its distribution allowed for reconstruction to Proto-Southern Nilotic, spoken until around 2,000 years ago. Franz Rottland, *Die Südnilotischen Sprachen: Beschreibung, Vergleichung und Rekonstruktion* (Berlin: Dietrich Reimer, 1982), 255, 400; Christopher Ehret, *Southern Nilotic History: Linguistic Approaches to the Study of the Past* (Evanston, IL: Northwestern University Press, 1971), 114, 146; John Albert Distefano, "The Precolonial History of the Kalenjin of Kenya: A Methodological Comparison of Linguistic and Oral Traditional Evidence" (PhD diss., University of California, Los Angeles, 1985). The chronology is from Ehret, *Southern Nilotic History*, 63; and Distefano, "Precolonial History," 105. For a fuller discussion of Kalenjin languages and their history, see chapter 5 of this work.

3. In technical terms, the Proto-Kalenjin bilabial plosive /p/ assimilated to the bilabial nasal /m/ because of the following alveolar nasal /n/. Ehret, *Southern Nilotic History*, 146.

4. Ehret, *Southern Nilotic History*, 80–85. See also John E. G. Sutton, "Becoming Masaailand," in *Being Maasai: Ethnicity and Identity in East Africa*, ed. Thomas Spear and Richard Waller (London: James Currey, 1993), 47–48.

5. For example, in Nandi the noun *kibananiat* means "poor person" and *bananet* means "orphan," while the intransitive verb *ke-banan* has the meanings "to look uncared for" and "to lack something." Jane Tapsubei Creider and Chet A. Creider, *A Dictionary of the Nandi Language* (Cologne: Rüdiger Köppe, 2001), 33.

6. In Nandi, the verb *ke-bönön-ji* that is derived from the same root means "to plead for someone," "to appeal," and "to beg," and in Kupsabiny, the noun *panan* refers to a beggar. Note that Nandi orthography is complicated by a lack of "functional distinction between voiced and voiceless stop consonants" and also by a twenty-vowel and four-tone system. Creider and Creider, *Dictionary of the Nandi Language*, 11. A more accurate phonological rendering of these words is: /_ki-pánan-yâ:t/, /_pánan-é:t/, /_ke:-panán/, and /ke:-panan-cì/, where /_/ indicates retracted tongue root pronunciation of the vowel (something Rottland marks with /ɑ/), the colon indicates a long vowel, and the diacritics indicate tone.

7. John E. G. Sutton, *The Archaeology of the Western Highlands of Kenya* (Nairobi: British Institute in Eastern Africa, 1973), 17; Sutton, "Becoming Masaailand," 47;

Gideon S. Were, *A History of the Abaluyia of Western Kenya* (Nairobi: East African Publishing House, 1967), 48, 58; John Osogo, *A History of the Baluyia* (Nairobi: Oxford University Press, 1966), 93–94, 107–8.

8. Rainfall would of course have fluctuated significantly across the centuries as we saw in the interchapter, but this area had one of Uganda's highest mean annual rainfalls in 1959 at 127 cm (50 inches). David N. McMaster, *A Subsistence Crop Geography of Uganda* (Bude, United Kingdom: Geographical Publications, 1962), 14. This pattern has continued into the twenty-first century, as can be seen in the rainfall for the long rainy season in March, April, and May in 2013. See Isaac Mugume et al., "Improving Quantitative Rainfall Prediction Using Ensemble Analogues in the Tropics: Case Study of Uganda," *Atmosphere* 9, no. 9 (2018), https://doi.org/10.3390/atmos9090328.

9. Erika Higenyi, "The History of the Banyole," trans. Elley Wesana-Chomi (unpublished manuscript, shared with author by Susan Reynolds Whyte. Original manuscript written in Luganda in 1936, English translation in 1968), 10.

10. For a summary of this history, see Michael A. Whyte, "The Ideology of Descent in Bunyole" (PhD diss., University of Washington, 1974), 22–24. See also Were, *History of the Abaluyia*.

11. See root 1 in the appendix for reflexes, meanings, and distributions.

12. See root 2 in the appendix for reflexes, meanings, and distributions.

13. This analysis is based on the model of diachronic semantic change that derives from prototype theory. See Dirk Geeraerts, *Diachronic Prototype Semantics: A Contribution to Historical Lexicology* (Oxford: Clarendon Press, 1997). For a discussion of its application in this context, see Rhiannon Stephens, "'Wealth,' 'Poverty' and the Question of Conceptual History in Oral Contexts: Uganda from c. 1000 CE," in *Doing Conceptual History in Africa*, rev. ed., ed. Axel Fleisch and Rhiannon Stephens (2016; Oxford: Berghahn Books, 2018), 27.

14. See root 14 in the appendix for reflexes, meanings, and distributions.

15. J. Curt Stager et al., "Solar Variability and the Levels of Lake Victoria, East Africa, during the Last Millennium," *Journal of Paleolimnology* 33, no. 2 (2005): 247; Rob Marchant et al., "Drivers and Trajectories of Land Cover Change in East Africa: Human and Environmental Interactions from 6000 Years Ago to Present," *Earth Science Reviews* 178 (2018): 339.

16. The Proto-Bantu form is *-gʉ̀- v. fall. Yvonne Bastin, André Coupez, Evariste Mumba, and Thilo C. Schadeberg, eds., *Bantu Lexical Reconstructions 3/Reconstructions lexicales bantoues 3* (Tervuren, Belgium: Musée Royale de l'Afrique Centrale, 2002), Main 1466, https://www.africamuseum.be/en/research/discover/human_sciences/culture_society/blr. For the Lunyole form, see Sylvester N. M. Musimami and Martin Diprose, *Ehyagi hy'Ebibono by'Olunyole/Lunyole Dictionary: Lunyole–English with English Index* (Entebbe, Uganda: Lunyole Language Association, 2011), 162.

17. As George Lakoff has noted, in English we tend to use "up-down" metaphors to express hierarchical structure. George Lakoff, *Women, Fire, and Dangerous Things: What Categories Reveal about the Mind* (Chicago: University of Chicago Press, 1987),

283. The *Oxford English Dictionary* has the following as one of the definitions of "fall": "To pass into or come to be in a specified state or condition, typically one which is unfavourable (as illness, poverty, decay, danger, etc.) or which comes about naturally or in the course of events (as silence, sleep, friendship, etc.)." It also includes a quotation from circa 1515 that reflects the antiquity of this meaning with particular reference to poverty. "fall, v." OED *Online*, June 2019, Oxford University Press, https://www.oed.com/view/Entry/67829?rskey=GGBrmd&result=3&isAdvanced=false.

18. See root 15 in the appendix for reflexes, meanings, and distributions. Musimami and Diprose, *Ehyagi hy'Ebibono by'Olunyole*, 182.

19. See root 4 in the appendix for reflexes, meanings, and distributions.

20. Musimami and Diprose, *Ehyagi hy'Ebibono by'Olunyole*, https://lunyole.webonary.org; entry: omwandu.

21. For an example of these developments and their entanglement with gender in eastern Uganda, see Pamela Khanakwa, "Reinventing *Imbalu* and Forcible Circumcision: Gisu Political Identity and the Fight for Mbale in Late Colonial Uganda," *Journal of African History* 50, no. 3 (2018): 357–89.

22. Sylvester N. M. Musimami, "Engero j'Abanyole n'endoma: Ey'ohubbimbirya n'amahulu gaabyo/Lunyole Proverbs and Sayings Explained" (unpublished manuscript, prepared November 2012), 57, no. 672.

23. Y. Nyango, "Family Life and Customs in Bunyole" (unpublished manuscript, Makerere University Library, n.d. but cited in Susan Reynolds Whyte and Michael A. Whyte, "Clans, Brides and Dancing Spirits," *Folk* 29 [1987]: 97–123, scan of original in author's possession), 4.

24. See root 5 in the appendix for reflexes, meanings, and distributions.

25. Musimami and Diprose, *Ehyagi hy'Ebibono by'Olunyole*, 59.

26. Musimami and Diprose, *Ehyagi hy'Ebibono by'Olunyole*, 59.

27. Cowpeas are indigenous to Africa and there does not seem to have been a single origin for domesticated varieties. Cowpeas are high in seed protein and carbohydrates, as well as in minerals, vitamins, and folic acid. Max Menssen et al., "Genetic and Morphological Diversity of Cowpea (*Vigna unguiculata* (L.) Walp.) Entries from East Africa," *Scientia Horticulturae* 226 (2017): 268–69.

28. Higenyi, "History of the Banyole," 10.

29. Musimami and Diprose, *Ehyagi hy'Ebibono by'Olunyole*, 184.

30. See root 16 in the appendix for reflexes, meanings, and distributions.

31. Bastin, Coupez, Mumba, and Schadeberg, eds., *Bantu Lexical Reconstructions 3*, Main 1916.

32. I am grateful to Kate de Luna for pushing my thinking on this etymology.

33. See root 17 in the appendix for reflexes, meanings, and distributions.

34. Kathryn M. de Luna, *Collecting Food, Cultivating People: Subsistence and Society in Central Africa* (New Haven: Yale University Press, 2016), 113–20.

35. Musimami and Diprose, *Ehyagi hy'Ebibono by'Olunyole*, 204.

36. See root 18 in the appendix for reflexes, meanings, and distributions.

37. On this practice in western Kenya, see Margaret Jean Hay, "Women as Owners, Occupants, and Managers of Property in Colonial Western Kenya," in *African Women*

and the Law: Historical Perspectives, ed. Margaret Jean Hay and Marcia Wright (Boston: Boston University, 1982), 110–23.

38. Sir Harry Johnston, *The Uganda Protectorate: An Attempt to Give Some Description of the Physical Geography, Botany, Zoology, Anthropology, Languages and History of the Territories under British Protection in East Central Africa, between the Congo Free State and the Rift Valley and between the First Degree of South Latitude and the Fifth Degree of North Latitude*, vol. 1 (London: Hutchinson, 1902), 59–60.

39. B. W. Langlands, "The Population Geography of Bugisu and Sebei Districts," occasional paper no. 28, Department of Geography, Makerere University (1971): 31; Martin S. Shanguhyia, *Population, Tradition, and Environmental Control in Colonial Kenya* (Rochester, NY: University of Rochester Press, 2015), 3–6.

40. This is a useful reminder that while bananas may have been a contributory factor in the emergence of Buganda as a centralized and expansionary state, they alone are not an adequate explanation as many other communities grew bananas but chose not to centralize political power in a similar manner.

41. Conrad P. Kottak, "Ecological Variables in the Origin and Evolution of African States: The Buganda Example," *Comparative Studies in Society and History* 14, no. 3 (1972): 356. On the deeper history of banana cultivation in the western Great Lakes region, see David L. Schoenbrun, "Cattle Herds and Banana Gardens: The Historical Geography of the Western Great Lakes Region, ca. AD 800–1500," *African Archaeological Review* 11, no. 1 (1993): 39–72. For banana cultivation in North Nyanza, see Rhiannon Stephens, *A History of African Motherhood: The Case of Uganda, 700–1900* (New York: Cambridge University Press, 2013), 67–70.

42. J. M. Tukahirwa, "Soil Resources in the Highlands of Uganda: Prospects and Sensitivities," *Mountain Research and Development* 8, no. 2/3 (1988): 170.

43. McMaster, *Subsistence Crop Geography of Uganda*, 4–5. The dangers of steep slopes accompanied by deforestation is all too apparent in the annual death tolls in this area from mudslide. See, for example, Yahudu Kitunzi, "Survivor of Landslide Talks about Ordeal," *Daily Monitor*, September 10, 2017, http://www.monitor.co.ug/Magazines/Full-Woman/Survivor-landslide-talks-about-ordeal/689842-4087424-kj8706/index.html. On historical soil erosion due to agriculture elsewhere in East Africa, see Marchant et al., "Drivers and Trajectories," 340, 350, 354.

44. Johnston, *Uganda Protectorate*, 59.

45. See root 1 in the appendix for reflexes, meanings, and distributions. The sound change from /k/ to /x/ is regular in Proto-North Luhyia, with the latter representing a velar fricative.

46. See root 19 in the appendix for reflexes, meanings, and distributions.

47. John Roscoe and J. B. Purvis were both struck by the importance of feasts (including crucially the communal consumption of beer) among the Bamasaaba. John Roscoe, *The Northern Bantu: An Account of Some Central African Tribes of the Uganda Protectorate* (Cambridge: University Press, 1915), 159–94; John Roscoe, *The Bagesu and Other Tribes of the Uganda Protectorate* (Cambridge: University Press, 1924), 1–50; J. B. Purvis, *Through Uganda to Mount Elgon* (London: T. Fisher Unwin, 1909), 338–39. On contestations over male circumcision and *imbalu* see Pamela Khanakwa, "Male Circumcision

among the Bagisu of Eastern Uganda: Practices and Conceptualizations," in *Doing Conceptual History in Africa*, rev. ed., ed. Fleisch and Stephens, 115–37.

48. Roscoe, *The Northern Bantu*, 167.

49. See also the discussion of Eastern Nilotic–speaking communities in Stephens, "'Wealth', 'Poverty,'" 32; and chapter 5 of this work.

50. The condemnation of poor men as bachelors was widespread in the region and by no means limited to Bantu-speaking communities as can be seen in the Lango compound adjective for a poor man, which translates as "have sex with ash." **Buru**. Ashes. Ngoto buru, to lie with ashes, i.e. to be too poor to possess a wife." J. H. Driberg, *The Lango: A Nilotic Tribe of Uganda* (London: T. Fisher Unwin, 1923), 374, emphasis in original.

51. See root 2 in the appendix for reflexes, meanings, and distributions.

52. While a connection with this is difficult to establish definitively, in the Eastern Nilotic languages, spoken to the west, north, and east of the North Luhyia languages, there is a similar semantic mapping of poverty and torture onto a single root (*-can-*). Stephens, "'Wealth', 'Poverty,'" 30–32, and elsewhere in this volume.

53. Thank you to Marcia Wright for our conversations about this that helped shape my thinking. For economic descriptions of the nineteenth century, see F. E. Makila, *An Outline History of the Babukusu of Western Kenya* (Nairobi: Kenya Literature Bureau, 1978), 41–45; Purvis, *Through Uganda to Mount Elgon*, 272–73; Roscoe, *The Bagesu*, 12–22. On a public display of wealth leading to conflict and splintering, see Gideon S. Were, *Western Kenya Historical Texts: Abaluyia, Teso and Elgon Kalenjin* (Nairobi: East African Literature Bureau, 1967), 170.

54. See root 20 in the appendix for reflexes, meanings, and distributions.

55. See root 5 in the appendix for reflexes, meanings, and distributions.

56. From Proto-Bantu: *-i(b)ʊ*. Thilo C. Schadeberg, "Derivation," in *The Bantu Languages*, ed. Derek Nurse and Gérard Philippson (London: Routledge, 2003), 78.

57. Bastin, Coupez, Mumba, and Schadeberg, eds., *Bantu Lexical Reconstructions 3*, Main 2113. See also Kathryn M. de Luna, "Affect and Society in Precolonial Africa," *International Journal of African Historical Studies* 46, no. 1 (2013): 131–38. Jan Vansina glossed the root as "big man" in Western Bantu languages, arguing that the original meaning in Proto-Bantu was chief. Vansina, *Paths in the Rainforests: Toward a History of Political Tradition in Equatorial Africa* (Madison: University of Wisconsin Press, 1990), 73–74, 274 no. 11. Marcos Abreu Leitão de Almeida offered a useful overview of the different analyses of *-kum-* in Bantu languages before concluding, in agreement with de Luna, that the meaning of leadership derived from lineal descent was derivative rather than original. Instead, *-kum-* was a condition of respect that could be held by people other than big men. Abreu Leitão de Almeida, "Speaking of Slavery: Slaving Strategies and Moral Imaginations in the Lower Congo (Early Times to the Late 19th Century)" (PhD diss., Northwestern University, 2020), 128–33.

58. See root 4 in the appendix for reflexes, meanings, and distributions.

59. See root 21 in the appendix for reflexes, meanings, and distributions.

60. Bastin, Coupez, Mumba, and Schadeberg, eds., *Bantu Lexical Reconstructions 3*, Main 1001. The relevant sound changes here are *d > t following Luyia Law (with a likely intermediate stage of /ɾ/) and *p> *h following p-lenition. See also Martin Mould, "Greater Luyia," in *Studies in the Classification of Eastern Bantu Languages*, by Thomas H. Hinnebusch, Derek Nurse, and Martin Mould (Cologne: Helmut Buske, 1981), 181–261.

61. See root 24 in the appendix for reflexes, meanings, and distributions.

62. Ehret, *Southern Nilotic History*, 144. See root 22 in the appendix for reflexes, meanings, and distributions. Note that this meaning of abundant wealth in livestock also appears in Lusaamia, but this is an example of independent innovation and occurred later.

63. Distefano, "Precolonial History," 105. See also chapter 5 of this work.

64. Bastin, Coupez, Mumba, and Schadeberg, eds., *Bantu Lexical Reconstructions 3*, Main 1646. See root 23 in the appendix for reflexes, meanings, and distributions.

65. On the complex relationship between metalworking and status, see Eugenia Herbert, *Iron, Gender, and Power: Rituals of Transformation in African Societies* (Bloomington: Indiana University Press, 1993); Colleen E. Kriger, *Pride of Men: Ironworking in 19th Century West Central Africa* (Portsmouth, NH: Heinemann, 1999); Peter R. Schmidt, *Iron Technology in East Africa: Symbolism, Science, and Archaeology* (Bloomington: Indiana University Press, 1997). In a number of Luyia-speaking societies in what is today western Kenya, the association between metal and social standing was made through political leaders and clan leaders wearing copper or brass bracelets as part of their insignia. See Were, *Western Kenya Historical Texts*, 13, 30, 35, 40, 56, 60.

66. Roscoe, *The Northern Bantu*, 162 (quote). See also Purvis, *Through Uganda to Mount Elgon*, 272–73.

67. Roscoe, *The Northern Bantu*, 162–63.

68. Roscoe, *The Northern Bantu*, 163.

69. See root 2 in the appendix for reflexes, meanings, and distributions.

70. On *imbalu* see Khanakwa, "Male Circumcision among the Bagisu."

71. See root 20 in the appendix for reflexes, meanings, and distributions.

72. Rhiannon Stephens, field notes.

73. See root 22 in the appendix for the full set of reflexes, meanings, and distributions.

74. Roscoe, *The Northern Bantu*, 168.

75. Purvis, *Through Uganda to Mount Elgon*, 274.

76. Roscoe, *The Northern Bantu*, 168.

77. Roscoe, *The Northern Bantu*, 173 (quote); Purvis, *Through Uganda to Mount Elgon*, 274.

78. Roscoe, *The Northern Bantu*, 173.

79. Roscoe, *The Northern Bantu*, 179–81.

80. See root 4 in the appendix for reflexes, meanings, and distributions.

81. See root 21 in the appendix for reflexes, meanings, and distributions.

82. See root 24 in the appendix for reflexes, meanings, and distributions.
83. See root 5 in the appendix for reflexes, meanings, and distributions.
84. See root 23 in the appendix for reflexes, meanings, and distributions.
85. Berthe Siertsema, *Masaba Word List: English–Masaba, Masaba–English* (Tervuren, Belgium: Musée Royale de l'Afrique Centrale, 1981), 44, 71.
86. Purvis, *Through Uganda to Mount Elgon*, 274.
87. See root 2 in the appendix for reflexes, meanings, and distributions. These translations, while highlighting the Christian moral condemnation of extramarital sexuality, do capture the social opprobrium of this kind of behavior.
88. Widow inheritance was prevalent in several Greater Luhyia societies, at least when they were first written about and likely for a significant period before that. Johnston, *Uganda Protectorate*, 2: 749; C. W. Hobley, *Eastern Uganda: An Ethnological Survey* (London: The Anthropological Institute of Great Britain and Ireland, 1902), 25; Roscoe, *The Northern Bantu*, 178; J. S. La Fontaine, *The Gisu of Uganda*, ed. Daryll Forde (London: International African Institute, 1959), 36.
89. See root 1 in the appendix for reflexes, meanings, and distributions.
90. Rhiannon Stephens, field notes.
91. See root 25 in the appendix for reflexes, meanings, and distributions.
92. See roots 22, 4, and 23 in the appendix for reflexes, meanings, and distributions.
93. See root 5 in the appendix for reflexes, meanings, and distributions.
94. See root 26 in the appendix for reflexes, meanings, and distributions.
95. Charles Okumu Wandera, personal communication, June 1, 2016. See root 2 in the appendix for reflexes, meanings, and distributions. This meaning is shared with Lugwere. It is difficult from the phonology to be certain of the direction of movement here, but given the same meaning is held in both Lugwe and Lusaamia, it is reasonable to posit that speakers of Lugwere borrowed from them, rather than the other way around.
96. See roots 3 and 1 in the appendix for reflexes, meanings, and distributions.
97. See root 5 in the appendix for reflexes, meanings, and distributions.
98. See root 4 in the appendix for reflexes, meanings, and distributions.
99. Bastin, Coupez, Mumba, and Schadeberg, eds., *Bantu Lexical Reconstructions 3*, Main 1997. See root 27 in the appendix for reflexes, meanings, and distributions.
100. Thilo C. Schadeberg and Koen Bostoen, "Word Formation," in *Bantu Languages*, 2nd ed., ed. Mark Van de Velde, Koen Bostoen, Derek Nurse, and Gérard Philippson (London: Routledge, 2019), 183–84.
101. David Lee Schoenbrun, *The Historical Reconstruction of Great Lakes Bantu Cultural Vocabulary: Etymologies and Distributions* (Cologne: Rüdiger Köppe, 1997), 138, Root 205.
102. See root 28 in the appendix for reflexes, meanings, and distributions.
103. Richard Nzita and Mbaga-Niwampa, "The Basamia-Bagwe," in *Peoples and Cultures of Uganda* (Kampala: Fountain Publishers, 1993), 73–76.
104. Johnston, *Uganda Protectorate*, 43.
105. Johnston, *Uganda Protectorate*, 44.
106. Joseph Thomson, *Through Masai Land: A Journey of Exploration among the Snowclad Volcanic Mountains and Strange Tribes of Eastern Equatorial Africa. Being*

the Narrative of the Royal Geographical Society's Expedition to Mount Kenia and Lake Victoria Nyanza, 1883–1884 (Boston: Houghton, Mifflin, 1885), 491.

107. The term Kavirondo was used by outsiders, and adopted by Europeans in the late nineteenth century, to refer to people living around the northeast of the Victoria Nyanza and their lands. A further distinction was made between those who spoke Bantu languages (i.e., people speaking Greater Luhyia and East Nyanza languages) and those who spoke Nilotic languages (i.e., people speaking Southern Luo languages).

108. N. Stam, "Bantu Kavirondo of Mumias District (near Lake Victoria)," *Anthropos* 14/15, no. 4/6 (1919): 969; cited in R. W. Moody, "Social and Political Institutions of the Samia" (PhD diss., Cambridge University, 1967), 6.

109. R. W. Moody, "Land Tenure in Samia" (unpublished manuscript, 1962), 1.

110. Thomson, *Through Masai Land*, 482.

111. R. W. Moody, "Samia Fishermen" (unpublished manuscript, 1963), 2.

112. Moody, "Samia Fishermen," 2.

113. Moody, "Samia Fishermen," 4.

114. Michael G. Kenny, "Pre-colonial Trade in Eastern Lake Victoria," *Azania* 14 (1979): 102.

115. Thomson, *Through Masai Land*, 492.

116. Thomson, *Through Masai Land*, 492–93.

117. Shanguhyia, *Population, Tradition, and Environmental Control*, 6; Moody, "Social and Political Institutions of the Samia," 6; Stam, "Bantu Kavirondo," 969.

118. Shanguhyia, *Population, Tradition, and Environmental Control*, 77.

119. See root 11 in the appendix for reflexes, meanings, and distributions.

120. See root 3 in the appendix for reflexes, meanings, and distributions.

121. Rhiannon Stephens, field notes.

122. Rhiannon Stephens, field notes.

123. See root 6 in the appendix for reflexes, meanings, and distributions.

124. See root 5 in the appendix for reflexes, meanings, and distributions.

125. See root 4 in the appendix for reflexes, meanings, and distributions.

126. See root 28 in the appendix for reflexes, meanings, and distributions.

127. See root 27 in the appendix for reflexes, meanings, and distributions.

128. See root 22 in the appendix for reflexes, meanings, and distributions.

Chapter Four: Gender and Honor

1. On the Proto-Rutara speaker community, see David Lee Schoenbrun, *A Green Place, A Good Place: Agrarian Change, Gender, and Social Identity in the Great Lakes Region to the 15th Century* (Portsmouth, NH: Heinemann, 1998), 217–53.

2. Schoenbrun, *A Green Place*, 79, 167; Rhiannon Stephens, *A History of African Motherhood: The Case of Uganda, 700–1900* (New York: Cambridge University Press, 2013), 38–39.

3. See root 6 in the appendix for reflexes, meanings, and distributions.

4. See root 7 in the appendix for reflexes, meanings, and distributions.

5. Rob Marchant et al., "Drivers and Trajectories of Land Cover Change in East Africa: Human and Environmental Interactions from 6000 Years Ago to the Present," *Earth Science Reviews* 178 (2018): 339.

6. David L. Schoenbrun, *The Names of the Python: Belonging in East Africa, 900 to 1930* (Madison: University of Wisconsin Press, 2021), 38.

7. See root 29 in the appendix for reflexes, meanings, and distributions.

8. For a different reconstruction of this, see David Lee Schoenbrun, *The Historical Reconstruction of Great Lakes Bantu Cultural Vocabulary: Etymologies and Distributions* (Cologne: Rüdiger Köppe, 1997), 245–46, no. 375. My reading of the evidence is that the original meaning was limited to evil and filth, with the references to poverty only emerging among speakers of Proto-North Nyanza.

9. Writing about a very different time and context, a number of scholars have highlighted the connection between neoliberal economics and witchcraft in postcolonial Africa. See, in particular, Maia Green and Simeon Mesaki, "The Birth of the 'Salon': Poverty, 'Modernization,' and Dealing with Witchcraft in Southern Tanzania," *American Ethnologist* 32, no. 3 (2005): 371–88; Maia Green, "Discourses on Inequality: Poverty, Public Bads and Entrenching Witchcraft in Post-adjustment Tanzania," *Anthropological Theory* 5, no. 3 (2005): 247–66; Peter Geschiere, *The Modernity of Witchcraft: Politics and the Occult in Postcolonial Africa*, trans. Peter Geschiere and Janet Roitman (Charlottesville: University of Virginia Press, 1997).

10. See root 30 in the appendix for reflexes, meanings, and distributions

11. Francis Katamba, "Bantu Nominal Morphology," in *The Bantu Languages*, ed. Derek Nurse and Gérard Philippson (London: Routledge, 2003), 115.

12. See root 31 in the appendix for reflexes, meanings, and distributions.

13. Yvonne Bastin, André Coupez, Evariste Mumba, and Thilo C. Schadeberg, eds., *Bantu Lexical Reconstructions 3/Reconstructions lexicales bantoues 3* (Tervuren, Belgium: Musée Royale de l'Afrique Centrale, 2002), Main 1084, https://www.africamuseum.be/en/research/discover/human_sciences/culture_society/blr.

14. Bastin, Coupez, Mumba, and Schadeberg, eds., *Bantu Lexical Reconstructions 3*, Derived 4809 *-pʊʊdɪʊ n. "cloth from ficus bark," from Main 2628 *-pʊʊd- "thresh (corn); beat with stick."

15. See root 4 in the appendix for reflexes, meanings, and distributions.

16. While Bantu languages tend to be gender-neutral in terms of morphology, this is not consistently the case and broad-based arguments about gender-neutral language proving the lack of significance of gender in a historical community require some nuancing. The prefixes *na* and *ise* (discussed below and denoting a male noun) initially meant mother and father (see Bastin, Coupez, Mumba, and Schadeberg, eds., *Bantu Lexical Reconstructions 3*, Main 3368 *-jinà "mother" and Main 501 *cé "his father"), but in North Nyanza languages the meaning has generalized to adult woman and adult man.

17. David Schoenbrun, Dictionary entry no. 71, personal communication, March 2017.

18. On changing marriage practices, see Rhiannon Stephens, "'Whether They Promised Each Other Some Thing Is Difficult to Work Out': The Complicated History of Marriage in Uganda," *African Studies Review* 59, no. 1 (2016): 127–53.

19. See root 9 in the appendix for reflexes, meanings, and distributions.

20. See root 32 in the appendix for reflexes, meanings, and distributions.

21. Bastin, Coupez, Mumba, and Schadeberg, eds., *Bantu Lexical Reconstructions 3*, Main 378.

22. Stephens, *A History of African Motherhood*, 74, 100; David William Cohen, *Womunafu's Bunafu: A Study of Authority in a Nineteenth-Century African Community* (Princeton: Princeton University Press, 1977), 41.

23. J. Curt Stager et al., "Solar Variability and the Levels of Lake Victoria, East Africa, during the Last Millennium," *Journal of Paleolimnology* 33, no. 2 (2005): 247.

24. See roots 6, 29, and 7 in the appendix for reflexes, meanings, and distributions.

25. See root 1 in the appendix for reflexes, meanings, and distributions.

26. See root 9 in the appendix for reflexes, meanings, and distributions.

27. See root 32 in the appendix for reflexes, meanings, and distributions.

28. See root 4 in the appendix for reflexes, meanings, and distributions.

29. Stephens, *A History of African Motherhood*, 84–85; Stephens, "'Whether They Promised,'" 134.

30. Bethwell A. Ogot, *History of the Southern Luo, Volume I: Migration and Settlement 1500–1900* (Nairobi: East African Publishing House, 1967), 73–74; David William Cohen, *The Historical Tradition of Busoga: Mukama and Kintu* (Oxford: Clarendon Press, 1972), 127–28.

31. Cohen, *Historical Tradition of Busoga*, 139.

32. Cohen, *Historical Tradition of Busoga*, 126 (quotes); citing Ogot, *History of the Southern Luo*, 53–57, and J. P. Crazzolara, *The Lwoo* (Verona: Missioni Africane, 1950–1954). Somewhat problematically, Cohen also attributed the migration to "wanderlust" and an inherent pattern of expansion and raiding.

33. Rhiannon Stephens, "A History of Motherhood, Food Procurement and Politics in East-Central Uganda to the Nineteenth Century" (PhD diss., Northwestern University, 2007), 136–70. See also Frederick Peter Batala-Nayenga, "An Economic History of the Lacustrine States of Busoga, Uganda: 1750–1939" (PhD diss., University of Michigan, 1976), 106.

34. Stephens, *A History of African Motherhood*, 127–28; Batala-Nayenga, "Economic History," 108.

35. David William Cohen, "The Face of Contact: A Model of a Cultural and Linguistic Frontier in Early Eastern Uganda," in *Nilotic Studies: Proceedings of the International Symposium on Languages and History of the Nilotic Peoples, Cologne, January 4–6, 1982*, part 2, ed. Rainer Voßen and Marianne Bechhaus-Gerst (Berlin: Dietrich Reimer, 1983), 344 (quote); Batala-Nayenga, "Economic History," 98.

36. Cohen, *Historical Tradition of Busoga*, 141–42. Note that in Busoga clans are named after a founder, with the prefix *abaise* glossing as "the people of."
37. Cohen, *Historical Tradition of Busoga*, 142.
38. Stephens, *A History of African Motherhood*, 116.
39. See root 4 in the appendix for reflexes, meanings, and distributions.
40. Cohen, "Face of Contact," 352–53.
41. See root 6 in the appendix for reflexes, meanings, and distributions.
42. Katamba, "Bantu Nominal Morphology," 115.
43. Katamba, "Bantu Nominal Morphology," 115.
44. See root 7 in the appendix for reflexes, meanings, and distributions.
45. See root 10 in the appendix for reflexes, meanings, and distributions.
46. For an exploration of this kind of borrowing in a southern African context, see Axel Fleisch, "Conceptual Continuities: About 'Work' in Nguni,'" in *Doing Conceptual History in Africa*, rev. ed., ed. Axel Fleisch and Rhiannon Stephens (2016; Oxford: Berghahn Books, 2018), 49–72.
47. See root 29 in the appendix for reflexes, meanings, and distributions.
48. See root 30 in the appendix for reflexes, meanings, and distributions.
49. See root 1 in the appendix for reflexes, meanings, and distributions.
50. See also Rhiannon Stephens, "'Wealth,' 'Poverty' and the Question of Conceptual History in Oral Contexts: Uganda from c.1000 CE," in *Doing Conceptual History in Africa*, rev. ed., ed. Fleisch and Stephens, 33–34.
51. See root 33 in the appendix for reflexes, meanings, and distributions.
52. See root 4 in the appendix for reflexes, meanings, and distributions.
53. Stephens, *A History of African Motherhood*, 133. For a fictional account of the impact of this raiding of women and girls on those stolen and their descendants, see Jennifer Nansubuga Makumbi, *A Girl Is a Body of Water* (Portland, OR: Tin House, 2020).
54. See root 9 in the appendix for reflexes, meanings, and distributions.
55. For wealth in people, see Igor Kopytoff and Suzanne Miers, "Introduction: African 'Slavery' as an Institution of Marginality," in *Slavery in Africa: Historical and Anthropological Perspectives*, ed. Suzanne Miers and Igor Kopytoff (Madison: University of Wisconsin Press, 1977), 3–81; Caroline Bledsoe, *Women and Marriage in Kpelle Society* (Stanford, CA: Stanford University Press, 1980); Jane I. Guyer, "Wealth in People, Wealth in Things – Introduction," *Journal of African History* 36, no. 1 (1995): 83–90.
56. See also Stephens, "'Wealth,' 'Poverty,'" 40–41.
57. See root 32 in the appendix for reflexes, meanings, and distributions.
58. See root 34 in the appendix for reflexes, meanings, and distributions.
59. Minah Nabirye, *Eiwanika ly'Olusoga: Eiwanika ly'Aboogezi b'Olusoga n'abo Abenda Okwega Olusoga* (Kampala: Menha Publishers, 2009), 308.
60. See root 16 in the appendix for reflexes, meanings, and distributions. The phoneme /k/ in Lusoga corresponds with /h/ in Lunyole in a regular manner.
61. Bastin, Coupez, Mumba, and Schadeberg, eds., *Bantu Lexical Reconstructions 3*, Main 1916.

62. J. C. D. Lawrance, *The Iteso: Fifty Years of Change in a Nilo-Hamitic Tribe of Uganda* (London: Oxford University Press, 1957), 10; William Fitzsimons, "Distributed Power: Climate Change, Elderhood, and Republicanism in the Grasslands of East Africa, ca. 500 BCE to 1800 CE" (PhD diss., Northwestern University, 2020), 119, 304.

63. For more on this, see Stephens, *A History of African Motherhood*, 131.

64. Ronald R. Atkinson, ed., "Bugwere Historical Texts," text 4, Ronald R. Atkinson Private Collection; see also Stephens, *A History of African Motherhood*, 113, 146–47.

65. For a detailed discussion of this, see Stephens, *A History of African Motherhood*, 148–50.

66. G. W. B. Huntingford, "The Orusyan Language of Uganda," *Journal of African Languages* 4, no. 3 (1965): 145. It was among this migrant population that Huntingford conducted his research on the language.

67. See root 29 in the appendix for reflexes, meanings, and distributions.

68. See root 30 in the appendix for reflexes, meanings, and distributions.

69. See root 1 in the appendix for reflexes, meanings, and distributions.

70. See root 9 in the appendix for reflexes, meanings, and distributions.

71. See root 4 in the appendix for reflexes, meanings, and distributions.

72. See root 32 in the appendix for reflexes, meanings, and distributions.

73. For more on this, see Stephens, *A History of African Motherhood*, 146, 148–49.

74. Atkinson, ed., "Bugwere Historical Texts," text 4.

75. Atkinson, ed., "Bugwere Historical Texts," text 13.

76. See root 1 in the appendix for reflexes, meanings, and distributions.

77. See root 29 in the appendix for reflexes, meanings, and distributions.

78. See root 31 in the appendix for reflexes, meanings, and distributions.

79. Richard Nzogi and Martin Diprose, *EKideero ky'oLugwere/Lugwere Dictionary: Lugwere–English with English Index* (Budaka, Uganda: Lugwere Bible Translation and Literacy Association, 2011), https://lugwere.webonary.org; Interview with Samuel Mubbala, May 21, 2013, Mbale, Uganda.

80. See root 2 in the appendix for reflexes, meanings, and distributions.

81. See root 3 in the appendix for reflexes, meanings, and distributions.

82. See root 9 in the appendix for reflexes, meanings, and distributions.

83. See root 4 in the appendix for reflexes, meanings, and distributions.

84. See root 32 in the appendix for reflexes, meanings, and distributions. Note that there is alternation between /f/ and /s/ in Lugwere, so we also find *kufuna*.

85. Stephens, *A History of African Motherhood*, 155.

Chapter Five: Orphans and Livestock

1. John Albert Distefano, "The Precolonial History of the Kalenjin of Kenya: A Methodological Comparison of Linguistic and Oral Traditional Evidence" (PhD diss., University of California, Los Angeles, 1985), 100. For earlier classifications with some

differences, including in terms of dating, see also Christopher Ehret, *Southern Nilotic History: Linguistic Approaches to the Study of the Past* (Evanston, IL: Northwestern University Press, 1971), 63–71; Franz Rottland, *Die Südnilotische Sprachen: Beschreibung, Vergleichung und Rekonstruktion* (Berlin: Dietrich Reimer, 1982), 19–24.

2. Ehret, *Southern Nilotic History*, 63, 65; Distefano, "Precolonial History," 105.
3. Distefano, "Precolonial History," 106.
4. Distefano, "Precolonial History," 108.
5. Ehret, *Southern Nilotic History*, 63–71, 144, 153, 157.
6. Ehret, *Southern Nilotic History*, 63–64, 75.
7. Ehret, *Southern Nilotic History*, 63–64. See also Angelika Mietzner, *Cherang'any: A Kalenjin Language of Kenya* (Cologne: Rüdiger Köppe, 2016), 39–40.
8. Christopher Ehret, *An African Classical Age: Eastern and Southern Africa in World History, 1000 B.C. to A.D. 400* (Charlottesville: University of Virginia Press, 1998), 163; Mietzner, *Cherang'any*, 40–41.
9. Ehret, *Southern Nilotic History*, 64.
10. See root 11 in the appendix for reflexes, meanings, and distributions.
11. Ehret, *Southern Nilotic History*, 105; Rottland, *Südnilotischen Sprachen*, 303; Jane Tapsubei Creider and Chet A. Creider, *A Dictionary of the Nandi Language* (Cologne: Rüdiger Köppe, 2001), 187–88. See root 35 in the appendix for reflexes, meanings, and distributions.
12. David M. Anderson and Vigdis Broch-Due, eds., *"The Poor Are Not Us": Poverty and Pastoralism in Eastern Africa* (Cambridge: Cambridge University Press, 1999).
13. Distefano, "Precolonial History," 105.
14. Distefano, "Precolonial History," 108–10.
15. Distefano, "Precolonial History," 111, 113 (quotation).
16. Distefano, "Precolonial History," 113–14.
17. Distefano, "Precolonial History," 184.
18. J. E. G. Sutton, "Sirikwa Holes, Stones Houses and Their Makers in the Western Highlands of Kenya," *Man* 65 (1965): 101.
19. John Sutton, *A Thousand Years of East Africa* (Nairobi: British Institute in Eastern Africa, 1990), 49.
20. J. E. G. Sutton, *The Archaeology of the Highlands of Western Kenya* (Nairobi: British Institute in Eastern Africa, 1973), 58.
21. J. E. G. Sutton, "Becoming Maasailand," in *Becoming Maasai: Ethnicity and Identity in East Africa*, ed. Thomas Spear and Richard Waller (Oxford: James Currey, 1993), 44.
22. Sutton, "Becoming Maasailand," 46 (quote). See also M. D. Kyule, "The Sirikwa Economy," *Azania* 32, no. 1 (1997): 21–30; Matthew Davies, "The Archaeology of Clan- and Lineage-Based Societies in Africa," in *The Oxford Handbook of African Archaeology*, ed. Peter Mitchell and Paul Lane (Oxford: Oxford University Press, 2013), 723–36.
23. Davies, "Archaeology of Clan- and Lineage-Based Societies," 728–31.
24. Davies, "Archaeology of Clan- and Lineage-Based Societies," 728–31.

25. See root 36 in the appendix for reflexes, meanings, and distributions.

26. A Southern Nilotic or Kalenjin root should consist of at most a consonant-vowel-consonant cluster (CVC) followed by a suffix, whereas this root consists of a CVCVC cluster.

27. I thank Christopher Ehret for his help in pointing me in the right direction on this. Personal communication, March 20, 2019.

28. Distefano, "Precolonial History," 184–86, citing Walter Goldschmidt, *The Culture and Behavior of the Sebei: A Study in Continuity and Adaptation* (Berkeley: University of California Press, 1976), 14.

29. Goldschmidt, *Culture and Behavior of the Sebei*, 22–23; Distefano, "Precolonial History," 194.

30. Walter Goldschmidt, *The Sebei: A Study in Adaptation* (New York: Holt, Rinehart and Winston, 1986), 13.

31. Goldschmidt, *The Sebei*, 15–16.

32. Goldschmidt, *The Sebei*, 16.

33. Goldschmidt, *The Sebei*, 16.

34. See root 36 in the appendix for reflexes, meanings, and distributions.

35. Interview with Kamuron Peter and Kurwa Charles, Kapchorwa, January 22, 2015.

36. See root 11 in the appendix for reflexes, meanings, and distributions.

37. William Fitzsimons, "Distributed Power: Climate Change, Elderhood, and Republicanism in the Grasslands of East Africa, c. 500 BCE to 1800 CE" (PhD diss., Northwestern University, 2020), 99–123. Fitzsimons's research updates the earlier classifications and locations in time and space set out by Rainer Vossen, *The Eastern Nilotes: Linguistic and Historical Reconstructions* (Berlin: Dietrich Reimer, 1982), 49 (quotes), citing Christopher Ehret et al., "Some Thoughts on the Early History of the Nile-Congo Watershed," *Ufahamu* 5, no. 2 (1974): 85–112; and Ehret, "Cushites and the Highland and Plains Nilotes to A.D. 1800," in *Zamani: A Survey of East African History*, ed. Bethwell A. Ogot (Nairobi, 1974), 150–69.

38. Fitzsimons, "Distributed Power," 130–33.

39. Fitzsimons, "Distributed Power," 116–17.

40. See root 10 in the appendix for reflexes, meanings, and distributions.

41. The causative form is marked by the *-ti-* infix, thus we can see that the noun is also derived from the causative verb. The same is true for *-si-* in the Ngakarimojong verb.

42. Peter Logiro and Joyce Ilukori, *A Simplified Ngakarimojong–English English–Ngakarimojong Dictionary* (Kampala: Fountain Publishers, 2007), 72.

43. Åshild Næss, *Prototypical Transitivity* (Amsterdam: John Benjamins, 2007), 8.

44. See Fitzsimons, "Distributed Power."

45. See root 37 in the appendix for reflexes, meanings, and distributions.

46. I am grateful to Will Fitzsimons for this suggestion.

47. See root 12 in the appendix for reflexes, meanings, and distributions.

48. Fitzsimons, "Distributed Power," 286, 293. Fitzsimons's research points toward a significantly earlier date for the emergence of Ateso as a distinct language than had previously been estimated, but is based on extensive fieldwork and a far more comprehensive set of data than other scholars have had access to.

49. J. B. Webster, "Usuku: The Homeland of the Iteso," in J. B. Webster, D. H. Okalany, C. P. Emudong, and N. Egimu-Okuda, *The Iteso during the Asonya* (Nairobi: East African Publishing House, 1973), 1.

50. Fitzsimons, "Distributed Power," 294. See also the overview of climate events in the interchapter of this work.

51. Fitzsimons, "Distributed Power," 118–19.

52. Fitzsimons, "Distributed Power," 123. This differs from earlier classifications and is based on a more comprehensive data set. See Vossen, *Eastern Nilotes*; Harald Hammarström, Robert Forkel, Martin Haspelmath, and Sebastian Bank, *Glottolog 4.2.1* (Jena, Germany: Max Planck Institute for the Science of Human History, 2020), http://glottolog.org.

53. The interviews appear to have been exclusively conducted with men.

54. Webster, "Usuku," 12.

55. Webster, "Usuku," 13.

56. Teso Historical Text no. 12, cited in Webster, "Usuku," 13.

57. Webster, "Usuku," 14.

58. See root 10 in the appendix for reflexes, meanings, and distributions.

59. Apuda Ignatius Loyola, *Bi-lingual Ateso Dictionary* (Entebbe, Uganda: Marianum Press, 2007), 166.

60. Simon Peter Ongodia and Austin Ejiet, *Ateso–English Dictionary* (Kampala: Fountain Publishers, 2008), 188, 248.

61. J. C. D. Lawrance, *The Iteso: Fifty Years of Change in a Nilo-Hamitic Tribe of Uganda* (London: Oxford University Press, 1957), 95.

62. Lawrance, *The Iteso*, 95–96.

63. Teso Historical Text no. 20, cited in Webster, "Usuku," 15.

64. See roots 39 and 12 in the appendix for reflexes, meanings, and distributions.

65. Ivan Karp, *Fields of Change among the Iteso of Kenya* (London: Routledge and Kegan Paul, 1978), 40–41; Fitzsimons, "Distributed Power," 336–37.

66. Jane I. Guyer, *Marginal Gains: Monetary Transactions in Atlantic Africa* (Chicago: University of Chicago Press, 2004), 131–51.

67. U'mista Cultural Society, "Living Tradition: The Kwakwaka'wakw Potlatch of the Northwest Coast," https://umistapotlatch.ca/potlatch-eng.php; H. G. Barnett, "The Nature of the Potlatch," *American Anthropologist* 40, no. 3 (1938): 349–58; Marshall Sahlins, "Poor Man, Rich Man, Big-Man, Chief: Political Types in Melanesia and Polynesia," *Comparative Studies in Society and History* 5, no. 3 (1963): 285–303. I am grateful to Jeffrey Hantman for his advice on this comparison.

68. See root 12 in the appendix for reflexes, meanings, and distributions.

69. Fitzsimons, "Distributed Power," 453, reconstruction PA 138.

70. See root 38 in the appendix for reflexes, meanings, and distributions. Fitzsimons, "Distributed Power," 465–66, reconstruction PT 10. I had previously mistakenly attributed words derived from this root in Ateso to an older root, **ker*. I am very grateful to Will Fitzsimons for correcting my error.

71. Fitzsimons, "Distributed Power," 336.
72. Loyola, *Bi-lingual Ateso Dictionary*, 295.
73. See root 39 in the appendix for reflexes, meanings, and distributions.
74. Webster, "Usuku," 20–21.
75. Paulo Ocoriai and Eriasaapu Oluny (cousins) Toroma, Teso Historical Texts no. 5; quoted in Webster, "Usuku," 24.
76. Webster, "Usuku," 21.
77. Lawrance, *The Iteso*, 135.
78. C. P. Emudong, "The Settlement and Organisation of Kumi during the Asonya," in Webster, Okalany, Emudong, and Egimu-Okuda, *The Iteso during the Asonya*, 88, 99.
79. Webster, "Usuku," 21.
80. Teso Historical Text no. 21, cited in Webster, "Usuku," 22.
81. Teso Historical Text no. 122, cited in Emudong, "Settlement and Organisation of Kumi," 89.
82. Webster, "Usuku," 17.
83. See root 37 in the appendix for reflexes, meanings, and distributions.
84. Webster, "Usuku," 21.
85. Webster, "Usuku," 23.
86. Ben Knighton, *The Vitality of Karamojong Religion: Dying Tradition or Living Faith?* (Aldershot, UK: Ashgate Publishing, 2005), 19. As Knighton notes, this region is larger than Burundi, Rwanda, Wales, or Israel.
87. Knighton, *Vitality of Karamojong Religion*, 19.
88. Knighton, *Vitality of Karamojong Religion*, 19.
89. Knighton, *Vitality of Karamojong Religion*, 19–20.
90. Knighton, *Vitality of Karamojong Religion*, 22; P. H. Gulliver, "Jie Agriculture," *Uganda Journal* 18 (1954): 66.
91. Gulliver, "Jie Agriculture," 66, quoted in John Lamphear, *The Traditional History of the Jie of Uganda* (Oxford: Clarendon Press, 1976), 5. Fitzsimons's research shows that this is an ancient practice that dated back to when Proto-Ateker was spoken. Fitzsimons, "Distributed Power," 143, 151–52.
92. Neville Dyson-Hudson, *Karimojong Politics* (Oxford: Clarendon Press, 1966), 38.
93. Dyson-Hudson, *Karimojong Politics*, 40.
94. Gulliver, "Jie Agriculture," 67.
95. Gulliver, "Jie Agriculture," 68, summarized in Lamphear, *Traditional History of the Jie*, 6.
96. Fitzsimons, "Distributed Power," 219–20.
97. Gulliver, "Jie Agriculture," 65.
98. Lamphear, *Traditional History of the Jie*, 5.
99. Lamphear, *Traditional History of the Jie*, 6.
100. Lamphear, *Traditional History of the Jie*, 7n16. Lamphear argued that the ritual significance of beer had been overlooked by scholars in favor of emphasizing the significance of cattle.

101. Fitzsimons, "Distributed Power," 123.
102. Knighton, *Vitality of Karamojong Religion*, 24; Fitzsimons, "Distributed Power"; William Fitzsimons, personal correspondence, June 14, 2020.
103. Knighton, *Vitality of Karamojong Religion*, 24.
104. Fitzsimons, "Distributed Power," 208.
105. Fitzsimons, "Distributed Power," 479, reconstruction PNA 12.
106. See root 10 in the appendix for reflexes, meanings, and distributions.
107. See root 40 in the appendix for reflexes, meanings, and distributions. See also Fitzsimons, "Distributed Power," 481, reconstruction PNA 19. Fitzsimons reconstructed this independently and with a reflex in Toposa, as well as Turkana and Ngakarimojong.
108. Akuremeri, Jie Historical Text no. 7, cited in Lamphear, *Traditional History of the Jie*, 65.
109. Lamphear, *Traditional History of the Jie*, 66.
110. Dyson-Hudson, *Karimojong Politics*, 86.
111. Dyson-Hudson, *Karimojong Politics*, 85.
112. Dyson-Hudson, *Karimojong Politics*, 86.
113. See root 12 in the appendix for reflexes, meanings, and distributions.
114. Dyson-Hudson, *Karimojong Politics*, 45 (quote); P. H. Gulliver, *The Family Herd: A Study of Two Pastoral Tribes in East Africa: The Jie and Turkana*, 2nd ed. (1955; London: Routledge and Kegan Paul, 1966), 69.
115. See root 37 in the appendix for reflexes, meanings, and distributions.
116. See root 41 in the appendix for reflexes, meanings, and distributions.
117. Fitzsimons, "Distributed Power," 143–44 (quote); 449–50 reconstruction PA 126.
118. Dyson-Hudson, *Karimojong Politics*, 42.
119. Dyson-Hudson, *Karimojong Politics*, 43.
120. Bethwell A. Ogot, *A History of the Luo-Speaking Peoples of Eastern Africa* (Kisumu, Kenya: Anyange Press, 2009), 421.
121. Ogot, *History of the Luo-Speaking Peoples*, 427.
122. Ogot, *History of the Luo-Speaking Peoples*, 428.
123. See root 10 in the appendix for reflexes, meanings, and distributions.
124. See root 13 in the appendix for reflexes, meanings, and distributions.
125. See root 42 in the appendix for reflexes, meanings, and distributions.
126. Chimamanda Ngozi Adichie, "The Danger of a Single Story," TEDGlobal, 2009, https://www.ted.com/talks/chimamanda_ngozi_adichie_the_danger_of_a_single_story.

Chapter Six: Wealth, Poverty, and the Colonial Economy

1. Rhiannon Stephens, *A History of African Motherhood: The Case of Uganda, 700–1900* (New York: Cambridge University Press, 2013), 149.

2. Dirk Verschuren, Kathleen R. Laird, and Brian F. Cumming, "Rainfall and Drought in Equatorial East Africa during the Past 1,100 Years," *Nature* 403, no. 6768 (2000): 412. I am currently engaged in a collaborative research project with Jason Smerdon and Edward Cook that aims to better delineate the onset, duration, and scope of this drought drawing on new paleoclimate reconstructions that offer higher resolution than the lake sediment cores.

3. Gideon S. Were, *A History of the Abaluyia of Western Kenya* (Nairobi: Africa Publishing House, 1967), 92. The initial settlement of the area by Ateso speakers happened by 1700, but the process of expansion lasted into the late nineteenth century. On the dating of the earlier settlement, see William Fitzsimons, "Distributed Power: Climate Change, Elderhood, and Republicanism in the Grasslands of East Africa, c. 500 BCE to 1800 CE" (PhD diss., Northwestern University, 2020), chapter 2.

4. Were, *History of the Abaluyia*, 135.

5. Were, *History of the Abaluyia*, 136.

6. See root 4 in the appendix for reflexes, meanings, and distributions.

7. R. W. Moody, "Land Tenure in Samia" (unpublished manuscript, 1962), 1; Simiyu Wandibba, "Some Aspects of Precolonial Architecture," in *History and Culture in Western Kenya: The People of Bungoma District through Time*, ed. Simiyu Wandibba (Nairobi: Gideon Were Press, 1985), 34–35; John Osogo, *A History of the Baluyia* (Nairobi: Oxford University Press, 1966), 85.

8. Moody, "Land Tenure in Samia," 1.

9. See root 15 in the appendix for reflexes, meanings, and distributions.

10. See root 25 in the appendix for reflexes, meanings, and distributions.

11. Henri Médard, *Le royaume du Buganda au XIXe siècle* (Paris: Karthala, 2007), 239–46; David Schoenbrun, *Names of the Python: Belonging in East Africa, 900 to 1930* (Madison: University of Wisconsin Press, 2021).

12. Joseph Thomson, *Through Masai Land: A Journey of Exploration among the Snowclad Volcanic Mountains and Strange Tribes of Eastern Equatorial Africa. Being the Narrative of the Royal Geographical Society's Expedition to Mount Kenia and Lake Victoria Nyanza, 1883–1884* (Boston: Houghton, Mifflin, 1885), 502–3.

13. Were, *History of the Abaluyia*, 143.

14. See, for example, David Schoenbrun, "Violence, Marginality, Scorn and Honour: Language Evidence of Slavery to the Eighteenth Century," in *Slavery in the Great Lakes Region of East Africa*, ed. Henri Médard and Shane Doyle (Athens: Ohio University Press, 2007), 38–75.

15. Were, *History of the Abaluyia*, 143; see also Thomson, *Through Masai Land*, 506–7.

16. See root 2 in the appendix for reflexes, meanings, and distributions.

17. Loburkan, Jie Historical Texts no. 122, quoted in John Lamphear, *The Traditional History of the Jie of Uganda* (Oxford: Clarendon Press, 1976), 221. Italics in original.

18. Lamphear, *Traditional History of the Jie*, 221–22.

19. Aringole, Lomulen (Puten), Loibok (Daudi), and others, Jie Historical Texts no. 26, quoted in Lamphear, *Traditional History of the Jie*, 223. Italics in original.

20. Loden (Kapelinyong) and Meron, Jie Historical Texts no. 127, quoted in Lamphear, *Traditional History of the Jie*, 223. Italics in original.

21. Although they date to the early twentieth century, the series of reports on ivory in Karamoja from the Governor of the Uganda Protectorate to London capture this perspective effectively: Governor of Uganda to the Secretary of State for the Colonies, 21 January 1911, CO 536/39; Governor of Uganda to the Secretary of State for the Colonies, 13 March 1911, CO 536/40; Governor of Uganda to the Secretary of State for the Colonies, 4 July 1911, CO 536/41; all in Records of the Colonial Office, National Archives, UK.

22. Lamphear, *Traditional History of the Jie*, 225. See also the summary of history of the ivory trade from the colonial perspective in a letter from the Governor of Uganda to the Secretary of State for the Colonies, July 4, 1911, CO 536/41, no. 24772, Records of the Colonial Office, National Archives, UK.

23. Lamphear, *Traditional History of the Jie*, 226.

24. Lamphear, *Traditional History of the Jie*, 226–27.

25. Lamphear, *Traditional History of the Jie*, 227–40.

26. W. D. M. Bell, *Karamojo Safari* (London: Gollancz, 1949), 132; Report of H. M. Tufnell, 4 October 1911; quoted in Lamphear, *Traditional History of the Jie*, 243.

27. Bell, *Karamojo Safari*, 140.

28. See root 12 in the appendix for reflexes, meanings, and distributions.

29. Georgina H. Endfield, David B. Ryves, Keely Mills, and Lea Berrang-Ford, "'The Gloomy Forebodings of this Dread Disease': Climate, Famine and Sleeping Sickness in East Africa," *The Geographical Journal* 175, no. 3 (2009): 181–95, here 184. For a detailed discussion of the variation of the lake's level since 1800 and its relationship to various climate factors, see Sharon E. Nicholson and Xungang Yin, "Rainfall Conditions in Equatorial East Africa during the Nineteenth Century as Inferred from the Record of Lake Victoria," *Climate Change* 48 (2001): 387–98.

30. Thomson, *Through Masai Land*, 482.

31. Thomson, *Through Masai Land*, 481.

32. Thomson, *Through Masai Land*, 487.

33. Sharon E. Nicholson, "Climate and Climatic Variability of Rainfall over Eastern Africa," *Review of Geophysics* 55 (2017): 619.

34. Sharon E. Nicholson, Amin K. Dezfuli, and Douglas Klotter, "A Two-Century Precipitation Dataset for the Continent of Africa," *Bulletin of the American Meteorological Society* 93, no. 8 (2012): 1127. Mount Kenya, for example, saw a drying trend start in the 1870s: Bronwen Konecky et al., "Impact of Monsoons, Temperature, and CO_2 on the Rainfall and Ecosystems of Mt. Kenya during the Common Era," *Palaeogeography, Palaeoclimatology, Palaeoecology* 396 (2014): 22–23.

35. H. Hanlon, "News from our Missions: Vicariate of the Nile. Letter from Bishop Hanlon to Our Superior General. In Camp Tabingwa's, Usoga, August 7th, 1898," *St Joseph's Advocate: A Quarterly Illustrated Record of Foreign Missions and of Life and Suffering in Heathen Lands* 3, no. 19 (1899): 376. Similar depictions of the agricultural and pastoral abundance of Busoga at this time are commonplace. See B. W. Langlands, "The

Banana in Uganda, 1860–1920," *Uganda Journal* 30, no.1 (1966): 39–63; Stephens, *A History of African Motherhood*, 127–28. See also Endfield, Ryves, Mills, and Berrang-Ford, "'Gloomy Forebodings,'" 181–95.

36. A. Vanterm, "News from Our Missions: Usoga and Uganda. Letter from Father Vanterm. St Francis Xavier's Mission, Usoga, Feast of St Joseph [19 March] 1900," *St Joseph's Advocate* 3, no. 23 (1900): 489.

37. H. Drontman, "News from Our Missions: Usoga and Uganda. Letter from Father Drontman. St Francis Xavier's Mission, Lubas, Usoga, Feast of the Sacred Heart 1900," *St Joseph's Advocate* 3, no. 25 (1900): 504.

38. Endfield, Ryves, Mills, and Berrang-Ford, "'Gloomy Forebodings,'" 188.

39. Drontman, "News from Our Missions," 504.

40. See root 1 in the appendix for reflexes, meanings, and distributions.

41. See root 2 in the appendix for reflexes, meanings, and distributions.

42. Lamphear, *Traditional History of the Jie*, 224.

43. Amuk (Atkitibuin), Jie Historical Texts no. 89, quoted in Lamphear, *Traditional History of the Jie*, 224.

44. Longoli (Apanyemuge), Jie Historical Texts no. 104, quoted in Lamphear, *Traditional History of the Jie*, 224.

45. J. B. Webster, "Usuku: The Homeland of the Iteso," in J. B. Webster, D. H. Okalany, C. P. Emudong, and N. Egimu-Okuda, *The Iteso during the Asonya* (Nairobi: East African Publishing House, 1973), 52.

46. David J. Vail, *A History of Agricultural Innovation and Development in Teso District, Uganda* (Syracuse, NY: Syracuse University Press, 1972), 15, cited in Joan Vincent, *Teso in Transformation: The Political Economy of Peasant and Class in Eastern Africa* (Berkeley: University of California Press, 1982), 163.

47. Webster, "Usuku," 52.

48. Webster, "Usuku," 36.

49. Webster, "Usuku," 50.

50. Webster, "Usuku," 51.

51. Teso Historical Text no. 25, quoted in Webster, "Usuku," 51.

52. Fitzsimons, "Distributed Power," 334–36.

53. Richard Waller, "Emutai: Crisis and Response in Maasailand 1883–1902," in *The Ecology of Survival: Case Studies from Northeast African History*, ed. Douglas H. Johnson and David M. Anderson (London: Lester Crook Academic, 1988), 75.

54. Waller, "Emutai," 76, citing Maasai Text MT/M/P25. See also Lamphear, *Traditional History of the Jie*, 220.

55. Maasai Text MT/M/DT5 cited in Waller, "Emutai," 76. Research on the impact of rinderpest in East Africa has focused heavily on Kenya and Tanzania; on Uganda, see Endfield, Ryves, Mills, and Berrang-Ford, "'Gloomy Forebodings,'" 186, 192. For a useful recent overview of the epidemic, see Thaddeus Sunseri, "The African Rinderpest Panzootic, 1888–1897," *Oxford Research Encyclopedia of African History* (2018), https://oxfordre.com/africanhistory/view/10.1093/acrefore/9780190277734.001.0001/acrefore-9780190277734-e-375.

56. Waller, "Emutai," 76–77.

57. Waller, "Emutai," 77.

58. J. C. D. Lawrance, *The Iteso: Fifty Years of Change in a Nilo-Hamitic Tribe of Uganda* (London: Oxford University Press, 1957), 93.

59. Webster, "Usuku," 20.

60. William Fitzsimons describes the importance of being married with an "honorable bridewealth." Fitzsimons, "Distributed Power," chapter 4.

61. D. A. Low, *Fabrication of Empire: The British and the Uganda Kingdom, 1890–1902* (Cambridge: Cambridge University Press, 2009), 75–76.

62. Were, *History of the Abaluyia*, 136–37.

63. For a detailed summary of these developments, see Samwiri Rubaraza Karugire, *A Political History of Uganda* (Nairobi: Heinemann Educational Books, 1980), 49–98.

64. Michael Twaddle, *Kakungulu and the Creation of Uganda: 1868–1928* (London: James Currey, 1993), 136.

65. Twaddle, *Kakungulu*, 136.

66. Twaddle, *Kakungulu*, 137.

67. Johnston to London, 6 April 1900, FO2/299, Foreign Office: Political and Other Departments: General Correspondence before 1906, Africa, National Archives, UK; quoted in Twaddle, *Kakungulu*, 138.

68. Vincent, *Teso in Transformation*, 45–61; Twaddle, *Kakungulu*, 138 (quote).

69. Vincent, *Teso in Transformation*, 59.

70. For the role of taxation in British colonial rule in Africa, including Uganda, see Leigh A. Gardner, *Taxing Colonial Africa: The Political Economy of British Imperialism* (Oxford: Oxford University Press, 2012).

71. Vincent, *Teso in Transformation*, 112–13.

72. See root 4 in the appendix for reflexes, meanings, and distributions.

73. R. A. Snoxall, *Luganda–English Dictionary* (Oxford: Clarendon Press, 1967), 233.

74. See roots 12 and 39 in the appendix for reflexes, meanings, and distributions.

75. Twaddle, *Kakungulu*, 144.

76. Twaddle, *Kakungulu*, 152.

77. See, for example, the case of Kidza of Budaka, Twaddle, *Kakungulu*, 178.

78. Vincent, *Teso in Transformation*, 115.

79. Twaddle, *Kakungulu*, 182–83; Vincent, *Teso in Transformation*, 116.

80. Governor Frederick Jackson to the Secretary of State for the Colonies, 14 July 1911, CO 536/41, Records of the Colonial Office, National Archives, UK.

81. "A Report by Major E. H. Gorges on the Wa-Kavirondo," 20 August 1901, 67, FO2/804, Foreign Office: Political and Other Departments: General Correspondence before 1906, Africa, National Archives, UK.

82. C. W. Hobley, *Kenya, from Chartered Company to Crown Colony: Thirty Years of Exploration and Administration in British East Africa* (London: H.F. and G. Witherby, 1929), 81–83; Were, *History of the Abaluyia*, 166–67.

83. Osogo, *History of the Baluyia*, 85.

84. Osogo, *History of the Baluyia*, 85.

85. Vincent, *Teso in Transformation*, 151.

86. On the consequences of the introduction of taxation in the Uganda Protectorate, focused on Buganda, see Michael W. Tuck, "'The Rupee Disease': Taxation, Authority, and Social Conditions in Early Colonial Uganda," *International Journal of African History Studies* 39, no. 2 (2006): 221–45.

87. Commissioner James H. Sadler to Marquis of Lansdowne, "Report on the Working of the Hut Tax," 16 November 1902, 8, FO 2/594, Foreign Office: Political and Other Departments: General Correspondence before 1906, Africa, National Archives, UK.

88. Special Commissioner Harry H. Johnston to the Marquis of Salisbury, "Preliminary Report on the Protectorate of Uganda," 27 April 1900, 7, FO 2/298, Foreign Office: Political and Other Departments: General Correspondence before 1906, Africa, National Archives, UK.

89. Johnston, "Preliminary Report on the Protectorate of Uganda," 6. The agreement also included a gun tax of three rupees per annum but that was primarily aimed at disarming Ugandans by encouraging people to sell their guns to the colonial administration rather than pay the tax.

90. Special Commissioner Harry H. Johnston, "Instructions to the Collectors of Districts in the Protectorate of Uganda Relative to the Rate at Which Local Labours or Produce May Be Accepted in Lieu of Cash in Payment of Hut and Gun Taxes," 16 March 1900, FO 2/297, Foreign Office: Political and Other Departments: General Correspondence before 1906, Africa, National Archives, UK.

91. Lawrance, *The Iteso*, 40.

92. Vincent, *Teso in Transformation*, 169–70.

93. Vincent, *Teso in Transformation*, 165. On the "ploughing school" see "Report on the Cotton Department of Uganda, for the Year Ending March 31, 1910," CO 536/33, Records of the Colonial Office, National Archives, UK.

94. Governor Frederick Jackson to the Secretary of State for the Colonies, 14 July 1911, CO 536/41, Records of the Colonial Office, National Archives, UK.

95. Fitzsimons, "Distributed Power," chapter 3.

96. Teso Historical Text no. 20, cited in Webster, "Usuku," 15.

97. Vincent, *Teso in Transformation*, 151.

98. Vincent, *Teso in Transformation*, 151.

99. Vincent, *Teso in Transformation*, 153.

100. Vincent, *Teso in Transformation*, 151.

101. Fr. Kestens, Budaka Diary I: 1901–1903, Mill Hill Missionaries' Archives, UK.

102. Pamela Khanakwa, "Male Circumcision among the Bagisu of Eastern Uganda: Practices and Conceptualizations," in *Doing Conceptual History in Africa*, rev. ed., ed. Axel Fleisch and Rhiannon Stephens (2016; Oxford: Berghahn Books, 2018), 119.

103. Vincent, *Teso in Transformation*, 109. See also entries in "Budaka Diary I: 1901–1903," Mill Hill Missionaries' Archives, UK.

104. Letter from R. J. N. Madaba to the District Commissioner, Bugisu District, 15 April 1957, Minute Paper No. C NAF 5; Chiefs' visits to UK, MBL/11/9, Mbale District Archives, Uganda.

105. Robert W. Strayer, "The Making of Mission Schools in Kenya: A Microcosmic Perspective," *Comparative Education Review* 17, no. 3 (1973): 314.

106. Strayer, "Making of Mission Schools in Kenya," 318.

107. Letter from R. J. N. Madaba to the District Commissioner, Bugisu District, 15 April 1957, Minute Paper No. C NAF 5; Chiefs' visits to UK, MBL/11/9, Mbale District Archives, Uganda.

108. Letter from R. J. N. Madaba to the District Commissioner, Bugisu District, 15 April 1957, Minute Paper No. C NAF 5; Chiefs' visits to UK, MBL/11/9, Mbale District Archives, Uganda. These administrative structures of chiefship were adapted from Buganda and introduced across the Uganda Protectorate.

109. Ronald R. Atkinson, "Bugwere before 1900: A Survey" (unpublished manuscript), in possession of the author.

110. Twaddle, *Kakungulu*, 166.

111. Interview with Israel Kabazi, in Ronald R. Atkinson, ed., "Bugwere Historical Texts," Ronald R. Atkinson Private Collection, text 4.

112. Interview with Alex Pokino, Atkinson, ed., "Bugwere Historical Texts," text 23.

113. Interview with Ezekeri Kageni, Atkinson, ed., "Bugwere Historical Texts," text 24.

114. See root 32 in the appendix for reflexes, meanings, and distributions.

115. This quote is from the following document, but a similar one could be found in multiple such documents: "Uganda Protectorate Intelligence Report No. 10: Appendix D: Report on the Busoga District of the Central Province. Compiled from Information Received from Mr W. Grant C.M.G.," 2 February 1902, FO2/804, Foreign Office: Political and Other Departments: General Correspondence before 1906, Africa, National Archives, UK.

116. Margaret Jean Hay, "Changes in Clothing and Struggles over Identity in Colonial Western Kenya," in *Fashioning Africa: Power and the Politics of Dress*, ed. Jean Allman (Bloomington: Indiana University Press, 2004), 67–68.

117. Hay, "Changes in Clothing," 68.

118. See, for example, J. B. Purvis, *Through Uganda to Mount Elgon* (London: T. Fisher Unwin, 1909), 307, 347.

119. Hay, "Changes in Clothing," 69.

120. Hay, "Changes in Clothing," 68–69.

121. See root 31 in the appendix for reflexes, meanings, and distributions.

122. Yvonne Bastin, André Coupez, Evariste Mumba, and Thilo C. Schadeberg, eds., *Bantu Lexical Reconstructions 3/Reconstructions lexicales bantoues 3* (Tervuren, Belgium: Musée Royale de l'Afrique Centrale, 2002), Main 1084, https://www.africamuseum.be/en/research/discover/human_sciences/culture_society/blr.

123. This is also reflected in Luganda proverbs about poverty; see Rhiannon Stephens, "'Wealth,' 'Poverty' and the Question of Conceptual History in Oral Contexts: Uganda from c. 1000 CE," in *Doing Conceptual History in Africa*, ed. Fleisch and Stephens, 36–37. On clothing in Buganda, see Richard Reid, *Political Power in Pre-Colonial Buganda: Economy, Society and Warfare in the Nineteenth Century* (Oxford: James Currey, 2002), 58–60.

Conclusion

1. Susan Reynolds Whyte, "Men, Women and Misfortune in Bunyole," in *Women's Religious Experience*, ed. Pat Holden (London: Croom Helm, 1983), 183.

Appendix: Reconstructed Vocabulary

1. Yvonne Bastin, André Coupez, Evariste Mumba, and Thilo C. Schadeberg, eds., *Bantu Lexical Reconstructions 3/Reconstructions lexicales bantoues 3* (Tervuren, Belgium: Musée royale de l'Afrique centrale, 2002), Main 418 and 9283; David Lee Schoenbrun, *The Historical Reconstruction of Great Lakes Bantu Cultural Vocabulary: Etymologies and Distributions* (Cologne: Rüdiger Köppe, 1997), 64, no. 80.

2. Bastin, Coupez, Mumba, and Schadeberg, eds., *Bantu Lexical Reconstructions 3*, Main 2747, Main 2751, Main 2754, and Main 2757; Schoenbrun, *Historical Reconstruction*, 66, no. 86; 163–64, no. 247; 239–40, no. 365 and no. 366.

3. Bastin, Coupez, Mumba, and Schadeberg, eds., *Bantu Lexical Reconstructions 3*, Main 2414.

4. David Lee Schoenbrun, personal correspondence. I am indebted to David for sharing with me this entry from his new dictionary.

5. Bastin, Coupez, Mumba, and Schadeberg, eds., *Bantu Lexical Reconstructions 3*, Main 2520; Schoenbrun, *Historical Reconstruction*, 251, no. 385.

6. Bastin, Coupez, Mumba, and Schadeberg, eds., *Bantu Lexical Reconstructions 3*, Main 6938.

7. Christopher Ehret, *A Historical-Comparative Reconstruction of Nilo-Saharan* (Cologne: Rüdiger Köppe, 2001), 313, no. 251 and no. 252.

8. Bastin, Coupez, Mumba, and Schadeberg, eds., *Bantu Lexical Reconstructions 3*, Main 3081 and Main 3131.

9. William Fitzsimons, "Distributed Power: Climate Change, Elderhood, and Republicanism in the Grasslands of East Africa, c. 500 BCE to 1800 CE" (PhD diss., Northwestern University, 2020), 418, PA 11.

10. Christopher Ehret, *Southern Nilotic History: Linguistic Approaches to the Study of the Past* (Evanston, IL: Northwestern University Press, 1971), 114; Franz Rottland, *Die Südnilotische Sprachen: Beschreibung, Vergleichung und Rekonstruktion* (Berlin: Dietrich Reimer, 1982), 400.

11. Fitzsimons, "Distributed Power," 402, PT 1.

12. Bastin, Coupez, Mumba, and Schadeberg, eds., *Bantu Lexical Reconstructions 3*, Main 1916.

13. See *-jàj-* v. plunder (Zone J languages only) in Bastin, Coupez, Mumba, and Schadeberg, eds., *Bantu Lexical Reconstructions 3*, 8091.

14. Bastin, Coupez, Mumba, and Schadeberg, eds., *Bantu Lexical Reconstructions 3*, Main 1001.

15. Ehret, *Southern Nilotic History*, 144.

16. Bastin, Coupez, Mumba, and Schadeberg, eds., *Bantu Lexical Reconstructions 3*, Main 1646.

17. Bastin, Coupez, Mumba, and Schadeberg, eds., *Bantu Lexical Reconstructions 3*, Main 1997.

18. Schoenbrun, *Historical Reconstruction*, 245–46, no. 375.

19. Bastin, Coupez, Mumba, and Schadeberg, eds., *Bantu Lexical Reconstructions 3*, Main 1084.

20. Ehret, *Southern Nilotic History*, 105; Rottland, *Die Südnilotischen Sprachen*, 303.

21. Bastin, Coupez, Mumba, and Schadeberg, eds., *Bantu Lexical Reconstructions 3*, Derived 2004.

22. Fitzsimons, "Distributed Power," 453, PA 138; 465–66, Teso 10.

23. Fitzsimons, "Distributed Power," 481, PNA 19.

24. Fitzsimons, "Distributed Power," 449–50, PA 126.

BIBLIOGRAPHY

Interviewees by Language Family

Greater Luhyia

Hihubbi Adam, Gesa Aristarchus, Gudoi Esau, Pamela Khanakwa, Henry Aloysius Mafwabi, Florence Naasambu, Peter Namaondo, George Okambo, Charles Okumu, Musumba Ouma, Samuel Siminyu, James Kangala Tuumuwa, Wanende, Timothy Wangusa, Sarah Maswere Wasake, Cornelius Wekunya, Gershom Ngolobe Zablon

North Nyanza

Tazenya Henry, Helen Kagino, Veronica Kanyana, Joyce Kawuledde, John Kunena, Samsom Luvunya, Henry Maganda, Tom Masaba, Madete Mohammed, Henry Mongo, Joram Mpande, Samuel Mubbala, Peter Michael Muloit, Yokulamu Mutemere, Sam Mwigo, Rehema Nakaima, Harriet Nakibanda, Ephraim Talyambiri, Abel Wanzige, Gertrude Yanga

Southern Nilotic

Kurwa Charles, Peter Kamuron, Masai Moses, Mutemo Robert

Eastern Nilotic

Stephen Akabway, Adyango Freda, Okalany David Hannington, Joseph Lomongin, Robert Osega

Western Nilotic

Jimmy Eribu, Carol Ilako, Laury Ocen, John Owor

Archives

Mbale District Archives, Mbale, Uganda

MBL/11/9 Chiefs' Visits to UK

Mill Hill Missionaries' Archives, Freshfield, United Kingdom
Budaka Diary I: 1901–1903
St Joseph's Advocate: A Quarterly Illustrated Record of Foreign Missions and of Life and Suffering in Heathen Lands

The National Archives, Kew Gardens, London, United Kingdom
CO 535, Records of the Colonial Office
FO 2, Foreign Office: Political and Other Departments: General Correspondence before 1906, Africa

Dictionaries and Wordlists

Anangwe, Alfred, and Michael R. Marlo. "Wanga–English Dictionary." Unpublished manuscript, last modified September 1, 2008. PDF.
Appleby, L. L. *A Luluhya–English Vocabulary*. Maseno, Kenya: Church Missionary Society, 1943.
Barrett, A. *English–Turkana Dictionary*. Nairobi: Macmillan Kenya, 1988.
Barrett, A. *Turkana–English Dictionary*. London: Macmillan, 1990.
Bastin, Yvonne, André Coupez, Evariste Mumba, and Thilo C. Schadeberg, eds. *Bantu Lexical Reconstructions 3/Reconstructions lexicales Bantoues 3*. Tervuren, Belgium: Musée Royale de l'Afrique Centrale, 2002. https://www.africamuseum.be/en/research/discover/human_sciences/culture_society/blr.
Bosire, Kennedy Momanyi, and Gladys Kwamboka Machogu. *Authoritative Ekegusii Dictionary/Endabaro endabasia y'Ekegusii*. Kenya: Ekegusii Encyclopedia Project, 2009.
Bukenya, Austin, and Leonard Kamoga. *Standard Luganda–English Dictionary*. Kampala: Fountain Publishers, 2009.
Capen, Carole J. *Bilingual Dholuo–English Dictionary*. Tucson, AZ: C. A. Capen, 1998.
Creider, Jane Tapsubei, and Chet A. Creider. *A Dictionary of the Nandi Language*. Cologne: Rüdiger Köppe, 2001.
De Blois, Kornelius Frans. "Bukusu." 1975. Comparative Bantu Online Dictionary. http://www.cbold.ish-lyon.cnrs.fr.
Dictionary: Lusoga–English English–Lusoga. Jinja, Uganda: Cultural Research Centre, 2000.
Downing, Laura. "Jita Wordlist." 1999. Comparative Bantu Online Dictionary. http://www.cbold.ish-lyon.cnrs.fr.
Ehret, Christopher. *A Historical-Comparative Reconstruction of Nilo-Saharan*. Cologne: Rüdiger Köppe, 2001.

Griffiths, Bruce, and Dafydd Glyn Jones. *Geiriadur yr Academi: The Welsh Academy English–Welsh Dictionary Online*. Bangor University on behalf of the Welsh Language Commissioner, 2012. https://geiriaduracademi.org.

Gulere, Cornelius W. *Lusoga–English Dictionary/Eibwanio*. Kampala: Fountain Publishers, 2009.

Hamilton, Alan. *Luganda Dictionary and Grammar: Luganda–English and English–Luganda Dictionary with Notes on Luganda Grammar*. With Naomi Hamilton, Phoebe Mukasa, and David Ssewanyana. Godalming, UK: Alan Hamilton, 2016.

Heasty, J. A. *English–Shilluk and Shilluk–English Dictionary*. 1937. Reprint, Dolieb Hill, South Sudan: American Mission, 1974.

Hilders, J. H., and J. C. D. Lawrance. *An English–Ateso and Ateso–English Vocabulary*. Nairobi: Eagle Press, 1958.

Huntingford, G. W. B. "The Orusyan Language of Uganda." *Journal of African Languages* 4, no. 3 (1965): 145–69.

Kagaya, Ryohei. *A Gwere Vocabulary*. Tokyo: Institute for the Study of Languages and Cultures of Asia and Africa, 2006.

Kaji, Shigeki. *Lexique Tembo I: Tembo–Swahili du Zaïre–Japonais–Français*. Tokyo: Institute for the Study of Languages and Cultures of Asia and Africa, 1985.

Kambale, Kavutirwaki. *Lexique nande–français/français–nande*. Kinshasa: Éditions du secretariat general de l'épiscopat du Zaïre, 1978.

KWL. "Bukusu–English Wordlist." 1998. Comparative Bantu Online Dictionary. http://www.cbold.ish-lyon.cnrs.fr.

Le Veux, Père. *Premier essai de vocabulaire luganda–français d'après l'ordre étymologique*. Maison Carrée, Algeria: Imprimerie des missionaires d'Afrique (Pères Blancs), 1917.

Logiro, Peter, and Joyce Ilukori. *A Simplified Ngakarimojong–English English–Ngakarimojong Dictionary*. Kampala: Fountain Publishers, 2007.

Loyola, Apuda Ignatius. *Bi-lingual Ateso Dictionary*. Entebbe, Uganda: Marianum Press, 2007.

Luragoli–English Vocabulary. Friends Africa Mission Press, 1940.

Makok, Stephen Dit, and Samuel Galuak Marial. *Thuɔŋjäŋ (Dinka) English Dictionary*. Nairobi: Sudan Literature Centre, 1999.

Marlo, Michael, and Alfred Anangwe. "Luyia Dictionary." Unpublished manuscript, last modified January 24, 2010. Excel file.

Marlo, Michael, Adrian Sifuna, and Aggrey Wasike, comps. and eds. "Bukusu Dictionary." Unpublished manuscript, last modified September 1, 2008. PDF.

Massamba, David P. B. *Eciruuri: Kamusi ya Ciruuri–Kiswahili–Kiingereza*. Dar es Salaam: Languages of Tanzania Project, University of Dar es Salaam, 2005.

Matasovic, Ranko. *Etymological Dictionary of Proto-Celtic*. Leiden: Brill, 2009. http://dictionaries.brillonline.com/proto-celtic.

Mdee, James S. *Kijita: Msamiati wa Kijita–Kiswahili–Kiingereza na Kiingereza–Kijita–Kiswahili*. Dar es Salaam: Languages of Tanzania Project, University of Dar es Salaam, 2008.

Mietzner, Angelika. *Cherang'any: A Kalenjin Language of Kenya*. Cologne: Rüdiger Köppe, 2016.

Mol, Frans. *Maa: A Dictionary of the Maasai Language and Folklore*. Nairobi: Marketing and Publishing, 1978.

Mous, Maarten, Martha Qorro, and Roland Kießling. *Iraqw–English Dictionary with an English and a Thesaurus Index*. Cologne: Rüdiger Köppe, 2002.

Muniko, S. M., B. Muita oMagige, and M. J. Ruel. *Kuria–English Dictionary*. Hamburg: LIT, 1996.

Murphy, John D. *Luganda–English Dictionary*. Washington: The Catholic University of America Press, 1972.

Musimami, Sylvester N. M., and Martin Diprose. *Ehyagi hy'Ebibono by'Olunyole/Lunyole Dictionary: Lunyole–English with English Index*. Entebbe, Uganda: Lunyole Language Association, 2011. https://lunyole.webonary.org.

Mutaka, Ngessimo M., and Kambale Kavutirwaki. *Kinanda/Konzo–English Dictionary: With an English–Kinande Index*. Trenton, NJ: Africa World Press, 2011.

Muzale, H. R. T. *Ikaningambo ya Oruhaya: Kamusi ya Kihaya–Kiingereza–Kiswhili/Ruhaya–English–Kiswahili and English–Ruhaya–Swahili Dictionary*. Dar es Salaam: Languages of Tanzania Project, University of Dar es Salaam, 2006.

Nabirye, Minah. *Eiwanika ly'Olusoga: Eiwanika ly'Aboogezi b'Olusoga n'Abo Abenda Okwega Olusoga*. Kampala: Menha Publishers, 2009.

Ndanyi, Joseph Olindo. *Lulogooli–English Translation (Dictionary)*. 2005. 2nd ed. Nairobi: Ndanyi Enterprises, 2010.

Ndoleriire, O., J. Kintu, J. Kabagenyi, and H. Kasande. *Runyoro-Rutooro–English Dictionary*. Kampala: Fountain Publishers, 2015.

Ŋakarimojong–English and English–Ŋakarimojong Dictionary. Moroto, Uganda: Comboni Missionaries-Verona Fathers, 1985.

Nzogi, Richard, and Martin Diprose. *EKideero ky'oLugwere/Lugwere Dictionary: Lugwere–English with English Index*. Budaka, Uganda: Lugwere Bible Translation and Literacy Association, 2011. https://lugwere.webonary.org.

Odaga, Asenath Bole. *Dholuo–English Dictionary*. Kisumu, Kenya: Lake Publishers, 2005.

Odaga, Asenath Bole. *English–Dholuo Dictionary*. Kisumu, Kenya: Lake Publishers, 1997.

Odden, David. "Kerewe Wordlist." 1994. Comparative Bantu Online Dictionary. http://www.cbold.ish-lyon.cnrs.fr.

Odonga, Alexander. *Lwo–English Dictionary*. Kampala: Fountain Publishers, 2005.

OED Online. December 2015. Oxford University Press. http://www.oed.com.

Oketcho, Phillip. *Dero ma Dhopadhola/Dhopadhola Dictionary*. Cape Town: Centre for Advanced Studies of African Society, 2010.

Okonye, G. *Lango–English Dictionary*. Kampala: Fountain Publishers, 2012.

Ongodia, Simon Peter, and Austin Ejiet. *Ateso–English Dictionary*. Kampala: Fountain Publishers, 2008.
Polak-Bynon, Louise. *Lexique shi–français, suive d'un index français–shi*. Tervuren, Belgium: Musée royale de l'Afrique centrale, 1978.
Robert, Businge Makolome, and Martin Diprose. *Ntongoli gya Lugungu/Lugungu Dictionary: Lugungu–English with English Index*. Hoima, Uganda: Lugungu Bible Translation and Literacy Association, 2011.
Rubanza, Yunus. *Luzinza: Msamiati wa Luzinza–Kiswahili–Kiingereza na Kiingereza–Luzinza–Kiswahili*. Dar es Salaam: Languages of Tanzania Project, University of Dar es Salaam, 2008.
Rubongoya, L. T. *Katondogorozi y'Orunyoro-Rutooro n'Orungereza/Runyoro-Rutooro-English and English–Runyoro-Rutooro Dictionary*. Kampala: Modrug, 2013.
Rugelimara, Josephat M. *Orunyambo: Msamiati wa Runyambo–Kiswahili–Kiingereza na Kiingereza–Runyambo–Kiswahili [Runyambo–Kiswahili–English and English–Runyambo–Kiswahili Lexicon]*. Dar es Salaam: Languages of Tanzania Project, University of Dar es Salaam, 2002.
Schoenbrun, David Lee. Field notes. Unpublished.
Schoenbrun, David Lee. *The Historical Reconstruction of Great Lakes Bantu Cultural Vocabulary: Etymologies and Distributions*. Cologne: Rüdiger Köppe, 1997.
Siertsema, Berthe. *Masaba Word List: English–Masaba, Masaba–English*. Tervuren, Belgium: Musée Royale de l'Afrique Centrale, 1981.
Snoxall, R. A. *Luganda–English Dictionary*. Oxford: Clarendon Press, 1967.
Stephens, Rhiannon. Field notes. Unpublished.
Taylor, C. *A Simplified Runyankore-Rukiga–English and English–Runyankore-Rukiga Dictionary*. 1959. Reprint, Kampala: Fountain Publishers, 1998.
Tucker, A. N., and J. Tompo Ole Mpaayi. *A Maasai Grammar with Vocabulary*. London: Longmans, Green, 1955.

General Bibliography

Abram, Nerilie J., Jessica A. Hargreaves, Nicky M. Wright, Kaustubh Thirumalai, Caroline C. Ummenhofer, and Matthew H. England. "Palaeoclimate Perspectives on the Indian Ocean Dipole." *Quaternary Science Reviews* 237 (2020). https://doi.org/10.1016/j.quascirev.2020.106302.
Abreu Leitão de Almeida, Marcos. "Speaking of Slavery: Slaving Strategies and Moral Imaginations in the Lower Congo (Early Times to the Late 19th Century)." PhD diss., Northwestern University, 2020.
Adichie, Chimamanda Ngozi. "The Danger of a Single Story." TEDGlobal, 2009. https://www.ted.com/talks/chimamanda_ngozi_adichie_the_danger_of_a_single_story.
Afigbo, A. E. *Ropes of Sand (Studies in Igbo History and Culture)*. Nsukka: University of Nigeria Press, 1981.

Allman, Jean. "Phantoms of the Archive: Kwame Nkrumah, a Nazi Pilot Named Hanna, and the Contingencies of Postcolonial History-Writing." *American Historical Review* 118, no. 1 (2013): 104–29.

Alpers, Edward A. *Ivory and Slaves: Changing Patterns of International Trade in East Central Africa to the Later Nineteenth Century*. Berkeley: University of California Press, 1975.

Amin, Samir. "The Class Struggle in Africa." In *Classes and Class Struggle in Africa*, by Samir Amin and Robin Cohen, 28–52. Lagos: Afrografika, 1977.

Amoah, Elizabeth. "African Traditional Religion and the Concept of Poverty." In *Religion and Poverty*, edited by Peter J. Paris, 111–27. Durham, NC: Duke University Press, 2009.

Anderson, David M., and Vigdis Broch-Due, eds. *"The Poor Are Not Us": Poverty and Pastoralism in Eastern Africa*. Cambridge: Cambridge University Press, 1999.

Ashby, Solange. "Dancing for Hathor: Nubian Women in Egyptian Cultic Life." *Dotawo: A Journal of Nubian Studies* 5, no. 1 (2018): 63–90.

Ashley, Ceri Z. "Towards a Socialised Archaeology of Ceramics in Great Lakes Africa." *African Archaeological Review* 27, no. 2 (2010): 135–63.

Atkins, Margaret, and Robin Osborne, eds. *Poverty in the Roman World*. Cambridge: Cambridge University Press, 2006.

Atkinson, Ronald R. "Bugwere before 1900: A Survey." Unpublished manuscript.

Atkinson, Ronald R., ed. "Bugwere Historical Texts." Ronald R. Atkinson Private Collection.

Austen, Ralph A., ed. *In Search of Sunjata: The Mande Oral Epic as History, Literature, and Performance*. Bloomington: Indiana University Press, 1999.

Barnett, H. G. "The Nature of the Potlatch." *American Anthropologist* 40, no. 3 (1938): 349–58.

Batala-Nayenga, Frederick Peter. "An Economic History of the Lacustrine States of Busoga, Uganda: 1750–1939." PhD diss., University of Michigan, 1976.

Bell, W. D. M. *Karamojo Safari*. London: Gollancz, 1949.

Bender, M. Lionel. "Nilo-Saharan." In *African Languages: An Introduction*, edited by Bernd Heine and Derek Nurse, 43–73. Cambridge: Cambridge University Press, 2000.

Bender, M. Lionel. *The Nilo-Saharan Languages*. Munich: LINCOM Europa, 1996.

Bernault, Florence. *Colonial Transactions: Imaginaries, Bodies, and Histories in Gabon*. Durham, NC: Duke University Press, 2019.

Bessems, Ilse, Dirk Verschuren, James R. Russell, Jozef Hus, Florias Mees, and Brian F. Cumming. "Palaeolimnological Evidence for Widespread Late 18th Century Drought across Equatorial East Africa." *Palaeogeography, Palaeoclimatology, Palaeoecology* 259 (2008): 107–20.

Blank, Andreas. "Why Do New Meanings Occur? A Cognitive Typology of the Motivations for Lexical Semantic Change." In *Historical Semantics and Cognition*, edited by Peter Koch and Andreas Blank, 61–90. Berlin: De Gruyter Mouton, 1999.

Bledsoe, Caroline. *Women and Marriage in Kpelle Society*. Stanford, CA: Stanford University Press, 1980.
Boyeldieu, Pascal. "Les langues nilo-sahariennes." In *Dictionnaire des langues*, edited by Emilio Bonvini, Joëlle Busuttil, and Alain Peyraube, 185–90. Paris: Presses universitaires de France, 2011.
Brown, Peter. *Treasure in Heaven: The Holy Poor in Early Christianity*. Charlottesville: University of Virginia Press, 2016.
Campbell, Lyle. *Historical Linguistics: An Introduction*. 2nd ed. Cambridge, MA: MIT Press, 2004.
Clark, J. Desmond, and Steven A. Brandt, eds. *From Hunters to Farmers: The Causes and Consequences of Food Production in Africa*. Berkeley: University of California Press, 1984.
Cohen, David William, ed. "Collected Texts of Busoga Traditional History." David William Cohen Private Collection.
Cohen, David William. "The Face of Contact: A Model of a Cultural and Linguistic Frontier in Early Eastern Uganda." In *Nilotic Studies: Proceedings of the International Symposium on Languages and History of the Nilotic Peoples, Cologne, January 4–6, 1982*, part 2, edited by Rainer Voßen and Marianne Bechhaus-Gerst, 339–55. Berlin: Dietrich Reimer, 1983.
Cohen, David William. *The Historical Tradition of Busoga: Mukama and Kintu*. Oxford: Clarendon Press, 1972.
Cohen, David William. *Towards a Reconstructed Past: Historical Texts from Busoga, Uganda*. Oxford: Oxford University Press, 1986.
Cohen, David William. *Womunafu's Bunafu: A Study of Authority in a Nineteenth-Century African Community*. Princeton: Princeton University Press, 1977.
de Cort, Gijs, Dirk Verschuren, Els Ryken, Christian Wolff, Robin W. Renaut, Mike Creutz, Thijs Van der Meeren, Gerald Haug, Daniel O. Olago, and Florian Mees. "Multi-basin Depositional Framework for Moisture-Balance Reconstruction during the Last 1300 Years at Lake Bogoria, Central Kenya Rift Valley." *Sedimentology* 65, no. 5 (2018): 1667–96.
Crazzolara, J. P. *The Lwoo*. Verona, Italy: Missioni Africane, 1950–1954.
Croft, William. *Explaining Language Change: An Evolutionary Approach*. Harlow, UK: Longman, 2000.
Dale, Darla, and Ceri Z. Ashley. "Holocene Hunter-Fisher-Gatherer Communities: New Perspectives on Kansyore Using Communities of Western Kenya." *Azania: Archaeological Research in Africa* 45, no. 1 (2010): 24–48.
Davies, Matthew. "The Archaeology of Clan- and Lineage-Based Societies in Africa." In *The Oxford Handbook of African Archaeology*, edited by Peter Mitchell and Paul Lane, 723–36. Oxford: Oxford University Press, 2013.
Decker, Corrie, and Elisabeth McMahon. *The Idea of Development in Africa: A History*. New York: Cambridge University Press, 2020.
Diké, K. O. "African History and Self-Government." *West Africa*, March 14, 1953, 225–26.

Diké, K. O. *Trade and Politics in the Niger Delta, 1830–1885: An Introduction to the Economic and Political History of Nigeria*. Oxford: Clarendon Press, 1956.

Dimmendaal, Gerrit J. *Historical Linguistics and the Comparative Study of African Languages*. Amsterdam: John Benjamins, 2011.

Dimmendaal, Gerrit J. "Reconstructing the Historical Development of Nilotic: A Testcase for Cladistic and Rhizotic Models of Genetic Affinity." *Sprache und Geschichte in Afrika* 19 (2008): 31–66.

Distefano, John Albert. "The Precolonial History of the Kalenjin of Kenya: A Methodological Comparison of Linguistic and Oral Traditional Evidence." PhD diss., University of California, Los Angeles, 1985.

Driberg, J. H. *The Lango: A Nilotic Tribe of Uganda*. London: T. Fisher Unwin, 1923.

Drontman, H. "News from Our Missions: Usoga and Uganda. Letter from Father Drontman. St Francis Xavier's Mission, Lubas, Usoga, Feast of the Sacred Heart 1900." *St Joseph's Advocate: A Quarterly Illustrated Record of Foreign Missions and of Life and Suffering in Heathen Lands* 3, no. 25 (1900): 504–5.

Dyson-Hudson, Neville. *Karimojong Politics*. Oxford: Clarendon Press, 1966.

Ehret, Christopher. *An African Classical Age: Eastern and Southern Africa in World History, 1000 B.C. to A.D. 400*. Charlottesville: University of Virginia Press, 1998.

Ehret, Christopher. *The Civilizations of Africa: A History to 1800*. Charlottesville: University of Virginia Press, 2002.

Ehret, Christopher. "Cushites and the Highland and Plains Nilotes to A.D. 1800." In *Zamani: A Survey of East African History*, edited by Bethwell A. Ogot, 150–69. Nairobi: East African Publishing House, 1974.

Ehret, Christopher. *History and the Testimony of Language*. Berkeley: University of California Press, 2011.

Ehret, Christopher. *Southern Nilotic History: Linguistic Approaches to the Study of the Past*. Evanston, IL: Northwestern University Press, 1971.

Ehret, Christopher. "Subclassifying Bantu: The Evidence of Stem Morpheme Innovation." In *Bantu Historical Linguistics: Theoretical and Empirical Perspectives*, edited by Jean-Marie Hombert and Larry M. Hyman, 43–147. Stanford, CA: CSLI, 1999.

Ehret, Christopher, Thomas Coffman, Laura Fliegelman, Alice Gold, Marinez Hubbard, and Douglas Johnson. "Some Thoughts on the Early History of the Nile-Congo Watershed." *Ufahamu* 5, no. 2 (1974): 85–112.

Ellis, Stephen. "Writing Histories of Contemporary Africa." *Journal of African History* 43, no. 1 (2002): 1–26.

Endfield, Georgina H., David B. Ryves, Keely Mills, and Lea Berrang-Ford. "'The Gloomy Forebodings of this Dread Disease': Climate, Famine and Sleeping Sickness in East Africa." *Geographical Journal* 175, no. 3 (2009): 181–95.

Fair, Laura. *Pastimes and Politics: Culture, Community, and Identity in Post-Abolition Urban Zanzibar, 1890–1945*. Athens: Ohio University Press, 2001.

Feierman, Steven. "Reciprocity and Assistance in Precolonial Africa." In *Philanthropy in the World's Traditions*, edited by Warren F. Ilchman, Stanley N. Katz and Edward L. Queen II, 3–24. Bloomington: Indiana University Press, 1998.

Fields-Black, Edda L. *Deep Roots: Rice Farmers in West Africa and the African Diaspora*. Bloomington: Indiana University Press, 2008.

de Filippo, Cesare, Koen Bostoen, Mark Stoneking, and Brigitte Pakendorf. "Bringing Together Linguistic and Genetic Evidence to Test the Bantu Expansion." *Proceedings of the Royal Society B: Biological Sciences* 279, no. 1741 (2012): 3256–63.

Fitzsimons, William. "Distributed Power: Climate Change, Elderhood, and Republicanism in the Grasslands of East Africa, c. 500 BCE to 1800 CE." PhD diss., Northwestern University, 2020.

Fleisch, Axel. "Conceptual Continuities: About 'Work' in Nguni'." In *Doing Conceptual History in Africa*, edited by Axel Fleisch and Rhiannon Stephens, 49–72. 2016. Revised edition, Oxford: Berghahn Books, 2018.

Fleisch, Axel, and Rhiannon Stephens, eds. *Doing Conceptual History in Africa*. 2016. Revised edition, Oxford: Berghahn Books, 2018.

Frankema, Ewout, and Marlous van Waijenburg. "Structural Impediments to African Growth? New Evidence from Real Wages in British Africa, 1880–1965." *Journal of African Economic History* 72, no. 4 (2012): 895–926.

Freu, Christel. *Les figures du pauvre dans les sources italiennes de l'antiquité tardive*. Paris: De Boccard, 2007.

Gadgil, Sulochana. "The Monsoon System: Land-sea Breeze or the ITCZ?" *Journal of Earth System Science* 127, no. 1 (2018): 1–29.

Gardner, Leigh A. *Taxing Colonial Africa: The Political Economy of British Imperialism*. Oxford: Oxford University Press, 2012.

Gebregeorgis, E. Gebrehiwot, I. Robertson, M. Koprowski, L. P. Zhou, P. Gao, A. P. Williams, Z. Eshetu, and T. H. G. Wils. "Historical Droughts Recorded in Extended *Juniperus procera* Ring-Width Chronologies from the Ethiopian Highlands." *International Journal of Biometeorology* 64, no. 5 (2020): 739–53.

Geeraerts, Dirk. *Diachronic Prototype Semantics: A Contribution to Historical Lexicology*. Oxford: Clarendon Press, 1997.

Geschiere, Peter. *The Modernity of Witchcraft: Politics and the Occult in Postcolonial Africa*. Translated by Peter Geschiere and Janet Roitman. Charlottesville: University of Virginia Press, 1997.

Goldberg, Rachel E., and Susan E. Short. "'The Luggage That Isn't Theirs Is Too Heavy...': Understandings of Orphan Disadvantage in Lesotho." *Population Research and Policy Review* 31, no. 1 (2012): 67–83.

Goldschmidt, Walter. *The Culture and Behavior of the Sebei: A Study in Continuity and Adaptation*. Berkeley: University of California Press, 1976.

Goldschmidt, Walter. *The Sebei: A Study in Adaptation*. New York: Holt, Rinehart, and Winston, 1986.

Green, Maia. "Discourses on Inequality: Poverty, Public Bads and Entrenching Witchcraft in Post-adjustment Tanzania." *Anthropological Theory* 5, no. 3 (2005): 247–66.

Green, Maia, and Simeon Mesaki. "The Birth of the 'Salon': Poverty, 'Modernization,' and Dealing with Witchcraft in Southern Tanzania." *American Ethnologist* 32, no. 3 (2005): 371–88.

Green, Toby. *A Fistful of Shells: West Africa from the Rise of the Slave Trade to the Age of Revolution*. Chicago: University of Chicago Press, 2019.
Greenberg, Joseph H. "Studies in African Linguistic Classification: IV. Hamito-Semitic." *Southwestern Journal of Anthropology* 6 (1950): 47–63.
Grollemund, Rebecca. "Nouvelles approches en classification: Application aux langues Bantu du nord-ouest." PhD diss., Université Lumière Lyon 2, 2012.
Gulliver, P. H. *The Family Herd: A Study of Two Pastoral Tribes in East Africa: The Jie and Turkana*. 1955. 2nd ed. London: Routledge and Kegan Paul, 1966.
Gulliver, P. H. "Jie Agriculture." *Uganda Journal* 18 (1954): 65–70.
Guyer, Jane I. *Marginal Gains: Monetary Transactions in Atlantic Africa*. Chicago: University of Chicago Press, 2004.
Guyer, Jane I., ed. *Money Matters: Instability, Values and Social Payments in the Modern History of West African Communities*. Portsmouth, NH: Heinemann, 1995.
Guyer, Jane I. "Pauper, Percentile, Precarity: Analytics for Poverty Studies in Africa." *Journal of African History* 59, no. 3 (2018): 437–48.
Guyer, Jane I. "Wealth in People, Wealth in Things – Introduction." *Journal of African History* 36, no. 1 (1995): 83–90.
Guyer, Jane I., and Samuel M. Eno Belinga. "Wealth in People as Wealth in Knowledge: Accumulation and Composition in Equatorial Africa." *Journal of African History* 36, no. 1 (1995): 91–120.
Hammarström, Harald, Robert Forkel, Martin Haspelmath, and Sebastian Bank. *Glottolog 2.7*. Jena, Germany: Max Planck Institute for the Science of Human History, 2016. http://glottolog.org.
Hammarström, Harald, Robert Forkel, Martin Haspelmath, and Sebastian Bank. *Glottolog 4.2.1*. Jena, Germany: Max Planck Institute for the Science of Human History, 2020. http://glottolog.org.
Hanlon, H. "News from Our Missions: Vicariate of the Nile. Letter from Bishop Hanlon to Our Superior General. In Camp Tabingwa's, Usoga, August 7th, 1898." *St Joseph's Advocate: A Quarterly Illustrated Record of Foreign Missions and of Life and Suffering in Heathen Lands* 3, no. 19 (1899): 376.
Hanson, Holly Elisabeth. *Landed Obligation: The Practice of Power in Buganda*. Portsmouth, NH: Heinemann, 2003.
Hartwig, Gerald W. "Demographic Considerations in East Africa during the Nineteenth Century." *International Journal of African Historical Studies* 12, no. 4 (1972): 653–72.
Hay, Margaret Jean. "Changes in Clothing and Struggles over Identity in Colonial Western Kenya." In *Fashioning Africa: Power and the Politics of Dress*, edited by Jean Allman, 67–83. Bloomington: Indiana University Press, 2004.
Hay, Margaret Jean. "Women as Owners, Occupants, and Managers of Property in Colonial Western Kenya." In *African Women and the Law: Historical Perspectives*, edited by Margaret Jean Hay and Marcia Wright, 110–23. Boston: Boston University, 1982.

Herbert, Eugenia. *Iron, Gender, and Power: Rituals of Transformation in African Societies*. Bloomington: Indiana University Press, 1993.

Higenyi, Erika. "The History of the Banyole." Translated by Elley Wesana-Chomi. Unpublished manuscript, shared with author by Susan Reynolds Whyte. Original manuscript written in Luganda in 1936, English translation in 1968.

Hobley, C. W. *Eastern Uganda: An Ethnological Survey*. London: The Anthropological Institute of Great Britain and Ireland, 1902.

Hobley, C. W. *Kenya, from Chartered Company to Crown Colony: Thirty Years of Exploration and Administration in British East Africa*. London: H. F. and G. Witherby, 1929.

Holden, Clare J., and Russell D. Gray. "Rapid Radiation, Borrowing and Dialect Continua in the Bantu Languages." In *Phylogenetic Methods and the Prehistory of Languages*, edited by Peter Forster and Colin Renfrew, 19–32. Cambridge: McDonald Institute for Archaeological Research, 2006.

Hopkins, A. G. *An Economic History of West Africa*. London: Longman, 1973.

Huntingford, G. W. B. "Introduction." In *The Periplus of the Erythraean Sea, by an Unknown Author: With Some Extracts from Agatharkhides "On the Erythraean Sea."* Translated and edited by G. W. B. Huntingford, 1–15. London: Hakluyt Society, 1980.

Ifversen, Jan. "About Key Concepts and How to Study Them." *Contributions to the History of Concepts* 6, no. 1 (2011): 65–88.

Iliffe, John. *The African Poor: A History*. Cambridge: Cambridge University Press, 1987.

Jerven, Morten. *Africa: Why Economists Get It Wrong*. London: Zed Books, 2015.

Jerven, Morten. "The History of African Poverty by Numbers: Evidence and Vantage Points." *Journal of African History* 39, no. 3 (2018): 449–61.

Jimenez, Raevin F. "Rites of Reproduction: Gender, Generation and Political Economic Transformation among Nguni-Speakers of Southern Africa, 8th–19th Century CE." PhD diss., Northwestern University, 2017.

Johnston, Sir Harry. *The Uganda Protectorate: An Attempt to Give Some Description of the Physical Geography, Botany, Zoology, Anthropology, Languages and History of the Territories under British Protection in East Central Africa, between the Congo Free State and the Rift Valley and between the First Degree of South Latitude and the Fifth Degree of North Latitude*. Vol. 1. London: Hutchinson, 1902.

Joseph, Brian D., and Richard D. Janda, eds. *The Handbook of Historical Linguistics*. Malden, MA: Blackwell, 2005.

Kagame, Alexis. *La poésie dynastique au Rwanda*. Brussels: Institut royal colonial belge, 1951.

Kalu, Ogbu U. "Poverty in Pre-colonial and Colonial West Africa: Perceptions, Causes and Alleviation." In *Themes in West African History*, edited by Emmanuel Kwame Akyeampong, 163–85. Athens: Ohio University Press, 2006.

Kalusa, Walima T., and Megan Vaughan. *Death, Belief and Politics in Central African History*. Lusaka: Lembani Trust, 2013.

Kanyoro, Rachel Angogo. *Unity in Diversity: A Linguistic Survey of the Abaluyia of Western Kenya*. Vienna: Afro-Pub, 1983.

Karp, Ivan. *Fields of Change among the Iteso of Kenya*. London: Routledge and Kegan Paul, 1978.

Karugire, Samwiri Rubaraza. *A Political History of Uganda*. Nairobi: Heinemann Educational Books, 1980.

Katamba, Francis. "Bantu Nominal Morphology." In *The Bantu Languages*, edited by Derek Nurse and Gérard Philippson, 103–20. London: Routledge, 2003.

Kenny, Michael G. "Pre-colonial Trade in Eastern Lake Victoria." *Azania* 14 (1979), 97–107.

Kessler, Brett. *The Significance of Word Lists*. Stanford, CA: CSLI Publications, 2001.

Khanakwa, Pamela. "Male Circumcision among the Bagisu of Eastern Uganda." In *Doing Conceptual History in Africa*, edited by Axel Fleisch and Rhiannon Stephens, 115–37. 2016. Revised edition, Oxford: Berghahn Books, 2018.

Khanakwa, Pamela. "Reinventing *Imbalu* and Forcible Circumcision: Gisu Political Identity and the Fight for Mbale in Late Colonial Uganda." *Journal of African History* 50, no. 3 (2018): 357–89.

Kisembe, Evelyne. "A Linguistic Analysis of Luyia Varieties Spoken in Western Kenya." MA diss., Memorial University of Newfoundland, 2005.

Kitunzi, Yahudu. "Survivor of Landslide Talks about Ordeal." *Daily Monitor*, September 10, 2017. http://www.monitor.co.ug/Magazines/Full-Woman/Survivor-landslide-talks-about-ordeal/689842-4087424-kj8706/index.html.

Kiwanuka, M. S. M. Semakula. *A History of Buganda from the Foundation of the Kingdom to 1900*. New York: Africana Publishing, 1972.

Knighton, Ben. *The Vitality of Karamojong Religion: Dying Tradition or Living Faith?* Aldershot, UK: Ashgate Publishing, 2005.

Kodesh, Neil. *Beyond the Royal Gaze: Clanship and Public Healing in Buganda*. Charlottesville: University of Virginia Press, 2010.

Konecky, Bronwen, James Russell, Yongsong Huang, Mathias Vuille, Lily Cohen, and F. Alayne Street-Perrott. "Impact of Monsoons, Temperature, and CO_2 on the Rainfall and Ecosystems of Mt. Kenya during the Common Era." *Palaeogeography, Palaeoclimatology, Palaeoecology* 396 (2014): 17–25.

Kopytoff, Igor, ed. *The African Frontier: The Reproduction of Traditional African Societies*. Bloomington: Indiana University Press, 1987.

Kopytoff, Igor, and Suzanne Miers. "Introduction: African 'Slavery' as an Institution of Marginality." In *Slavery in Africa: Historical and Anthropological Perspectives*, edited by Suzanne Miers and Igor Kopytoff, 3–81. Madison: University of Wisconsin Press, 1977.

Kottak, Conrad P. "Ecological Variables in the Origin and Evolution of African States: The Buganda Example." *Comparative Studies in Society and History* 14, no. 3 (1972): 351–80.

Kriger, Colleen E. *Cloth in West African History*. Lanham, MD: AltaMira Press, 2006.

Kriger, Colleen E. *Pride of Men: Ironworking in 19th Century West Central Africa*. Portsmouth, NH: Heinemann, 1999.
Kuhanen, Jan. *Poverty, Health and Reproduction in Early Colonial Uganda*. Joensuu, Finland: University of Joensuu Publications, 2005.
Kusimba, Chapurukha M. *The Rise and Fall of Swahili States*. Walnut Creek, CA: AltaMira Press, 1999.
Kyule, M. D. "The Sirikwa Economy." *Azania* 32, no. 1 (1997): 21–30.
La Fontaine, J. S. *The Gisu of Uganda*. Edited by Daryll Forde. London: International African Institute, 1959.
Lakoff, George. *Women, Fire, and Dangerous Things: What Categories Reveal about the Mind*. Chicago: University of Chicago Press, 1987.
Lamphear, John. *The Traditional History of the Jie of Uganda*. Oxford: Clarendon Press, 1976.
Lane, Paul. "The 'Moving Frontier' and the Transition to Food Production in Kenya." *Azania: Archaeological Research in Africa* 39, no.1 (2004): 243–64.
Lane, Paul, Ceri Ashley, and Gilbert Oteyo. "New Dates for Kansyore and Urewe Wares from Northern Nyanza." *Azania: Archaeological Research in Africa* 41, no. 1 (2006): 123–38.
Lane, Paul, Ceri Ashley, Oula Seitsonen, Paul Harvey, Sada Mire, and Frederick Odede. "The Transition to Farming in Eastern Africa: New Faunal and Dating Evidence from Wadh Lang'o and Usenge, Kenya." *Antiquity* 81, no. 311 (2007): 62–81.
Langlands, B. W. "The Banana in Uganda, 1860–1920." *Uganda Journal* 30, no.1 (1966): 39–63.
Langlands, B. W. "The Population Geography of Bugisu and Sebei Districts." Occasional paper no. 28. Department of Geography. Kampala: Makerere University, 1971.
Lawrance, J. C. D. *The Iteso: Fifty Years of Change in a Nilo-Hamitic Tribe of Uganda*. London: Oxford University Press, 1957.
Leakey, M. D., W. E. Owen, and L. S. B. Leakey. *Dimple-based Pottery from Central Kavirondo, Kenya Colony*. Occasional paper no. 2. Nairobi: Coryndon Memorial Museum, 1948.
Lee, Rebekah, and Megan Vaughan. "Death and Dying in the History of Africa since 1800." *Journal of African History* 49, no. 3 (2008): 341–59.
Levin, Naomi E. "Environment and Climate of Early Human Evolution." *Annual Review of Earth and Planetary Sciences* 43, no. 1 (2015): 405–29.
Lonsdale, John. "The Moral Economy of Mau Mau: Wealth, Poverty and Civic Virtue in Kikuyu Political Thought." In *Unhappy Valley: Conflict in Kenya and Africa; Book Two: Violence and Ethnicity*, by Bruce Berman and John Lonsdale, 315–504. Oxford: James Currey, 1992.
Low, D. A. *Fabrication of Empire: The British and the Uganda Kingdom, 1890–1902*. Cambridge: Cambridge University Press, 2009.
Lubogo, Y. K. *A History of Busoga*. Translated by Eastern Province (Bantu Language) Literature Committee. Jinja: East African Literature Bureau, 1960.

de Luna, Kathryn M. "Affect and Society in Precolonial Africa." *International Journal of African Historical Studies* 46, no. 1 (2013): 123–50.

de Luna, Kathryn M. *Collecting Food, Cultivating People: Subsistence and Society in Central Africa.* New Haven: Yale University Press, 2016.

de Luna, Kathryn M. "Hunting Reputations: Talent, Individuals, and Community in Precolonial South Central Africa." *Journal of African History* 53, no. 3 (2012): 279–99.

de Luna, Kathryn M., and Jeffrey Fleisher. *Speaking with Substance: Methods of Language and Materials in African History.* New York: Springer, 2018.

MacEachern, Scott. "Genes, Tribes, and African History." *Current Anthropology* 41, no. 3 (2000): 357–84.

MacEachern, Scott. "States and Their Genetic Consequences in Central Africa." *Proceedings of the National Academy of Sciences of the United States of America* 116, no. 2 (2019): 356–57.

MacGaffey, Wyatt. "A Note on Vansina's Invention of Matrilineality." *Journal of African History* 54, no. 2 (2013): 269–80.

Maho, Jouni. *A Comparative Study of Bantu Noun Classes.* Gothenburg, Sweden: Acta Universitatis Gothoburgensis, 1999.

Makila, F. E. *An Outline History of the Babukusu of Western Kenya.* Nairobi: Kenya Literature Bureau, 1978.

Makumbi, Jennifer Nansubuga. *A Girl Is a Body of Water.* Portland, OR: Tin House, 2020.

Mandala, Elias C. *The End of Chidyerano: A History of Food and Everyday Life in Malawi, 1860–2004.* Portsmouth, NH: Heinemann, 2005.

Marchant, Rob, Suzi Richer, Oliver Boles, Claudia Capitani, Colin J. Courtney-Mustaphi, Paul Lane, Mary E. Prendergast, et al., "Drivers and Trajectories of Land Cover Change in East Africa: Human and Environmental Interactions from 6000 Years Ago to Present." *Earth Science Reviews* 178 (2018): 322–78.

de Maret, Pierre. "Histoires des croisettes." In *Objets-signes d'Afrique*, edited by Luc de Heusch, 133–45. Tervuren, Belgium: Musée Royale de l'Afrique Centrale, 1995.

Marten, Lutz. "Bantu Classification, Bantu Trees and Phylogenetic Methods." In *Phylogenetic Methods and the Prehistory of Languages*, edited by Peter Forster and Colin Renfrew, 43–56. Cambridge: McDonald Institute for Archaeological Research, 2006.

The Masaaba M. R. Association. "The History of Bugisu." Unpublished manuscript, 1973. Shared with author by Pamela Khanakwa.

Mathez, Edmond A., and Jason E. Smerdon. *Climate Change: The Science of Global Warming and Our Energy Future.* 2nd ed. New York: Columbia University Press, 2018.

McIntosh, Susan Keech. "Pathways to Complexity: An African Perspective." In *Beyond Chiefdoms: Pathways to Complexity in Africa*, edited by Susan Keech McIntosh, 1–30 Cambridge: Cambridge University Press, 1999.

McMahon, April, and Robert McMahon. *Language Classification by Numbers*. Oxford: Oxford University Press, 2005.
McMaster, David N. *A Subsistence Crop Geography of Uganda*. Bude, UK: Geographical Publications, 1962.
Médard, Henri. *Le royaume du Buganda au XIXe siècle*. Paris: Karthala, 2007.
Menssen, Max, Marcus Linde, Emmanuel Otunga Omondi, Mary Abukutsa-Onyango, Fekadu Fufa Dinssa, and Traud Winkelmann. "Genetic and Morphological Diversity of Cowpea (*Vigna unguiculata* (L.) Walp.) Entries from East Africa." *Scientia Horticulturae* 226 (2017): 268–69.
Miers, Suzanne, and Igor Kopytoff, eds. *Slavery in Africa: Historical and Anthropological Perspectives*. Madison: University of Wisconsin Press, 1977.
Miller, Joseph C. *Way of Death: Merchant Capitalism and the Angolan Slave Trade, 1730–1830*. Madison: University of Wisconsin Press, 1988.
Mollat, Michel. *Études sur l'histoire de la pauvreté (Moyen Age – XVIe siècle)*. Vol. 2. Paris: Publications de la Sorbonne, 1974.
Mollat, Michel. *The Poor in the Middle Ages: An Essay in Social History*. Translated by Arthur Goldhammer. New Haven: Yale University Press, 1986.
Moody, R. W. "Land Tenure in Samia." Unpublished manuscript, 1962.
Moody, R. W. "Samia Fishermen." Unpublished manuscript, 1963.
Moody, R. W. "Social and Political Institutions of the Samia." PhD diss., Cambridge University, 1967.
Morley, Neville. "The Poor in the City of Rome." In *Poverty in the Roman World*, edited by Margaret Atkins and Robin Osborne, 21–39. Cambridge: Cambridge University Press, 2006.
Morrison, Kathleen D. "Provincializing the Anthropocene: Eurocentrism in the Earth System." In *At Nature's Edge: The Global Present and Long-Term History*, edited by Gunnel Cederlöf and Mahesh Rangarajan, 1–18. New Delhi: Oxford University Press, 2018.
Mould, Martin. "Greater Luyia." In *Studies in the Classification of Eastern Bantu Languages*, by Thomas H. Hinnebusch, Derek Nurse, and Martin Mould, 181–261. Hamburg: Helmut Buske, 1981.
Mugume, Isaac, Michel d. S. Mesquita, Yazidhi Bamutaze, Didier Ntwali, Charles Basalirwa, Daniel Waiswa, Joachim Reuder, Revocatus Twinomuhangi, Fredrick Tumwine, Triphonia Jakob Ngailo, and Bob Alex Ogwang. "Improving Quantitative Rainfall Prediction Using Ensemble Analogues in the Tropics: Case Study of Uganda." *Atmosphere* 9, no. 9 (2018). https://doi.org/10.3390/atmos9090328.
Musimami, Sylvester N. M. "Engero j'Abanyole n'endoma: Ey'ohubbimbirya n'amahulu gaabyo/Lunyole Proverbs and Sayings Explained." Unpublished manuscript, prepared November 2012.
Musisi, Nakanyike B. "Women, 'Elite Polygyny,' and Buganda State Formation." *Signs* 16, no. 4 (1991): 757–86.

Mutongi, Kenda. *Worries of the Heart: Widows, Family, and Community in Kenya.* Chicago: University of Chicago Press, 2007.
Næss, Åshild. *Prototypical Transitivity.* Amsterdam: John Benjamins, 2007.
Nicholson, Sharon E. "Climate and Climatic Variability of Rainfall over Eastern Africa." *Reviews of Geophysics* 55 (2017): 590–635.
Nicholson, Sharon E. "The ITCZ and the Seasonal Cycle over Equatorial Africa." *Bulletin of the American Meteorological Society* 99, no. 2 (2018): 337–48.
Nicholson, Sharon E. "A Review of Climate Dynamics and Climate Variability in Eastern Africa." In *The Limnology, Climatology and Paleoclimatology of the East African Lakes,* edited by Thomas C. Johnson and Eric O. Odada, with Katherine T. Whittaker, 25–56. Amsterdam: Gordon and Breach Science Publishers, 1996.
Nicholson, Sharon E., Amin K. Dezfuli, and Douglas Klotter. "A Two-Century Precipitation Dataset for the Continent of Africa." *Bulletin of the American Meteorological Society* 93, no. 8 (2012): 1219–31.
Nicholson, Sharon E., and Xungang Yin. "Rainfall Conditions in Equatorial East Africa during the Nineteenth Century as Inferred from the Record of Lake Victoria." *Climate Change* 48 (2001): 387–98.
Nietzsche, Friedrich. "Second Essay: 'Guilt,' 'Bad Conscience,' and the Like." In *The Genealogy of Morals: A Polemic,* translated by Horace B. Samuel, 40–93. New York: Boni and Liveright, 1918.
Nikis, Nicolas, and Alexandre Livingstone Smith. "Copper, Trade and Politics: Exchange Networks in Southern Central Africa in the 2nd Millennium CE." *Journal of Southern African Studies* 43, no. 5 (2017): 895–911.
Nurse, Derek. *Swahili and Sabaki.* Berkeley: University of California Press, 1993.
Nurse, Derek, and Gérard Philippson. "Towards a Historical Classification of the Bantu Languages." In *The Bantu Languages,* edited by Derek Nurse and Gérard Philippson, 164–81. London: Routledge, 2003.
Nurse, Derek, and Thomas Spear. *The Swahili: Reconstructing the History and Language of an African Society, 800–1500.* Philadelphia: University of Pennsylvania Press, 1985.
Nyakwada, W., L. A. Ogallo, and R. E. Okoola. "The Atlantic-Indian Ocean Dipole and Its Influence on East African Seasonal Rainfall." *Journal of Meteorology and Related Sciences* 3 (2009): 21–35.
Nyango, Y. "Family Life and Customs in Bunyole." Unpublished manuscript, Makerere University Library, n.d. Shared with author by Susan Reynolds Whyte.
Nyerere, Julius K. "Socialism and Rural Development." In *Freedom and Socialism/Uhuru na Ujamaa: A Selection from Writings and Speeches, 1965–1967,* 337–66. Dar es Salaam: Oxford University Press, 1968.
Nzita, Richard, and Mbaga-Niwampa. *Peoples and Cultures of Uganda.* Kampala: Fountain Publishers, 1993.
Ogot, Bethwell A. *A History of the Luo-Speaking Peoples of Eastern Africa.* Kisumu, Kenya: Anyange Press, 2009.
Ogot, Bethwell A. *History of the Southern Luo, Volume I: Migration and Settlement.* Nairobi: East African Publishing House, 1967.

O'Grady, William. "Semantics: The Analysis of Meaning." In *Contemporary Linguistics: An Introduction*, edited by William O'Grady, Michael Dobrovolsky, and Francis Katamba, 268–312. London: Longman, 1996.
Ogundiran, Akinwumi. *Archaeology and History in Ìlàrè District (Central Yorubaland, Nigeria), 1200–1900 A.D.* Oxford: Archaeopress, 2002.
Osogo, John. *A History of the Baluyia*. Nairobi: Oxford University Press, 1966.
Palmer, Robin, and Neil Parsons. "Introduction. The Roots of Rural Poverty: Historical Background." In *The Roots of Rural Poverty in Central and Southern Africa*, edited by Robin Palmer and Neil Parsons, 1–32. Berkeley: University of California Press, 1977.
Palmer, Robin, and Neil Parsons, eds. *The Roots of Rural Poverty in Central and Southern Africa*. Berkeley: University of California Press, 1977.
Philippson, Gérard, and Rebecca Grollemund. "Classifying Bantu Languages." In *The Bantu Languages*, 2nd ed., edited by Mark Van de Velde, Koen Bostoen, Derek Nurse, and Gérard Philippson, 335–54. London: Routledge, 2019.
Pikirayi, Innocent. *The Zimbabwe Culture: Origins and Decline of Southern Zambezian States*. Walnut Creek, CA: AltaMira Press, 2001.
"Poverty in Depth: New International Perspectives." *International Journal of Historical Archaeology* 15, no. 4 (2011).
Prestholdt, Jeremy. *Domesticating the World: African Consumerism and the Genealogies of Globalization*. Berkeley: University of California Press, 2008.
Purvis, J. B. *Through Uganda to Mount Elgon*. London: T. Fisher Unwin, 1909.
Ranger, Terence O. "Towards a Usable Past." In *African Studies since 1945: A Tribute to Basil Davidson*, edited by Christopher Fyfe, 17–30. London: Longman for the Centre of African Studies, Edinburgh, 1976.
Ray, Benjamin. *Myth, Ritual, and Kingship in Buganda*. New York: Oxford University Press, 1991.
"Reduce Rising Level of Poverty in Uganda." *Monitor*, January 30, 2021. https://www.monitor.co.ug/uganda/oped/editorial/reduce-rising-level-of-poverty-uganda-3211864.
Reid, Andrew, and Ceri Ashley. "Islands of Agriculture on Victoria Nyanza." In *Archaeology of African Plant Use*, edited by Chris J. Stevens, Sam Nixon, Mary Anne Murray, and Dorian Q. Fuller, 179–88. Walnut Creek, CA: Left Coast Press, 2014.
Reid, Richard. "Human Booty in Buganda: Some Observations on the Seizure of People in War, c.1700–1890." In *Slavery in the Great Lakes Region of East Africa*, edited by Henri Médard and Shane Doyle, 145–60. Oxford: James Currey, 2007.
Reid, Richard. *Political Power in Pre-colonial Buganda: Economy, Society and Warfare in the Nineteenth Century*. Oxford: James Currey, 2002.
Richter, Melvin. "*Begriffsgeschichte* and the History of Ideas." *Journal of the History of Ideas* 48, no. 2 (1987): 247–63.
Robertshaw, Peter, David Collett, Diane Gifford, and Nubi B. Mbae. "Shell Middens on the Shores of Lake Victoria." *Azania* 18 (1983): 1–43.
Rodney, Walter. *How Europe Underdeveloped Africa*. Washington: Howard University Press, 1972.

Roscoe, John. *The Bagesu and Other Tribes of the Uganda Protectorate*. Cambridge: University Press, 1924.

Roscoe, John. *The Northern Bantu: An Account of Some Central African Tribes of the Uganda Protectorate*. Cambridge: University Press, 1915.

Rosenblatt, Paul C., and Busisiwe Catherine Nkosi. "South African Zulu Widows in a Time of Poverty and Social Change." *Death Studies* 31, no. 1 (2007): 67–85.

Rottland, Franz. *Die Südnilotischen Sprachen: Beschreibung, Verglechung und Rekonstruktion*. Berlin: Dietrich Reimer, 1982.

Russell, James M., and Thomas C. Johnson. "A High-Resolution Geochemical Record from Lake Edward, Uganda Congo and the Timing and Causes of Tropical African Drought during the Late Holocene." *Quaternary Science Reviews* 24, no. 12–13 (2005): 1375–89.

Russell, James M., Thomas C. Johnson, Kerry R. Kelts, Tine Lærdal, and Michael R. Talbot. "An 11 000-yr Lithostratigraphic and Paleohydrologic Record from Equatorial Africa: Lake Edward, Uganda–Congo." *Palaeogeography, Palaeoclimatology, Palaeoecology* 193 (2003): 25–49.

Ryner, Maria, Karin Holmgren, and David Taylor. "A Record of Vegetation Dynamics and Lake Level Changes from Lake Emakat, Northern Tanzania during the Last c. 1200 Years." *Journal of Paleolimnology* 40, no. 2 (2007): 583–601.

Sá, Ana Lúcia. "The Concept of 'Land' in Bioko: 'Land as Property' and 'Land as Country.'" In *Doing Conceptual History in Africa*, edited by Axel Fleisch and Rhiannon Stephens, 138–61. 2016. Revised edition, Oxford: Berghahn Books, 2018.

Sahlins, Marshall. "Poor Man, Rich Man, Big-Man, Chief: Political Types in Melanesia and Polynesia." *Comparative Studies in Society and History* 5, no. 3 (1963): 285–303.

Salih, Abubakr A. M., Marta Baraibar, Kenneth Kemucie Mwangi, and Guleid Artan. "Climate Change and Locust Outbreak in East Africa." *Nature Climate Change* 10, no. 7 (2020): 584–85.

Schadeberg, Thilo C. "Derivation." In *The Bantu Languages*, edited by Derek Nurse and Gérard Philippson, 71–89. London: Routledge, 2003.

Schadeberg, Thilo C. "Historical Linguistics." In *The Bantu Languages*, edited by Derek Nurse and Gérard Philippson, 143–63. London: Routledge, 2003.

Schadeberg, Thilo C., and Koen Bostoen. "Word Formation." In *Bantu Languages*, 2nd ed., edited by Mark Van de Velde, Koen Bostoen, Derek Nurse, and Gérard Philippson, 172–203. London: Routledge, 2019.

Schmidt, Peter R. *Iron Technology in East Africa: Symbolism, Science, and Archaeology*. Bloomington: Indiana University Press, 1997.

Schoenbrun, David Lee. "Cattle Herds and Banana Gardens: The Historical Geography of the Western Great Lakes Region, ca. AD 800–1500." *African Archaeological Review* 11, no. 1 (1993): 39–72.

Schoenbrun, David Lee. "Great Lakes Bantu: Classification and Settlement Chronology." *Sprache und Geschichte in Afrika* 15 (1994): 39–72.

Schoenbrun, David Lee. *A Green Place, A Good Place: Agrarian Change, Gender, and Social Identity in the Great Lakes Region to the 15th Century.* Portsmouth, NH: Heinemann, 1998.

Schoenbrun, David Lee. "Mixing, Moving, Making, Meaning: Possible Futures for the Distant Past." *African Archaeological Review* 29, no. 2 (2012): 293–317.

Schoenbrun, David Lee. *The Names of the Python: Belonging in East Africa, 900 to 1930.* Madison: University of Wisconsin Press, 2021.

Schoenbrun, David Lee. "Pythons Worked: Constellating Communities of Practice with Conceptual Metaphor in Northern Lake Victoria, ca. A.D. 800 to 1200." In *Knowledge in Motion: Constellations of Learning across Time and Place*, edited by Andrew Roddick and Ann Stahl, 216–46. Tucson: University of Arizona Press, 2016.

Schoenbrun, David Lee. "Violence, Marginality, Scorn and Honour: Language Evidence of Slavery to the Eighteenth Century." In *Slavery in the Great Lakes Region of East Africa*, edited by Henri Médard and Shane Doyle, 38–75. Oxford: James Currey, 2007.

Schoff, Wilfred H., trans. *The Periplus of the Erythraean Sea: Travel and Trade in the Indian Ocean by a Merchant of the First Century.* New York: Longmans, Green, 1912.

Seligman, Andrea Felber. "Encircling Value: Inland Trade in the Precolonial East African-Indian Ocean World, ca. 1st–17th Centuries." PhD diss., Northwestern University, 2014.

Seligman, Andrea Felber. "Wealth Not by Any Other Name: Material Aesthetics in Expanding Commercial Times, ca. 16th–20th Centuries." *International Journal of African Historical Studies* 48, no. 3 (2015): 449–69.

Serels, Steven. *The Impoverishment of the African Red Sea Littoral, 1640–1945.* Cham, Switzerland: Palgrave Macmillan, 2018.

Shanguhyia, Martin S. *Population, Tradition, and Environmental Control in Colonial Kenya.* Rochester, NY: University of Rochester Press, 2015.

Sheriff, Abdul. *Slaves, Spices, and Ivory in Zanzibar: Integration of an East African Commercial Empire into the World Economy, 1770–1873.* London: James Currey, 1987.

Shipton, Parker. *Mortgaging the Ancestors: Ideologies of Attachment in Africa.* New Haven: Yale University Press, 2009.

Shipton, Parker. *The Nature of Entrustment: Intimacy, Exchange, and the Sacred in Africa.* New Haven: Yale University Press, 2007.

Shorter, Aylward. *Chiefship in Western Tanzania: A Political History of the Kimbu.* Oxford: Clarendon Press, 1972.

Sihler, Andrew L. *Language History: An Introduction.* Amsterdam: John Benjamins, 2000.

Sisòkò, Fa-Digi, and John William Johnson. *Son-Jara: The Mande Epic.* Bloomington: Indiana University Press, 1986.

Ssemmanda, Immaculate, David B. Ryves, Ole Bennike, and Peter G. Appleby. "Vegetation History in Western Uganda during the Last 1200 Years: A Sediment-Based Reconstruction from Two Crater Lakes." *Holocene* 15, no. 1 (2005): 119–32.

Stager, J. Curt, Brian F. Cumming, and L. David Meeker. "A 10,000 Year High-Resolution Diatom Record from Pilkington Bay, Lake Victoria, East Africa." *Quaternary Research* 59, no. 2 (2003): 172–81.

Stager, J. Curt, David Ryves, Brian F. Cumming, L. David Meeker, and Juerg Beer. "Solar Variability and the Levels of Lake Victoria, East Africa, during the Last Millennium." *Journal of Paleolimnology* 33, no. 2 (2005): 243–51.

Stam, N. "Bantu Kavirondo of Mumias District (near Lake Victoria)." *Anthropos* 14/15, no. 4/6 (1919): 968–80.

Stephens, Rhiannon. "Bereft, Selfish, and Hungry: Greater Luhyia Concepts of the Poor in Precolonial East Africa." *American Historical Review* 123, no. 3 (2018): 789–816.

Stephens, Rhiannon. *A History of African Motherhood: The Case of Uganda, 700–1900*. New York: Cambridge University Press, 2013.

Stephens, Rhiannon. "A History of Motherhood, Food Procurement and Politics in East-Central Uganda to the Nineteenth Century." PhD diss., Northwestern University, 2007.

Stephens, Rhiannon. "Poverty's Pasts: A Case for *Longue Durée* Histories." *Journal of African History* 59, no. 3 (2018): 399–409.

Stephens, Rhiannon. "'Wealth,' 'Poverty' and the Question of Conceptual History in Oral Contexts: Uganda from c.1000 CE." In *Doing Conceptual History in Africa*, edited by Axel Fleisch and Rhiannon Stephens, 21–48. 2016. Revised edition, Oxford: Berghahn Books, 2018.

Stephens, Rhiannon. "'Whether They Promised Each Other Some Thing Is Difficult to Work Out': The Complicated History of Marriage in Uganda." *African Studies Review* 59, no. 1 (2016): 127–53.

Stephens, Rhiannon, and Axel Fleisch. "Introduction: Theories and Methods of African Conceptual History." In *Doing Conceptual History in Africa*, edited by Axel Fleisch and Rhiannon Stephens, 1–20. 2016. Revised edition, Oxford: Berghahn Books, 2018.

Strayer, Robert W. "The Making of Mission Schools in Kenya: A Microcosmic Perspective." *Comparative Education Review* 17, no. 3 (1973): 313–30.

Sunseri, Thaddeus. "The African Rinderpest Panzootic, 1888–1897." *Oxford Research Encyclopedia of African History*. 2018. https://oxfordre.com/africanhistory/view/10.1093/acrefore/9780190277734.001.0001/acrefore-9780190277734-e-375.

Sutton, John E. G. *The Archaeology of the Western Highlands of Kenya*. Nairobi: British Institute in Eastern Africa, 1973.

Sutton, John E. G. "Becoming Masaailand." In *Being Maasai: Ethnicity and Identity in East Africa*, edited by Thomas Spear and Richard Waller, 38–60. London: James Currey, 1993.

Sutton, John E. G. "Sirikwa Holes, Stones Houses and Their Makers in the Western Highlands of Kenya." *Man* 65 (1965): 113–15.
Sutton, John E. G. *A Thousand Years of East Africa*. Nairobi: British Institute in Eastern Africa, 1990.
Swadesh, Morris. "Lexico-Statistic Dating of Prehistoric Ethnic Contacts: With Special Reference to North American Indians and Eskimos." *Proceedings of the American Philosophical Society* 96, no. 4 (1952): 452–563.
Tantala, Renée L. "Verbal and Visual Imagery in Kitara (Western Uganda): Interpreting 'The Story of Isimbwa and Nyinamwiru.'" In *Paths Toward the Past: African Historical Essays in Honor of Jan Vansina*, edited by Robert W. Harms, Joseph C. Miller, David B. Newbury, and Michele D. Wagner, 223–43. Atlanta: African Studies Association Press, 1994.
Thomson, Joseph. *Through Masai Land: A Journey of Exploration among the Snowclad Volcanic Mountains and Strange Tribes of Eastern Equatorial Africa. Being the Narrative of the Royal Geographical Society's Expedition to Mount Kenia and Lake Victoria Nyanza, 1883–1884*. Boston: Houghton, Mifflin, 1885.
Tierney, Jessica E., James M. Russell, Jaap S. Sinninghe Damsté, Yongsong Huang, and Dirk Verschuren. "Late Quaternary Behavior of the East African Monsoon and the Importance of the Congo Air Boundary." *Quaternary Science Reviews* 30 (2011): 798–807.
Traugott, Elizabeth Closs, and Richard B. Dasher. *Regularity in Semantic Change*. Cambridge: Cambridge University Press, 2002.
Tuck, Michael W. "'The Rupee Disease': Taxation, Authority, and Social Conditions in Early Colonial Uganda." *International Journal of African History Studies* 39, no. 2 (2006): 221–45.
Tukahirwa, J. M. "Soil Resources in the Highlands of Uganda: Prospects and Sensitivities." *Mountain Research and Development* 8, no. 2/3 (1988): 165–72.
Twaddle, Michael. *Kakungulu and the Creation of Uganda: 1868–1928*. London: James Currey, 1993.
U'mista Cultural Society. "Living Tradition: The Kwakwaka'wakw Potlatch of the Northwest Coast." https://umistapotlatch.ca/potlatch-eng.php.
Vail, David J. *A History of Agricultural Innovation and Development in Teso District, Uganda*. Syracuse, NY: Syracuse University Press, 1972.
Van de Velde, Mark. "Nominal Morphology and Syntax." In *The Bantu Languages*, 2nd ed., edited by Mark Van de Velde, Koen Bostoen, Derek Nurse, and Gérard Philippson, 237–69. London: Routledge, 2019.
Vansina, Jan. *How Societies Are Born: Governance in West Central Africa before 1600*. Charlottesville: University of Virginia Press, 2004.
Vansina, Jan. *Oral Tradition as History*. Madison: University of Wisconsin Press, 1985.
Vansina, Jan. *Oral Tradition: A Study in Historical Methodology*. London: Routledge and Kegan Paul, 1965.

Vansina, Jan. *Paths in the Rainforests: Toward a History of Political Tradition in Central Africa*. Madison: University of Wisconsin Press, 1990.
Vanterm, A. "News from Our Missions: Usoga and Uganda. Letter from Father Vanterm. St Francis Xavier's Mission, Usoga, Feast of St Joseph [19 March] 1900." *St Joseph's Advocate: A Quarterly Illustrated Record of Foreign Missions and of Life and Suffering in Heathen Lands* 3, no. 23 (1900): 488–89.
Verschuren, Dirk. "Reconstructing Fluctuations of a Shallow East Africa Lake during the Past 1800 Yrs from Sediment Stratigraphy in a Submerged Crater Basin." *Journal of Paleolimnology* 25, no. 3 (2001): 297–311.
Verschuren, Dirk, and Dan J. Charman. "Latitudinal Linkages in Late Holocene Moisture-Balance Variation." In *Natural Climate Variability and Global Warming: A Holocene Perspective*, edited by Richard W. Battarbee and Heather A. Binney, 189–231. Chichester, UK: Wiley, 2008.
Verschuren, Dirk, Thomas C. Johnson, Hedy J. Kling, David N. Edgington, Peter R. Leavitt, Erik T. Brown, Michael R. Talbot, and Robert E. Hecky. "History and Timing of Human Impact on Lake Victoria, East Africa." *Proceedings of the Royal Society B: Biological Sciences* 269, no. 1488 (2002): 289–94.
Verschuren, Dirk, Kathleen R. Laird, and Brian F. Cumming. "Rainfall and Drought in Equatorial East Africa during the Past 1,100 Years." *Nature* 403, no. 6768 (2000): 410–14.
Vidal, Claudine. "Alexis Kagame entre memoire et histoire." *History in Africa* 15 (1988): 493–504.
Vincent, Joan. *Teso in Transformation: The Political Economy of Peasant and Class in Eastern Africa*. Berkeley: University of California Press, 1982.
Vossen, Rainer. *The Eastern Nilotes: Linguistics and Historical Reconstructions*. Berlin: Dietrich Reimer, 1982.
van de Walle, Dominique. "Lasting Welfare Effects of Widowhood in Mali." *World Development* 51 (2013): 1–19.
Waller, Richard. "Emutai: Crisis and Response in Maasailand 1883–1902." In *The Ecology of Survival: Case Studies from Northeast African History*, edited by Douglas H. Johnson and David M. Anderson, 73–112. London: Lester Crook Academic, 1988.
Walser, Ferdinand. *Luganda Proverbs*. Berlin: Reimer Verlag, 1982.
Wandibba, Simiyu. "Some Aspects of Precolonial Architecture." In *History and Culture in Western Kenya: The People of Bungoma District through Time*, edited by Simiyu Wandibba, 34–41. Nairobi: Gideon Were Press, 1985.
Webster, J. B., D. H. Okalany, C. P. Emudong, and N. Egimu-Okuda. *The Iteso during the Asonya*. Nairobi: East African Publishing House, 1973.
Weiss, Brad. "Forgetting Your Dead: Alienable and Inalienable Objects in Northwest Tanzania." *Anthropological Quarterly* 70, no. 4 (1997): 164–72.
Were, Gideon S. *A History of the Abaluyia of Western Kenya*. Nairobi: East African Publishing House, 1967.

Were, Gideon S. *Western Kenya Historical Texts: Abaluyia, Teso and Elgon Kalenjin.* Nairobi: East African Literature Bureau, 1967.
Whyte, Michael A. "The Ideology of Descent in Bunyole." PhD diss., University of Washington, 1974.
Whyte, Susan Reynolds. "Men, Women and Misfortune in Bunyole." In *Women's Religious Experience*, edited by Pat Holden, 175–92. London: Croom Helm, 1983.
Whyte, Susan Reynolds, and Michael A. Whyte. "Clans, Brides and Dancing Spirits." *Folk* 29 (1987): 97–123.
World Bank. "GDP (Current US$) – Sub-Saharan Africa." https://data.worldbank.org/indicator/NY.GDP.MKTP.CD?locations=ZG.
World Bank. "Gini Index (World Bank Estimate)." https://data.worldbank.org/indicator/SI.POV.GINI.
World Bank. "Poverty Headcount Ratio at $1.90 a Day (2011 PPP) (% of Population) – Sub-Saharan Africa." https://data.worldbank.org/indicator/SI.POV.DDAY?locations=ZG.
Wrigley, Christopher. *Kingship and State: The Buganda Dynsasty*. Cambridge: Cambridge University Press, 1996.
Wynne-Jones, Stephanie. *A Material Culture: Consumption and Materiality on the Coast of Precolonial East Africa*. Oxford: Oxford University Press, 2016.
Zeleza, Paul Tiyambe. *A Modern Economic History of Africa Volume I: The Nineteenth Century*. Dakar: CODESRIA, 1993.

INDEX

Page locators in italics refer to figures, maps, and tables.

The African Poor (Iliffe), 56
age sets, 2, 59, 122
agriculture: *amio* (wealth in crops and food), 6–7, 134–35, 156, 160–61, 204; banana cultivation, 81, 100–101, 106, 108, 126, 231n40; beer, production of, 62, 87, 100, 122, 137, 231n47, 243n100; cash crops introduced by colonial administration, 2, 6, 95, 159–60, 162; communal feasts, 82, 87, 231n47; cotton production, 159–60; cowpeas, 78, 230n27; crop failures, 50, 69, 71, 137, 140, 146; food, search for, 49–50; food, wealth in, 6–7, 20, 78, 133–34, 135–36, 143, 156, 204; intercropping of legumes with staples, 54; iron hoe trade, 6–7, 135; millet, 5, 6–7, 59–60, 75, 101, 128, 135; sesame, 5, 6, 167; sorghum, 5–7, 59, 108, 128, 137, 159, 167; time and season, 56, 101; women's wealth in crops, 7, 10–11, 80, 120, 133–36, 139. *See also* drought; livestock
Amin, Samir, 13
Amoah, Elizabeth, 13
Anglican Church Missionary Society (CMS), 161
archaeology, 12, 14, 17–18, 23, 85, 209n21, 224n52; excavations near Uganda, 40–41; individual level not possible, 25–26; migration, record of, 46–48; and reconstruction of languages, 34; Sirikwa Holes evidence, 124–25
Ashby, Solange, 44

Ashley, Ceri, 41
Ateker languages: and colonialism, 137; concepts of poverty and wealth through the nineteenth century, 130–31; genetic classification of, 31, *32*, 131; glottochronological dates for, 34; Highland Northern Ateker concepts of poverty and wealth, 136–41; modern dialect chaining, 129; Ngakarimojong (modern language), 2, *3*, 20, 31, *121*, 131; Northern, *32*, 129; Proto-Ateker, 20, 31, 60–61, 120, *121*, 128–31; Proto-Highland Northern Ateker, 31, *32*, *121*, 131, 138; Proto-Kyoga-Bisina Teso, 131; Proto-Lowland Northern Ateker, 31, *32*, 131, 138; Proto-Northern Ateker, 31, *32*, 130, 131, 138–40, 204; Toposa, Nyangatom, and Turkana dialects, 131, 216n32. *See also* Ateso languages
Atengorit (wealthy Iteso woman), 133–34, 160
Ateso languages, 2, *3*, 6–7, 20, 83, *121*, 128–29, 241n48; Atesyo (Tororo) language, 31, *32*; concepts of poverty and wealth through the nineteenth century, 131–36; dialects of Pallisa, Usuku, and Ngora, 31, 131; genetic classification of, 31, 131; migration by speakers of, 131–32; Proto-Ateso, 31, *32*, *121*, 130–36, 203; Proto-Teso, 31, *32*; wealth in harvested crops, 120. *See also* Ateker languages; Iteso communities

Atlantic-Congo languages, 30, 31–32, *33*. *See also* Bantu language family
attachment, ideologies of, 15

Babukusu communities, 89–91, 90, 146, 157–58
Baganda communities, 81, 147–48, 158, 160
Bagwe communities, 93
Bagwere communities, 116, 118, 144, 157. *See also* Lugwere
Balalaka polity, 116, 162
Bamasaaba communities, 82, 86–89, 116, 157, 231n47
Bantu language family, 2, 8, 28, *29*, *30*, *33*, *73*, 214n21, 234n95; Atlantic-Congo languages, genetic classification of, 30, 31–32, *33*; gender neutrality of, 221n15, 236n16; isiZulu, 28; Kalenjin speakers among, 122, 124; Kiswahili, 16, 28, 87, 144, 162; modern, 32; noun classes in, 38–40, 52, 102–3, 109; pre-Gungu, 33, *33*; Proto-East Bantu, 28, 32; Proto-East Nyanza, 32, *33*, 55, 125; protolanguages, map of, *47*; Proto-Nguni, 28; Proto-Northeast Coast Bantu, 28; Proto-Western Lakes, 32, *33*; Proto-West Nyanza, 17, 32, *33*, 54–58, 156; West Nyanza, 31. *See also* Greater Luhyia languages; Great Lakes Bantu languages; Lubukusu; Ludadiri; Luganda; Lugwe; Lugwere; Lumasaaba; Lunyole; Lusaamia; Lusoga; North Nyanza; Proto-Bantu; Proto-Greater Luhyia languages; Proto-Great Lakes Bantu; Rushana; West Nyanza languages
Banyole people, 5, 75–80, 77, 118, 164–65, 167, 169
Basaamia communities, 93–97, 147
Bashana people, 115, 116, 144. *See also* Rushana

Basoga traders, 7, 135
Bastin, Yvonne, 55, 84
beggars and begging, 20, 60, 74, 123; *-panan-* (pauper, bereavement, kinlessness), 59–60, 122–24, 127–28, 186–88, 224n63, 228nn5–6
Belinga, Samuel M. Eno, 14
Benue-Congo, 32
bereavement, 1, 11, 50–51, 63, 72, 74–75, 120, 123, 169; *khutàmbà* as word root for, 86, 173; *-panan-* as word root for, 59–60, 122–24, 127–28, 186–88, 224n63, 228nn5–6; and slave trade, 148, 165; *-tak* as word root for, 75–76, 172; *-tamb-* as word root for, 75–76, 83, 86, 91, 118, 148, 173–74; *umudambiro* (greeting to bereaved person), 86; *umutambi* (destitute person, bereaved person), 86, 173–74; and vulnerability, 11, 50–51, 60, 74, 80, 122–23, 221n15
Blank, Andreas, 36–37
bridewealth, 6, 10, 19, 77–80; effect of cattle diseases on, 154, 165–66; head of household's power over, 139–40; **omwaandu* (plunder, captive women), 22, 23, 77, 103–4, 112–13, 116, 156, 158, 168, 175–76; **-yaand-* (bridewealth, military plunder, material goods), 52–54, 77, 79–80, 84, 88, 92, 96, 103–5, 107, 109, 112, 119, 146–47, 156, 167–68, 175–76. *See also* livestock; women
British Protectorate of Uganda, 155–56, 159. *See also* colonial era
British Special Commissioner to Uganda, 81
Buganda (central Uganda), 2, 4, 25; and banana cultivation, 231n40; economic and political power of, 57–58; nineteenth-century military conflicts, 147–48, 155–56; seventeenth-century conquests by, 105, 112–13; Uganda Agreement (1900), 159

Bugwere (eastern Uganda), 156, 161–63
Bukedi (east Uganda), 155–60
Bukooli, eastern Uganda, 107
Bulegenyi communities, 115, 144
Bunyala (Port Victoria), 146
Bunyole, 75, 77–78; prayer for wealth, 5–6, 167
Bunyoro (western Uganda), 4, 25, 155
Burun, 31, *32*, 62
Busaamia (eastern Uganda), 93–95, 147–48, 163
Busoga (eastern Uganda), 75, 107–8, 151, 157
Buxton High School (CMS, Mombasa), 162

capitalism, 168, 169
ceramics: Contact Urewe ware, 41; Kansyore ware, 41; Urewe ware, 41, 48
charity and almsgiving, 13–14
Cherangany Hills (Kenya), 122
chiefs, 89, 158; colonial creation of, 160–63, 164, 169
Christian missionaries, 111, 144–45, 157, 159, 165; Mill Hill missionary station, 93–94, 151, 161
Church Missionary Society (CMS), 161
clans, 4, 86, 104, 108–9, 116, 133, 138
climate conditions, 12, 56, 64–71, 212n55; from start of Common Era to eleventh century, 49, 67–68; from eleventh to sixteenth century, 68–69; from sixteenth to nineteenth century, 69–71; African and Indian Ocean monsoons, 66; and banana cultivation, 108; Congo Air Boundary, 65–66; dendrochronology, emphasis on, 64–65, 225n1; diatom evidence, 67; economic and social responses to, 4, 10, 18, 45, 49, 64, 69–71; El Niño-Southern Oscillation (ENSO), 66, 70; and glottochronological dates, 34; Indian Ocean Dipole (IOD), 66, 70; Inter-Tropical Convergence Zone (ITCZ), 65–66, 70, 226n5; Lake Kyoga, 106; leaf wax records, 70; Medieval Climate Anomaly (circa 950–1250 CE), 67, 68, 131; mountain ranges and volcanic craters, 66–67; and negative views of poverty, 61; in oral traditions, 116; palynological (pollen) records, 34, 68; rain-shadows, 66; Rift Valleys, 66; and solar activity, 67, 68; variability, 49, 67, 69–70, 101–2, 229n8. *See also* drought
clothing, 44, 103, 145, 157, 163–64
coastal traders, 21, 148
cognate words, 11–12, 28–29, *29*, 35, 224n52
cognitive semantics, 36–40
Cohen, David William, 108
colonial era, 13, 144–66; administrative appointments, 162–63; cash crops introduced, 2, 6, 95, 159–60, 162; as cause of famine, 95; chiefs as creation of, 160–63, 164, 169; and drought of late nineteenth century, 95, 150–54, 165–66; and Highland Northern Ateker speakers, 137; material poverty and wealth under, 163–65; missionary education, 161–63; natural and social disruption, concepts of, 146–47; new forms of power, 157–61, 162, 166, 168–69; nineteenth and early twentieth centuries, 20–21; police force, 157; racism of, 4, 61, 159; rule of, 154–57, 168–69; slave and ivory trades, 147–50, 165; structural poverty caused by, 4, 207n6; taxation, 2, 156–61, 249n89; violence of colonial conquest, 144–45, 157, 166
comparative historical linguistics, 1, 11–12, 17, 26–27, 40, 214n17; comparative method, 29–31, 34–35; interdisciplinary approach, 11, 16, 169
composition of wealth, 10, 14, 15, 57, 165

conceptual history, 4; complexity of, 8–9, 26, 40; ideas, reconstruction of, 23; of poverty and wealth, 7–11
conjunctural poverty, 56, 207n6
contact languages, 28
contingency of poverty, 50–51, 76–77, 79, 99–100, 102–3
continuity: of languages, 22–23, 52; of practices, 16, 43–44
core vocabulary, 28–29, *29*, 34
COVID-19 pandemic, 2, 207n2
Crabtree, William, 161
credit, debt, and land in western Kenya, 15
Crescent Island Basin (Lake Naivasha), 67, 70
Croft, William, 22
Cushitic languages, Eastern and Southern, 59–60

Dahl's Law, 35
Dale, Darla, 41
Dasher, Richard, 36
Datooga dialect cluster, 31
Davies, Matthew, 125
debt relations, 15, 55, 58, 175, 183
deceitful, poor as, 1, 9, 75, 76, 80, 170, 189
de Luna, Kathryn, 15, 24, 79
dendrochronology, 64–65, 225n1
desire, 49, 117, 220n9
Dhopadhola, *121*, 141–42
diachronic semantics, 17, 36, 38
Diké, K. O., 12–13, 22
Distefano, John, 85, 126
Dodos dialect, 131
Dodosŏ, 138
Doing Conceptual History in Africa (Fanego Palat), 8
Drontman, Father, 151
drought, 67–68, 130–31, 146–47, 245n2; *bukwikwi* famine (1830s), 116; century-scale, 68; colonial era, 95, 150–54, 165–66; concepts of poverty and wealth formed during times of, 12, 49–50, 69, 74, 76, 107, 119, 140–41; *matyama* famine (1780s), 116; mid-1800s, 116, 144, 146–47; multidecadal, 12, 18, 68, 70, 76, 106, 119, 122, 131, 146, 165, 168. *See also* agriculture; climate conditions
Dyson-Hudson, Neville, 137
Dyson-Hudson, Rada, 140

Early Iron Age, 13
egalitarian depiction of Africa, 4–5, 13, 87
Egimu-Okuda, N., 131
Ehret, Christopher, 14, 59, 85, 224n52
elderhood, wealth connected with, 19, 92–93, 122, 125–26
"elite polygyny," 4
elopement, 5, 6
Elureko (Western Kenya), 148
emaciation, poverty as, 10
Emudong, C. P., 131
emuron (foreteller), 152–53
engoba (olukoba) (walled villages), 94, 147
equality, prosperity in terms of, 134
Equatorial Africa, 14
Equatorial Guinea, 23
ethnography, 12, 23, 38, 42–44, 82, 93, 127–28, 133, 154
Europe, histories of poverty and wealth, 15
evil, poverty connected with, 101, 102, 111, 199–200, 236
exchange, 7, 20, 48, 53, 55, 62–63

Fair, Laura, 16
"Family Life and Customs in Bunyole" (Nyango), 77–78
Fanego Palat (née Fleisch), Axel, 8
Fields-Black, Edda, 25, 213n9

Fitzsimons, William, 31, 34, 61–62, 128–29, 130–31, 134, 137, 138, 153, 224n52
frontier situation, 41

Ganda society, 164–65. *See also* Luganda
Geeraerts, Dirk, 37
gendered forms of poverty, 9–10, 132–33, 154, 173, 185, 186, 187; and bereavement, 50–51, 221n15; *nambadi* (irresponsible husband), 118; women's contravention of social norms linked to, 90, 151–52, 165, 170
gendered forms of wealth, 19–20, 100, 163, 190; and hunters, 15, 79; *omwandu* (plunder, captive women), 22, 23, 77, 103, 112–13, 116, 156, 158, 168, 175–76; plunder, wealth as product of, 19, 57, 79, 103, 107, 112, 156, 158; and power, 108–9; women, wealth in, 4, 52–54, 56–58, 77, 96, 103–5, 109, 112, 146–47, 167–68, 175; **-yaand-* (bridewealth; military plunder, material goods), 52–54, 77, 79–80, 84, 88, 92, 96, 103–5, 107, 109, 112, 119, 146–47, 156, 167–68, 175–76. *See also* bridewealth; livestock
genetic classifications of languages, 11, 17, 27–33, *32, 33*, 214n21, 216n36; Atlantic-Congo languages, 30, 31–32, *33*; Nilo-Saharan, 215n29; Nilotic languages, 30–31, *32*
Ghana Living Standards Survey, 134
gift exchange, 20, 142, 189
Gikuyu society, 13
Gisu clans, 155
Goldschmidt, Walter, 126–27
grammaticalization, 36
Greater Luhyia languages, 9–10, 17, *29*, 29–31, *30*, 72–98, 124, 217n38; Dahl's Law, 35; frontier situation, 410–600 CE, 41; genetic classification of, 33, *33*; Lubukusu concepts of poverty and wealth, 89–91; Lukisa, Luwanga, and Lutsotso dialect cluster, 33; Lumasaaba concepts of poverty and wealth, 86–89; Lunyole concepts of poverty and wealth, 75–80; Lusaamia concepts of poverty and wealth, 93–97; Lutirichi, Lwidakho, and Lulogooli, 33; Luyia Law, 35, 233n60; modern, 35, 72; oral traditions of societies, 42–43; proximity to other language speakers, 97–98; use of root **-yaand-*, 146–47. *See also* Lubukusu; Ludadiri; Lugwe; Lumasaaba; Lunyole; Lusaamia; Proto-North Luhyia
Great Lakes Bantu languages, 9, 31–33, *33*, 57, 76, 223n50; proximity to other language speakers, 97–98. *See also* Greater Luhyia languages; North Nyanza
grief, 51, 110
Grollemund, Rebecca, 30
Gulliver, P. H., 137
Guyer, Jane, 14–15, 134, 208n10
Gwe-Saamia, 19, 33, 50

Habaci, 148–49
Haji, Muyaka bin, 16
Hanlon, Henry, 151
Hathor, worship of in Nubia, 44
Hay, Margaret Jean, 163–64
healers, access to, 88
Heligoland Treaty of 1890, 155
heritable wealth, 10, 52–54, 58, 63, 90–91, 103, 112, 116, 167, 175–76, 234n88
Highland Northern Ateker concepts of poverty and wealth, 138–41
History in Africa: A Journal of Debates, Methods, and Source Analysis, 42
"History of Bugisu," 43
Hobley, Charles W., 158
honor, and wealth, 11, 19, 73, 80, 84–85, 89–90
Hopkins, A. G., 13

hunter-gatherer communities, 41, 48, 124
hunters, 15, 79
Hyrax Hill (western Kenya), 125

Ibwala (wealthy hoe trader), 6–7
ideas, reconstruction of, 23
Ifversen, Jan, 26
Igbo-speaking regions, 12–13
Ik communities, 139
Ikumama communities, 136
Iliffe, John, 13, 56
Imperial British East Africa Company, 154–55
imperialism, European, 20–21
Indo-European family of languages, 27–28, 34
insignia, 11
intellectual work of ordinary people, 4–7, 9, 12, 22, 53, 119, 169–70
iron production, 94–95
Iteso communities, 6–7, 116, 133, 157, 160–61, 245n3; asonya period, 136; and drought of 1890s, 152; economic equilibrium, 153; growth and expansion in nineteenth century, 146; oral traditions, 42, 116; Teso Historical Texts project, 43, 131–36. *See also* Ateso languages
ivory trade, 7, 21, 135, 148–50, 149, 151, 165

Jackson, Frederick, 154–55, 160
Japadhola communities, 141
jewelry, references to, 85, 194, 233n65
Jie communities, 148–50, 152
Jie dialect, 31, 43, *121*, 131, 136–39, 148–50, 152, 155, 210n33, 216n32
Johnston, Harry H., 81, 93, 155, 159

Kabareega, Mukama (King), 155
Kagame, Alexis, 25
Kageni, Ezekeri (colonial administrator), 163

Kagera River, 46
Kakungulu, Semei (military leader), 155–57, 162
Kalenjin: Bantu-speaking communities, interactions with, 122, 124; modern, 123, 228n2; Proto-Central Kalenjin, 31; Proto-Elgon Kalenjin, 31, *121*, 124; Proto-Elgon-Mau Kalenjin, 20, 31, 85, *121*, 122, 124–28; Proto-Kalenjin, 20, 31, 59–60, 63, 74, 85, 97–98, 120–28, *121*; Proto-Northern Kalenjin, 31, 85, 121–22; Proto-Southern Kalenjin, 31; speakers of as refugees, 74. *See also* Proto-Elgon-Mau Kalenjin
Kalu, Ogbu, 14
Kampala, Uganda, 2
Karimojong communities, 20, 136–41, 149
Kateregga, King (Buganda), 112
Katonga River, 99
Kavirondo region (northeast of Victoria Nyanza), 93–94, 158, 235n107
Kenya, 31, 46, 120; climate conditions over time, 67–68; credit, debt, and land in western, 15; Hyrax Hill, 125; Luo speakers, 141; Mombasa, 16, 162; Mumias settlement, 148, 154–55, 157–58; Sirikwa Holes, 124–25
Kenyan Rift Valley, 59
Khanakwa, Pamela, 23
Kihaya, 33, *33*
Kinare, 31
kinlessness, 9, 59–60, 63, 74, 80, 143; of orphans, 11, 20, 60, 74, 122–23, 128
Kipsigis, 31
Kiswahili, 16, 28, 87, 144, 162
Kivu Rift Valley, 46
Kizenguli, 107
Kizinza, 33
Knighton, Ben, 138
knowledge, wealth in, 15
Koki province (southern Uganda), 155

Konecky, Bronwen, 67
Kony, 124
Kopytoff, Igor, 46
Krapf, Johann, 16
Kupsabiny (Kupsapiny), 2, *3*, *32*, *121*, 124, 126–28, 228n6

Labwor Acholi communities, 149
Lake Bogoria area (Kenya), 68, 70
Lake Emakat area (northern Tanzania), 68
Lake Kyoga (eastern Uganda), *100*, 106, 107, 128
Lake Mwitanzige (Edward) (western Uganda), 67, 68
Lake Naivasha (central Kenya), 67, 68, 70
Lake Nakuru (Kenya), 66
Lake Tanganyika, 66
Lake Turkana (Kenya), 66
Lake Victoria Nyanza, 8; boat fishing on, 94; and climate conditions, 67–70, 102, 108, 150–51; littoral and islands of, 41; migration patterns and languages, 46–49, *47*, 52, 54, 75, 91, 93, 99, *100*, 102, 104–8, 114
Laki Omugobera (Teso man), 116
Lamphear, John, 137, 139, 149, 152, 243n100
"land hunger," 12–13
Lango people, 155
languages: cognate words, 11–12, 28–29, *29*, 35, 224n52; dialects, 27; genetic classification of, 11, 17, 27–30, *32*, *33*, 216n36; genetics applied to African history, 214n18, 216n36; Indo-European family of, 27–28; loan words, 57–60, 74, 95, 127; map of modern, *3*; morphology, 8, 27, 29–30, *30*, 236n16; phonemes, 11–12, 34–35; sound changes in (sounds, pronunciation, and phonemes), 11–12, 17, 22–23, 27, 34–35; spoken, continuity of, 22–23, 52; synonyms, 12, 15–16, 38. *See also* Bantu language family; modern languages; Nilotic language family; protolanguages; specific languages and language families
Lawrance, J. C. D., 133, 135, 154
leadership: hereditary, 36, 54, 142, 232n57; wealth linked with, 10, 15, 19, 85, 89–91, 127, 140–41, 142, 143; words not linked with wealth, 127. *See also* power
lexicostatistics, 28, 29–30, 34
lineality, 51, 54, 63, 86, 104, 109, 232n57
linguistics. *See* comparative historical linguistics
livestock, 6; *abar* (wealth in cattle), 7; cattle, privileging of, 123; changes in ownership patterns, 62–63; as communal property (*esipan*), 139–40; diseases and drought, effect on, 21, 88, 108, 149, 152–54, 166; goats, 41, 88, 94, 125, 131, 133, 135–36; poverty and lack of, 20, 63, 123–24, 126; and Proto-Kalenjin speaking communities, 122; Proto-West Nyanza speakers' expertise, 54; raids on herds of others, 126–27, 128, 138, 153–54; wealth in, 85, 87–88, 96, 127, 130, 134, 139, 149–50, 160–61. *See also* agriculture; bridewealth
loan words, 57–60, 74, 95, 127
loincloth (*-*doobe*), 103, 117, 164
longue durée, 2, 12–13, 169; large-scale changes, 15, 20–21. *See also* climate conditions
Lonsdale, John, 13
Loriang (war-leader), 149
Lotuko, 31
Lubukusu, 19, *29*, *30*, 33, *33*, 73, *73*, 81, 86; concepts of poverty and wealth through the nineteenth century, 89–91
Lúcia Sá, Ana, 23

Ludadiri, 2, 3, *29*, *30*, 33, *33*, *73*, 81, 84, 86
Lugabula dialect, 107, 156
Luganda, 19, *33*, 99, 105, 111–12; clothing, terms for, 164–65; gendered forms of wealth, 104; loan words, 57–58; proverb about poverty and climate, 56
Lugungu, 57, 223n50
Lugwe, 2, 28, *29*, *30*, *33*, *73*, 118, 234n95
Lugwere, 33, *33*, *100*, 105, 234n95; concepts of poverty and wealth through the nineteenth century, 116–19; more words for poverty than wealth, 117, 119; pre-Lugwere, 144; verb and subject agreement, 39
Luhyia languages. *See* Greater Luhyia languages; Proto-Greater Luhyia languages
Lukisa, *30*, 33, *33*
Lulamoogi dialect, 107
Lulogooli, *30*, 33, *33*
Lumasaaba, 2, *3*, 19, *29*, *30*, 33, *33*, *73*, 81, 84, 90; concepts of poverty and wealth through the nineteenth century, 86–89
Lunyole, 1, 2, *3*, 19, 28, *29*, *30*, *33*, *73*, 83, 113, 141; antiquity of, 75–76, 147; concepts of poverty and wealth through the nineteenth century, 75–80; land conflicts and speakers of, 75; prayer for wealth, 5–6, 167; pre-Lunyole, 33, 72, 106; Proto-Lunyole, 75, 80
Luo (modern language), 62
Luo communities (western Kenya), 15
Lusaamia, *30*, 33, *33*, *73*, 118, 234n95; concepts of poverty and wealth through the nineteenth century, 93–97; population density reflected in, 93–94
Lusiki dialect, 107
Lusoga, 19–20, 96, *100*, 105; banana cultivation by speakers of, 108; concepts of poverty and wealth, 107–14; fluid borders, 108; immorality and poverty linked, 151; noun classes, 39; Owiny Karuoth group, 109
Lutenga dialect, 107
Lutirichi, *30*, 33, *33*
Lutsotso, *30*, 33, *33*
Luwanga, *30*, 33, *33*
Luyia, 33, 50, 90
Luyia Law, 35, 233n60
Lwidakho, *30*, 33, *33*
Lyada (Balalaka polity ruler), 162

Maasai communities, 123, 153
Maasailand, 124
Macdonald, J. R. L., 155
Madaba, R. J. N. (enslaved man, colonial administrator), 161–62
Makerere University, 43
Mali empire, 25
Mambruki (porter, enslaved man), 147–48
Marchant, Rob, 67
marriage: exogamous, 109; *ókusuná, ókusuna mukalí, ókusuna musaizá* (get a woman or man; wealth by acquisition), 119, 163; polygynous households, 104, 113, 127; restrictions on, 109; senior wife (*-jidù*), 55; as wealth, 104–5; and wealth in livestock, 133, 135; without cattle, 154, 165; wives retain property, 80. *See also* bridewealth
Masaaba communities, 87–89
Masaaba Word List (Siertsema), 89
Mbaga-Niwampa, 93
Mbale (district), 7, 157, 162–63
meaning: cognitive linguistics applied to, 36–40; and diachronic semantics, 17, 36, 38; and grammaticalization, 36; and lexical gaps, 37; and noun classes, 38–40; prototype theory, 37–38; reconstruction of, 35; typology of motivations, 36–37
methodologies, 22–44; archaeology, 25–26, 34, 40–41; archive of

reconstructed words, 24; cognate words, 11–12, 28–29, *29*, 35, 224n52; comparative method, 29–31, 34–35; concepts, meaning, and cognitive semantics, 36–40; core vocabulary, 28–29, *29*, 34; diachronic semantics, 17, 36, 38; documentary baseline, 25, 45; ethnography and history, 43–44; glottochronology, 34; history from words, words from history, 26–34; individual level attributes not possible, 24–26; interviews with modern speakers, 38; lexicostatistics, 28, 29–30, 34; morphology, comparison of, 8, 27, 29–30, *30*, 236n16; and oral traditions, 42–43; semantic maps, 38, 165, 232n52

migration, 131–32; by Ateso speakers, 131–32; by Dhopadhola speakers, 141; due to violence, 146–47; "Internal African Frontier," 46; Lake Victoria Nyanza patterns of, 46–49, *47*, 52, 54, 75, 91, 93, 99, *100*, 102, 104–8, 114; social networks left behind because of, 49–50, 52; Southern Luo, 107–8; by wealthy people, 133

Mill Hill missionary station, 151, 161

modern languages, 2, *3*, 11–12, 19, 22–24, 144; Kalenjin, 123, 228n2; maps of location, *73*, *100*, *121*; modern dialect chaining, 129; relationships between, 27–28, 31–33, *32*, *33*; word roots for poverty and wealth in, 38, 45, 50, 53, 138

Mollat, Michel, 15–16

Mombasa (Kenya), 16, 162

Moody, R. W., 94, 147

Morrison, Kathleen, 65

Mould, Martin, 35

Mount Elgon-Masaaba, 89, 116, 121, 124, 126, 128, 131, 144; British expedition to, 155

Mount Kenya, 68, 70

Mount Moroto, 8, 128

Mpologoma River, 107, 116

Mumia (chief), 148, 158, 164

Mumias settlement (western Kenya), 148, 154–55, 157–58

Musa, Mansa (ruler), 5

Musimami, Sylvester, 77

Musisi, Nakanyike, 4

Mwanga (deity), 88

Nabumali (eastern Uganda), 161–63

Nabumali High School (CMS, Mbale), 162

Nabuso Nabagereka (Queen Mother) (Buganda), 112

Nakuru (western Kenya), 124

Nalundiho (rainmaker), 93

Namajanja (member of Bukhoone clan), 158

Namwangala (medium, priest), 88

narrowness, thinness, 90, 109, 147, 196, 197

natural phenomenon, poverty as, 10, 19–20, 96, 99–100, 102, 109–11, 114, 119

Ngakarimojong, 2, *3*, 20, 31, *121*, 131, 138

Ngikuliak communities, 139

Nicholson, Sharon, 66

Nietzsche, Friedrich, 8

Nile River, *3*, 8, *73*, 99, *100*, 107

Nilotic language family, 2, 8, 98, 120–43; Ateso concepts of poverty and wealth, 131–36; Dhopadhola, 2, *3*, 20; early concepts of poverty and wealth, 58–63; Eastern Nilotic, 9, 17, 31; Elgon-Mau Kalenjin concepts of poverty and wealth, 124–26; genetic classification of, 30–31, *32*; Highland Northern Ateker concepts of poverty and wealth, 138–41; Kupsabiny concepts of poverty and wealth, 126–28; Ngakarimojong, 2, *3*, 20, 31, *121*, 131; pastoralism associated with, 142–43; Proto-Ateker concepts of poverty and

Nilotic language family (continued)
wealth, 128–31; Proto-Eastern Nilotic, 20, 31, 45, *47*, 58, 60–62, 63, 120, 128–29; Proto-Kalenjin concepts of poverty and wealth, 120–24; protolanguages, map of, *47*; Proto-Nilotic, 22, 30–31, *47*, 58–63, 110, 129–30, 132, 141, 185, 188, 224n52; Proto-Southern Luo concepts of poverty and wealth, 141–42; Proto-Western Nilotic, 20, 31, *32*, 45, *47*, 61–62, 64, 120; Southern Nilotic (Kalenjin branch), 9; Western Nilotic, 9, 17, 20, 61, 204. *See also* Ateker languages; Ateso language; Kalenjin; Kupsabiny (Kupsapiny); Proto-Kalenjin; Proto-Southern Nilotic; Southern Luo
North Nyanza, 9, 17, *33*, 99–119; contingency of poverty, 99–100, 102–3; gendered forms of wealth, 100, 103–5, 107, 112–13; gradations of poverty, 99, 111–12; Lugwere concepts of poverty and wealth, 116–19; Lusoga concepts of poverty and wealth, 107–14; modern, 33; poverty as natural, 96, 99–100, 102, 109–11, 114, 119; Proto-East Kyoga concepts of poverty and wealth, 114–16; Proto-North Nyanza concepts of poverty and wealth, 100–105; Proto-South Kyoga concepts of poverty and wealth, 105–7; wealth as acquired, 99, 105–7, 113, 116, 119; widespread poverty, 100–103. *See also* Lugwere; Lusoga; Rushana
Nubia, 44
Nyerere, Julius, 13
Nzita, Richard, 93
Nzoia River, 8

Ocopo, war with (1890s), 6
Ogot, Bethwell, 107, 141
O'Grady, William, 37

Okadaro (Iteso leader), 152–53
Okalany, D. H., 131
Olokotum (wealthy Iteso man), 152–53
Omoding (of Ogooma, Nyero, informant), 133–34
Omotik (extinct language), 31
Ongamo, 31
oral traditions, 12; continuity of, 22–23; in methodologies, 42–43; multiple interpretations of, 25; stories about histories, 23; transcriptions of, 42–43; violent encounters referenced in, 106
orphans, 173, 181, 186–87, 221n16, 228n2, 228n5; kinlessness of, 11, 20, 60, 74, 122–23, 128; lack of livestock, 124
Orwatum (leader, *emuron*), 153
Owiny Karuoth (Southern Luo group), 109

Päkot, 31
Palmer, Robin, 13
palynological (pollen) records, 34, 68
Papa Eunyat of Moruita (wealthy Iteso man), 135–36
Parsons, Neil, 13
pastoralism, 2, 11, 20–21, 68, 71; in colonial era, 152–54, 165; of Nilotic speakers, 58–59, 120, 122–28, 130, 136, 139; transition to from subsistence practices, 25–26; western Kenya, 124–25
patrilineal descent, 51, 54, 63, 86, 104, 109
"The Periplus of the Erythraean Sea," 42
Peters, Carl, 155
phonemes, 11–12, 34–35; reconstructing, 34–35
pity, 51
plunder, wealth as product of, 19, 57, 79, 103, 107, 112, 156, 158
"The Poem of What Poverty Does" (Siti binti Saad), 16
Pokino, Alex, 163

poor, the: communal attitudes toward, 16; as deceitful, 1, 9, 75, 76, 80, 170, 189; as disruptive to community, 20, 61, 63, 83, 138, 143; gradations of, 19, 20; individual failings of, 101; lack of social standing, 123; little trace on historical record, 15; negative concepts of, 11, 19–20, 72–73; as not fully adult, 55–56; as not fully human, 9, 101, 102–3, 109; physical consequences of poverty for, 19, 99, 110–12, 117, 132, 147; as selfish, 72, 81–83, 90; sympathy for, 86, 109; as threat to collective, 9; very poor, 20. *See also* poor, words for derived from roots

poor, words for derived from roots: *amule* (poor woman), 132–33; *ekulyakana* (poor person), 138, 204; *ekulyakit* (pauper), 138, 204; *jachandi* (poor person), 141; *kùwe'jjera* (breathe hard, gabble), 111–12; *lukyôló* (poor person), 109, 111, 178; **lunkúpe* (pauper, very poor person), 102, 110, 115, 117–18, 200; *maskini* (from Arabic *miskīn*) (very poor person), 144; **mɛ:R* (to die), 124, 202; *mudambi* (very, very poor person), 118, 173; *mughedhere* (very poor person), 201–2; *munyerere, omunyerere* (thin), 96–97, 196–97; *mupaati* (nonrelative [no connection with poor]), 118–19, 175; *mutambi* (worker), 118, 174; *nairange* (poor person lacking respect), 117–18; *nambadi* (irresponsible husband), 118; *natang'wali* (very poor person), 87; *óbútáki* (deficiency or failing), 111; **obwavu* (poor, poverty), 115; *omugadi* (poor person), 76, 189; *omúghédhére* (pant or wheeze, destitution), 111–12; **omulyasi* (someone who eats all the food), 82; *omumanani, abamanani*, 73, 74, 95, 98, 187; *omúnakú* (wretch; without friends), 110, 180; *ómunyelele* (someone who is thin), 90, 196; **omupaati* (poor person), 51; *omusakandu* (poor person), 95, 96; *ómutaambi* (poor person), 152; **ómútáki* (poor person), 22, 23, 106, 115, 117, 172, 173; **omutambi* (hard worker, needy person, bereaved person), 22, 23, 50, 92, 173, 174; **omwaati* (poor person), 92, 95, 175; *umurasyi* (destitute person), 87; **umutali* (poor person), 83, 87, 192; *umutambi* (destitute person, bereaved person), 86, 173–74; *yandaba* (destitute person), 96

poverty: as absence of clothing, 157, 163–65; ahistorical projections about, 4; caused by colonial disruption, 145–46; causes and consequences of, 54; coexistence with grief and adversity, 132; conjunctural, 56, 207n6; consequences of for community, 61; as contingent condition, 50–51, 76–77, 78, 79, 99–100, 102–3; degrees of, 87; destitution, 4, 13, 20, 51, 55, 86–87, 96, 101, 103, 110–12, 117–19, 132, 138–39, 164–65; as disturbing or disruptive to others, 20, 61, 63, 83, 138; earliest concepts of, 45–63; emotional terms for, 72–73; evil and filth connected with, 101, 102, 111, 199–200, 236; gradations of, 19, 20, 99, 111–12; histories of, 12–18; immorality as concept of, 151–52, 165; as kinlessness, 9, 59–60, 63, 74; as lack, 10, 16, 49, 54, 74, 75; and lack of livestock, 20, 63, 123–24, 126; as long-term condition, 56, 102, 103; and misery, 20, 56, 101, 110, 119, 132, 172, 173, 179–81, 185–86; narrowness, thinness linked with, 10, 90, 109, 147, 196, 197; as natural phenomenon, 10, 19–20, 96, 99–100,

288 *Index*

poverty (continued)
102, 109–11, 114, 119; negative concepts of, 11, 19–20, 51, 59, 61, 72–73, 76, 82, 89–90, 96, 97–98, 101–3, 110, 132, 141; and physical condition, 19, 99, 110–12, 117, 132, 147; as punishment or torture, 20, 61, 83, 87, 89, 129, 132, 141; structural, 4, 56, 207n6. *See also* beggars and begging; bereavement; gendered forms of poverty; orphans; poverty, word roots for; poverty, words for derived from roots; suffering

poverty, word roots for: *-bak-* (poverty and misery), 132; **-bánjà* (courtyard, plot of land, debt), 55; **-càk-* (desire, wish; search for), 49, 117, 172; **-can-* (suffering, punishment and torture), 58–61, 90, 98, 110, 132–33, 138, 140–42, 185–86, 232n52; *-chan-* (suffering, poverty), 141; **-daha* (being in want), 92; *-damb-* (severe poverty or destitution), 118; **-dòb-* (disappear; get lost), 103, 164, 200; **-doobe* (loincloth), 103, 117, 164, 200; *ecanit* (poverty), 132, 185; *-gwa* (fall, lose wealth, become poor), 76; **-gad-* (deceit), 1, 76, 80, 170, 189; **-jidù* ([male] follower, client), 55; **-jódò* (weak person, smooth person, poor person), 55, 101, 106, 109, 111, 115, 117, 178–79; *-jódozi* (one who causes another to be soft or weak; guardian), 56; **-jolo* (weak person, smooth person, poor person), 55, 101, 106, 109–11, 115, 117, 178–79; **-ka-yar-an* (to be alive or to subsist), 138; **kulyak* (poverty, destitution, poor or destitute person), 138, 204; **-lyasi* (selfish, mean; entirely, all), 82, 192; **-manan-*, 73; **me:i-* (person without cattle), 123, 126, 202; **-naku* (poverty, sorrow, and misery; time and season), 56, 101, 106, 110–11, 115, 117, 179–81; **-nyerere* (narrow, thin), 90, 147, 196, 197; **-ŋat-* (to become emaciated; suffer in exile, be ostracized), 77, 147, 189–90; **-pát-* (hold, be jammed, be wedged), 51, 174; **-paat-*, 51–52, 92, 118, 174–75; **pan-* (pauper), 59, 224; **-panan-* (pauper, bereavement, kinlessness, destitution), 59–60, 74, 95, 122–24, 127–28, 186–88, 224n63, 228n2, 228n5–6; **-sàka* (find food, trade or work for food), 49, 50; *-sakandu* (poverty), 96; **-tak-* (lack, want; social and spiritual failings), 49–50, 75–76, 80–82, 87, 89–90, 92, 106, 110–11, 115, 117, 151, 172–73; **-tali* (poor man, poverty), 83, 192; **-tamb-* (call; take; receive; walk; and play, dance, jump; bereavement work hard), 50–52, 75–76, 83, 86–87, 89–92, 118, 148, 152, 173–74; **-tamba* (work hard without resting), 50, 91–92; **-yavu* (evil, filthy), 102, 106, 111, 115, 117, 199–200; **-yabu* (evil, filthy), 102, 199. *See also* poor, words for derived from roots; poverty, words for derived from roots

poverty, words for derived from roots: *acanaanu* (poverty), 138, 185; *aiticanet* (punishment; inconvenience), 129, 132, 185; *akayaran* (one who lives on someone), 138; *akicana* (to lack or be lacking), 138, 185; *akicanut* (to trouble, disturb, annoy, molest, afflict, or cause to be sad), 138, 185; *akilokit lo ican* (poor man), 133; *akisican* (to afflict or punish), 129, 138, 185; *akulyakanut* (poverty due to lack of cattle), 138, 204; *akulyako* (poverty or abject poverty), 138, 204; *budòobi* (destitution), 117, 200; *burasyi* (destitution), 87; *butami* (condition of being poor), 90; *buutakha* (avarice, selfishness, meanness, lack, poverty, and want), 90, 172; *bwavu* (poverty),

115, 117, 199; *chandi* (poverty, misery), 141, 186; *chandirok* (sufferings or trouble), 141, 186; *chandò* (punish, make miserable, torment, and annoy), 141, 186; **-doob-* (become destitute), 103, 117, 164, 200; *ibakor* (both poverty and misery), 132; *icana* (scarce or rare, troublesome), 132, 185; *khutàmbà* (to be poor, bereaved, helpless), 86, 173; *khutàmbísà* (disturb, trouble, torture, interrupt), 87, 173, 174; *khúumanana* (to become poor), 73, 187; *kidoobi* (destitute), 117, 200; *kudambadamba* (to suffer a lot), 118, 174; *kudambya* (to disturb, vex, or cause trouble), 118, 174; *kùdoòba* (be stripped of everthing, be destitute), 117, 164–65; *kupaatiika* (set a limit or boundary), 119, 175; *kutamba* (work), 118, 174; *lo-na-ibako* (destitute), 132; *lu-* prefix, 110; *maskini wa mungu* (God's poor) (Kiswahili), 87; *nambadi* (irresponsible husband), 118; *ŋican* (grief, suffering, trouble), 61, 129, 138, 185; *obugadi* (poverty), 76, 189; *obumanani* (poverty), 95, 187; *obúnakú* (destitution, afflictions, anguish, misery, grief), 110, 180; *obusakandu* (poverty), 96; **óbútáki* (poverty and need), 106, 115, 117, 172; **obutaxa* (avarice, selfishness, lack), 82; **obwaati* (poverty), 92, 95, 175; *obwávú* (poverty, being needy), 110, 199; *ohumanana* (become poor), 95, 187; *ohuŋata* (living a life of poverty), 77, 189; *ohwandaba* (destitution), 96; *òkutakíwálá* (become poor), 117, 172; *omutaamba* (harlot, prostitute), 90, 152, 234n87; **omutaxa* (poor person, selfish person), 82, 83; **-paata* (be poor), 51; *pánánɛ:t* (poverty, orphanhood), 128, 187; *sisa* (poverty and suffering), 90; **ubutali* (poverty), 83, 87; *umudambiro* (greeting to bereaved person), 86

poverty and wealth: ancient vocabulary for, 4; as complex concepts, 1, 5, 8–9, 52–53, 63; conceptual history of, 7–11; in eastern Uganda, 5–7; European histories of, 15–16; histories of, 12–18; from indigenous African perspective, 14; multiple meanings of, 8, 16; in social, material, and emotional terms, 9–11, 46, 51, 63, 72, 99–100, 136; between and within societies, 2; understandings of, 1–2, 4, 8–11, 16, 45. *See also* poverty; wealth

power: and age grades, 122; and authority, 78; of Buganda, 57–58; colonial forms of, 157–61, 162, 166, 168–69; of elders, 19, 122; and gendered concepts of wealth, 108–9; of head of household, 139–40; Proto-Greater Luhyia words for, 53–54, 93; Proto-Gwe-Saamia words for, 93, 96, 198–99; of royal families, 101, 104; wealth as, 10–11, 54, 72, 92–93, 130, 136, 139–43; wealth delinked from, 142, 152. *See also* leadership

practices, continuity of, 16, 43–44

Prestholdt, Jeremy, 16

Proto-Ateker, 20, 60–61, 120, *121*; concepts of poverty and wealth, 128–31. *See also* Ateker languages

Proto-Ateso, 31, *32*

Proto-Bantu, 5, 32, *33*, 49–57, 76, 79, 84–85, 92, 97, 103, 105, 109, 113, 117, 164. *See also* Bantu language family; Proto-Great Lakes Bantu; Proto-West Nyanza

Proto-Eastern Nilotic, 20, 31, 45, *47*, *48*, 58, 60–62, 63, 120, 128–29; Proto-Bari, 31. *See also* Proto-Tung'a

Proto-East Kyoga, 19, 20, *100*, 107, 114–16, 144. *See also* Proto-South Kyoga; Rushana

Proto-Elgon Kalenjin, 31, *121*, 124
Proto-Elgon-Mau Kalenjin, 20, 31, 85, *121*, 122; concepts of poverty and wealth, 124–26, 127, 128
Proto-Greater Luhyia languages, 10, 17–19, 45, *47*, 85, 86, 91, 103, 118; bereavement, concept of, 50–51; early concepts of poverty and wealth, 46–55; and exchange patterns, 48; migration of speakers of, 46–48; neighboring languages, 106; poverty, word roots for, 49–52; poverty and the poor, new words for, 17, 48–49; power, words for, 53–54, 93; Proto-Gwe-Saamia, 19, 33, 72, 93, 96, 198–99; protolanguages from, 72–73; Proto-Luyia, 19, 33, 72; Proto-North Luhyia, 19, 33, 50, 96, 126; wealth, word roots for, 52–54. *See also* Bantu language family; Greater Luhyia languages
Proto-Great Lakes Bantu, 22, 32–33, *33*, 46, 49–50, 102, 167; pre-Gungu, 33, *33*; Proto-East Nyanza, 32, *33*, 55, 125; Proto-Western Lakes, 32, *33*; Proto-West Nyanza, 32, *33*, 54–58, 156. *See also* Proto-Greater Luhyia languages
Proto-Gwe-Saamia, 72, *73*, 96, 106, 198–99; concepts of poverty and wealth through the nineteenth century, 91–93
Proto-Iraqw, 59, 122, 128, 186
Proto-Kalenjin, 20, 31, 59–60, 63, 74, 85, 97–98, *121*; concepts of poverty and wealth, 120–24, 126, 128. *See also* Proto-Southern Nilotic
protolanguages, 9, 11, 17, *47*; archive of reconstructed words, 24–25; diversity among and between vocabularies, 46; reconstruction of from modern languages, 27; reconstruction of sound in, 34–35. *See also* languages; Proto-Greater Luhyia languages; specific protolanguages

Proto-Luyia, 72, *73*
Proto-Lwo, 140
Proto-Ngikatapa Teso (pre-Teso), 129–30, 136
Proto-Nguni, 28
Proto-Nilotic, 22, 30–31, *47*, 58–63, 110, 129–30, 132, 141, 185, 188, 224n52
Proto-Northeast Coast Bantu, 28
Proto-Northeast Savanna Bantu, 32
Proto-Northern Kalenjin, 31, 85, 121–22
Proto-North Luhyia, 19, 33, 50, 72, 86, 91, 96, 126; concepts of poverty and wealth through the nineteenth century, 81–85
Proto-North Nyanza, 19, 99, *100*, 100–105, 109; Proto-East Kyoga, 19, 20, *100*, 107, 114–16, 144; Proto-South Kyoga, 19–20, 99, *100*, 105–7, 109, 115. *See also* Lugwere; Lusoga
Proto-North Rutara, 56
Proto-Omotik-Datooga, 31, 120
Proto-Pok-Ong'am, 124
Proto-Rutara, 99
Proto-Sabiny-Kony, 124, 126
Proto-Southern Luo, 55, 62, 110, 120, *121*, 141–42, 188–89
Proto-Southern Nilotic, 9, 20, 31, *32*, 45, *47*, 58, 59–60, 120, 127–28, 228n2; pre-Southern Nilotic, 59. *See also* Proto-Kalenjin
Proto-South Kyoga, 19–20, 99, *100*, 105–7, 109, 115. *See also* Proto-East Kyoga
Proto-Tato, 31
Proto-Tung'a, 31, *47*, 60, 61–62, 129–30, 134, 138, 188, 224n52, 224n64; wealth in general terms, 130, 134, 188. *See also* Proto-Eastern Nilotic
prototype theory, 37–38
Proto-Western Nilotic, 20, 31, *32*, 45, *47*, 58, 61–62, 64; Anywa, 31; Dinka-Nuer, 31; Jieng (Dinka), 31, 62; Luo, 31; Luo-Burun, 31; Naadh (Nuer), 31, 62; Northern, 31; Nuer-Dinka, 31; Ocolo

(Shilluk), 31; Proto-Northern West Nilotic, 62. *See also* Western Nilotic
Proto-West Nyanza, 17, 18, 32, 45, *47*, 54–58, 79, 101, 103, 156; dialects by eighth century, 99; loan words, 57–58. *See also* Proto-Bantu
Proto-West Nyanza speakers: early concepts of poverty and wealth, 54–58
proverbs, 16
punishment or torture, poverty as, 20, 61, 83, 87, 89, 129, 132, 141
Purvis, J. B., 87–88, 89

rainmaking ceremonies (*elelekeja*), 152
Ranger, Terence, 8
reproduction, 5–6, 119, 128, 139; poverty and inability to contribute to, 9, 82, 141, 154, 166; as wealth, 6. *See also* bridewealth
respect, 11, 83–84, 87–89, 91–92, 96, 192–95, 232n57; *-ifu* extension, 87–88; *-kasa* (respect), 89, 192–95; *-kum* (respect), 84, 232n57
Richter, Melvin, 7, 8
Rift Valleys, 46, 59, 66, 121, 124
Rodney, Walter, 13
Roscoe, John, 44, 82, 86, 87–88
Rottland, Franz, 59–60
Royal Geographic Society expedition, 154
Rub languages, 138–39
Rukiga, 56, 112
Runyankore, 56, 112
Runyoro, 57
Rushana, 2, *3*, 33, *33*, *100*, 105, 116, 144
Rwanda, 25

Saamia communities, 147
Sacred Lake (Mount Kenya), 68, 70
scarcity, 13, 56, 132, 136
Schoenbrun, David, 26, 53, 54, 101, 103, 223n50
Sebei communities, 124–28, 155
semantic maps, 38, 165, 232n52

semantics, cognitive, 36–40
Shanguhyia, Martin, 95
Shilluk, 62, 203
Shipton, Parker, 15
Siertsema, Berthe, 89
Sirikwa Holes (western Kenya), 124–25
Siti binti Saad, 16
slavery, 147–50, 161–62; and bereavement, 148; *-jidù* as word root for, 55
slave trade, transatlantic, 13, 21
social death, 120, 123, 124, 143, 170
social networks: age sets and age grades, 2, 59, 122; and kinlessness, 9, 59–60, 63, 74, 80, 120, 122–23, 143; left behind because of migration, 49–50, 52; Proto-South Kyoga speakers, 105–7; sharing of wealth expected, 16, 133–34, 142, 152–53; through marriage, 104, 105, 113–14
social status, 5–6, 43, 53, 59, 60, 133–36; and clothing, 163–64; colonial era education and conversion to Christianity, 162; communal feasts, 82, 87; junior, 6, 170; *mokoriondet* (leader), 127. *See also* bridewealth; gendered forms of poverty; gendered forms of wealth; livestock; marriage
So communities, 139
Soga kingdoms, 112–13
sorrow, poverty as condition of, 56, 63, 101, 179–80
sound, changes in, 11–12, 17, 22–23, 27; loan words, 57–58, 74; reconstruction of, 34–35; word root for bereavement, 50
South Central Africa, 15
Southern Luo, 9, 62, 107–12, 114; clans, 108–9; Dhopadhola, *121*, 141–42; and migration, 107–8; Proto-Southern Luo, 55, 62, 110, 120, *121*, 141–42, 188–89. *See also* Lusoga; Western Nilotic
South Sudan, languages spoken in, 31, 46, 58, 62, 128, 131

Spire, Frederick, 157–58
Stager, J. Curt, 68
Stam, Father N., 93–94
sub-Saharan Africa: ahistorical narratives about poverty of, 1, 4; egalitarian depiction of, 4–5, 13, 87; poverty rate until COVID-19 pandemic, 2, 207n2
Sudi (chief), 158
Sudi of Pangani (slave raider), 158
suffering, 11, 17, 63, 119; *-can- (suffering, punishment and torture), 58–61, 90, 98, 110, 132–33, 138, 140–42, 185–86, 232n52; -chan- (suffering, poverty), 141; *-ŋat- (to become emaciated; suffer in exile, be ostracized), 77, 147, 189–90; poverty as one of many forms of, 20, 56, 101, 106, 110–11, 115, 117, 179–81
Sundiata, epic of, 25
Sutton, John, 125
Swadesh, Morris, 28
Swadesh list, 28
Swahili traders (Acumpa), 148–49

Tanganyika, 155
Tanzania, 124; Datooga dialect cluster, 31
Teso communities. *See* Iteso communities
Teso Historical Texts project, 43, 131–36
Thomson, Joseph, 93, 147, 150, 153, 154
time and season, 56, 101–2, 180–81, 223n41
trade networks, global, 1–2, 13, 20–21, 87, 144, 168
Traugott, Elizabeth Closs, 36
Turkana, 129, 131, 140, 149
Twaddle, Michael, 155

Uganda, eastern, 2; Bantu and Nilotic language families, 2, 8; Budama, 141; Bugwere, 156, 161–63; defined, 8; ethnographies of, 44; Karamoja area, 136–37; Kavirondo region, 93–94, 158, 235n107; map of in nineteenth and early twentieth centuries, *145*; multilingualism, 9, 110–11; Mumias settlement, 148, 154–55; Nabumali, 161–63; political centralization, aversion to, 25; poverty and wealth in, 5–7; as refuge for objectors to British protectorate, 155; relief map, *3*; trade networks, nineteenth and early twentieth centuries, 20–21; Usuku region, 130–31
Uganda Agreement (1900), 159
Uganda History Project (Makerere University Department of History), 43
Ukimbu (western Tanzania), 69
Usenge, excavations at, 41
Usuku region (eastern Uganda), 130–31

Vansina, Jan, 13
Vanterm, Anthony, 151
Vincent, Joan, 156, 159
violence: of colonial conquest, 144–45, 157, 166; migration due to, 74, 146–47; referenced in oral traditions, 106; wealth acquired through, 19, 57, 79, 91, 113, 126–27, 146–47, 153–54, 166, 169
visiting, 20, 62, 141–42

Wakida, Leo (colonial administrator), 162
Waller, Richard, 153
wealth: acquired, 6, 19, 77–79, 91, 99, 101, 104–5, 105–7, 113, 119; acquired through violence, 19, 57, 79, 91, 113, 126–27, 146–47, 153–54, 166, 169; ancient vocabulary for, 4; in bananas, 101, 108; causes and consequences of, 54; chance or luck, connection with, 91; children as, 5–6, 53, 96, 97, 100, 104, 114, 127, 167; colonial forms of, 157–61, 163; composition of, 10, 14, 15, 57, 165; in crops, 7, 11, 120, 136, 139;

elderhood connected with, 19, 92–93, 122, 125–26; equality, prosperity in terms of, 134; exportation of from Africa, 14; in food, 6–7, 78, 133–34, 135; generational transmission of, 10, 36, 52, 54, 58, 63, 134; heritable, 10, 52–54, 58, 63, 90–91, 103, 112, 116, 161, 167, 175–76, 234n88; in land, 11, 75, 78; in livestock, 85, 87–88, 96, 127, 130, 134, 139, 149–50, 160–61; marriage as, 104–5; material, 9–11, 46, 75, 78, 88; multiple forms of, 6–7, 209n14; negative terms for, 11, 79–80, 91, 134; numerical largeness, quantity, 78; obligation to share, 133–34; in people, 6, 10–11, 14–15, 20, 38, 53, 107, 113–14, 127, 208n10; as power, 10–11, 54, 72, 92–93, 130, 136, 139–41, 143; power delinked from, 142, 152; power intertwined with, 140–43; as product of plunder, 19, 57, 79, 103, 107, 112, 156, 158; redistribution of, 62, 109, 112, 116, 142; sharing of expected, 16, 62, 133–34, 142, 152–53; skill linked with, 134–35; status-enhancing, 5–6, 43, 53; through tax collection, 158–60; translation of from one form to another, 5–6, 11, 97, 98, 127, 134–36, 154; and visiting, 20, 62; in women, 4, 10, 52–54, 56–58, 77–78, 96, 103–5, 109, 112, 146–47, 167–68, 175. *See also* gendered forms of wealth; livestock wealth, word roots for: **-bahi* (great wealth in livestock), 85; *-bar-* (increase in size; wealth in general terms; wealth in livestock), 61–62, 130, 134, 139–41, 150, 156, 168, 188; **-bayi* (to keep cattle), 85, 97–98, 193–94; **-bún* (break; snap), 105; *-dip-* (pay, compensate), 84, 192; **-fún-* (acquisition of wealth), 105, 106–7, 113, 116, 119, 200–201; **-gaig-* (wealth in general), 105, 106, 113, 116, 119, 184–85, 223n51; **-gáìga* (general term), 57–58; **-gaigawala* (becoming wealthy), 105; **-hinda* (rich or wealthy), 53; **-hind-* (fold, hem, plait; turn, invert, change), 53–54, 78, 83–84, 89, 91–92, 96, 176–78, 222n28; **-hul-* (grow), 92; **-hulahula* (growing, process of), 92; **-hulahulana* (prosper, prosperity), 97, 198; **-ifu* extension (respected), 87–88; **-jàandu* (wealth in women; wealth obtained through war), 52, 56–58, 175; **-kabi* (prosperity through chance or luck), 91, 197; **-kác-* (dry up, coagulate, be hard), 85, 194; **-kasa* (respect), 89, 192–95; **-kerian* (be rich, skillful, wealthy), 203–4; **-kómb-* (scrape, dig; lick [food] with finger), 79, 113, 190; **-kor* (grow or age), 125; **-kúd-* (grow up), 92, 198; **-kum* (respect), 84, 232n57; **lim-* (wealth and visiting), 62, 141–42, 188–89; *-lóka* (sprout), 113; **-losela* (prosperity [material]), 84–85, 195–96; *-mio* (wealth in food), 135, 204; *mo-* (singular person class prefix), 125; **mokor-* (rich person, wealth, riches), 125–27, 202–3; **mukasa* (jewelry), 85, 194, 233n65; **-nyal-* (power), 93, 96–97, 198–99; *-ɲang'-* (rich), 142; **-pind-* (authority, power, able person), 53–54, 176; **-polo-* (many, numerous, wealth and power), 140, 204; **-rian-* (equal [in size, height, etc.]), 134, 203; **-tihi* (great wealth in things, material wealth), 89, 192–93; **-tunga* (be wealthy), 57–58, 181–84; *-túng-* (put through; thread on string; plait; sew; tie up; build, close (in)), 57, 181; **-yaand-* (military plunder, material goods), 79–80, 84, 88, 92, 109, 119, 146–47, 156, 167, 175–76; **-yàandu* (wealth in women; wealth obtained

wealth, word roots for (continued)
through war), 52–54, 77, 96, 103–5, 107, 109, 112, 167; *-yaay- (hunting, plunder, and loot), 79–80, 191–92. *See also* wealth, words for derived from roots; wealthy, words for derived from roots

wealth, words for derived from roots: *abar* (wealth in cattle), 7, 134, 188; *ajakaania* (become wealthy), 140, 203; *akapolon* (chief), 140, 204; *akerianut* (to be rich, successful), 134–35, 204; *amio* (wealth in crops and food), 6–7, 134–35, 156, 160–61, 204; *aŋaŋg'o* (rich), 142, 205; *apolokin* (be in charge of), 140, 204; *apoloor* (prosper), 140, 204; *apolou* (honor), 140, 204; *búbwaayi* (great wealth in livestock), 90, 193; *bubwáhi* (wealth in livestock), 87, 193; *buhindifu* (wealth and respect), 89, 177; **buhinda* (rich or wealthy), 53; *bukasa* (wealth, honor, and leadership), 85, 90, 195; *bukásyà* (wealth, respect, and honor), 89; **butihi* (riches, great wealth in things), 84, 89, 192–93; *bya kusuná* (wealth), 119; *ebarar* (to be plenty or numerous), 139, 188; *eekhabi* (prosperity, good luck), 91, 197–98; **ehulahulana* (prosperity), 92, 198; *emyaando* (general term), 96, 175; *epol* (big, great, or large), 130, 204; *ibarasit* (head of cattle), 134, 188; *ibaren* (wealth in livestock), 134–36, 139, 156, 160, 188; *inzilò(o)sèlà* (accumulation), 89, 196; **isemwandu* (widower), 103–4; *khulò(o)sèlà* (add, increase, develop), 89, 196; *khunyola zikhabi* (be fortunate, be prosperous), 91, 197; *kimihándù* (possessions), 88, 175; *kúmùhàndù* (material property), 88, 175; *kúmwáandu* (property or possesssions), 90, 175; *lím* (gift or present), 142, 189; *límó* (receive, pay a visit), 142, 189; *mokoriondit* (wealth), 127, 203; *mokoriondit toga* (wealth in livestock), 127; *mokoron* (prosper), 127; **muhinda* (rich person), 53; *muyiinda ali n'engombe* (wealth in cattle), 96, 177; *namwándú* (widow), 112, 176; **namwandu* (widow), 103, 119, 175; *ngango* (wealth, riches, or immense wealth), 142, 205; *ŋibaren* (livestock, wealth, and good luck), 139; **obúfuní* (wealth and possession of property), 107, 201; **óbugáigá* (riches), 22, 23, 58, 105, 116, 119, 184; *obunyali* (wealth), 96–97, 199; *obuyiinda* (riches or wealth), 96, 177; *obuyindifu* (prosperity), 96; **ohuhulahulana* (prosper), 92, 198; *ohunyalira* (becoming wealthy), 97, 199; *ohuyaaya* ("greedily grab food at a communal meal"), 80, 191; **ohuyiindiyala* (becoming wealthy), 92, 177; *ohuyindiyala* (prospering), 96, 177; *ókugaigáwála* (become rich), 119, 184; *ókusuná* (prosper), 119, 163, 201; *omuyaaya* (prosperity), 79, 83, 191; **omwaandu* (bridewealth), 22, 23, 77, 103–4, 112–13, 116, 156, 158, 168, 175–76; *sémwándú* (widower), 112

"Wealth in People, Wealth in Things – Introduction" (Guyer), 14

wealthy, the: emotional terms for, 73; as honorable, 11, 19, 73, 80, 84–85, 89–90; limits on accumulation by, 16; negative terms for, 82–83; *ohuŋiindigirisa* (to influence), 78; positive views of, 83–84; respect for, 83–85, 87–89, 91–92, 96, 192–95, 232n57; as those with influence, 78; women as, 10, 80, 133–34, 192

wealthy, words for derived from roots: *abaran* (rich person), 134, 188; *ajakait* (wife of ejakait), 136, 203; *dhako jaŋang'o* or *dhako mu ngang* (rich woman), 142, 205; *ebarit* (someone wealthy in livestock), 134, 188; *ejakait* (head of ojakait), 136, 140, 203; *jaŋang'o* or *ja ngango* (very rich person), 142, 205; *jichwo jaŋang'o* (rich man), 142, 205; *khuuyiinda* (to squeeze through, to displace, to take someone's place), 91; *mokoriondet* (wealthy person), 127, 203; **obukait* (respected person, leader), 85; *ojakait* (big home), 136, 203; *omokoro* (elder), 125–26, 203; *omúfuní* (rich man with many wives), 113, 201; **omugáiga* (**abagaiga*) (rich person), 58, 105, 113, 116, 119, 184; *omugerama* (rich woman), 80, 192; *omuhombe* (extremely wealthy person), 79–80, 113, 190–91; *omukasa* (respected person, wealthy person, leader), 85, 90, 195; *omúkombé ow'ábákazí* (man wealthy in wives), 113, 191; *ómúlokí* (rich man with many wives), 113, 202; *omunyali* (rich person), 93, 97, 199; *omúsaadha byâgi* (man of granaries), 113; **omutungi* (wealth, wealthy person), 57, 181–82; **omuyiinda* (wealthy person, respected person), 91, 92, 96, 177; **umuhindifu* (respected person), 83–84, 89; *umukásyà* (respected person), 89

Webster, J. B., 130, 131, 135, 154
Were, Gideon, 42–43, 146, 148
West Africa, 25
West Central Africa, 13
Western Nilotic, 9, 17, 20, 61, 204. *See also* Proto-Western Nilotic; Southern Luo
West Nyanza languages, *3*, 33, 90; East Kyoga, 33, *33*; genetic classification of, 33, *33*; Kihaya, 33, *33*; Kizinza, 33, *33*; North Nyanza, 33, *33*; Proto-North Nyanza, 33, *33*; Proto-South Kyoga, 33, *33*; Runyoro, 33, *33*; Rushana, 2, *3*, 33, *33*, *100*, 105, 116, 144; Rutara, 33, *33*. *See also* Luganda; Lugwere; Lusoga; North Nyanza; Proto-East Kyoga; Rushana

white, as cognate example, 28–29, *29*
Whyte, Susan Reynolds, 5, 208n9
widows, 10, 52–53, 103, 112, 234n88
witchcraft, 102–3, 236n9
women: captive, as wealth, 4, 57, 104, 112; colonial treatment of, 144–45; contravention of social norms linked to poverty, 90, 151–52, 165, 170; crops and wealth of, 7, 10–11, 80, 120, 133–36, 139; inherited by husband's heir, 10, 52, 58, 90, 103–4, 112, 116, 175, 234n88; **-jàandu* (wealth in women; wealth obtained through war), 52, 56–58, 175; **omukelema* (women of honor and respectability), 80, 192; *omwandu* (plunder, captive women), 22, 23, 77, 103, 112–13, 116, 156, 158, 168, 175–76; violent acquisition of in host communities, 146–47; wealth in, 4, 10, 52–54, 56–58, 77–78, 96, 103–5, 109, 112, 146–47, 167–68, 175; wealthy, 10, 80, 133–34, 192; widows, 10, 52–53, 103, 112, 234n88; **-yàandu* (wealth in women; wealth obtained through war), 52–54, 77, 96, 103–5, 107, 109, 112, 167. *See also* bridewealth
words-and-things approach, 12, 24
written sources, 11–13, 27, 33–34, 40, 42–43, 65
Wynne-Jones, Stephanie, 16

Zanzibar, 16

www.ingramcontent.com/pod-product-compliance
Lightning Source LLC
Chambersburg PA
CBHW050208240426
43671CB00013B/2250